SECOND EDITION

INTERCULTURAL
INTERACTIONS

CROSS-CULTURAL RESEARCH AND METHODOLOGY SERIES

Series Editors

Walter J. Lonner, *Department of Psychology, Western Washington University (United States)*
John W. Berry, *Department of Psychology, Queen's University, Kingston, Ontario (Canada)*

Volumes in this series:

SECOND EDITION

INTERCULTURAL INTERACTIONS

A Practical Guide

Kenneth Cushner
Richard W. Brislin

First edition, published in 1986, was authored by
Richard W. Brislin, Kenneth Cushner, Craig Cherrie,
and Mahealani Yong.

Cross-Cultural Research and Methodology   Volume 9

SAGE Publications
International Educational and Professional Publisher
Thousand Oaks   London   New Delhi

For information address:

SAGE Publications, Inc.
2455 Teller Road
Thousand Oaks, California 91320
E-mail: order@sagepub.com

SAGE Publications Ltd.
6 Bonhill Street
London EC2A 4PU
United Kingdom

SAGE Publications India Pvt. Ltd.
M-32 Market
Greater Kailash I
New Delhi 110 048 India

Printed in the United States of America

Library of Congress Cataloging-in-Publication Data

Cushner, Kenneth
    Intercultural interactions: A practical guide / Kenneth Cushner
and Richard W. Brislin.—2nd ed.
        p.   cm.—(Cross-cultural research and methodology series; v. 9)
    Rev. ed. of: Intercultural interactions / by Richard W. Brislin
. . . [et al.]. c1986.
    Includes bibliographical references and indexes.
    ISBN 0-8039-5990-7 (C: acid-free paper).—ISBN 0-8039-5991-5 (P:
acid-free paper)
        1. Intercultural communication. 2. Ethnopsychology—Methodology.
3. Social interaction. 4. Cross-cultural studies. I. Brislin,
Richard W., 1945- . II. Intercultural interactions. III. Title.
IV. Series.
GN496.I57   1995
303.4′82—dc20   95-35480

This book is printed on acid-free paper.

96 97 98 99 10 9 8 7 6 5 4 3 2 1

Sage Production Editor: Astrid Virding
Sage Typesetter: Andrea D. Swanson

CONTENTS

SERIES EDITORS' INTRODUCTION

Suppose you are about to enter a labyrinth. It is dark inside, and the only thing you know for certain is that you will face many twists and turns as you try to grope your way through the maze. Would you consider this situation as a thrilling and welcome personal and individual challenge, or would you prefer to get some expert guidance before taking your first cautious step?

This book is a helpful guide to the labyrinth of culture. While not usually as foreboding as negotiating a real labyrinth, entering the frequently baffling and often strange domain of a rather different way of looking at the world— that is, entering a culture different from your own—can be worrisome, confusing, and generally not very pleasant. It can also be delightful, invigorating, and the thrill of a lifetime. In either case, a guidebook can make the "lows" not as precipitous and the "highs" more exhilarating. And that is the intent of this second edition of *Intercultural Interactions: A Practical Guide.* The first edition, published in 1986, and prepared by Richard Brislin, Kenneth Cushner, Craig Cherrie, and Mahealani Yong, was a very big success. As a unique approach to learning about other cultures, the authors developed the original book around 100 "critical incidents" that were spread across 18 themes of human interaction. It proved to be a large help to students, academics, people in business, and others who were novices when faced with intercultural interactions. The revision, developed by Kenneth Cushner and Richard Brislin, has the same goals as the first edition. However, this new version introduces a number of new incidents and uses an expanded definition of "subjective culture." For instance, it includes incidents that will be helpful to understand the "culture" of the deaf. This unique addition serves as a reminder that the labyrinth of culture need not cross national boundaries or involve the show of a passport or currency exchanges to be different and potentially bewildering.

The **Sage Series on Cross-Cultural Research and Methodology** was inaugurated in 1975, and was designed to satisfy a growing need to integrate research method and theory and to dissect issues in comparative analyses across cultures. The ascent of the cross-cultural method in the social and behavioral sciences can largely be attributed to a recognition of methodological power inherent in the comparative perspective; a truly international approach to the study of behavioral, social, and cultural variables can be done only within such a methodological framework.

Each volume in the series has presented substantive cross-cultural studies, considerations of the strengths, interrelationships, and weaknesses of its various methodologies, drawing upon work done in various disciplines. Both individual researchers knowledgeable in more than one discipline and teams of specialists with differing disciplinary backgrounds have contributed to the series. While each individual volume has represented the integration of only a few disciplines, the cumulative totality of the series reflects an effort to bridge gaps of methodology and conceptualization across the various disciplines and many cultures.

Thus we welcome this book into the cross-cultural literature, and into this series. Culture training programs, as one aspect of the growing interest in cross-cultural psychology, have become quite popular in the past decade. The original *Intercultural Interactions* found a solid place in such programs, and this revision will be even more warmly welcomed by those who serve as culture guides as well as by those unseasoned sojourners who choose not to enter the labyrinth of culture without some expert guidance. May this book help make your journey more pleasant, productive, and memorable.

Walter J. Lonner
Western Washington University

John W. Berry
Queen's University

PREFACE

The efforts that led to *Intercultural Interactions: A Practical Guide* (1986), and to this second edition, began at the East-West Center in Honolulu, Hawaii. As a group of people from a variety of academic disciplines, professions, and cultural backgrounds, we agreed, and the research literature supported, that there are a number of interesting facts about intercultural interactions and the ways people learn to behave in such interactions, including the following:

1. Whether people like it or not, they are increasingly being expected to engage in interpersonal interactions with individuals from cultures other than their own. Reasons for this phenomenon include developments in the global marketplace, increases in international tourism, affirmative action policies, changes in school curricula in response to demands for cultural sensitivity, changes in immigration policies, and the movements of international students.

2. There has been a history of success in developing programs to prepare people for such interactions in a variety of contexts, and there has been vigorous discussion concerning the best ways to design and administer these programs.

3. In virtually all these preparation efforts, most commonly called *cross-cultural training programs,* trainers frequently use the method of relating stories about situations similar to those that are likely to happen to trainees when they cross cultural boundaries. Often, these stories are from the trainers' personal experiences.

4. However, there is a danger in total reliance on such stories. In any given program, they are limited to the experiences of one or a few people, and the conclusions trainees should draw from them are often not clear. The ultimate danger is that trainees will conclude, We heard a lot of interesting stories, but I don't know what to expect when I interact with people from other cultures.

There was thus a need to go beyond the stories to examine ways they could be used as instructional devices.

5. There is some overlap between the material covered in cross-cultural training programs and the content found in college courses on topics such as cross-cultural psychology, intercultural communication, multicultural education, and international management. Consequently, materials from training programs can be of use to professors developing college course work, and trainers can benefit from the materials developed by professors.

Given these observations, a group of four people (Richard Brislin, Kenneth Cushner, Craig Cherrie, and Mahealani Yong) made an attempt to maximize the advantages and minimize the disadvantages they contain. We attempted to prepare a set of training materials based on interesting stories that were organized around a set of 18 concepts that provide a framework for understanding cross-cultural interactions and for developing effective cross-cultural training programs. We moved beyond our own personal experiences by integrating stories gathered from large numbers of people and also from the published literature in such fields as cross-cultural psychology, intercultural communication, and international business. We placed the specific occurrences typical of individuals' stories into a broader framework in the hopes that this would be a model for people to follow during their own intercultural experiences. As we discuss more fully in Chapter 1, we benefited from the approach to cross-cultural training known as the *culture assimilator,* a method in which stories constitute critical incidents that should be of widespread interest to people moving across cultural boundaries.

We were pleased with the positive reaction to the first edition of *Intercultural Interactions,* which appeared in 1986. That book went through 10 printings, and we were asked to write numerous articles about its use for diverse groups such as international businesspeople, teachers and teacher education students, psychology professors, cross-cultural trainers, and health care professionals. It was widely used in both cross-cultural training programs and college courses. For the latter, professors often used the approach of introducing a topic through the use of the incidents as a key point in understanding complex concepts. Then, with the importance of the topic underscored, they could expand on the scope of key concepts through assigned readings, lectures, and classroom exercises and demonstrations. Classroom exercises often took the form of having various students role-play the people in the incidents and explain their behavior from particular cultural viewpoints; students also were asked to prepare incidents themselves, based upon their own knowledge and experience.

Perhaps most memorable and gratifying for us, because of their immediate impact, have been people's personal responses to the book. People have stopped us in organizations, at conventions, and on campuses, and have written and telephoned, to express their appreciation for our efforts. They have told us, "I was having a terrible time adjusting to my new coworkers from cultures very different from my own. I thought that it might be due to some unrecognized prejudice on my part. But reading your book, I discovered that lots of people have problems similar to mine, and that many miscommunications can be understood through the framework you provided." Or people in large multicultural organizations and schools would comment, "Your framework has helped me to understand better the complexity underlying the range of potential cross-cultural interactions I might encounter." Sometimes someone would stop us and say, "I had terrible anxiety and stress readjusting to my own country after being abroad for 2 years. I never had a clue that this would happen. But you covered this in your book, and I learned both that many people have reentry culture shock *and* that it can be understood."

For this second edition, we have added new critical incidents, reviewed research studies that used materials and concepts from the first edition, and integrated recent research studies and analyses related to the 18 themes in our framework for interpreting intercultural interactions. Much of this new material represents expansion into areas that our colleagues have identified through their use of the materials. Examples include interactions between members of the deaf culture and hearing individuals, the delivery of health care across cultural boundaries, differences among ethnic groups within a large and complex nation such as the United States, and misunderstandings between males and females who think they are communicating but are not as effective as they would wish. We hope that readers continue to find these materials and concepts useful in their teaching, training activities, and interpretation of their own intercultural encounters. We are eager to continue receiving your comments and feedback.

Kenneth Cushner
Richard W. Brislin

ACKNOWLEDGMENTS

This second edition of *Intercultural Interactions: A Practical Guide* has been prompted by continuously changing events worldwide as people have continued to explore and grapple with issues of intercultural interaction and cultural diversity, within as well as between nations. This updated edition expands upon the successful culture-general framework and critical-incident approach of the first edition by recognizing changes in world events as well as integrating issues of cultural diversity within given nations, including issues surrounding gender and exceptionality.

Our most pleasant task in the preparation of this book is to thank the many people who have generously offered assistance. The following individuals helped in one or more ways: They participated as members of the validation sample (for the original and/or this edition), suggested first drafts of incidents, offered editorial assistance, made suggestions that were incorporated into essays, and offered encouragement during frustrating moments. This book would not exist without their able contributions.

Rosita Daskal Albert	Frances Biedler
Diane Allensworth	J. Sam Biedler
John Allensworth	Mary G. F. Bitterman
Michael Argyle	Michael Bond
Fale Asaua	Betsy Brandt
Gale Awaya	Alice Brislin
Michelle Barker	Ann Brislin
Jim Baxter	Darrell Broaddus
Patricia Bergh	Arlene Cabacungan
John Berry	Robyn Carl

Gail Bartking Carter

Craig Cherrie

Elizabeth Christopher

Leeva Chung

Jo Ann Craig

Hyla Cushner

Christopher Deegan

Juris Draguns

C. Jeffrey Dykhuizen

Anne-Katrin Eckermann

Linda Husain Ehrlich

Jeanne Erdman

Katinka Evensen

Roxanne Fand

Caroline MeiMei Fox

Jan Fried

Seiko Furahashi

Cannon Garber

Jayne Garside

John Gould

Dennis Grossman

Neal Grove

Jean Haas

Michael Hamnett

Lisa Hancock-Leung

Betsy Hansel

Charles T. Hendrix

Ikumi Hitosugi

Naomi Horoiwa-Taguchi

Ann Marie Horvath

Martha Horvath

John James

S. Susan Jane

Marion Korllos

Charles Nieman

McCarthy Nitsa

R. Michael Paige

Pauli Stewart

Nestor G. Trillo

Kozie Ueki

Sheldon Varney

Mary Wang

Sonja Wiley

David Williams

Melinda Wood

Glenn Yamashita

1

INFORMATION FOR PEOPLE
ABOUT TO INTERACT EXTENSIVELY
IN ANOTHER CULTURE

Since the first edition of *Intercultural Interactions: A Practical Guide* (Brislin, Cushner, Cherrie, & Yong, 1986), debate, discussion, and training efforts centered on issues of intercultural interaction and cultural diversity have intensified. It has become clear to many people that, like it or not and ready or not, the conditions of the world are such that we are all increasingly coming into contact with those who are different from ourselves. Such changes are evident in a wide variety of contexts, both internationally and intranationally around the globe: The international business community continues to expand; international refugees and immigrants swell national populations; organizations such as the Peace Corps and various missionary groups send increasing numbers of people to overseas destinations; schools within many nations are increasingly addressing the needs of individuals and groups from cultures other than the mainstream; and businesses and communities worldwide struggle as their workforces become increasingly diverse, mixing nationalities, genders, ethnicities, races, sexual orientations, and abilities/disabilities.

Recent conceptions of the influence of culture on people's behavior have followed these phenomena and have expanded to consider a variety of contexts beyond national culture to include issues related to ethnicity, social class, exceptionality, and gender (Brislin, 1993; Cushner, McClelland, & Safford, 1992; Pedersen, 1988; Tannen, 1990). The theoretical field of cross-cultural psychology and the applied field of cross-cultural or intercultural training have both continued to grow in response to these circumstances. In this second edition of *Intercultural Interactions,* we recognize the many different contexts in which intercultural interactions are likely to occur; we have designed this volume with this expanded audience in mind. The changes that have been taking place worldwide, along with many of our own experiences in conducting hundreds of workshops and training programs employing this model and the considerable research we and others have conducted using the framework presented in this book, provide the impetus for this second edition.

The materials presented in this book are intended to assist people when they must adjust to life in countries other than their own, to assist people who need to interact extensively with people from other cultural backgrounds, and to provide a foundation of knowledge concerning the nature of culture as well as cross-cultural interaction. The materials are designed to be helpful regardless of (a) the cultural backgrounds of the people involved in a given interchange, (b) the country or culture in which the reader moves or interacts, and (c) the particular role the reader assumes in another country or within another group.

We recommend that persons preparing to live in countries other than their own, or to interact extensively with members of other cultures, examine the collection of critical incidents presented in this book and analyze the issues that they raise. The cross-cultural encounters depicted in the incidents are typical of the kinds faced by people living and working in other cultures, and they summarize common emotional experiences, communication difficulties, and challenges to preexisting knowledge. The assumption is that as people read and analyze the incidents, all drawn from the actual experiences of others who have moved across cultures, they will become better prepared for their own upcoming intercultural interactions. They will thus develop broader vocabularies and conceptual bases about intercultural interactions that will empower them to understand and solve their own cross-cultural problems more efficiently.

People typically have difficulties when moving across cultures. Suddenly, and with little warning, they find that behaviors and attitudes that proved necessary for obtaining goals in their own culture are no longer useful. Further, familiar behaviors that marked well-adjusted persons in their own culture may even be seen as indicative of ill-mannered persons in their new surroundings. Even with all the typical difficulties, however, most people who have had cross-cultural experiences look back on them as an enriching, challenging part of their lives. Many people make career changes as a result of extensive intercultural interaction, and many become more interested in international affairs. A possible reason for such positive developments is that most people who interact cross-culturally successfully overcome barriers to adjustment and consequently develop images of themselves as competent individuals who can understand the viewpoints of people in various parts of the world. They also become more knowledgeable about others' perspectives and ways of life, and are thus better able to understand the issues and conflicts that others may face. Individuals differ as to how quickly they begin to overcome the inherent difficulties of cross-cultural interaction and begin to obtain the benefits it offers. A basic assumption behind the development of the materials in this book, substantiated by much of the research on this topic (see Chapter 2), is that all people can successfully overcome the difficulties if they are aware of the range of challenges they will face. They will also benefit if they analyze how various experienced people have obtained their goals during intercultural assignments.

The materials presented here were developed to improve formal efforts to prepare people for extensive interaction with individuals from cultures other than their own. Such efforts are most commonly referred to as cross-cultural training, diversity training, or multicultural education programs.

WHAT WE HAVE LEARNED FROM CROSS-CULTURAL TRAINING PROGRAMS

Various researchers and practitioners have designed programs to prepare people for successful sojourns in other countries or to prepare people for extensive interaction with members of other cultural groups within any one country (Bhawuk, 1990; Brislin & Pedersen, 1976; Brislin & Yoshida, 1994a, 1994b; Landis & Brislin, 1983). The ultimate purpose of these programs is to increase the probability of people's successful adjustments in dealing with other cultures. *Successful adjustment* is defined as a combination of four factors (Brislin, 1981, 1993; Ruben & Kealey, 1979):

1. *Good personal adjustment,* marked by feelings of contentment and well-being. If a person can say to him- or herself, "Yes, I feel comfortable here and feel that I'm doing well," this would be an indication that this *one* criterion of successful adjustment is being met.

2. *Development—and maintenance—of good interpersonal relations with hosts,* marked by respect for people in the other culture, good collegial relations in the community or on the job, free time spent with those of the other culture, and sharing of personal information with others. Especially important is the other's point of view. If *others* say, "This person interacts well in this context and gets along with others," this would be an indication that this aspect of cross-cultural success is being met.

3. *Task effectiveness,* or the completion of work goals in the other country or with the other culture. This aspect of cross-cultural success concerns the attainment of task-related goals, and these will differ from person to person. Foreign students want to obtain high school diplomas or college degrees. Overseas businesspeople want to establish trade agreements. Technical assistance advisers want to complete development projects. Teachers in diverse settings want to help their students succeed in school. In the last two examples, for instance, this aspect will include the sharing of knowledge with others along with the accompanying need to adjust one's teaching style to accommodate a different learning style, as in the transfer of information for the maintenance of a successfully completed development project (Hawes & Kealey, 1981) or in teaching in a culturally diverse school setting (Cushner, 1994; Cushner et al., 1992). This is but one example of how the materials in this book highlight the cross-cultural differences individuals must understand in order to achieve subsequent success.

4. *No greater stress or experience of culture shock than would occur in the home culture when moving into a similar role.* People experience adjustment difficulties, for example, whenever they move into new positions, no matter where they are. Teachers of adolescents will have difficult moments whether they teach in Seoul, New Delhi, or New York. Likewise, air traffic controllers have stressful jobs whether they are in Tokyo, Cairo, or Atlanta. This fourth criterion of success is met when the individual experiences only the natural period of culture shock or adjustment *any* person would experience, with no greater stress than would be caused by the same circumstances in his or her own culture.

Readers should keep all four criteria for success in mind when thinking about cross-cultural adjustments. People may make seemingly adequate progress in one area, but may have difficulties because of inattention to the other three. For instance, a person may think he or she is making a good adjustment (the first criterion), but may be disliked by hosts (the second criterion). A strong-willed person may overcome obstacles and achieve task-related goals (the third criterion), but at the cost of his or her physical and mental health (the first criterion) or relations with others (the second criterion). Professionals who work with people crossing cultures (e.g., foreign student advisers, personnel officers in multinational or multicultural organizations) should make sure that attention is paid to all four criteria. This attention is especially important for the future of cross-cultural interaction. Often in international work, individuals who are overly concerned with one of the aspects of successful adjustment (e.g., they work to the exclusion of good interpersonal relations) do not receive appropriate feedback from hosts because of local norms demanding politeness and congeniality. Subsequently, the programs that brought the troublesome sojourners to the host country are jeopardized, and there are fewer opportunities for the next wave of potential sojourners. Or social service providers may be so intent on their task that they ignore critical aspects of communication and relationship building, and thus alienate and distance clients. Put another way, the next wave of people crossing cultures pay for the sins of their predecessors. Many cultures have "war stories" about past sojourners or workers that make it difficult, if not impossible, for today's sojourners to establish themselves and to have a chance to meet the four criteria of successful adjustment.

THE NATURE OF CULTURE
AND CULTURE LEARNING

The process by which we all come to believe that there is a "right" way to think, express ourselves, and act is called *socialization.* It is the process by which individuals learn what is required of them in order to be successful members of a given group, what is right and good. Socialization is a unique process in that it simultaneously looks to the future and the past. It looks forward to where people are expected to be and backward to determine what behaviors, values, and beliefs are important to continue. Socialization is such a potent process that once people have been socialized they are hardly aware that other realities can exist. This results in the presence of *ethnocentrism,* the tendency of people to judge others from their own culture's perspective, believing theirs to be the only "right" or "correct" way to perceive the world.

We consider most people to be potentially multicultural, as we are all socialized by many different groups that influence our behaviors and thought patterns; gender, nationality, ethnicity, socioeconomic status, and religion, for example, all play roles in our socialization. Brislin (1993) provides a list of culture's features that is useful in helping us to understand the influence of culture on behavior; these features apply across all of the categories of groups by which we are socialized. The list is summarized below; readers are advised to apply it to the various groups with which they interact.

Culture usually refers to something that is made by human beings rather than something that occurs in nature. The place where a body of water meets a shore provides an example. The naturally occurring components of this environment are not considered culture—the water itself, the beachfront (usually), or the horizon. How we *think about* and what we *do with* this natural environment, however, are usually dependent upon culture. Consider the beachfronts of Miami Beach, Florida, and Malaga, Spain, and their various waterfront condominiums, piers and boardwalk, boats, shoreline litter (including medical waste that may wash ashore), and even the thin layer of suntan lotion left floating on the water's surface. All of these would be considered part of culture. Furthermore, the condos, the boats, and the litter are not only products of culture, they also represent attitudes toward the natural environment. Thus human culture and the natural environment are always connected, usually in a variety of ways.

Clearly, then, culture consists of interrelated components of material artifacts (the condos and boats), social and behavioral patterns (we have medical waste and we dump it in the ocean), and mental products (it's all right to dump litter in the ocean because, somehow, the water will take care of it, and anyway, the ocean is so large).

The most critical dimension of culture concerns itself with people's assumptions about life. Culture consists of the ideals, values, and assumptions about life that are widely shared and that guide specific behaviors. Triandis (1977) points out the distinction between objective and subjective culture. The term *objective culture* refers to the visible, tangible aspects of culture, and includes such things as the artifacts people make, the food they eat, the clothing they wear, and even the names they give to things. It is relatively easy to pick up, analyze, and hypothesize about the uses and meanings of objective elements of culture.

Subjective culture, on the other hand, refers to the invisible, less tangible aspects of a group of people. People's values, attitudes, norms of behavior, and adopted roles—the things generally kept in people's minds—fall into this category. It is much more difficult for people to speak about, observe, and understand what is going on when it is the subjective elements of their culture that are in conflict with those of another. It is thought that most cross-cultural misunderstandings occur at the subjective cultural level, and that this should be the focus of good cross-cultural training.

Culture is a collective creation. Culture is *socially constructed* by human beings in *interaction with others.* Cultural ideas and understandings are shared by groups of people who recognize the knowledge, attitudes, and values of one another, and who also agree on which cultural elements are better than others. Culture is, thus, transmitted across generations by parents, teachers, respected elders, and religious leaders, and is mediated through a variety of sources, including the media, the stories parents tell their children, and the various experiences individuals have in a given culture's schools.

There exist clear childhood experiences that individuals can identify that help to develop and teach particular values and practices. Consider the characteristics of individualism and self-reliance so highly prized in the United States. Most people who have grown up in the United States can identify specific experiences from their childhoods that helped them to develop such traits, such as early jobs (paper routes, baby-sitting), and proverbs extolling the virtues of individuality that were influential as they grew up ("God helps those who help themselves"; "The early bird catches the worm").

Aspects of persons' cultures that guide their behavior are not frequently spoken about. In many ways, culture is a secret. Because one's culture is generally widely shared and accepted as "normal" and "natural," there is little reason to discuss it frequently. Consequently, people generally lack the vocabulary to discuss issues when cross-cultural problems emerge. It thus becomes a major responsibility of cross-cultural trainers and educators to help individuals develop categories and vocabularies that will allow them to discuss freely the encounters they experience, thus enabling them to resolve problems before they get out of hand.

Owing to the lack of common vocabulary and the fact that most people are uncomfortable with discussing or unable to discuss culture with others, culture becomes most evident in well-meaning clashes. Such clashes occur when people from different cultures interact in ways that each believes are proper and appropriate *from his or her own perspectives* but are different from what is expected by the other. A problem emerges, then, when people confront differences with which they are unfamiliar. Lacking both an outsider's perspective on the elements of their own culture and a vocabulary with which to discuss that culture, they are unable to speak with others about the situation. People typically respond first on an emotional level; they may become quite frustrated, make negative judgments about others, and then end an interaction at this point of frustration. This must be avoided if productive encounters are to result. A major goal of this book is to help people develop vocabularies of related terms that they can begin to utilize in their interactions with others, thus establishing the groundwork for more effective communication and understanding.

Culture allows people to fill in the blanks, so to speak. That is, people who share common knowledge and who are in agreement about many cultural elements can communicate a considerable amount of information with just a few words or phrases. For instance, when someone from work suggests that people get together on Friday at the local pub or bar, it is clear that the gathering will consist of a relatively small in-group of people who will meet for no more than a couple of hours, share in a few drinks and snacks, relate a few jokes, and generally let off some steam after a busy week. Notice that there is probably no expectation that anyone will receive a formal invitation, or that people will go home to change clothes before arriving at the bar. Nor is there an expectation that people will make an entire evening of the activity. These gaps in the communication are filled in by the knowledge commonly shared by the people in the group; they need not be spoken of.

Cultural values tend to remain in practice in spite of compromises or slip-ups. For instance, even though most organizations in the United States today profess to abide by a variety of affirmative action or equal rights rulings, something we might now consider a cultural value, it is widely known that many job vacancies are "wired" ahead of time and go to individuals known by influential people in the firm. Even though this practice occurs, the cultural value of affirmative action or equal rights still exists.

People experience strong emotional reactions when their cultural values are violated or when their cultures' expected behaviors are ignored. This is the basis for the strong and often unexpected emotional responses people experience in cross-cultural encounters. People expect specific things to occur in certain ways as a result of their behaviors. When things do not unfold according to their expectations, they often have strong emotional responses.

People's acceptance of their cultures' values can vary at certain times. It is widely expected, for instance, that adolescents will challenge authority and go to endless means to create identities unique to their group. Such behavior, however, does not preclude them from being considered members of a given culture, as it is widely understood that most will eventually adopt the majority of mainstream values and practices. A teenage boy may be a genuine juvenile delinquent, wearing leathers, carrying a switchblade, and so forth, and still reenter the mainstream and become a fully contributing member of society— as was the case with one of the authors of this book.

When changes in cultural values are contemplated, a likely reaction is, "This will be an uphill battle." Think back to the definition of culture given above. A hallmark of the general attitude of Western civilization for at least 500 years has been the belief that human beings are, in some sense, apart from nature—indeed, nature is something to be "conquered," something to be put into our service, something to be *used*. Many indigenous groups around the world, as well as many cultural groups outside the West, on the other hand, have an entirely different view of the natural environment. Rather than seeing themselves as opposed to nature, many believe strongly in the place of human beings *within* the natural world. And, because in their view we are a part of nature, it behooves us not to interfere with it too much.

This is an interesting example, because it shows not only that different sociocultural groups perceive the world in very different terms, but also that cultural beliefs and attitudes are dynamic and that they can and do change. Many people in the West are now beginning to see the damage they have caused to the environment and to consider not only ways of cleaning it up, but ways of rethinking the relation of human beings to nature. This rethinking has taken considerable effort on the part of many special interest groups and activists who have worked endlessly in hopes of changing people's thinking about the environment.

Or consider recent debates about the ownership of guns in the United States. Gun ownership, long valued by many Americans as a given right, is under considerable review in light of recent escalations of violence. Many understand the uphill battle that will be fought to change the laws, but are quite willing to put forth considerable time and effort to push for such measures as bans on assault weapons and waiting periods before the purchase of handguns.

When we look at expected behaviors across cultures, some observations can be summarized in clear contrasts. Such examples as people's use of time, their orientation in space, and deference to youth or age all provide clear instances of divergent practices. Such contrasts are the bases of many of the critical incidents in this book.

A BROADENED DEFINITION OF DIVERSITY AND THE PROCESS OF INTERCULTURAL INTERACTION

The definition of *cultural diversity* that we use in this book encompasses not only those individuals whose ethnic or cultural heritages originate in countries other than those in which they are living, but also those within a given country who may have been socialized by different groups—those who may have special educational and other needs (e.g., those who are deaf), those who may share significantly different lifestyles from the majority (e.g., rural and urban children, people who live in extreme poverty, substance abusers), those whose identities are critically influenced by their genders, and those who are significantly influenced by variations in class and religion. By this definition, everyone in a pluralistic society—such as that in the United States, Australia, New Zealand, Great Britain, or Israel—is multicultural to some degree. Each person may have a distinct subjective culture, or combination of cultures, including a unique value system, norms of behavior, modes of interaction, socialization practices, and linguistic patterns. Understanding how culture influences people in the many worlds in which they live is critical to developing skills for learning in a multicultural environment.

Culture, then, as used in this book, follows the definition provided by Triandis, Kurowski, Tecktiel, and Chan (1993): "a set of human-made objective and subjective elements that in the past have (a) increased the probability of survival, (b) resulted in satisfaction for the participants in an ecological niche, and thus (c) become shared among those who communicate with each other because they had a common language and lived in the same time-place" (p. 219). Each specific socializing group, thus, has its unique historical experience and current relationships from which to draw.

Cushner and colleagues (1992) use the deaf population as an example of a group that has developed a unique culture with both subjective and objective elements. People often think of deaf persons as being just like persons who can hear well, except that they sign instead of speak. In most situations, this is not the case; the deaf community has a culture specific to its members. Speech, for instance, is not valued, and is often considered inappropriate. Most people who are deaf do not sign Standard English (that is, they do not put signs together in Standard English word order) except when signing with hearing people. When interacting with other deaf people, they use American Sign Language (ASL), which has its own syntax. Accompanying the use of a distinct language among the deaf population are patterns of behavior that are particular to the group, including early childhood socialization practices. Children of deaf parents may grow up in environments with much greater visual orientation than those in the hearing culture; lights may accompany ringing telephones or doorbells, and people may depend upon gestures in interpersonal communication. The deaf community is also very close-knit, placing strong emphasis on social and family ties. Some 80-90% of people who are hearing-impaired marry others with hearing losses. Thus a strong in-group orientation develops, making it difficult for outsiders who do not know ASL to enter. Interactions between hearing and deaf populations are often filled with feelings of anxiety, uncertainty, and threat of loss. These feelings are all similar to those encountered in other cross-cultural exchanges. Using this as an example, it is easy to see the range of possible cross-cultural interactions that can occur between individuals and groups that have distinct subjective cultures. The culture-general framework presented in this book has been used as a tool to train interpreters for the deaf as they prepare for interactions across hearing and hard-of-hearing cultures.

Let's imagine what might happen in any intercultural interchange. People have certain expectations of the outcomes of their own behavior as well as the motivations of others. These expectations are based upon the behavior they observe in others. Such expectations come primarily from their own socialization, which predisposes them to view the world from a particular perspective. When people's expectations are not met, they must reconcile the difference between the reality and their expectations. This is the basis of the strong emotional reactions found in cultural conflict. Many outcomes are possible, including the following: (a) People may feel extreme emotional upset, often without knowing what is at play (culture is a secret!); as a result, they may have a tendency to avoid further cross-cultural situations, which they perceive to be unpleasant. (b) People may make faulty attributions, or assign inaccurate interpretations, to the meaning and intentions of others' behavior, accusing them of lacking sufficient knowledge, cheating, or being pushy; in other words, people may interpret events from their own ethnocentric perspectives and thus judge others by inappropriate standards. (c) People may begin to inquire as to how others interpret or find meaning in their world; as they begin to learn how others understand and operate from their own perspectives or subjective cultures, they begin to take part in true culture learning. This suggests that people have a need to broaden their knowledge base, to learn more about both their own socialization and that of others. The culture-general framework presented in this book provides one such foundation of knowledge concerning issues at play in intercultural interaction. Building such a knowledge base enables individuals taking part in cross-cultural interactions to understand and overcome the often unexpected but strong emotions they are certain to encounter in themselves, to be more precise and accurate in their interpretations of others' behavior, and thus to interact more effectively with those who are different from themselves.

THE IMPORTANCE OF
CROSS-CULTURAL PREPARATION

One major feature of the world today, as we have noted, is that increasing numbers of people at some time during their lives will have extensive interaction in cultures other than their own. Difficulties inevitably arise whenever there is extensive cross-cultural interaction. People are socialized within their own cultures to accept as "proper and good" relatively narrow ranges of behaviors. Those behaviors not labeled as good are perceived as less desirable or, in extreme cases, absolutely wrong. Further, others who engage in those less desirable behaviors may be seen as backward, ignorant, or ill-mannered. In other words, people become accustomed to doing things (eating, courting, working, teaching, learning, interacting with others) in certain ways, and they see the behaviors surrounding these activities as proper. When they interact with people from other cultures, however, what they perceive to be proper behaviors are not always forthcoming. In addition, behaviors that one group of people consider improper may be practiced on a routine basis by those in another group. Common responses to this confrontation of past learning and present experiences include intense dislike of culturally different others (leading to prejudice), negative labels (stereotypes), and refusal to interact with the others (discrimination).

The reactions of prejudice, stereotype formation, and discrimination occur even with people who voluntarily, and with the best intentions, move into cultures other than their own. People of goodwill who live in other cultures will inevitably encounter differences in behavior that are at odds with their expectations, but they must adjust their own behaviors so as to avoid behaving in discriminatory or judgmental ways. There are a great many adjustments to be made: The other people make friends in different ways; they have different work and eating habits; they do not communicate their desires in familiar ways; and they come up with decisions in ways that boggle the mind. The demand on individuals to make so many adjustments is one reason for the phenomenon commonly called *culture shock*. No single one of these demands is overwhelming: People make adjustments every day to new pressures or to new information in their own cultures. But the multiple demands, coming within a short period of time, cause frustration during extensive cross-cultural interaction. That frustration occasionally leads to negative feelings about members of other cultures, no matter how egalitarian the cross-cultural adjuster happens to be.

CULTURE ASSIMILATORS
AND THE ATTRIBUTION PROCESS

The culture assimilator is a cross-cultural training strategy that employs a critical-incident approach to present examples of culture clashes between individuals from different backgrounds. Trainees read short vignettes, or critical incidents, in which individuals from different cultures interact with the intent of pursuing some common goal. Toward the end of each incident a clash of cultures is evident and the two parties are unable to accomplish their task. More often than not, an unintended misinterpretation of events or a misunderstanding of the subjective meaning given to a particular behavior is at the base of the problem. The reader is presented with a number of alternative explanations and is asked to select the one that best accounts for the problem *from the point of view of the actor in the vignette who is not a member of the reader's own culture.*

A typical training program making use of the culture assimilator will have trainees read a number of such critical incidents, the assumption being that as the trainee receives feedback on his or her responses, he or she will begin to understand the *subjective culture* of the target group and subsequently select more appropriate responses. The trainee is thus making *isomorphic attributions,* or judgments about another's behavior that are similar to those the actor would make about him- or herself.

Such an approach to training encourages individuals to develop more sophisticated understanding of the distinction between objective and subjective culture, which we discussed earlier. Subjective elements of culture are most evident when people make judgments or attributions about others based on the behaviors they observe. People judge others to be well-intentioned, ill-mannered, well educated, hardworking, and so forth relatively quickly—generally within the first few minutes of an encounter. It must be kept in mind, however, that behavior itself, with no understanding of the reasons behind it or the context in which it occurs, is relatively meaningless. That is, an individual behaves in ways that meet his or her needs. In order to understand accurately what a person's intentions are when he or she behaves in certain ways, one must understand the context in which the behavior occurs. Culture provides one such context. Without an adequate cultural context, behavior is just noise—rather meaningless. Knowledge about the culture in which behavior is observed enables one to be accurate in judgments of others. Misunderstanding the reasons or motivations for people's behaviors, or making misattributions, is a common problem in intercultural contexts.

Perhaps an example related recently to one of the authors will be helpful. An 11-year-old boy would become rather rowdy and disruptive in the classroom each day at about 2:00 p.m. Inevitably, his teacher would send him to the school's office, and from there he was promptly sent home. Here was a boy perceived as a troubled child, labeled so by all in the school, until an astute and inquisitive counselor did some inquiry. It turned out that the boy's mother's live-in boyfriend would come home every day about 2:45, often drunk and quite violent. In his rage, the boyfriend often abused the mother. The boy figured out that if he was sent home by 2:30, he would arrive before the boyfriend and would thus be able to protect his mother. Suddenly, and with greater understanding of the context, our so-called troubled boy is viewed as a hero—he figured out how to protect his vulnerable mother. His behavior was judged by inappropriate or inaccurate standards until its context was fully understood.

In the cross-cultural context, understanding another's culture can make us more accurate in our interpretations of and attributions about that person's behavior. For instance, most Euro-Westerners are disdainful toward the idea of arranged marriage, viewing it as antiquated, until they understand the reasons behind this custom. From the perspective of some cultures, arranged marriage makes sense, because parents understand their children *and* the demands placed upon adults far better than most young people do. Parents, then, are best suited to select a mate who will be compatible with their child. Young people who marry as a result of such practice learn to love one another and thus grow into love, rather than fall in love and then marry. Helping people to understand the motivations or reasons behind others' behaviors in their appropriate context—in other words, enabling them to make isomorphic attributions—improves intercultural understanding and relations; this is the major goal of the culture-general assimilator.

We have prepared a number of critical incidents to introduce readers to the range of experiences they will have as they cross cultures. These vignettes are designed to assist readers in making intercultural adjustments and developing more comprehensive understanding of the processes involved in cross-cultural interaction. We have tried to identify central issues in cross-cultural interactions, no matter the exact places where any given incidents take place. That is, the incidents are designed to be relevant to all readers, no matter what their specific roles in cultures other than their own (e.g., foreign students, overseas businesspersons, teachers, social workers, diplomats, technical assistance advisers). An advantage of the critical incidents is that they depict cross-cultural encounters in an interesting way.

The incidents include named people who are trying to adjust, and it is inherently interesting to read about what happens to them. The twin concerns of relevance to many different types of people and human interest should be clear in the following example, an incident that was originally written as part of materials to prepare foreign students for life in the United States (Gosnell, 1983).

Dubud desperately wanted to make friends with U.S. students, especially with American girls, but he failed in all his attempts at being friendly. He could never get a date with an American girl. He couldn't even seem to make friends with American male students. He became very lonely and missed his home, where he had been very popular. Dubud became very bitter about the way the American students treated him. He felt lonely and isolated from everyone. He began to withdraw from any contact with other students. He felt totally rejected.
Why did the American students seem to reject Dubud?

1. Dubud probably had not bothered to go through a third person in order to arrange a date, as is the usual American custom. Therefore, the American girls probably were insulted at being approached directly.
2. The American students probably considered Dubud to be in a different social and economic class from themselves. Therefore, they did not feel free to make friends with him.
3. The American students probably were too busy with their studies to make friends with Dubud.
4. The American students probably had their own friends already and assumed that Dubud had international student friends.

Readers of such incidents want to know what happened to the people involved. The best critical incidents have a human relations appeal that encourages people to ask what happened and why. The procedure of choosing among alternatives can also be very interesting. Matching one's choices with the correct answer or answers is challenging.

The preferred alternative answer in the example above is 4: American hosts already have networks of friends and do not often go out of their way to welcome newcomers to their country and to integrate them into the community. Note that this incident brings up a common experience that virtually all people crossing cultures have: the problem of making friends. Because the issue faced is common to many who cross cultures and attempt to live and work closely with others, this critical incident is of widespread relevance even though the particular character involved is a foreign student. All of the incidents in this book deal with such common concerns. We validated the alternative explanations we offer for the incidents by asking a number of very experienced people to rate the adequacy of each alternative (60 for the first edition and 21 for the new incidents added to this edition). In reading the incidents and choosing among alternatives, then, people using these materials will be comparing their choices with those of highly experienced individuals who have lived and worked extensively in cultures other than their own.

ORGANIZATION OF
THE CRITICAL INCIDENTS

Many of the points raised in the last few pages (e.g., experiences common to all who interact across cultures, the validation of the critical incidents) are discussed in more depth in Chapter 2, "Information for Teachers and Cross-Cultural Trainers." Of course, all readers are invited to examine that material, but those who do not desire such detail should have sufficient information at this point to begin analysis of the critical incidents, and may wish to move ahead to Chapter 3.

The incidents are arranged according to what typically happens during extensive cross-cultural experiences. People become participants in many cross-cultural incidents and then *later* become interested in why things are happening to them as they do. The alternative direction—analyzing why things happen and then reading the critical incidents—is too abstract: The incidents are what interest people in analyzing the underlying reasons for the issues raised. Given this reasoning, the critical incidents are organized according to the contexts of where and when they happen (e.g., at work or with family members). After examining the incidents, the reader may want to explore the 18 themes that organize the information presented in the incidents, which we discuss in the final three chapters. The framework provided by these 18 themes leads to analysis of the underlying reasons that things happen as they do.

The assumption behind these materials is that reading the incidents best mimics actual long-term, cross-cultural encounters: Things happen, and then people want to know why. However, we realize that some readers will want to turn to in-depth discussion of underlying reasons after reading incidents that especially interest them, so we identify the essays within Chapters 11-13 that discuss the issues raised in each incident in the explanation section for that incident. Active involvement with the incidents will result in a great deal of reader cross-referencing, an activity we want to encourage.

The critical incidents are presented in Chapters 3-10. Each chapter begins with a brief introduction, followed by a number of incidents and their alternative explanations. The incidents are arranged according to degree of difficulty; that is, selecting correct explanations should be easier for the incidents in the first part of each chapter than for those that come later. Incidents that fall toward the end of a chapter may require more sophisticated and careful analysis, or may have more than one preferred alternative. Each chapter ends with discussions of the various alternatives corresponding to the different incidents.

For those using the set of learning materials offered in this volume, we recommend the following steps (other suggested uses are discussed in Chapter 2):

1. Readers should read each item separately, mark their reactions to all of the alternatives, and then compare their responses with the developers' explanations and the responses of the validation sample. All of the alternatives should be considered, for two reasons. First, in many cases, two (or even more) of the alternative explanations may be considered correct or appropriate. After all, in everyday life people do not find only one exact explanation for every incident they encounter. Second, successful cross-cultural adjustment is dependent upon the individual's ability to reject incorrect explanations as well as to find correct ones. Readers might want simply to mark each alternative with words such as *very good, good, bad,* or *very bad.* Or they may want to use the same format as the members of the validation sample. Members of the sample were given this suggestion: "Ask yourself, How likely is it that this alternative is correct?" Then check in one of the six spaces for *each* alternative according to the scale:

_____ I am certain that this is correct.
_____ Very likely.
_____ Likely.
_____ Unlikely.
_____ Very unlikely.
_____ I am certain this is not correct.

Thus, you will have either four or five checks for each incident, depending upon whether there are four or five alternatives.

2. If training is taking place in a group, trainees can compare results, discuss their reactions, and perhaps role-play some of the incidents.

3. After reading all the incidents and the discussions of the alternative explanations, readers will have been exposed to a great deal of information. To help put this in perspective, they should read (and perhaps discuss) the 18 essays presented in Chapters 11-13, which develop broad themes useful in analyzing cross-cultural experiences. Within each essay we review the relevant critical incidents and provide information useful for analyzing the many specific events people will encounter in their actual cross-cultural interactions subsequent to training.

4. Readers may also want to make notes concerning how the points raised in the incidents may be related to their own specific cross-cultural assignments or events in their prior experiences. The incidents begin in Chapter 3.

2

INFORMATION FOR TEACHERS
AND CROSS-CULTURAL TRAINERS

This chapter presents considerable background information for trainers, educators, and those interested in a broader understanding of issues related to intercultural education and training. Included is a general overview of cross-cultural training strategies and, in particular, an overview of the development and use of culture assimilators. We also present in this chapter the rationale for the development of a culture-general assimilator capable of preparing people for a variety of extensive cross-cultural experiences, information on how the materials were originally developed and validated, a survey of how the research literature supports the use of this instrument, and suggested uses and modification of these materials based on the extensive experiences of the developers.

COMMONALITIES IN
CROSS-CULTURAL EXPERIENCES

It is possible to develop a set of materials usable by many people about to live abroad, or about to interact extensively with culturally different others, because of the commonalities in people's cross-cultural experiences. These commonalities include intense personal experiences, such as emotional upheaval, an occasional sense of displacement, and confrontation with the fact that one's previous learning may be insufficient for effective functioning within another culture. All of the incidents in this book are designed to identify common concerns, as the example provided in Chapter 1 illustrates. Even though Dubud, the person involved in that incident, was a foreign student, his underlying concern of developing friendships is common to all people, especially sojourners in countries other than their own. Indeed, so is the reason Dubud had difficulty in forming friendships: Hosts or those who have been in the setting for a long time very often have well-established social networks and do not need to go out of their way to integrate newcomers.

The assumption that a set of materials of widespread usefulness is possible differs from the assumption behind most available materials designed to prepare people for cross-cultural interaction. Most existing materials are targeted for specific audiences (e.g., businesspeople, diplomats, foreign students) about to interact in specific countries (e.g., Japan, Australia, Great Britain). In cases where the purpose is to prepare people for interactions with culturally different others within their own countries, cultural groups are usually specified (e.g., African Americans and European Americans in the United States). The best of these existing materials are extremely useful, and the present volume is meant to complement such country- or culture-specific and audience-specific materials when they are available. Before we describe the set of materials offered here, we believe a short introduction to various cross-cultural training programs and to existing materials is necessary.

THE CONTENT OF
CROSS-CULTURAL TRAINING PROGRAMS

Given the desire to prepare people to live and work in other cultures, the obvious question becomes, What is the best approach to, and content for, cross-cultural training programs? Researchers and practitioners have identified a number of programs that are commonly offered to those about to interact with people from cultures other than their own (Bhawuk, 1990; Brislin, Landis, & Brandt, 1983; Brislin & Yoshida, 1994a, 1994b; Gudykunst & Hammer, 1983). Keep in mind that all of these approaches to training basically have the same goals: to help trainees (a) manage the stress of cross-cultural interaction and thus make good personal adjustments, (b) develop and maintain interpersonal relationships, (c) complete the tasks they originally set out to accomplish, and (d) restrict the time they need for successful adjustment to what would be expected in a more familiar context. (These four criteria of successful adjustment are also discussed in Chapter 1.) In designing actual training programs, most trainers choose a combination of ways to accomplish these goals.

Cognitive training. Cognitive training places emphasis on facts about the host country or target culture, as well as information about what commonly happens to sojourners in that culture. Typical teaching methods include lectures, group discussions, presentation of written materials, and question-and-answer sessions with "old hands" who have worked within the culture for some time. A considerable amount of accurate information can be transferred to trainees in a relatively short period of time through such an approach. Unfortunately, there seems to be little correlation between the mere accumulation of information and people's subsequent ability to function effectively in another context.

Behavior modification. This approach looks at the roles of rewards and punishment in a person's life. Typical methods involve asking trainees to visualize what is rewarding and what is punishing for them in their own culture. Trainees would be asked to learn about the other culture in terms of obtaining rewards and avoiding (or at least mitigating) punishments. Such an approach can be highly effective in helping people achieve the goals of training. One major drawback of this approach is the high degree of specificity required, and thus the relatively few trainees who can benefit from such programs.

Experiential training. Experiential training emphasizes activities in which trainees participate. Typical methods include having trainees role-play potentially problematic situations (such as negotiations between a boss from one culture and a subordinate from another), take part in simulations of other cultures for up to 2 weeks at a time, and take field trips into other cultures. Also included are such classic cross-cultural simulations as Bafa Bafa (or the children's version, Rafa Rafa; Shirts, 1976) and Barnga (Thiagarajan & Steinwachs, 1990), which effectively re-create many of the experiences encountered in real cross-cultural encounters and can be quite engaging for participants. Culture-specific simulations in which trainees spend periods of time living as they would in a new setting can be highly effective, but are extremely costly and time-consuming. Execution of the more "classroom-oriented" simulations requires significant skill and practice, as does the critical debriefing stage. Experiential activities can provide a good foundation for subsequent learning.

Cultural self-awareness. In this type of training, trainees learn about the importance of culture by examining common experiences people have in their own countries and cultures. Typical methods include group discussions in which Americans might explore the roots of the value placed on individualism and Asians might discuss the value placed on the collectivity. These discussions often stimulate an expansion of people's thinking, as when Americans bring up examples where the collective good is paramount (such as in team sports) and Asians discuss those aspects of their culture where a premium is placed on individuality (such as when passing individualistic examinations is a requirement for securing limited slots in good colleges and universities). This approach is especially useful when trainees are aware that they will be leaving their own country but do not know their exact destination, as is the case for many refugees; military personnel, who often do not receive specific orders until a very short time before actual assignment; and overseas businesspeople on troubleshooting missions.

Attribution training. In this approach, trainees learn about how people make judgments concerning the causes of behavior. The assumption behind attribution training is that many misunderstandings stem from differing perceptions of, or attributions about, given events. Cross-cultural adjustment is facilitated when people learn how and why others make attributions about a wide variety of events so that they can learn to make the same attributions (called *isomorphic attributions*; see Triandis, 1977, and our discussion in Chapter 1). For example, a student may voice disagreement with a position taken by a teacher. This behavior may be attributed to disrespect of authority in one culture, whereas in another it would be seen as desirable individualism. Misunderstanding is reduced when people know when, how, and why certain attributions will be made in cases such as this one. Given the incredibly wide range of situations in which sojourners will find themselves, cross-cultural training cannot give enough information so that trainees can learn to make isomorphic attributions quickly whenever a potential misunderstanding arises. Rather, training can deal with the how, why, and when of attributions so that trainees will understand some general principles that lie behind the thousands of specific behaviors they will observe. The typical method of attribution training (called the *culture assimilator* or *intercultural sensitizer*) involves reading short case studies, called *critical incidents,* that involve cross-cultural interaction and potential misunderstandings on the part of hosts and sojourners. Trainees are asked to choose from among a range of alternative explanations for each incident, each explanation representing a different attribution concerning the causes of behavior.

There is no one ideal type of training. Most good orientation programs will use more than one of the five approaches reviewed above. In our experience, for instance, trainees enjoy talking about their own backgrounds (cultural self-awareness) because thoughts about the importance of "culture" can be triggered by their upcoming experience. Culture is much like the air people breathe: It is taken for granted until there is an external stimulation that forces people to think about it. Although frequently used as the point of departure for more innovative approaches, there is a place in good programs for stimulating lecturers and discussions with old hands (cognitive training). Trainees can use the information learned through this method as their training moves on to more active approaches (experiential training). It is difficult, and not particularly beneficial, for trainees to participate in active training methods when they have no basic information on how people might behave in certain situations (Kerrick, Clark, & Rice, 1967). After they have lived through simulated experiences in other cultures, discussions concerning the possibilities of finding rewards and avoiding punishers (behavioral training) are more meaningful. The various bits of knowledge learned through these different approaches can sometimes be integrated as trainees learn how and why hosts and sojourners think and make judgments about cross-cultural encounters (attribution training).

More information on the various approaches to cross-cultural training can be found in the work of Gudykunst and Hammer (1983) and Brislin and Yoshida (1994a, 1994b). For reasons to be explained in forthcoming sections of this chapter, we chose the culture assimilator method (from the attribution approach) for the development of these training materials. Consequently, we focus more on the research literature concerning the culture assimilator than on the literature concerning other approaches to training.

CULTURE ASSIMILATORS:
DEVELOPMENT AND USE

Given their choices of one or a combination of the five approaches, cross-cultural trainers will be eager to find specific materials to help meet their program goals. Despite years of experience, however, there are very few sets of materials in widespread use. Rather, different trainers use different materials. Further, there has long been a tradition of homemade and do-it-yourself materials that have had little distribution outside given trainers' social networks. Although undoubtedly meeting the needs of individual trainers, this approach means that there are few materials of which many trainers are aware and that they have used in actual programs. Consequently, when they meet at conventions and workshops, trainers rarely talk about similar experiences and share notes so that a commonly used set of materials can be improved. The culture assimilator is, perhaps, the exception to this rule.

The culture assimilator is a cross-cultural training strategy that employs the critical-incident approach to present culture clashes between individuals from different backgrounds. Trainees read short vignettes, or critical incidents, in which individuals from different cultures interact with the intent of pursuing some common goal. Toward the end of each incident, a clash of cultures is evident and the two parties are unable to accomplish their task. More often than not, an unintended misinterpretation of events is at the base of the problem, or a misunderstanding of the subjective meaning given to a particular behavior. The reader is presented with a number of alternatives and is asked to select the one that best explains the problem *from the point of view of the person in the vignette who is not from the reader's own culture.*

The history of the culture assimilator goes back to 1962 at the University of Illinois, where researchers proposed the development of a computer program that could be used to provide cross-cultural training to students (Albert, 1983). It was here that the term *culture assimilator* was proposed. The first assimilator was developed to address communication and interaction between Arab and American students. Construction of such instruments has not altered much over the years. In the development of the first assimilator, Arab students were asked to relate a variety of culture clashes they had encountered with their American peers, and to explain the problems as best they could from their own perspective. American students were then asked to review the incidents and to explain them as best they could from their perspective. Episodes were constructed with a number of alternative explanations or attributions offered, generally four or five. One of the attributions presented was the one provided by the Arab respondents, and the remaining three or four came from those most often presented by the Americans. Such has been the general format for creating most culture assimilators.

A typical training program has trainees read a number of such critical incidents, perhaps as many as 30 or more. The assumption is that as trainees receive feedback on their responses, they begin to understand the *subjective culture* of the target group and subsequently select more appropriate responses. They are thus making isomorphic attributions and developing an insider's perspective.

TYPES OF CULTURE ASSIMILATORS

Prior to the mid-1980s, culture assimilators were developed for highly specific purposes. That is, they were designed to prepare individuals from one cultural group for interactions with people from another specific group. A variety of culture-specific assimilators have been developed for a variety of uses, including to prepare French bankers to live and work in Thailand, to prepare American adolescents about to embark on volunteer health programs in Honduras, and to prepare white and black servicemen to live and work together in the U.S. military (for comprehensive lists of culture-specific assimilators, see Albert, 1983; Cushner & Landis, in press).

Culture-specific assimilators have demonstrated considerable effectiveness at helping sojourners achieve the goals of their intercultural experiences when the target or host culture is well known (some of the research is reviewed below). The difficulty with the use of culture-specific assimilators seems to be one of availability. Developed for particular audiences and often for highly specific purposes (e.g., to prepare adolescent volunteer medical workers to work in Honduras in the Amigos de las Americas Program), these assimilators are generally not readily applicable to or easily obtained by the general public. An individual needs to have a wide network of colleagues in the field of cross-cultural training to gain access to the culture-specific assimilators that have been developed.

Development of the Culture-General Assimilator

Stimulated by large-scale programs such as the Peace Corps (e.g., Textor, 1966) as well as by organizations that support foreign students (e.g., Lambert & Bressler, 1956), a rich and diverse body of research has developed that focuses on the experiences of people who spend large amounts of time in cultures other than their own. In reviewing this literature, Brislin (1981) was struck by the similarities in people's experiences despite the wide range of roles they had and the many different countries in which they lived. Despite such diverse roles as businessperson, diplomat, Peace Corps worker, teacher in an urban setting, social worker, foreign student, and technical assistance adviser, people go through similar experiences when adjusting to life in countries other than their own and/or to extensive interaction with people from other cultures. Among these experiences are a sense of uprootedness, feelings that one has been singled out for special attention, difficulties in developing relationships (as presented in the incident related in Chapter 1), and the realization that one's previous knowledge may be inadequate. The range of such experiences forms the basis for the critical incidents prepared for this book, as well as for the 18 essays that review general themes brought out in the incidents. Brislin (1981) organizes his treatment of the commonalities in cross-cultural experiences according to nine broad categories:

1. the historical myths people bring with them to another culture;
2. people's attitudes, traits, and skills;
3. their thought and attribution processes;
4. the groups they join;
5. the range of situations in which they must interact;
6. their management of cross-cultural conflict;
7. the tasks they want to accomplish;
8. the organizations of which they are a part; and, given an understanding of the above,
9. the processes of short- and long-term adjustment.

Brislin has urged that people involved in one specific type of experience (e.g., foreign student advisers) should not think of their clientele as so unique that communication with other specialists (e.g., Peace Corps staff members) is undermined. Rather, a focus on commonalities allows interaction among specialists and opens up the possibility of mutual enrichment. Other developments have pointed to the possibility of greater attention to commonalities. And especially because culture is so secret from most people (see Chapter 1), it becomes necessary to establish and develop a common vocabulary among people engaged in extensive intercultural contact if they are to begin to converse with one another about such issues.

In addition, various summer programs designed to introduce professionals to cross-cultural training and to offer advanced instruction for experienced people have been offered over the years. During the summer of 1983, Drs. Dan Landis and Richard Brislin hosted a program designed to increase the skills of cross-cultural trainers, and more than 40 people participated. The specific training technique given the most attention was the culture assimilator. At this workshop, the possibility of a culture-general assimilator was introduced, and many of the participants thought such a project feasible. This was especially encouraging given that participants came from eight different countries and had worked in a wide variety of training programs for many types of target audiences. Attempts were made to write culture assimilator items of widespread usefulness, and this experience was helpful in the development of the final package. Several items from this summer program were used as first drafts in later efforts.

In September 1983, the four authors of the first edition of this book decided to meet regularly and to push forward on the development of a culture-general assimilator. Work proceeded smoothly, with the developers drawing from their own past experiences, reading, and interviews with experienced sojourners. Despite their experiences with very different target audiences, the authors found that the task of writing items of potential widespread use was by no means the most difficult aspect of the work. The most difficult task was creating a variety of alternative explanations for each item, just as this has always been the most difficult step in the development of the culture-specific assimilators already discussed. The team approach was very helpful in lessening the difficulties of writing alternative explanations.

All of us had worked with foreign students. In addition, the team had experience with overseas businesspeople and missionaries (Mahealani Yong); adolescents in youth exchange programs and students and teachers in international and intercultural education programs (Kenneth Cushner), immigrants and foreign-language instructors about to begin teaching students from other cultures (Craig Cherrie), and military personnel, researchers about to carry out experiments and surveys in other countries, and cross-cultural trainers wishing to improve their skills (Richard Brislin). A typical scene at a project meeting would involve one team member reading a draft of an item, together with one or two suggested alternative explanations. Responses of the other team members would often be something like, "I can see that you wrote that item based on your work with foreign students, but it would also work for overseas businesspeople." Other comments might be along the lines of "Just change one or two phrases, add another piece of background information, and the item will be of more widespread use." Team members also suggested additional alternative explanations of the incidents, some of them correct and some of them incorrect. The challenge of writing good alternatives is twofold: to highlight correct attributions of the causes of the behavior depicted and to indicate (through incorrect alternatives) common misconceptions that should be corrected. At the same time, good incident-alternative combinations should bring up general points that will be of use to sojourners as they adapt to life in other cultures. We undertook the step of alternative construction so frequently as a team that, although we can remember who wrote the first drafts of various items, we cannot remember who suggested which alternative explanations for many of the incidents.

RECENT THINKING
ABOUT EDUCATIONAL MATERIALS

In developing these materials, we were faced with the need to make difficult decisions at a number of points. One concerned the focus of the assimilator's core element: Should each of the critical incidents be concerned with specific people in a specific country, or should each incident be more general? One insightful colleague who examined all the incidents (but not the alternative explanations or the 18 essays) mentioned that he saw a possible discrepancy between the goal of a general assimilator and the path-to-goal of the incidents based on specific countries. Our reasoning at the time of the initial decision to develop incidents concerning interactions between people from specific cultural backgrounds living in specific countries was based on a combination of vague intuition and pragmatics. The latter was due to our experience during the 1983 summer program and the pretesting of incidents with colleagues: Specific incidents were preferred. We tried out more general incidents, involving, for instance, a person described as being from "a highly industrialized nation" interacting in a country described as a "less technologically developed Asian nation," but readers kept asking, "Which industrialized country and which nation in Asia?" We accepted their feedback as an indication that there is more interest in reading and discussing specific rather than general incidents, and so we chose to write all incidents with this feedback in mind.

While we were writing incidents for the first edition, an article appeared that made clear some of the vague intuitions that also led to the decision in favor of specific materials. In that article, Glaser (1984) analyzes how educational programs can improve reasoning and problem-solving skills, or, in everyday language, how education can help people to think better. A conclusion from past research is that when general skills develop, the path to skills is often knowledge in a specific domain. For instance, some general skills might be to avoid stereotyped thinking about a problem, to be willing to seek out more information, and to be unsatisfied with an obvious explanation based on the most colorful or vivid (not necessarily the most important) part of a problem. These general skills are often best developed during the study of a specific content area, whether it be automobile maintenance, algebra, or English literature. This suggests that it may not be as effective to approach the development of general skills through coverage of general principles. For example, the general skill of avoiding stereotyped thinking could be introduced through the examination of a wide variety of problems in many different areas, using puzzles, games, and everyday tasks that people must complete. Although intuitively appealing, this approach appears to be less successful than one that encourages skills development during the study of one specific content area of interest to the learner.

Interestingly, past efforts in cross-cultural training have moved from general to specific materials in the quest for general goals. One training approach (reviewed by Brislin & Pedersen, 1976) has been to have staff members role-play persons who are generally different from trainees (in the United States, called the *contrast-American* technique). For instance, where the American is individualistic, the staff member plays a person who defers to the collectivity. Where the American wants to hire workers based on their ability, the staff member makes recommendations based on the status of family name. In the past, trainees were uncomfortable with the level of generality of the roles played by staff members who act in an opposite manner. A trainee would ask, "Where is this person from? I must know to decide how to be as sensitive as I can." Given this feedback, the staff member in such role-play training is now introduced, for example, as a well-educated professional from South Asia who comes from a good family. We interpreted this feedback as another indication of the importance of specific content.

One goal of this training package is to encourage more sophisticated thinking about cross-cultural interaction and about life in other cultures. The most frequently mentioned general skill is *cross-cultural sensitivity*. Ideally, trainees bring an interest to the development of this skill, given their realization that their success in another culture will be dependent upon their sensitivity to their hosts' viewpoints. Like Glaser, we believe that the general skill is best developed through work with specific content—in our case, the critical incidents. Glaser (1984) goes further to indicate the way in which specific materials can be used in the development of general skills:

> I would like to refer particularly to the self-regulatory or metacognitive capabilities present in mature learners. The abilities include knowing what one knows and does not know, predicting the outcome of one's performance, planning ahead, efficiently apportioning time and cognitive resources, and monitoring and editing one's efforts to solve a problem or to learn. To develop these skills, one approach is to teach specific knowledge domains in interactive, interrogative ways so that general self-regulatory skills are exercised in the course of acquiring domain-related knowledge. (p. 102)

We feel that the culture assimilator format meets the elements in Glaser's recommendation. Specific materials (the critical incidents) are examined that should be of interest to many different trainees, and trainees are encouraged to interact with the teaching materials as much as possible through their choices among the alternative explanations of the incidents. There is also interaction given the comparison of trainees' choices of the correct explanations with our choices and our defense of those choices. Of course, there can be even more interaction if trainees discuss the incidents with each other and with program staff, and if they role-play some of the incidents that are of particular interest to them. Our explanations of the various alternatives, and the 18 essays in Chapters 11-13, are designed to bring up general points that people can use no matter where they find themselves.

A review of two incidents that were designed either during the summer of 1983 program or as part of our subsequent efforts to develop the total package should make these points clear. Both incidents could have been used in the final package, but they were not, for reasons to be specified. The first incident involves the interaction of a white, middle-class Australian with traditional Aboriginal Australians.

Jim, a non-Aboriginal consultant to a mining company in Australia, was given the task of negotiating with a traditionally oriented Aboriginal community for the right to mine a specific tract of land. A meeting of community leaders, all men, was called so that Jim might put his case. Some of the younger men were appointed spokespersons at the meeting because of their knowledge of English; some of the women gathered on the periphery to listen. At this meeting the older men decided that they would need more time to discuss this matter. Jim agreed to return in 3 days.

On his return, further discussions took place; more meetings were arranged. Jim reported to the community periodically for the next 2 months. Each time the talks proceeded a little further. It was indicated to Jim by spokespersons that it would be possible for the company to mine specific areas provided no other tracts of land were harmed; the debate turned to access rights, compensation, and the rules and regulations for the conduct of company staff. The proceedings were followed with intense interest, and only one old lady tended consistently to leave the meetings early. Finally, Jim returned to his company with the good news that the community had reached a consensus, the level of compensation had been agreed upon, and the first teams of support staff could move into the area. When the teams arrived 3 weeks later, they were told by the community that no mining could take place.

Why did the community reject the mining permit?

1. The spokesperson misled Jim into thinking mining had been approved.
2. Aboriginal people just cannot make decisions.
3. Jim had not obtained approval from the custodian of the land.
4. The community decided that the compensation offered was inadequate and were stalling as part of a bargaining strategy.

The correct choice is 3. After choosing this alternative, trainees read the following: "This is the most probable explanation. Aboriginal people are often considered to own land collectively; that is, the right to use land is vested in the group rather than the individual. However, the more realistic approach would be to see Aboriginal 'ownership' in terms of custodianship. Custodianship implies that people, as a group and as individuals, are responsible for the care of certain tracts of land for their own and their groups' spiritual and economic welfare. As such, alienation of land, in a non-Aboriginal sense, is inconceivable. However, should people decide to make a compromise with non-Aboriginal demands, as well as the changing demands of their own groups, then that decision must be made ultimately by the custodians of any particular tract of land. Such custodians are most frequently male, though they may be female. Due to the fairly dramatic reduction of Aboriginal populations during colonization, the numbers of custodians over any one tract of land may be small. In this particular example, it had been reduced to one old lady sitting on the sidelines who listened to the debate, took little active part, but made the decision to leave the meetings early, indicating that she did not agree with what was going on. If this old woman's agreement cannot be received, no decision can be reached, even though discussions by prospective or related custodians may continue. Jim, misunderstanding the process of decision making and the principle of custodianship, paid little attention to the old lady's actions. Consequently, he failed to get the permission of the land's custodian, though he tried hard to attain community consensus."

If they choose 1, they read: "It sometimes happens that Aboriginal people, familiar with the English language, are appointed interpreters by non-Aboriginal negotiators in order to make the process of discussion 'easier,' that is, more manageable. At times these spokespersons may be presenting a decision that does not represent the community's perceptions. In this case, however, the story indicates that the meeting men appointed the young men as interpreters only. There is no absence of the rest of the community. Please choose again."

If they choose 2, they read: "It is true that the story indicates that there have been some obstacles to the process that most non-Aborigines recognize as decision making. Among non-Aboriginal groups in Australia, decision making is generally based on majority rule, determined by designated/elected leaders/spokespersons or committees. Aboriginal decision-making processes are generally based on consensus; that is, everybody who has a real interest has a voice, and no decision is taken unless everybody agrees. This is time-consuming and it may mean at times that no definite decision is reached. The decision, then, is made to suspend judgment until the situation again arises to demand that the process of discussion is recommended. Aboriginal people, then, operate on principles very different from those to which most people are accustomed. It therefore becomes easy to assume that they are unable to make decisions. Please choose again."

If they choose 4, they read: "It can happen that the level of compensation becomes contentious. Aboriginal people are aware of economic manipulations. They are certainly aware that monetary compensation can be used by the community for all sorts of advantages. However, whenever levels of compensation become an issue, the courts, particularly the Land Councils, are called in for negotiations. If this had been the case, then the company would have been notified early through legal channels and would have been spared the expense of sending out exploratory teams for nothing. Please choose again."

This incident brings up all the different tightropes we had to walk in developing specific incidents for a general assimilator. We felt that this item, although excellent for a culture-specific assimilator for interaction with Aboriginal Australians, dealt with issues that had less widespread usefulness than other incidents. We felt that Glaser's suggestion about using specific items to develop general skills would not be well applied here because of the very detailed points being made about Aboriginal Australians. There are general points made by this incident. One is that people should seek more information and should not make quick decisions based on stereotypes. Another is that sojourners should be prepared for differences in how decisions are made. We feel, however, that these points are better handled in other incidents. Another consideration in not using this item was that people might find it difficult to put themselves in Jim's shoes because of the nature of his specialized task. The best incidents, we feel, encourage the reader to empathize with one or more of the characters.

To reiterate, this is an excellent item for use in training people to interact with Aboriginal Australians, but it is less useful for a culture-general assimilator. On the other hand, we feel that the following item does meet the demands of culture-general training. This is one of the more difficult items we developed. Trainees can readily choose the correct explanations from the alternatives offered on the easier incidents; they make more mistakes, or must expend more thought, on the difficult ones.

"Did you see the notice about this program to be held in Samoa?" a friend of Jack Edwards asked him at lunch. Jack had seen the announcement, because his boss had earlier told him that, should Jack request it, a trip to Samoa would be funded for his attendance at a conference on indigenous technology. Jack worked for a company in New York City involved in heavy industry, and his boss felt that having someone current in indigenous technology would provide a beneficial broadening of perspective. The boss chose Jack because of Jack's good relations with coworkers, which would make the eventual sharing of information possible. Jack was also highly respected by his coworkers.

Jack flew to Samoa and settled into the hotel near the conference headquarters. He was mildly surprised, at looking over the registration list, that he did not know any other conference participants. Many of the participants were from Asian countries.

The meetings started and Jack took his place along with about 100 other participants. He contributed to conversations and discussions about as much as 80% of the other participants. As at any conference, a certain percentage (here about 20%) had little to say. In a private conversation after dinner one night, Jack happened to find himself one-on-one with one of the quiet participants, an engineer from Thailand. Jack did not mind getting into the conversation, as his company had dealings in Thailand. But Jack found that the English of the Thai engineer was not very good, and he began to become patronizing in his conversation, berating Thailand for not being more careful about who it sends to international conferences. People who happened to overhear these remarks later made an opportunity to apologize to the Thai engineer.

What could have contributed to Jack's behavior in the one-on-one conversation with the Thai engineer? Of the four explanations, choose the one that takes as much information into account as possible.

1. Jack was a rude and insensitive individual.
2. Jack's sense of his own personal identity was not allowed to be expressed at the conference.

3. It is a very frustrating challenge to keep up a conversation with someone whose English is not very good.
4. People trained in heavy industry have a difficult time grasping concepts about indigenous technology.

If they choose 2, the correct alternative, trainees are told: "There are a number of factors that threaten Jack's identity, and so this is the best answer. Identity is a quality that is partly given to us by others, through their affection, respect, and feedback concerning the behaviors in which we engage. In this story, Jack is a high-status person who becomes one of many participants on the same level in Samoa. He does not have his status group with him to continually reinforce him, as he does in his home environment. He knows no one else at the meeting who could remind the conference of his status and good standing in his profession. A term social psychologists have used when identity given to us by others is stripped is *deindividuation.* When people are not recognized as the individuals they know themselves to be, and when they are away from the people who give them their identity, they may act in atypical ways. At this conference, Jack is confronted with a major temptation: It is easy to lash out against someone who has a difficult time defending himself and who is unlikely to retaliate. Here, of course, that target person is the Thai engineer. But such temptations must be resisted. A professor accustomed to working with foreign students once said, 'I have to be very careful since working with Asian students always brings out my inherent bossiness.' This professor was wise to recognize this quality in himself so that he could take preventive measures. Recognizing the potential negative features of the deindividuating experience, as exemplified in this story, should also allow people to catch themselves before engaging in rude behavior."

If they choose 1, trainees read: "Jack certainly acted in a rude manner. However, the early part of the story presents evidence that Jack was considered a valued coworker with good relations with peers in his home environment. There are factors affecting his behavior associated with this trip. Please choose again."

If they choose 3, trainees read: "It is frequently frustrating to keep up a conversation with someone who does not speak the same language well. But there are other factors presented throughout the entire story that lead to a better answer. Most sojourners learn to keep up conversations gracefully with people who do not speak a common language well."

If they choose 4, trainees are presented with this information: "While it may be difficult to shift one's thinking from heavy industry to indigenous technology, this is too much of an overgeneralization to be of much help. If people trained in one specialty were always thought unable to benefit from the insights of another, there would not be much hope for the advancement of knowledge. Please choose again."

Even though not all trainees will have ever meet a person from Thailand, or have been to Samoa, we feel that the issues raised in this incident are of general usefulness. Most sojourners will go through periods during which their identities are threatened and during which they feel deindividuated. Further, it is fairly easy to identify with Jack Edwards because virtually all readers have been away from home in places where nobody knows them. Consequently, the interaction with specifics that leads to general skills, as suggested by Glaser, is possible with this incident. The possibility of such interaction was sought for all of the incidents created for the final training package.

THE RELATIONSHIP BETWEEN
GENERAL AND SPECIFIC TRAINING

The differences between the two items reviewed above also highlight a point about the place of a culture-general assimilator in a training program. The general assimilator cannot be a complete substitute for specific information about the culture in which a person is about to live and/or work. For example, specific information about Japan is extremely desirable in a good training program for people about to live in that country. Specific knowledge about Latino culture is necessary for social workers who work extensively with Latino communities. Or, in reference to one of the critical incidents already covered, a culture-specific component of a training program to prepare people for interaction with Aboriginal Australians could employ materials that depict key areas of possible miscommunication between sojourners and hosts.

A culture-general assimilator is useful in many different ways, as we discuss below.

A culture-general assimilator can be of use when a culture-specific training program is not available. In our experience, this is a common predicament, because there often are not enough sojourners preparing to live in the same country to make a specific program financially feasible. The present training package can be used when a group of trainees are about to travel to a number of different countries. Or it can be used by individual sojourners who have no access to a formal training program.

A culture-general assimilator can serve as a basis for coverage of culture-specific information in newly developed programs. At times, professionals involved in cross-cultural training are asked to prepare people to spend time in countries where the staff members themselves have not lived. In such cases, experienced sojourners who have lived in the particular countries are hired as consultants. But because these experienced sojourners may have had little experience with cross-cultural training, they are often at a loss to know what material they should cover. A general assimilator can be used to remind the experienced person of key problems encountered when adjusting to other cultures. The specific coloring to, or specific examples of, the general problem can then be covered in training. For instance, the example item presented in Chapter 1 deals with friendship formation. Primed by this general incident, experienced people can then be specific about the problems of friendship formation in particular countries or cultures.

A culture-general assimilator provides a way of integrating a great deal of specific information. Sometimes, the complaint about specific cross-cultural training programs is that too much information is presented without any attempt to integrate the information. Consequently, trainees' memories become taxed and fatigue becomes a problem. The themes presented in the culture-general assimilator can assist trainers in organizing specific information.

The three uses of the culture-general assimilator described above emphasize the relation between culture-general and culture-specific training. In addition, there are at least two uses of the culture-general assimilator that result directly in benefits to the user.

The culture-general assimilator provides a way of encouraging the development of a global, multicultural perspective for those who work with people from many cultures within a short period of time. Examples would include teachers who work in culturally diverse schools, businesspeople who travel frequently, social workers who interact extensively with members of many different ethnic groups, foreign student advisers, and college professors who attract students from many different countries.

The culture-general assimilator provides a way of involving students in courses such as cross-cultural psychology, international education, cultural anthropology, and so forth. Courses such as these are often difficult

to teach, as students may not have experienced much cross-cultural interaction. Consequently, discussions about the influence of culture on human
behavior are very abstract for them. But if they can become acquainted with
the problems and prospects of extensive cross-cultural interaction through
a culture-general assimilator, they may be interested in pursuing research
on some of the topics raised in the critical incidents. Our experience, in
common with other trainers, also suggests that many people have not had
extensive intercultural interaction prior to training, or if they have, they
have not stopped to reflect upon that experience in such a way that it
becomes a meaningful learning experience. This means that they enter
training sessions without a foundation upon which to build. This is a critical
element to consider in any educational setting. Bransford (1979) suggests
that up to 80% of what a person learns in any educational session is directly
dependent upon what that individual already knows. It becomes the task of
the teacher or trainer to stimulate students' memories of those prior
experiences, which then act as a foundation for further learning. If trainees
have not had extensive cross-cultural experiences, they may be missing a
critical element in the learning process. The critical incidents, then, provide
the necessary foundation upon which further learning can build. Put another way, after working through the incidents, students who have not had
cross-cultural experiences may become more similar to those who have,
such as foreign students, former Peace Corps volunteers, and sons and
daughters of overseas businesspeople. Such people, who are unfortunately
in the minority, have long done well in international or cross-cultural
course work. For instance, a number of the critical incidents deal with
misunderstandings stemming from differing views concerning how interpersonal relationships are developed in different cultures. After reading
these incidents and empathizing with the people involved in the stories,
students may find the cross-cultural research literature on interpersonal
relationships (e.g., Triandis, 1977) to be of more interest.

Even though it may appear that we are setting culture-general and
culture-specific materials in opposition to each other, that is not our
intention. Our recommendation is that training and educational programs
include specific information whenever possible. This can include specific
information on the upcoming country of assignment, the demands of
certain jobs (e.g., social workers or foreign student advisers), and the
results of very specific research studies. Most training programs use a
variety of methods so as to both achieve different goals and maintain
trainee/student interest and enthusiasm. There is no competition between
specific and general approaches. Rather, each can complement the other.

In their review of recent work in personnel decision making within organizations, which includes decisions about training, Zedeck and Cascio (1984) conclude:

> We are attempting to find generalities in the field. . . . At the same time, emphasis on details and processes is a positive step to further our understanding. We do not see a contradiction between the movement toward generalization and the emphasis on specific processes. Hopefully, the two will move our field from an applied, reactive orientation to one that has a theoretical formulation incorporating resources, tasks, environments, and systems. (p. 506)

The generalizations to which Zedeck and Cascio refer are exemplified in this work by the themes brought out in the explanations of the alternatives and in the 18 essays. The specific processes include details on how the general themes (e.g., learning styles, prejudice) will be encountered in a particular country or context.

There is, of course, a large step to be taken in moving from ideas about a culture-general assimilator, as already discussed, to its actual development. We felt that a poor way to start would be to collect or write a haphazard set of incidents that each of us thought might be useful. We felt that there would be too much wasted time in such an effort because there could easily be (a) duplication of effort and (b) spotty coverage of important areas. Instead, we began with the themes we wanted to include, and then wrote critical incidents that exemplified each of the themes in people's actual cross-cultural interactions. We decided that 18 themes would provide good coverage, and these themes were developed in the 18 essays presented later in this volume. The 18 essays were also designed to integrate key points brought out in the critical incidents. The 18 themes were identified based on their centrality in the literature examining cross-cultural experiences. Previously, one of us had been involved in extensive literature searches in the preparation of several books (Brislin, 1981; Landis & Brislin, 1983) and had identified key studies and literature reviews as the best resources for each of the 18 essays. Especially helpful were chapters in the *Handbook of Intercultural Training* (Landis & Brislin, 1983).

We present a brief introduction to the 18 themes immediately below. However, because knowing the themes may cue readers to the correct alternative explanations for some of the incidents, those wishing to use the materials without these cues may want to skip over this introductory treatment and go to the section headed "The Creation of the Incidents."

The 18 themes can themselves be organized around three broad headings:

1. experiences people are likely to have that cause intense feelings and that engage their emotions;
2. knowledge areas that people learn are right and appropriate as they are socialized within any given culture, yet that incorporate many cross-cultural differences that people find difficult to understand; and
3. some bases of cultural differences, especially concerning how people think about and process information.

Organized around these three broad headings, the 18 themes are as follows.

People's Intense Feelings

In adjusting to life and work within cultures other than their own, people are likely to experience a number of emotional reactions owing to feelings of displacement and unfamiliarity, and because of their status as outsiders.

- *Anxiety:* As people encounter many unfamiliar demands, they are likely to become anxious about whether or not their behavior is appropriate.
- *Disconfirmed expectations:* People may become upset or uncomfortable not because of the specific circumstances they encounter, but because their experiences in the other culture differ from what they had expected.
- *Belonging:* People have the need to fill a niche, to feel that they belong and are accepted by others, but they often cannot when interacting in another culture because they have the status of outsider.
- *Ambiguity:* In their own cultural contexts, people learn appropriate responses to a wide variety of social stimuli. When living and working across cultures, they may receive messages that are often unclear, yet they must still make decisions and take appropriate actions. People who are effective at working across cultures are known to have a high tolerance for ambiguity.
- *Confrontation with one's prejudices:* Part of socialization into a culture involves treating others who are noticeably different with reserve. People may discover that their previously held beliefs about certain groups may not be accurate or useful once they find themselves interacting with other cultures.

Knowledge Areas

Again and again, reports of people working in a variety of different cultures include difficulties and misunderstandings concerning a number

of commonly mentioned topics. Our shorthand for these frequently discussed topics is *knowledge areas,* and because people are socialized within
their own cultures to learn that certain things are appropriate, many specific
cross-cultural differences exist within these areas. People about to live and
work across cultures should realize that many potential misunderstandings
abound in these knowledge areas.

- *Work:* Many people crossing cultures spend a great deal of time in various
  workplaces, whether these are schools, factories, offices, or social service
  agencies. Differences in the amounts of time people spend on task versus time
  spent socializing, who has the obligation of control, and the manner in which
  decisions are made are examples of differences that may occur in this area.

- *Time and spatial orientation:* Various attitudes exist regarding the importance
  of adhering to clock time in certain situations, as well as the proper spatial
  orientations people adopt with respect to one another during different interpersonal encounters. These important areas have been well examined in the
  seminal works of Edward Hall (1959, 1966).

- *Communication and language use:* Communication differences are probably
  the most obvious problem that must be overcome in the crossing of cultural
  boundaries. Cross-cultural verbal and nonverbal communication, attitudes
  toward language use, and the difficulties of learning another language as it is
  actually spoken rather than read from a book are part of this knowledge area.

- *Roles:* There are generally accepted sets of behaviors people perform in relation
  to the roles they adopt. Examples of roles include the family provider, the boss,
  the volunteer, and the leader. Tremendous differences may exist with respect to
  the occupants of such roles and how they are enacted in different cultures.

- *Importance of the group and the importance of the individual:* All people act at
  times in their individual interest and at other times according to their group
  allegiances. The relative emphasis on group versus individual orientation varies
  from culture to culture and may have a significant impact on people's decision-
  making processes, choices of peers and associates, and the degree to which they
  perform effectively on their own. Of all the differences found to exist between
  cultures, group versus individual orientation seems to be one of the most significant. Another set of terms frequently used in discussing this distinction is indi-
  vidualism/collectivism (Bhawuk & Brislin, 1992; Triandis, Brislin, & Hui, 1988).

- *Rituals versus superstition:* All cultures have rituals that help people meet their
  needs as they cope with life's everyday demands. People in all cultures also
  engage in behaviors that outsiders may label superstitious. One culture's
  "intelligent practices" may be seen as another culture's rituals and superstition.

- *Hierarchies—class and status:* Whenever a large number of people have to
  interact frequently, leaders emerge and power becomes unevenly distributed.

One manifestation of the unequal access to power is the division of people into various social class groupings. People often make distinctions based on various markers of high and low status, and these distinctions differ from culture to culture.

- *Values:* As part of their socialization, people learn to accept as proper a small set of ideas within such broad areas as religion, economics, aesthetics, political organization, and interpersonal relationships. Such learning becomes internalized and affects attitudes, preferences, and views of what is desirable and undesirable. Understanding these internalized views, or values, is critical in cross-cultural adjustment.

Bases of Cultural Differences

People everywhere are bombarded with immense amounts of information every day, not all of which they can possibly give their full attention. Understanding the ways in which they respond to and organize this information, and then communicate the information to others, provides a great deal of insight into the cultural differences that people find puzzling as they try to adjust to life in other cultures.

- *Categorization:* Because they cannot attend to all pieces of information, people group bits of information into categories for more efficient organization. People in different cultures place the same individual elements into different categories (e.g., who is a friend, what a good worker does), causing confusion for people accustomed to any one given set of categories.
- *Differentiation:* Given that people become accustomed to one set of categories, they are likely to use those categories when faced with new information. One reason for the possible misuse of a category is that people in another culture may differentiate pieces of information, treating those pieces as if they were quite distinct. One result of increased interest in, or importance of, a certain knowledge area is that more and more information is differentiated within that area such that new categories are formed. Examples are types of obligations that accompany various kinship relations and the various ways to overcome red tape. If sojourners do not differentiate information in the same manner as hosts, they may be treated as naive or ignorant.
- *In-group/out-group distinction:* One of the major bases for forming categories about other people, and for differentiating information within those categories, is the ubiquitous tendency to form in-groups and out-groups. In-groups are made up of those people with whom interaction is sought. Out-group members are held at a distance and are often the targets of rejection. People the world over divide others into in-groups and out-groups. Those entering other cultures

or new groups must recognize that they will often be considered out-group members and that there are some behaviors associated with in-group membership in which sojourners will never participate.

- *Learning styles:* Change and growth, as well as the possibility for self-improvement, involve new learning. Even though people desire change and improvement, the styles in which people learn best may differ from culture to culture. People involved in change efforts (e.g., teachers, social workers, technical assistance advisers) may find that information presented in ways attractive and efficient to them may be awkward to others and may not lead to desired outcomes.

- *Attribution:* People observe the behavior of others, and they also reflect upon their own behavior. Judgments about the causes of behavior are called *attributions*. The same behavior, such as a firm handshake and a pleasant chat with the newcomer to an organization, may be attributed to different underlying causes by the parties involved. The person offering the handshake may consider the greeting polite. The newcomer may label it insincere, especially if norms concerning the proper length of time for the chat differ according to people's cultural backgrounds. Because research on attribution is central to thinking about the culture assimilator in cross-cultural training, we have presented more information on this topic earlier in this chapter.

THE CREATION OF THE INCIDENTS

Given the decision to develop the incidents around the 18 themes described above, we created each individual incident with the purpose of making a point associated with a given theme. For instance, one of us would take the work theme and develop an incident involving differing cultural views about some aspect of work. The most common technique was to start with the conclusion, such as a misunderstanding based on differing work attitudes, and to build an incident leading up to that conclusion. Characters would be created and a plot line developed with a beginning, middle, and end, with the conclusion always involving some difficulty experienced by a sojourner, host, or both.

Some incidents are based on our own experiences, our own misunderstandings and attempts to cope with them, and our interpretations of cross-cultural difficulties that we have observed. Others are based on episodes related to us by colleagues in various work settings and by participants in various summer programs. Still others are based on research findings. For instance, Hawes and Kealey (1981) found that certain traits and behaviors mark successful technical assistance advisers, so we wrote an incident that deals with the difficulties brought about by the absence of these traits and behaviors. Lambert and Bressler (1956), as well as Kelman and Ezekiel (1970), found that if sojourners are treated in certain specified ways by hosts, they feel their cross-cultural experiences are enjoyable and worthwhile, so we wrote incidents in which sojourners were or were not treated in these ways. Still other incidents are modeled after some found in existing culture-specific assimilators that we felt had broader applicability than to just one country. And some incidents have been developed over the years as we have become increasingly engaged in work that confronts issues of cultural diversity within a given nation.

In writing alternative explanations for the incidents, we did not always try to develop only one correct explanation. Rather, we assumed that some misunderstandings and difficulties occur for more than one reason. Individuals should be aware of such complexity and should not expect one clear reason for every problem in cross-cultural interactions. (In many of the workshops we have conducted, a common response reflects just this notion. Many people have noted that they think the reason for the problem in a given incident is something beyond the alternatives provided, and that they would prefer to give open-ended answers, without having to choose among particular set alternatives. Of course this is always a possibility, and users are encouraged to be creative and use these materials in whatever ways best suit their needs. Users of these materials must keep in mind, however, that one of the primary reasons for their development was to help create a common base for discussion while building a common vocabulary and conceptual foundation. The various incidents are designed to *teach* about given concepts or issues, and we fully recognize that other possible explanations for the incidents might exist. If the incidents are used in an open-ended manner, subsequent discussion may lack focus and direction.)

After our development efforts for the first edition, we had about 150 incidents from which to choose. After eliminating those we felt were unclear or too country specific, or that duplicated the points made in others, we retained 106 incidents. We then submitted the items to a validation sample to assess their usefulness. Our goal was that 80 items would survive the validation procedure; the fact that 100 survived was one of the very pleasant results of this work.

THE VALIDATION SAMPLE
FOR THE INCIDENTS

We modified slightly the classic method of validating a culture assimilator (as detailed by Albert, 1983). Experienced people, adult hosts in the case of country-specific assimilators, examined each incident and gave their judgments as to the correct alternative explanation or explanations. Items for which there was too much disagreement concerning the correct explanation(s) were eliminated with the charge that they are too unclear or too ambiguous. Items that were retained, then, were those that the validation sample felt were clear and about which they agreed concerning the correct explanation or set of explanations. Trainees later working through a culture assimilator were asked to choose the correct explanation(s), *correctness* being defined as the clear choice(s) of hosts in the country where sojourners will be living (e.g., Thai nationals for the Thai culture assimilator). In developing a culture-general assimilator, we chose a validation sample of experienced sojourners who had lived in many different countries and who had held a wide variety of jobs in those countries. Such a sample selection, of course, follows from our assumptions about the possibility of a culture-general assimilator. If the assimilator is to be of use for people about to live in many different countries, about to interact with people of different backgrounds, and about to assume a wide variety of jobs, then the assimilator should be validated by people with a great deal of experience along those same dimensions. Our basic criterion in choosing members of the validation sample was that each person should have had an intense cross-cultural experience of at least 2 years' duration. At least one of us knew each member of the sample and felt that each was a sensitive, thoughtful person whose judgments concerning the 106 incidents should be respected. There were 60 people (32 females and 28 males) in the validation sample; they ranged in age from 25 to 72, with the average age being 42. Table 2.1 gives descriptions of the sample members' cross-cultural experiences. In addition to the information presented in the table, we should note that 3 members of the sample were involved in the development of culture-specific assimilators and 28 have published materials in respected books and journals related to cross-cultural communication, international behavior, or training. Members of the sample had experienced the wide range of roles discussed throughout this chapter: They included teachers, foreign students, social workers, businesspeople, diplomats, counselors, researchers, and immigrants.

EXPLANATION OF THE PROJECT
TO THE VALIDATION SAMPLE

Members of the validation sample were recruited either at the East-West Center in Honolulu, Hawaii, or through the mail. After a brief introduction

Table 2.1 Cross-Cultural Experiences of the Validation Sample

Number of Respondents	Descriptions of Sojourner Experiences
13	*Teachers:* involved in teaching, from foreign-language tutoring to professorship at a university
11	*Peace Corps workers:* involved in several capacities, including teaching, technical advising, and directing in-country training for new volunteers
7	*Students:* traveled into another cultural area to pursue education
5	*Social workers:* involved in working with refugees or immigrants
5	*Counselors:* involved in working with exchange students and other types of sojourners with individual problems
5	*Grew up in another culture:* either born and raised in one environment and later immigrated to another culture or born in one culture and families immigrated to another where they grew up, later to return to original culture
4	*Educational administrators:* involved in duties relating to the educational system but not directly as teachers
3	*Businesspeople:* involved in profit-oriented ventures but not technical assistance
3	*Researchers:* involved in postgraduate academic endeavors
2	*Military personnel:* involved in defense efforts (not families—they are included elsewhere)
1	*Diplomat:* responsibilities different from purely business, military, or technical assistance
1	*Seeker of self-growth:* personal sojourn for information and travel experience; more than two years

Total: 60

to the idea of materials development for cross-cultural training, they were told (or they read) of the possibility of a culture-general assimilator:

> We feel that the materials will be useful in training programs no matter which countries are the locales for people's sojourns. This assumption is based upon two broad issues. We feel that there are commonalities in the emotional experiences of people no matter where they sojourn (e.g., loneliness, sense of uprootedness) and that there is a set of concepts that are useful to have in mind since they come up again and again in people's retrospective discussions of their sojourns. Such concepts include differentiation of roles, decision making, and in-group/out-group distinctions. The exact coloring of these concepts, of course, is dependent upon the exact locale of the sojourn. But we feel that it is useful to be introduced to the concepts so that sojourners have a framework to which they can add the specific coloring either on their own or in the culture-specific part of a long training program.

We have prepared 106 short critical incidents and four or five alternative explanations for each in the culture assimilator format. We are now seeking out a validation sample of people who have spent a long period of time in a culture other than the one in which they were born. We wonder if you would like to be part of the validation sample. The final editing of the incidents will be done with the input from this sample. Items will be discarded if the validation sample finds them unclear. If the answers of the validation sample disagree with our own "contenders" for correct explanations to incidents, the validation sample will be considered correct.

Of the 71 people approached, 60 agreed to participate and completed the task of reading and responding to the alternatives. After they agreed to undertake the task, they were given the following instructions:

The answer sheets are in grid form, stapled together. The numbers on the answer sheets match up to the numbers of the incidents. After reading each incident, you will then read a question. Consider each of the alternatives— either four or five such alternatives. Then check off the likelihood *of each* alternative on the answer sheet. Ask yourself, "How likely is it that this alternative is correct?" Then check in one of the six spaces for *each* alternative according to the scale:

_____ I am certain that this is correct.

_____ Very likely.

_____ Likely.

_____ Unlikely.

_____ Very unlikely.

_____ I am certain this is not correct.

Thus you will have either four or five checks for each incident, depending upon whether there are four or five alternatives.

Also enclosed is a short biographical sheet that we would like you to complete. Of course, we are most interested in your cross-cultural experience. Cross-cultural experience can include work within one's own country with either people from another country or minority groups. Examples would be foreign student advisers at an American university, or people in Australia who work with Aboriginal Australians, or people from the well-established middle class in any country who work with the very poor, or with immigrants/refugees, and so on.

For each of the 106 incidents we have a "contender" (sometimes two contenders) for the best alternative. The purpose of giving the items to you, of course, is to validate our choices. In cases of disagreement, the validation sample is considered correct.

Respondents gave their choices for explanations on a form like the one below.

How likely is it that this alternative is correct?

	I am certain that this is correct.	Very Likely	Likely	Unlikely	Very Unlikely	I am certain that this is not correct.
Item #1						
Response 1						
2						
3						
4						

Respondents then filled out such a scale for each of the 106 incidents, making a judgment about each alternative for each incident. Although not explicitly given the option, a number of respondents wrote "I don't know" or "unsure" for some alternatives. Anticipating this, we had developed the following numerical scale for statistical analysis of the validation sample's response:

I am certain that this is correct.   = 7
Very likely   = 6
Likely   = 5
Don't know, or unsure, or ?   = 4
Unlikely   = 3
Very unlikely   = 2
I am certain that this is *not* correct. = 1

Of the 106 incidents, we judged 100 as clear to the respondents based on statistical analysis of their answers. This judgment was based on three factors:

1. *An explanation or set of explanations clearly preferred by the validation sample for each incident:* According to our numerical scale, this meant an average score of 5 or greater for at least one of the explanations, with some explanations being clearly not preferred (i.e., average score less than 3).

2. *Agreement with our contenders for correct explanations:* When writing the incidents and alternatives, we had correct alternatives in mind. In all of the 100 retained incidents, the validation sample agreed with our main choice or with one of our choices if we wrote an incident with two explanations in mind. In some cases the validation sample saw wisdom in an explanation that we

did not have in mind as correct. In these cases, we accepted the validation sample's opinion and included those additional explanations as contributing to the correct interpretation of incidents.

3. *Lack of negative criticism of an item by more than one person:* Individual members of the validation sample expressed discomfort with individual incidents, but only one incident (dropped from the original 106 and so not included here) was criticized by more than one person. We gave special attention to the incidents criticized by an individual respondent, but concluded from the responses of the total sample that they were clear to most members of the validation sample.

For this second edition, we have eliminated 10 incidents that appeared in the first edition because for one reason or another we have concluded that they have limited usefulness. We have added 19 new incidents that have been developed to reflect greater diversity *within* a given nation as well as to consider recent changes in world events. We followed a validation process for these newly developed incidents similar to that described above; our second validation sample included 25 respondents.

RESEARCH IMPLICATIONS
OF THE CULTURE ASSIMILATOR

The culture assimilator has been the most thoroughly researched of all the cross-cultural training strategies that have been developed. Time and time again, and across a variety of audiences, the culture assimilator has proven to have positive impacts on people's cognitive, affective, and behavioral domains. Specifically, a number of studies have been undertaken with a variety of culture-specific assimilators. Albert (1983) provides a review of studies undertaken with a variety of culture-specific assimilators, a few of which will be summarized here. Fiedler, Mitchell, and Triandis (1971) found that Americans who received culture assimilator training prior to going to Honduras were better adjusted and performed their work better than did untrained individuals. Worchel and Mitchell (1970) found that persons trained with a Thai assimilator gave more favorable self-reports concerning contacts with members of the Thai culture and their work in Thailand than did untrained persons. Fiedler et al. (1971) found that persons using a Greek assimilator saw themselves as significantly better adjusted and as having better interpersonal relations and higher productivity than untrained individuals. In yet other studies, whites trained with an assimilator designed to improve white-black inter-actions made attributions that were more similar to those made by members of the target culture than did untrained whites (Weldon, Carlston, Rissman, Slobodin, & Triandis, 1975). Trained participants refused to engage in racial stereotyping more often than did untrained individuals. In addition, trained individuals perceived the attitudes of blacks and whites involved in conflict episodes as more positive than did untrained individuals.

Recent studies of the culture-general assimilator, too, have shown it to be of considerable use in preparing individuals for interactions in culturally diverse settings. A number of studies have been undertaken to analyze the impact of the culture-general assimilator in the preparation of teachers and teacher education students for the kinds of cross-cultural interactions they are certain to encounter in the increasingly diverse classrooms found in the United States. These studies have demonstrated that trainees are more knowledgeable about concepts relevant to cross-cultural interaction; are better able to generate, analyze, and apply such concepts to personal cross-cultural incidents; and are more sophisticated in their thinking about and analysis of cross-cultural issues present in diverse classroom settings (Bhatkal, 1990; Ilola, 1991; Pacino, 1989; Yarbro, 1988).

Cushner (1989) used a modified version of the culture-general assimilator in the preparation of adolescent exchange students from 14 countries about to spend one year living in New Zealand. The trained group spent 6 hours analyzing 19 cultural-general critical incidents rewritten to speak directly to the experiences of adolescents (Cushner, 1990b) as the basis of their orienta-tion and training for life in an overseas setting. The control group participated in the more traditional, yet quite comprehensive, AFS orientation to life in New Zealand. Data and interviews were collected on subjects over a period of 6 months after training. Results of this study indicated that, compared with the control group, trained individuals were more knowledgeable about concepts relevant to cross-cultural interaction, better able to apply those concepts to personal cross-cultural misunderstandings, better adjusted to their new envi-ronment as evidenced on one of four scales of the Cross-Cultural Adjustment Inventory, and more proficient in handling hypothetical interpersonal prob-lem-solving situations. An additional observation centered on the number of transfers required by students throughout the year. Although not significant, seven from the control group required changes in host families, whereas only three members of the trained group required such changes. This is certainly an outcome that would be welcomed by anyone working in adolescent exchange programs, considering the significant upheavals, embarrassment, and stresses such unanticipated family changes bring about.

In an empirical study designed to test the usefulness of the materials in university undergraduate courses, Broaddus (1986) compared an assimilator-trained group with a control group. He introduced the culture-general assimilator to half the students in a large lecture course in social psychology. The other half became a "wait control" group that received the culture-general assimilator at a later time. Assignment to the two groups was done on a random basis. At the point when half of the class had been exposed to the materials (the trained group) and half had not, Broaddus administered various dependent variable measures. Using a criterion introduced by Malpass and Salancik (1977), Broaddus found that trained students answered 15 of the more difficult items (which they had not seen before) more accurately than did the controls.

This finding suggests that trained people are better able to analyze new cross-cultural problematic encounters to which they have not been previously exposed after they have analyzed many other critical incidents and relevant essays during training. Trained students also scored significantly higher than controls on a newly developed scale that measures various aspects of people's attitudes toward, and behaviors concerning, intercultural interaction. Trained students scored higher on a factor concerned with cross-cultural sensitivity and acceptance of cultural relativity as measured by such items as the following:

- It is important to consider people's feelings before making decisions.
- There is usually more than one good way to get things done.
- I may defend the viewpoint of others.
- I think people are basically alike.
- Certain prejudices I have hinder the way I interact with people. (negatively scored)

These items were mixed in with many others that did not discriminate trained from untrained students, so it is unlikely that students were simply responding to these items in ways that would flatter themselves or to present themselves in a desirable light. Rather, our interpretation is that because many of the critical incidents examine the nature of cultural relativity, sensitivity to the viewpoint of others, and understanding the attributions made by others, this result reflects internalization of the ideas presented during training.

On the basis of investigations such as those cited above, we believe that the culture-general assimilator is capable of bringing about marked improvement in individuals' knowledge about factors related to cross-cultural interaction and adjustment. In addition, trained individuals seem better able to achieve their goals in intercultural settings, in part because they can confront unfamiliar situations with more confidence and view them from a more complex frame of reference than can untrained persons. Thus the culture-general assimilator is a good tool for preparing people to live and work in highly diverse settings.

Common to all culture assimilator training is that trainees from a given cultural background learn about others by examining a large number of critical incidents that identify potential areas of misunderstanding and interpersonal conflict. By learning the reasons for the behaviors depicted in the incidents, with special attention to attributions about the behaviors from the target culture's point of view, trainees accrue a number of benefits (see the research literature reviewed by Brislin et al., 1983), including the following:

1. greater understanding of hosts, as judged by the hosts themselves;
2. a decrease in the use of negative stereotypes on the part of trainees;
3. the development of complex thinking about the target culture, which replaces the oversimplified, facile thinking to which hosts react negatively;
4. greater enjoyment in interacting with members of the target culture, a feeling reciprocated by hosts;
5. better adjustment to the everyday stresses of life in other cultures; and
6. better job performance in cases where performance is influenced by specific cultural practices that can be covered in the training materials (Aoki, 1991; Brislin, Cushner, Cherrie, & Yong, 1986; Brislin & Yoshida, 1994b; Cushner, 1989; Ramirez, 1992).

OTHER CONCERNS IN THE
DEVELOPMENT OF THE MATERIALS

Prior to the publication of the first edition of *Intercultural Interactions,* an early draft of the manuscript was circulated for comments by experienced scholars and practitioners. Some of those comments bring up additional points we would like to address here.

One concern was that some incidents may have explanations that are easy to eliminate, and thus the choices of correct alternatives for those incidents are based on the elimination of poor answers rather than analysis of good explanations. Our response is that we made careful efforts to develop alternative explanations (four or five per incident) that *might be and have been used* by sojourners. Further, our instructions to the validation sample that more than one answer can be correct forced consideration of all alternatives. As will be seen in the discussions of the incidents, many do have more than one good explanation. The validation sample also was asked to make distinctions among possibly incorrect answers (unlikely, very unlikely, certain that this is not correct), again forcing careful thought rather than careless elimination of alternatives.

Another question dealt with the composition of the validation sample. The possibility was raised that the sample consisted of people who shared a common set of concepts, with an attendant jargon, and so would choose alternatives that included familiar terms in that jargon. Several facts argue against this possibility. As we have noted, there is no widely shared set of concepts or widely shared materials that would lead to like-mindedness. Further, only about one-third of the validation sample had extensive experience in formal cross-cultural training programs. The rest were highly experienced and thoughtful international sojourners, as has been discussed previously, but they had not served as staff members in formal training programs. Thus the validation sample did not consist of a large collection of people who might be exposed to the same concepts and jargon, even if such a group existed.

Another query concerned the possibility of an ethnocentric tone in some items. Many of the people in the incidents have Euro-American names. Many of the explanations draw on research done in the United States, Europe, and Australia, but less attention seems to be given to research from other parts of the world. This issue points to another tightrope we had to walk. How could we best present useful information to sojourners that is based on solid research, not just on our whims? We chose to do this by (a) drawing upon concepts from the published literature and translating these into incidents and (b) gathering incidents from experienced sojourners and analyzing them according to established, helpful concepts from the research literature. Our use of certain names and research concepts results from these decisions. The fact remains that most cross-cultural research continues to be done by Euro-Americans or by people who received their training in the United States, Europe, Australia, or New Zealand. A great many sojourners come from these parts of the world, and highly industrialized nations are also the recipients of many sojourners. Our hope, as we have noted previously, is that these incidents identify common concerns and that readers can go beyond particular names in the quest for issues relevant to them and to their assignments. However, as interest in cross-cultural encounters develops in other parts of the world, on the part of both practitioners and researchers, future training materials will benefit from additional points of view that are not currently treated in cross-cultural training programs.

APPROACHES TO THE
USE OF THESE MATERIALS

The materials in this book are presented to reflect the actual manner in which people are likely to encounter intercultural difficulties. Life is such that experiences are generally not encountered in a precisely organized and orderly sequence. Rather, difficulties may occur in a variety of unexpected and unplanned environments. Thus the organization of the incidents in this book reflects the places and situations where people are most likely to encounter difficulties (at work, with family members, and so on).

These materials, however, can be organized and presented in an alternative manner: according to the 18 themes that run throughout the incidents and that are discussed in the essays found in Chapters 11-13. This approach may be advantageous in particular circumstances, for instance, when certain concepts or themes seem most appropriate to the purposes of training, when the amount of time available for a program is limited, or when trainees are particularly inexperienced and might benefit from a more focused approach. Further, different trainers will, because of their backgrounds and formal educations, be more comfortable covering some themes than others. For example, a focus on psychological dynamics affected during intercultural interaction might draw upon the incidents specific to attribution, differentiation, categorization, and in-group/out-group distinctions. Likewise, a program emphasis on emotion could use specific incidents from the essays on anxiety and related emotional states, emotional experiences and disconfirmed expectations, and ambiguity. Trainees might read the incidents related to a specific concept or theme, discuss them as a group, attempt to draw their own conclusions or discover underlying concepts, and then read the accompanying essay or essays. We have used this approach with success in short-term programs (e.g., 1-2 days) during which we could not cover all of the incidents. Given the need to select among incidents, we based our choices on the themes we thought most appropriate for the particular audiences.

Over the years, trainers have used these materials in a variety of contexts and in many different ways. The culture-general framework and subsequent training materials have been developed with the idea that they *should* be modified to meet the demands of people working in a variety of situations. As such, these materials have been used in a variety of diverse contexts, including the following:

> high school, undergraduate, and graduate-level classes in psychology, sociology, anthropology, counseling, health, and education;
>
> to prepare health workers assigned to rural Alaskan villages as well as other settings;
>
> as the foundation for a curriculum to prepare Israeli Arab and Jewish young people to understand one another's situations;
>
> to train interpreters for the deaf for their interactions between hearing and deaf individuals;
>
> for businesspeople as well as diplomats about to be assigned to a variety of overseas posts;
>
> for teachers, counselors, and school administrators who work with young people in highly diverse settings in many different countries and in many different kinds of schools (Cushner, 1994; Cushner, McClelland, & Safford, 1992);
>
> as preparation for adolescent exchange students moving between many different countries (Cushner, 1990b); and
>
> in training a variety of cross-cultural trainers who assist others in improving their skills as they prepare for their sojourns.

Those who have employed the incidents and the framework of these materials have been very creative. As we have noted, the critical incidents can simply be read and referred to by lecturers or related to subsequent readings. They can also become the basis for a variety of role plays in which participants in training sessions can take part.

An alternative to reading a single incident is to group a number of related incidents, perhaps three to five, according to specific themes, and follow this procedure. In small groups, individuals read *each* incident and, before reviewing the rationales, discuss (a) their understanding of the situation, (b) how the incident may remind them of something else they have experienced or observed, and (c) their preferred choices of the correct alternative(s). Participants then read the rationales and gain further information for discussion. This procedure is repeated for three to five preselected and related incidents, after which participants attempt to identify the theme or themes common across all the incidents they just read. They then read the appropriate theme essay, which provides substantial information about the theme, and—perhaps the most critical activity—relate the theme to their present or anticipated work or

Table 2.2 Organization of Incidents by Essay Titles/Themes

Essay Title/Theme	Incident Numbers
Anxiety and related emotional states	40, 51, 52, 56, 73, 75
Emotional experiences and disconfirmed	
expectations	25, 29, 34, 41, 89, 99, 108, 109
Belonging	29, 38, 39, 48
Ambiguity	31, 46, 50, 85, 105, 106
Prejudice and ethnocentrism	36, 42, 50, 55, 67, 110
Work	59, 60, 61, 62, 70, 72, 74, 77, 97
Time and space	9, 24, 41, 66, 103
Language and communication	13, 15, 16, 33, 35, 44, 45, 59, 69, 78, 95, 102, 104
Roles	8, 18, 22, 23, 26, 27, 28, 30, 63, 79, 81, 82, 84, 93
Importance of the group and importance	
of the individual	1, 2, 5, 6, 11, 20, 37, 64, 80, 101, 107, 110
Ritual and superstition	3, 4, 68, 92
Hierarchies among people; class and status	12, 19, 32, 36, 43, 50, 51, 65, 69, 94, 96
Values: the integrating force	10, 17, 21, 27, 87
Learning styles	83, 86, 90, 91
Categorization	10, 14, 49, 54, 67, 88, 98
Differentiation	58, 67, 76, 100
In-group/out-group distinction	10, 21, 27, 87
Attribution	7, 17, 53, 57, 71, 72, 84

living situation. In other words, the task for trainees here is to make the themes as practical and real as possible. How does their new understanding of a particular theme help them to understand or anticipate interactions they are certain to encounter? The importance of stressing the themes cannot be overemphasized. As we have noted, one of the primary purposes of these materials is to help individuals to develop the capacity to think beyond their own experiences to concepts that are common in cross-cultural interaction. It is through their application of these themes to their own experiences that true growth and understanding begin to occur.

Incidents specific to each theme are identified in the section headed "Application to the Culture Assimilator Incidents" within each essay. In Table 2.2, we identify the numbers of the incidents that apply to the various themes.

CRITICAL INCIDENT CONSTRUCTION

Individuals should also be encouraged to create their own incidents reflecting 1 or more of the 18 themes. Incidents found in these materials that remind participants of situations with which they are familiar can be rewritten to reflect those situations. Alternatively, participants can use these incidents as models and develop new ones that speak to their specific needs. Individuals can also prepare a number of critical incidents specific to their own work settings that can subsequently become a training and orientation package designed for a given group. In any case, the following guidelines for preparing critical incidents may be helpful.

1. *Identify relevant themes/issues* for your purposes. You may select from the 18-theme cultural-general framework or identify specific themes/issues of relevance to your needs. *Remember, you wish to use the incident to inform others about a cultural issue or theme underlying the incident—not merely to relate the story.*

2. *Generate episodes* by identifying incidents based in personal experience, interviews with others, the research and/or ethnographic literature, or observation and analysis.

3. *Construct episodes or stories,* being certain to include only relevant information. Be sure to verify content; refine generalizations, abstractions, and specifics; and speak to your intended audience. The resulting incident should be clear, concise, straightforward, interesting, and believable, while maintaining the original conflict situation.

4. *Elicit attributions* by identifying different interpretations of the incident through interviews, ethnographic data, and open-ended questions completed by experienced and inexperienced individuals.

5. *Select attributions* to use.

6. *Complete the critical incident with feedback and explanations,* remembering that it is through the explanation that relevant cultural knowledge can be transmitted.

3

HOST CUSTOMS

As used here, *customs* refers to habitual ways of going about everyday activities. Individuals learn their cultures' customs at a very early age and come to take them for granted as the appropriate ways of accomplishing the tasks people face on a regular basis. Some of the clearest examples of cultural differences occur when people encounter different customary ways of working, entertaining, or interacting with others. Especially important for the individuals involved are those customs that are understood to be totally appropriate, with any other behaviors seen as boorish or ignorant. What may be understood in one culture to be impolite behavior may be seen as appropriate and acceptable in another. When people begin to understand others' customs and to see how they make sense, they begin to internalize the concept of cultural relativity. That is, one cannot judge the customs of others from a preconceived set of ideas learned elsewhere; rather, one must understand how various customs have developed to contribute to the smooth functioning of a society.

1

A Packed Lunch

An American family living in Japan for a year wanted their son (age 10) to attend a Japanese elementary school. When they so indicated to their landlord, he sent his English-speaking daughter to act as a go-between (*chukaisha*). The boy was duly enrolled and began school. He had to take a lunch (*bento*) every day, so he took a regular American meal of sandwich, chips, cookies, and drink. The teacher subsequently contacted the go-between to have her talk with the parents about the

inappropriateness of the lunch and to request that the parents provide a more Japanese-style *bento*.
Why was the schoolteacher perturbed by the child's American-style lunch?

1. The teacher feared that the Japanese children would become dissatisfied with their own lunches.
2. The teacher felt the lunch was not sufficiently nutritious.
3. The typical Japanese *bento* has symbolic significance, and the teacher felt that the child was breaking with tradition.
4. In Japanese society, conformity is valued more than individuality.

The discussions of these alternative explanations begin on page 63.

2

The Unsuccessful Dinner Party

Having been treated to a wonderful time by Mei-ying's family on her first visit to the Orient, Alice wanted to return their hospitality. She invited them out for a meal, but they politely refused, knowing that her travel budget could not afford it. Being aware of the Chinese emphasis on food, Alice volunteered to make the family a genuine American meal. They agreed to this, saying that they would get whatever she needed. Alice made a list, and Mei-ying took her to the marketplace. There seemed to be a horde of people pushing and grabbing at the various items displayed in every available spot, right there in the street. Mei-ying attempted to maneuver Alice to the meat section, where she could get some steaks. However, as she neared the area, Alice spotted a man who had just wrung a chicken's neck and then hung it up to bleed it. Alice was aghast but continued on, her gaze now directed to the street they were about to cross. There in the gutter, a man was scaling and cleaning out a large fish. At this, Alice remarked on the unsanitary conditions of the place. She nonetheless made her way to the booth with the beef, where she was met with the blank stare of a dead steer's head. Totally repulsed at this, she queasily asked Mei-ying to take her to another market, preferably one that was indoors. Mei-ying hesitantly agreed, saying that there was a Western-style supermarket on the next block, but that she rarely went there as she was unsure of the freshness of the items. To her delight, Alice found all the items she needed. However, she noticed Mei-ying poking and pinching and squeezing items, with a

worried look on her face. When all was prepared and served, Alice noticed that Mei-ying's family just picked at the food.
How would you help explain the family's reluctant feelings?

1. Mei-ying and her family were unaccustomed to eating American food, and they really did not want Alice to cook for them.
2. Mei-ying's family thought that Alice should pay for the items she needed to cook the treat for them.
3. Alice had insulted Mei-ying's family by suggesting that she cook for them, implying that their manner of cooking was not really acceptable.
4. Mei-ying and her family and Alice have different ideas about sanitary conditions and freshness of food.

The discussions of these alternative explanations begin on page 64.

3

Betting on the Bull

George is an American salesman working for a multinational company in Spain. He had expressed an interest to his Spanish colleagues in attending a bullfight, so when the first *corrida* (fight) of the season was announced, they invited him to accompany them. As the first bull was let out, George jokingly asked the others, "So who's going to win? I'll put my money on the bull." The rest suddenly became silent, and one of his fellow salesmen remarked tartly, "You Americans know nothing." George did not know what he had said to offend them and felt very uneasy throughout the *corrida*.
What explanation would you give to George as to how he had given offense?

1. His colleagues thought George was suggesting they bet on the outcome.
2. George was viewing the event as a sport; the Spanish view bullfighting more as a ritual.
3. His colleagues obviously thought the bull had no chance, and so George was being very ignorant.
4. It is regarded as very unlucky for the matador for someone to proclaim publicly that the bull will win.

The discussions of these alternative explanations begin on page 65.

4

A Few Beers

It was not long after John moved to Indonesia that he found himself in the company of two of his local acquaintances at a nearby marketplace. The older of the two Indonesians was named Soleh. After walking around for some time observing the local crafts and food items that were for sale, the men stopped for a few beers. The conversation swayed between such topics as aid to developing nations and the role of women in society. Just after initiating a discussion of local politics, John excused himself to go buy a round of beers, thus treating everyone at the table. He returned clutching three bottles in his right hand. While still holding the bottles, John suddenly remembered a point he wanted to stress with Soleh. Leaning forward and reaching for Soleh's shoulder with his hand before sitting down, he proceeded to talk. Soleh and his companion began to appear uncomfortable. The conversation began to move away from John. When the two Indonesians finished their beer, they politely excused themselves and left. Neither made contact with John again.

How can you explain this incident?

1. Touching a person of the same sex is understood to mean a sexual advance in the local culture. Both men were put off by John's apparent advance.

2. The left hand is considered unclean in some cultures, and there is a taboo against personal contact with it. Both Indonesian men were insulted when John touched Soleh with his left hand.

3. Soleh perceived John as flaunting his wealth by paying for the drinks. He was obviously insulted by John's purchase.

4. Both men were insulted that John would get up and leave just after initiating a discussion. It is preferable to signal to the waiter rather than leave your friends.

The discussions of these alternative explanations begin on page 65.

5

One Good Turn Deserves Another

Mr. Wong and Mr. Chang have known each other for a good number of years. They both have several children of about the same ages. Mr.

Chang has two brothers who live in the United States and have small family businesses. Both Mr. Chang and Mr. Wong have businesses that seem fairly prosperous. In fact, it was the capital that Mr. Chang provided that enabled his brothers to get started in their own flourishing livelihood. In recent times, however, Mr. Chang has had several difficulties. Interest rates are up and the unstable character of his country's monetary unit has caused him much financial loss. He has the opportunity to invest in a very promising venture, but at the moment does not have enough cash. This venture could pull his whole operation out of the slump he finds himself in, but his brothers do not have the large sum that he needs. Even though they seem to be doing well, their cash-flow situations prevent them from making additional investments. Mr. Chang considers carefully and then goes to Mr. Wong, who gladly lends him the money. The venture does indeed turn out very profitably for Mr. Chang, who is then able to repay Mr. Wong, with interest, immediately.

Later that year, when both men's sons are applying for colleges, Mr. Wong calls on Mr. Chang, whose other son is already attending a university in the United States, to help get Mr. Wong's son into the school by using his connections. Mr. Chang acquiesces and secures a place for Mr. Wong's younger son. A few months later, Mr. Wong's nephew plans to go to the United States by himself. Mr. Wong asks Mr. Chang if perhaps his brothers could help the nephew out and give him a job when he gets there. Again Mr. Chang complies without hesitation. The two men's relationship continues in this manner, with Mr. Wong calling on Mr. Chang for assistance in several more instances and Mr. Chang in some instances asking for several small favors as well.

How can one explain Mr. Wong's attitude?

1. Mr. Wong was simply taking advantage of Mr. Chang's good fortune.
2. Mr. Chang had obligated himself to Mr. Wong and it was his duty to help, which also obligated Mr. Wong to him.
3. This just shows the spirit of friendship and cooperation, of friends helping one another.
4. Mr. Chang was just taking as much as he could, but he was planning a way to get back at Mr. Wong.

The discussions of these alternative explanations begin on page 66.

6

The Invitation to Dinner

Mr. Yung had come to the United States from Korea about 7 years ago. Being hardworking and adaptable, he had found work and was able to bring the rest of his family over about 4 years ago. Despite their language difficulties, members of his family were able to get along fairly well in the community. The Yungs made a number of new friends who gladly helped them to adjust to various aspects of the new culture. In addition, the Yungs enjoyed their company, accepting and reciprocating invitations to dinner and to such festivities as birthday celebrations. The Yungs also discovered many other Korean immigrants and joined a few immigrants' organizations. However, the family still did not feel comfortable in this new society. They felt that in general people were always too busy and had no time for one another. They missed their old friends in Korea, who would often casually stop by to chat and stay for hours. Although they had new friends here, everyone seemed very business oriented and not really like friends at all. When Mr. Yung mentioned this to a neighbor "friend," the neighbor responded by inviting Mr. Yung to dinner "next week." Mr. Yung replied, "That's exactly what I mean." Although he accepted the invitation, his expression showed his disappointment. The neighbor was totally bewildered and frustrated about what to do.

How would you intervene and help explain? Don't be satisfied with overly general explanations.

1. Mr. Yung and his family expect too much from their friends.
2. Mr. Yung and family are used to a much more socially oriented society, where people do not have to make formal plans to spend time with friends.
3. Mr. Yung and his family are experiencing culture shock and adjustment problems.
4. Mr. Yung was upset at the vagueness of the reference to "next week." He wanted a specific date and time to be set.

The discussions of these alternative explanations begin on page 66.

7

Foreign Bureaucracy

Robert, an Englishman, has recently arrived in a Middle Eastern country and obtained a position as a private English teacher. He is required to obtain a work permit, and so presents himself at the appropriate government office to apply. He is told to fill out a form and return in a few days. When he returns and asks if the permit is granted, he is told there are some problems and to return in a few days. On two more visits he meets the same response and exasperatedly asks another teacher if this is normal. He is told that such delaying tactics are frequent and that he can avoid them by giving the official a small amount of money to expedite the process. Robert becomes very indignant at this and declares he will never resort to such bribery. However, after several more fruitless visits he slips the official some money and is subsequently granted his permit. He feels very bitter about the incident, however, and constantly denounces the corruption of "these people" to his fellow expatriates.

How would you interpret the official's action so as to make it more acceptable to Robert?

1. The official is not being discriminatory, as everybody is obliged to pay such bribes. Robert should not take it so personally.

2. The payment could be regarded as equivalent to a tip for services, such as that given to a waiter or porter.

3. Such behavior is probably not seen as unethical by the official, so Robert should not try to impose his culturally influenced values upon someone from another culture.

4. The official does not demand any large sums of money, so he is not really doing anything seriously wrong.

The discussions of these alternative explanations begin on page 67.

Incident 1 (p. 57): Rationales for the Alternative Explanations

1. This is possible, but it was probably not uppermost in the teacher's mind. Please choose again.

2. It probably is less nutritious, but there is no indication that this was the concern of the teacher. There is a more likely explanation. Please choose again.

3. The *bento* is usually made in the traditional manner, but it is not the breaking of tradition or desecrating of any symbol that upset the teacher. There is a more fundamental factor arising from the difference between the American lunch and *bento*. Please choose again.

4. This is the best choice. Conformity is a dominant characteristic of Japanese society, and the teacher possibly feared that such individuality could set a bad example or lead to teasing or ostracism of the boy. Many cultures stress strict conformity to group or societal norms as essential for the smooth functioning of the society. The socialization of children in such cultures is highly controlled, and any deviance from norms, values, or appearance is severely criticized and may lead to ostracism if continued. Although hosts may view sojourners much more leniently (and accept them despite their differences), in situations where they feel sojourners' actions may adversely influence group behavior (such as encouraging differences in children, as in this example), they will probably attempt to isolate, change, or criticize sojourner behavior so as to reduce its influence. Sojourners should be sensitive to such issues and not unduly contradict local norms merely for the sake of asserting their own individuality.

Incident 2 (p. 58): Rationales for the Alternative Explanations

1. It is probable that Mei-ying and her family were not accustomed to eating American food and perhaps did not care very much for it. They were, however, all aware of the gesture that Alice was trying to make, and they all indicated that they would be happy to try some genuine American cooking. There is an answer that more fully explains the situation. Please choose again.

2. It may have been more usual for Alice to pay, but considering this particular situation, and also the fact that Mei-ying's family already knew of Alice's financial status, this is not the case here. Please choose again.

3. There is no indication of this in this incident. The family seemed to appreciate Alice's plan when she first introduced it. Please choose again.

4. This seems to be the overriding problem. Food and the outdoors (certainly not the street) with no refrigeration do not seem to meet sanitary conditions from Alice's point of view. On the other hand, the Western-style market has food that may have been refrigerated for an indefinite period of time or in unknown places of storage. This food does not meet standards of freshness and cleanliness from Mei-ying and her family's perspective. The vegetables seem dried up and everything is covered or packaged so one cannot really tell how fresh things are. Mei-ying and Alice have different ideas about what constitutes sanitary or fresh food.

Incident 3 (p. 59): Rationales for the Alternative Explanations

1. Although they may be offended by such ideas, to the Spanish there is no notion of either bull or man "winning," so they would not conceive the event as anything to gamble on. Please select another response.
2. This is the best response. To the *aficionados* (devotees) bullfighting is a ritual, not a sport. It is viewed as a ceremony or drama in which the form, skill, and intensity of the performance are regarded as more important than the outcome. If the ritual is correctly performed, the bull's death is inevitable, but he will be allowed to exhibit dignity in this final act. Thus the concept of a "winner" is irrelevant, and George's colleagues saw his flippant remarks as debasing the event and were offended. Modern secular societies have stripped their cultures of many of the rituals that were formerly significant or have trivialized them to such a degree that they have largely lost their meaning. Sojourners from such societies are apt to view rituals of other cultures as quaint, amusing superstition or mere spectacle or sport. Failure to take them seriously can easily cause offense, so sojourners should be sensitive to their hosts' regard for such events.
3. George's colleagues would probably not expect George to know anything of the relative merits of individual bulls or matadors, nor would they be likely to take offense at George's ignorance of such matters. There is a more probable explanation. Please select again.
4. Although many matadors have their own personal superstitions, and our validation sample found this a possibility, there is nothing in the story to indicate that such statements are thought of as unlucky. There is a more substantial explanation for the Spaniards' reaction to George's remark. Please choose again.

Incident 4 (p. 60): Rationales for the Alternative Explanations

1. On the contrary, in Indonesia physical contact is often acceptable between members of the same sex. Neither would have been insulted merely because he was touched. Please select a better response.
2. This is the best answer. There is a taboo about personal contact with the left hand in many nations of Asia and Africa. The left hand is considered hygienically unclean and should not contact either people or food. An individual could expect a similar reaction if he or she is seen eating with the left hand.
3. There is no indication in the incident that this would be the case. In fact, it is common practice to share the purchase of beer. Please select another response.
4. This could be a possible explanation. One should be aware of social customs when interacting with host nationals. However, this is not the overriding issue

in this incident, as there is a much more critical point. Please choose a better response.

Incident 5 (p. 60): Rationales for the Alternative Explanations

1. Although this may seem like what is happening, we must remember that Mr. Chang is also a successful businessman and that he did not become one by letting other people take advantage of him. There is nothing in this story that would make one think of Mr. Chang as a good-natured fool. There is more going on here; please choose again.

2. A very complex system of reciprocity is at work here. Yes, Mr. Chang had obligated himself to Mr. Wong, but Mr. Wong's requests were not entirely annoying to him, because in the process Mr. Wong's requests were also obligating him to Mr. Chang. As the two had long been friends and were also very wealthy men, this could work to the advantage of both. In this system, one reciprocating act does not necessarily pay back another. There can be many rounds of requests, and at the same time those requests could be incurring other obligations. If it seems that this could go on forever, that is precisely the point. It could pass on through generations. This choice makes the most sense.

3. That is a very nice thought, and our validation sample found this explanation a possibility. However, it is doubtful that either Mr. Wong or Mr. Chang is so idealistic. Friendship is not necessary for the relationship between Mr. Wong and Mr. Chang to continue. Please consider again and make another choice.

4. If Mr. Chang really did not like or want to stand any more of Mr. Wong's actions, he certainly did not have to take them. He could have curtailed them right at the start, especially if he was planning to get back at Mr. Wong, which would have certainly ended their relationship. There is a better choice.

Incident 6 (p. 62): Rationales for the Alternative Explanations

1. Although this may seem true, Mr. Yung and his family are well liked in the community and are not demanding of their friends in any way. There is more going on in the situation than this. Please choose again.

2. This is the best answer. Mr. Yung and his family seem fairly adjusted into the society except for this one aspect. Many people in the United States work hard to accomplish goals they set for themselves. Although Americans may also be interested in leisure and enjoyment, even time with friends is often carefully scheduled. Mr. Yung and his family are used to a more socially oriented society, where it is more important to be together with other people.

They are used to a society where people drop in on friends without calling ahead. This occurs even to the extent of dropping in at dinnertime and joining in the meal with the family.

3. Although there may be some aspects of culture shock operating here, and our validation sample found this possible, this is too broad a generalization to explain this specific situation adequately, as Mr. Yung and his family seem fairly well adjusted in other areas. Please choose again.

4. The lack of an exact date and time is not the problem. In fact, such a formal approach to scheduling social interaction is what Mr. Yung dislikes. Please choose again.

Incident 7 (p. 63): Rationales for the Alternative Explanations

1. This is a partial explanation. Robert's negative reaction is more a result of a perceived violation of his ethics than because he feels discriminated against. Such practices are very common in many countries, and Robert probably realizes this. However, this knowledge probably will not go far toward making the actions more acceptable to him. There is another explanation. Please choose again.

2. This could be the best way to view such behavior. If one can relate certain customs to actions that are similar or parallel to some in one's own culture, one may see previously unacceptable behaviors in a better light. Tipping for various services is very common in England and accepted as an ethical practice, yet visitors from countries that do not have such practices feel very uneasy at being obliged to tip. The reason for such financial supplements is generally to compensate the worker for a low basic remuneration. The official in the Middle Eastern country probably requests such supplementary payments for the same reason.

3. This alternative has a good deal of merit, and our validation sample selected this as the best possible response. This explanation, however, will probably not help reduce Robert's feeling that his values are being violated. Although such explanations are often given to attempt to endorse such behaviors, they are very abstract—it is preferable to find an explanation that Robert can relate to more specifically. In light of this, please try again.

4. It is unlikely that the size of the sum will decrease Robert's perception of the act as corrupt. There is a better suggestion.

4

INTERACTING WITH HOSTS

Very few people can have successful cross-cultural experiences without engaging in extensive interaction with others and developing good interpersonal relationships with them. All definitions of successful cross-cultural adjustment (e.g., Ruben & Kealey, 1979) include such components as good relations with others, an ability to show respect, and a good reputation among others as a culturally sensitive individual. People want to interact with others and to go beyond superficial exchanges of pleasantries in their interpersonal relationships. The loneliness brought on by an absence of close friends is a frequent problem for sojourners. Further, the tasks that sojourners want to accomplish often necessitate the involvement of hosts. Foreign students want to ask hosts about the best courses to take. Technical assistance advisers need to transfer skills to hosts. Businesspeople want to develop joint ventures that are beneficial to all the parties involved. Social workers want to find out what is available in a particular community. Appropriate ways of developing and maintaining good relations differ across cultures, as can be seen in the following set of critical incidents.

8

Healing Wounds

An elderly immigrant from Saudi Arabia, Mr. Halim Mohamed, has come in for physical therapy. Mr. Mohamed was in a motorcycle accident and suffered partial paralysis. As a result, he needs someone to guide him in rehabilitation exercises, as well as to help him bathe and use the restroom. The supervisor of the respected Australian clinic where he is being treated assigns a fairly new intern, Sylvia, to the task. Sylvia, who has worked mostly with fellow Australians so far, approaches the work with her usual enthusiasm. However, by the end of the day she is exhausted. Mr. Mohamed seems to fight her every step of the way. Sylvia tells Mr. Mohamed that his rehabilitation cannot possibly be a success without his willing cooperation, but he reacts violently to her suggestions, even swearing at her at times. Sylvia goes home feeling utterly defeated, with no ideas of how to improve the situation. The next morning, her supervisor calls her into the office to talk. The supervisor says that Mr. Mohamed has complained about Sylvia's incompetence and is demanding a new therapist, a young man who really knows what he is doing. The supervisor takes Sylvia off the job, explaining that she will suffer no repercussions. That day, the supervisor assigns Mr. Mohamed to a young male therapist and hears no complaints from either party.

Why did Sylvia's attempt to provide therapy for Mr. Mohamed fail?

1. If the supervisor had introduced Sylvia to Mr. Mohamed properly, he would not have become so upset. Introductions are very important in Saudi Arabian culture.

2. Sylvia did not explain sufficiently to Mr. Mohamed how he would benefit from the therapy. He thought the entire procedure useless.

3. It is unacceptable for an Arab man to be assisted in such tasks as bathing and dressing by any woman other than a family member.

4. Mr. Mohamed is clearly a sexist individual and prefers males to females. There was no way that the supervisor or Sylvia could have known this ahead of time.

5. Sylvia is not a competent physical therapist, and so Mr. Mohamed demanded someone with more experience and expertise.

The discussions of these alternative explanations begin on page 95.

9

The Final Advance

Jane was asked to represent her company at a conference that was to take place in the capital city. Having just transferred to this Latin American country, she was understandably flattered that her boss would ask her to participate and excited that she would have the opportunity to see the city.

Everything went well—travel to the city, checking into the hotel, and so on—until the preconference cocktail party. Jane was approached by a young woman executive from a local firm who introduced herself as Dinorah. Immediately upon striking up a conversation she appeared to be making a physical advance. It seemed that every time Jane moved away, Dinorah moved forward. After some time, Jane found herself against a wall, unable to retreat any further. Dinorah kept her close distance. Having experienced enough discomfort, Jane curtly excused herself, returned to her room, and refused to attend any other social functions.

How can you best explain this incident?

1. Dinorah's advance was of a sexual nature.

2. It is very unusual in a Latin American country that a woman would be asked to represent her firm. Dinorah resented seeing another woman present and wished to make Jane feel as uncomfortable as possible, hoping she would leave.

3. The comfortable social distance usually kept between two Latin Americans is much closer than that for Americans. Both Jane and Dinorah were seeking a comfortable distance.

4. Jane was probably responding to the garlic on Dinorah's breath.

The discussions of these alternative explanations begin on page 95.

10

Foreign Policy Discussions

Never much interested in newspaper reading or current events, Betty Bradley from the United States had still done quite well in her undergraduate studies in anthropology and won a scholarship for overseas study in Germany. Again reflecting her academic abilities, she was quite fluent in German, having studied it in both high school and college. Upon her arrival in Germany, she settled in well and began her graduate studies. During four or five informal gatherings of students at the local beer hall, German colleagues asked her about U.S. policy on nuclear arms in Europe, the U.S. president's seeming unsureness in foreign policy, and recent trade agreements between the United States and the former Soviet republics. Betty was unprepared for such questions and had little to say, and so was not so frequently included in beer hall gatherings later on during her sojourn. Betty was puzzled by the fact that she was not included.

If Betty asked you what was going on, what would you say?

1. The German students expected that Betty would have a great deal to say about the issues raised and were surprised that she did not contribute to discussions.
2. The German students were baiting Betty, trying to catch her in an inconsistency so that they could then counter her arguments vigorously and show her to be poorly informed.
3. The Germans' concern with politics and foreign policy is a reflection of the authoritarianism they still have as a national characteristic.
4. The German students were very anti-American and rejected Betty for this reason.

The discussions of these alternative explanations begin on page 96.

11

The Trip to the Mountains

David, an American university student studying Chinese in Taiwan, met Chen Li-men, a young man from Taipei, at a local food stand. Chen Li-men, anxious to have a foreign acquaintance and perhaps practice some English, struck up a conversation. David also wanted to familiarize himself with Chinese cultural norms and to experience the local lifestyle. As the two were talking, David mentioned his interest in the outdoors: climbing, hiking, and camping. Chen Li-men suggested that they go hiking together on the nearby mountain, just outside the city, and promised to arrange everything. David, who was looking forward to getting to know someone who could give him some insights into the culture, as well as having some time away from the noise and congestion of the city, eagerly agreed. When they finally met to go hiking, however, they were greeted by some of Li-men's friends, the whole group numbering around 25. Many were anxious to talk to David. There were also several other large groups of people enjoying the hiking area. David, though visibly disappointed, said nothing, but tended to withdraw from the rest of the group. Chen Li-men noticed his disappointment and reclusive behavior and was bewildered. He could not understand why, when he had gone to such lengths to call his friends and arrange everything to make the hiking party possible, David was still not pleased.

How would you help interpret David's disappointment?

1. Chen Li-men's orientation to activities is group related, whereas David's tends to be individualistic.
2. The area that Chen Li-men had chosen was not the kind of hiking terrain that David was used to.
3. David is being selfish, thinking he will receive less attention from Chen Li-men.
4. David is too shy to interact with the others, who are speaking excitedly among themselves.

The discussions of these alternative explanations begin on page 97.

12

His First Job

Having just graduated with a master's degree in engineering, 25-year-old Mark Burke took a job in the Philippines on a technical assistance development project concerned with low-cost housing. Because he knew a number of Filipino academics, having gone to school with them back in the United States, Mark went out to the university early in his sojourn to visit them. Quickly, he was invited to give guest lectures at the university in topics related to his field: to physics classes, to urban development classes, even to chemistry classes. As his academic friends knew quite a few officials in the government, Mark was invited to parties and pretty soon was included on the guest lists of many elaborate gatherings of Filipino policy makers and community leaders. Mark was frequently asked to comment on various development plans for the Philippines. In his own job, for which he had originally come to the Philippines, Mark made few contributions. He began to arrive at work a few hours late each day. Mark's coworkers became unhappy with his contributions to the project, but tried their best to hide their feelings.

Why did Mark behave as he did in his job with the low-cost housing project?

1. He was reacting to an increase in status, over and above what he expected.
2. Through his contacts with policy makers at parties, he learned that the low-cost housing project was poorly conceived.
3. Policy makers had Mark in mind for a big promotion to a much higher position, and he began to give his attention to preparations for this new position.

4. Mark was anxious to make a good impression on his coworkers, and he felt that he could help the project most by keeping up close contact with high-level policy makers.

The discussions of these alternative explanations begin on page 97.

13

The Helpful Classmate

Heather Silva had a childhood disease that led to paralysis in both her legs and also affected her ability to move her arms. Now 20 years old, she was studying at a university where almost all the buildings were wheelchair accessible. There was one building on her campus, however, that necessitated that she ask people to carry her and her wheelchair up a set of stairs.

Heather was taking a class in Oriental philosophy, and the professor clearly had never won any awards for "exciting teacher of the year." Heather nevertheless attended the class faithfully. One day, toward the end of class, she found that a wastebasket was blocking the path between herself and the classroom door. Because the chairs in the room were bolted to the floor, she could not see an alternative path to the door. There were four other students sitting near Heather: John, Algea, Bruce, and Tiffany. After the lecture and the exit of the professor, John got out of his chair, yawned, said, "That lecture was more boring than most!" and then left the room. Algea made eye contact with Heather, smiled, and then left the room. Bruce left his seat, moved the wastebasket out of Heather's way, and moved Heather's wheelchair in the direction of the door. While Bruce was doing this, Tiffany waited near Heather and then asked Bruce, "Do you have notes for the lecture I missed last Wednesday?"

According to the norms of many people in the United States who have physical disabilities, who was most polite toward Heather, or most accepting of her disability?

1. John, who spoke out openly about an opinion shared by all the students.
2. Algea, who made eye contact with Heather and then left.
3. Bruce, who moved the wastebasket out of the way.
4. Tiffany, who waited near Heather until Bruce had moved the wastebasket.

The discussions of these alternative explanations begin on page 98.

14

It's a Great Day for the Irish

Henry Lee from Hong Kong was assigned by his company to live in the United States in order to examine the possibilities of joint business ventures. Henry had a specific place to go, an organization in Boston whose representatives had earlier visited Hong Kong and who had suggested the idea of a person like Henry visiting the Boston organization for an extended period.

Henry was made to feel at home. This was his first time out of Southeast Asia, but he had done some reading about the United States. He was invited to a cocktail party at which many of the important figures in the Boston organization would be present. Henry remembered from his reading that many important conversations that later might lead to actual business decisions were held at cocktail parties. Henry was anxious to make a good impression. Sure enough, at the party he was introduced to Sean O'Neil, a company vice president. Recognizing the name as Irish and remembering from his reading that a good way to get others into a conversation is to discuss matters they know about, Henry directed the conversation toward O'Neil's Irish heritage. Henry brought up matters such as the Irish immigration in the mid-1800s, which had Boston as a major target; Roman Catholicism; the distilling of Irish whiskey; and the current struggles in Northern Ireland. Henry also brought up a few facts about the plans of his organization in Hong Kong. Mr. O'Neil kept the conversation as short as possible and moved on to others at the party. Henry sensed that the conversation had not gone well and that he had not made a good impression on the vice president. What mistake did Henry make?

1. He should have met Mr. O'Neil's wife before talking to the vice president.
2. He should have met others lower in the organization hierarchy before meeting O'Neil.
3. His English was not good enough for him to keep up the conversation.
4. He used a stereotype in choosing topics for conversation.
5. The material he had read about business at parties had been wrong—one should not discuss business matters at such events.

The discussions of these alternative explanations begin on page 99.

15

Party Problems

Ronald Richards worked in the personnel department of a large multinational firm that was beginning to make plans for expansion into Brazil. In such a position, he had considerable influence concerning who would be given interviews for high-level positions in the company once plans had proceeded to the point where hiring could start. Ronald was at a party one evening with a Brazilian woman, Rosalita, whom he had known for a long time. Ronald felt comfortable enough with Rosalita that he felt he could tell jokes, share personal thoughts, and make observations about Brazil and Brazilian life without always feeling on guard about offending her. At the party, Rosalita said to him, "I'd like to introduce you to one of my good friends," indicating a woman on the other side of the room. "She is very capable, and she is thinking of going back to work, having raised her children for the last 10 years. She is very interested in your company." Ronald replied, "Okay—I just hope I don't get hustled." Rosalita was noticeably upset at this remark. She excused herself as politely as she could and did not speak with Ronald for the rest of the evening.

If Ronald asked you to help him interpret this obvious misunderstanding, on what would you focus your attention?

1. Rosalita felt that Ronald might like some female companionship and felt that Ronald and her friend would make a good pairing.
2. Rosalita and Ronald were spending too much time together at the party. In Brazil, the norm is to speak with many people over the course of an evening.
3. Rosalita thought that Ronald was making sexual advances toward her.
4. Rosalita interpreted Ronald's use of the word "hustled" in a very negative manner.

The discussions of these alternative explanations begin on page 100.

16

New Friends

Edson and Maria Nasciemento recently arrived in New Orleans from Brazil in order for Edson to pursue graduate studies in Latin American history. At a welcome party given by the graduate school in honor of new students, the Nasciementos met Trish and Tom Johnson, an American couple, who were also new to New Orleans. The Johnsons were very interested in learning more about Brazil and invited the Nasciementos to join them for lunch the following Sunday. The Brazilians were very happy about their good fortune in meeting an American couple so quickly.

On Sunday afternoon, the Johnsons picked up their guests and brought them to their off-campus apartment, where a pleasant lunch had been prepared. The lunch over, Tom drove his guests home. As they were leaving the car, Tom said, "We really enjoyed ourselves today. Drop in anytime."

The following weekend, the Nasciementos invited the Johnsons to dinner for a typical Brazilian meal. Everyone seemed to enjoy themselves. Edson and Maria were enthusiastic about the long-term possibilities for the friendship.

Classes began and a month went by, during which the two couples did not seem to have the time to get together. Edson had seen Tom on campus a couple of times when in passing Tom shouted, "Let's get together some time!" as he ran off to class.

After another month, the Nasciementos purchased a car. While out on a drive one Friday evening, they realized they were in the Johnsons' neighborhood. They stopped by the Johnson house and rang the bell, and a surprised Tom opened the door. He asked Edson and Maria to come in, but kept them standing in the hall while he "straightened up the room." After about 5 minutes, Tom asked the Nasciementos to be seated, but offered them no refreshments, saying he had nothing in the apartment. Trish did not appear at all, and Tom offered no explanation for her absence. The conversation remained rather strained and awkward. The Nasciementos left after 10 minutes, feeling very hurt by Tom's rudeness, and reassessed the friendship in negative terms.

What do you think is behind the uncomfortable situation?

1. Tom was probably studying for an exam. He should have explained this to the Nasciementos, who probably would have understood.
2. The surprise visit probably embarrassed Tom. After all, his house was a mess and he felt a need to clean up.
3. The Nasciementos probably misunderstood the Johnsons' invitation.
4. Tom was really insincere in his invitation.

The discussions of these alternative explanations begin on page 101.

17

A Natural Disaster?

Frank, a British engineer, works for an international aid agency. He had been assigned to a 6-month program in Guatemala to help develop disaster preparedness schemes following a particularly severe earthquake. Although he had some success in convincing local government leaders of the necessity for the measures, he was continually frustrated in trying to initiate preventive building and health programs among the largely Indian rural population. Frank was impressed with their rebuilding efforts after a disaster, but could not interest them in preparation for disaster. These people were ardent Catholics and believed that natural disasters were acts of God and their survival was determined absolutely by God's will. Preparations intended to minimize the effects of calamities thus seemed futile, as no person could subvert God's will. Frank himself was a practicing Christian and respected the strong faith of the people, but he could not accept or understand what seemed to him blind fatalism.

How could you help Frank to interpret this difference in religious beliefs?

1. The Guatemalans did not have sufficient education or sophistication to appreciate his viewpoint.

2. The Guatemalans had been repressed so long by political and economic forces that they had lost the will to act on their own behalf.

3. The Guatemalans probably had an inherent distrust of outsiders and were using their religious beliefs as an excuse not to cooperate.

4. The Guatemalans had an intense religiosity that pervaded their lives to a degree that Frank was not likely to experience in his culture.

The discussions of these alternative explanations begin on page 101.

18

A Borrower or a Lender Be?

Bill, a European American, works in a car assembly plant in California. Many of his coworkers are recent immigrants. Some of these coworkers have strong senses of humor, and Bill enjoys their company; their jokes and easy manner make the rather monotonous job seem less oppressive. One Samoan, Fua, has become quite a constant companion, and Bill often goes for a drink with him after work. Recently, however, Bill has become concerned about the relationship, as Fua has frequently been asking him for loans because Fua tends to spend his wages before the next payday arrives. Although Fua has always paid him back, Bill feels that Fua should be a bit more responsible and should live within his means. The next time Fua asks for a loan, Bill tries to suggest that he should budget a bit better and start putting some money aside for future needs or emergencies. Fua just laughs and says, "Why bother? . . . Good friends like you always help me out if need be." Bill says nothing but feels that Fua's attitude is very irresponsible and that he is being taken advantage of to some degree.

How would you explain to Bill Fua's apparent lack of concern over managing his money?

1. Samoans do not appreciate the value of money, as they are unaccustomed to living and working in a cash economy.
2. Fua probably spends a lot of money on beer but is unwilling to admit this weakness to Bill.
3. Samoans feel that possessions, including money, should be shared according to their availability.
4. Fua plans to leave California and return to Samoa, thus leaving his debts behind him.

The discussions of these alternative explanations begin on page 102.

19

The Woman in Black

While attending a reception for some visiting officials to the Philippines, Fred, who was a consultant to the Department of Education, was approached by Manuel, a lecturer at the university he had met through his work. Obviously a bit tipsy from a few drinks he had earlier in the evening, Manuel, surveying those attending the function, quietly asked Fred who he thought was the most beautiful woman present. Fred singled out a woman standing near the food tables and pointed to her.

"Who?" asked Manuel. Again Fred pointed to the woman dressed in black who was standing across the room by the food tables.

"Who?" Manuel asked again, obviously growing impatient.
"That woman right there. Don't you see her?" Fred asked in disbelief.
"Her?" asked Manuel. "Why she's just a server. I'm asking you about women."

Uncertain of what to say or do next, Fred politely ended his conversation with Manuel and mingled with others at the reception.

If you were to talk with Fred about this incident, what would you focus on as his main concern?

1. Fred was hurt because Manuel thought very little of his choice of women.
2. Fred was surprised that Manuel did not consider this woman a person, so to speak, as she was below his social status.
3. There is an obvious cultural preference for women that Fred is not yet aware of.
4. Fred was uncertain how to continue his interaction with someone who was so heavily under the influence of alcohol.

The discussions of these alternative explanations begin on page 103.

20

The Rock Concert

Judy is a 15-year-old U.S. high school student spending a month in Mexico as part of an international living program. She lives with a middle-class Mexican family and has become a good friend of the 14-year-old daughter, Rosa and, through her, her circle of girlfriends. Judy finds life in Mexico interesting because of the novelty of the situation but feels a little frustrated at the restricted range of activities she is permitted to indulge in compared with her life back home. Whenever she suggests to Rosa and her friends that they do something a little different or daring the others seem very uncomfortable and refuse to discuss it. Judy is excited to learn that a popular American rock group is scheduled to play in the city and suggests to Rosa and her friends that they should all go. Although they admit they would like to go, the others look very apprehensive and say that they could never get permission to attend such an event. Judy then proposes that they pretend to be visiting someone else and sneak off to the concert. The group refuses even to consider the idea, and Judy concludes exasperatedly that they are a very unadventurous lot.

What is the source of the Mexican girls' reluctance to consider Judy's proposal?

1. They are much more conscious of conforming to social norms than Judy is.
2. They resent Judy (a foreigner) trying to tell them what to do.
3. They do not really want to go to the rock concert and are just making excuses so as not to offend Judy.
4. They are afraid of what might happen at the concert but do not wish to admit their fears.

The discussions of these alternative explanations begin on page 103.

21

The Welcomed Visitor

It had taken some getting used to—the transition to living on a small Pacific island was not easy, and to top it off, Dave was the only European with whom the locals had any experience (except for the occasional tour boat, which would drop eager spenders ashore for a few hours at a time).

At first, everything had seemed special. Wherever Dave went, people would rush about making certain he was comfortable. The best welcome mats were put out when he came near, the best food was made available to him, and everyone seemed to clean their homes whenever he was expected. The villagers seemed so attuned to his needs that he was usually the only one given a chair to sit upon. But now, 6 months later, things were different. He was not showered with the attention to which he had grown accustomed. People seemed almost indifferent toward him, as if he were hardly there. He became moodier and often entertained the idea of returning home and forgetting the development work he had set out to do. He had to make a decision.

Which of the following explanations would help Dave analyze what has happened?

1. The villagers had obviously grown tired of Dave's presence. They attempted to ignore him in hopes that he would just go away.
2. Six months is a long time for Dave to be in such a different environment. He was probably lonely and experiencing some culture shock, and was undoubtedly due for a change.

3. The villagers were resentful of outside aid in the form of self-help programs. Once they realized that Dave had no handouts for them, they decided they did not need him.

4. The villagers were showing their acceptance of Dave by not treating him any differently than they would treat their own. He was finally one of the locals after 6 months of residence.

The discussions of these alternative explanations begin on page 104.

22

A Night Out

Soon after transferring to a small town in Belize, a small Central American country, the Thomas family (husband, wife, and two children, ages 10 and 8) was invited to the home of their neighbors, Mr. and Mrs. Usher, for dinner. Assuming that this was an opportunity to meet the Ushers and to learn more about the local area and customs, the Thomases eagerly accepted.

Upon arriving and being welcomed into the Usher home, the adults were offered beer to drink. The three Usher children (ages 5, 7, and 12) sat quietly, observing their new neighbors. The conversation turned to a discussion of Mr. Thomas's and Mr. Usher's work. Mr. Thomas, an expert on fisheries management, and Mr. Usher, head of the local fishing cooperative, had much in common to talk about. The Thomas children, meanwhile, impatient and eager to know more about their new surroundings, began exploring the house, picking up unfamiliar items and asking their purposes. Mr. and Mrs. Thomas encouraged their inquisitiveness, thinking that any new knowledge they acquired under these safe conditions would help make their transition easier.

Dinner consisted of foods that were new to the Thomas family, not so much what they were, but how they were prepared. When the Thomas children displayed their displeasure at the food offered, Mrs. Thomas urged them to try it, assuring them that they would probably enjoy it. After much encouragement and mild resistance by the children, they reluctantly ate their meal. Conversation around the table was still focused on the husbands' work, but it lacked the warmth and friendliness of the predinner talks.

The Thomas family left soon after dinner, assuming they had made friends with their neighbors. Weeks passed, however, before they heard from the Ushers again.

How would you explain the long lag in time before the Thomases heard from the Ushers?

1. In this culture, the needs of children are put below those of adults. The Ushers were put off by the forwardness of the Thomas children and the attention given them by their parents.
2. The conversation was considered too personal for an initial meeting.
3. It is usual to reciprocate an invitation by having the other party to one's home within 2 weeks. As the Thomases did not issue an invitation, the Ushers were insulted.
4. The Ushers sensed that the Thomases were not comfortable with the food they were served and did not wish to put them in an uncomfortable position again.

The discussions of these alternative explanations begin on page 104.

23

The Personal Touch

Jack had received his assignment to Manila, in the Philippines, from his company on rather short notice, and so had come ahead of his family, as he and his wife did not want to pull their children out of school in the middle of the year. Missing his wife and children, Jack accepted a friend's invitation to attend a party. Shortly after he and his friend arrived at the party, Jack was introduced around and soon fell into conversation with a very attractive Filipino woman. While speaking with Jack, this woman was very animated and very attentive to Jack's observations on various topics. When Jack mentioned something about his personal life, the woman matched it with an incident from her own life and added more detail than did Jack in his stories. Occasionally, the woman touched Jack when talking with him. Jack thought things were going well, but when he suggested that he and the woman go to a nightclub after the party by themselves, the woman cut off the conversation as quickly as politeness permitted and walked off to chat with friends in another part of the room. Jack was not sure what had happened.

If Jack asked you to help him understand what had happened, what would you say?

1. Jack misinterpreted the meaning of the woman's behavior.

2. The woman was trying to tease Jack so as to flatter herself when Jack made the inevitable suggestion.

3. Jack's behavior reflected his ambivalent feelings about his wife.

4. The friend who brought Jack to the party should have prepared Jack for such an eventuality.

The discussions of these alternative explanations begin on page 104.

24

A Kiss Away

James, an American student, met Zhiang, a recently arrived visitor from the People's Republic of China, and they decided to lunch together at the university cafeteria. On their way, they encountered James's girlfriend, Carol, who was on her way to a dance class. James and Carol carried on a lively, intimate conversation, virtually ignoring Zhiang, who followed behind them. When they reached the cafeteria, Carol said she had to go and James embraced her and gave her a long and passionate kiss. Zhiang turned away and then walked off toward the cafeteria. James looked up, saw that Zhiang had left, and looked puzzled. "Hey," he called, "wait for me!" Zhiang stopped, looked down, and said nothing, and then continued on by himself. James shrugged his shoulders and went off to eat by himself.

How would you explain Zhiang's behavior to James?

1. Zhiang was shocked by the display of physical affection between James and Carol.

2. Zhiang was offended by the manner in which James and Carol excluded him from their conversation.

3. Zhiang was annoyed by having to wait around while James chatted with his girlfriend.

4. Zhiang felt it appropriate to give James and Carol some privacy, so he went ahead to wait for James in the cafeteria.

The discussions of these alternative explanations begin on page 105.

25

Do I Really Want to Study This?

John Solomon was a hearing student who was studying American Sign Language at a 4-year college in the United States. He was in an advanced-level course, and he was considering the possibility of preparing for a career as a sign-language interpreter to assist deaf people with their communication needs in schools, hospitals, courts, and so forth. As part of his advanced studies, he was working on a class project involving the preparation of videotapes depicting deaf people using ASL in informal conversational settings. He asked two of his deaf friends, who were also students at the college, to appear in the instructional video and they agreed.

John scheduled a time for taping that was convenient for both his deaf friends and his technical crew. On the day of the taping, John asked his friends to sit in chairs and discuss an issue of interest as they were videotaped. The friends started their conversation by talking about their classes. After this, they quickly moved into a discussion concerning the difficulties they were having obtaining good interpreters who could attend classes with them and interpret what the professors and other students were saying. Some of the complaints were about specific interpreters, and John knew enough sign language to realize that the complaints were very intense. John happened to know one of the interpreters about whom his two deaf friends were complaining, and he knew that this interpreter was a person who put a great deal of time, concern, and effort into his work. John began to wonder if interpreting was a good choice for his career.

Of these possible explanations, is there one that represents a general viewpoint shared by many in deaf culture that John (and others planning careers as sign-language interpreters) should know about?

1. There are syntactic points in American Sign Language that deaf people can communicate very clearly when the topic is interpreters.
2. Deaf people have what can easily be called a love-hate relationship with interpreters.
3. The two deaf students probably had a recent negative experience with an interpreter.
4. John inadvertently communicated to the deaf students, in a way clear to the two of them, that he wanted them to have a conversation about interpreters.

The discussions of these alternative explanations begin on page 106.

26

The Southern Gentleman

Tamako arrived at her American university from Tokyo along with several other new freshmen who were bright eyed and excited about starting college life. She had this opportunity because her uncle lived in Florida, where he had started a business, and Tamako was to live with her uncle's family.

Tamako took part in an orientation program offered for all freshmen, and there she met Jack, a young man from Alabama who was equally excited about this new stage of life. As they were going through the orientation, Tamako noticed that when Jack was in her vicinity, he often would open doors for her or pull her chair out for her. She thought that this was very nice and began to enjoy the attention; unconsciously, she found herself conveniently in his vicinity as they were making the tour of campus buildings. Jack seemed attentive, always answering her questions with a smile. At one point, when they were crossing a street amid the confusion of many other students changing classes, he even took her elbow to help guide her across. Tamako was very excited indeed when she returned home that day, announcing to her cousin that she even had an American boyfriend now. Her cousin was shocked to think that she had not known of this before, and wondered how this could be, as Tamako had arrived in Florida from Japan only 2 weeks before. Tamako's cousin felt that her family's reputation in the community would be damaged.

How would you help to clarify the situation?

1. Tamako had been involved with Jack secretly because she thought this knowledge would upset her cousin.
2. Jack was a typical "playboy type" college man and was trying to take advantage of Tamako.
3. Tamako misinterpreted Jack's actions.
4. Life in the United States is fast paced. Even personal relationships can happen quickly.
5. Tamako was expressing her newfound freedom from her former personal inhibitions and restricted society.

The discussions of these alternative explanations begin on page 107.

27

Next-Door Neighbors

Chris and Margaret are two English teachers currently working in Barcelona, Spain. They live in a small but comfortable apartment in a building near the center of the city and are pleased to find that their neighbors (on the same floor) often stop to exchange pleasantries on the stairs. Chris and Margaret feel they should get to know their neighbors better, and on several occasions they invite neighbors over to their apartment for a drink or a meal. Although the neighbors thank them for their offers, none of them ever comes over. What is more, although the neighbors seem to be very social—often entertaining large gatherings of their relatives during the weekends—Chris and Margaret are never invited to these functions. As a consequence, the two women begin to feel uneasy in any interactions with the neighbors, believing that they are not really liked or wanted in the building.

How would you explain to Chris and Margaret the neighbors' apparent unwillingness to have any extensive personal interaction with them?

1. The neighbors are accustomed to restricting home-based social activities to those involving family.
2. The neighbors are probably wary of any intimate contact with foreigners.
3. The neighbors probably feel that they would not know how to talk to or entertain foreigners and so are reluctant to invite them over.
4. Chris and Margaret have probably unwittingly offended their neighbors in some way.

The discussions of these alternative explanations begin on page 107.

28

Rooming In—or Out?

Jack, a rather boisterous but well-liked American student, shared a room in an international dormitory with a Thai student, Pitchit. The two seemed to get on fairly well, and Jack remarked to one of his American friends how easy Pitchit was to live with compared with some of his previous roommates, as he and Pitchit seemed to have similar routines and interests. However, halfway through the semester, Pitchit suddenly announced he had asked for a room transfer and would be moving out the following week. Jack was quite upset and puzzled and asked Pitchit why. At first, Pitchit was reticent about saying anything, but after persistent questioning he told Jack he could not tolerate Jack's habits—he was always playing loud music, had friends visiting at all hours, and was very untidy. Jack asked Pitchit why he had not told him this before, as he had not realized he was disturbing Pitchit in any way. Pitchit said nothing.

Why did Pitchit not tell Jack sooner about his dissatisfaction?

1. He was afraid of angering Jack.
2. He felt overwhelmed by Jack's boisterous behavior.
3. As a foreigner, he felt inferior to Jack and so felt he should not complain.
4. He was not assertive enough to be able to confront Jack directly with his complaints.

The discussions of these alternative explanations begin on page 108.

29

Pizza for Dinner

Joshua, who was 12 years old, traveled with a group of elementary students from Ohio to visit with his pen pal in Belize, Central America. After an initial few days of adjustment, he began to feel quite comfortable in the home and with his host family. Joshua's teacher, the group leader, made daily visits to the home.

In the spirit of cross-cultural learning, Joshua had brought with him many items that he considered typically American to share with his host family. At the top of the list, as it would be for most 12-year-olds, was food. Wishing to treat his host family to a prepackaged pizza dinner, Joshua assumed control of the meal. After readying the ingredients, he prepared the oven by lighting a match, turning the valve, and holding the match close to the burner. To his surprise, there was a small explosion as the gas ignited, singeing the hair on his arm as well as his eyebrows. Seemingly unaffected by this slight mishap, the host family encouraged Joshua to keep on, as they were anxious to taste this meal. This he did, although not with the spirit with which he originally set out.

Soon after the meal was completed, Joshua's teacher stopped by the house on his daily rounds for a short visit. Immediately upon seeing his teacher, Joshua ran to him, pulled him outside, and burst into tears. The Belizean family was confused by his tears.
How would you interpret the situation?

1. The tears had nothing to do with the incident. Rather, they were due to Joshua's homesickness and his having to adjust to new people and places.
2. Joshua felt embarrassed, thinking that he had ruined the event he had planned for so long and that he had not lived up to his mission as a cultural teacher.
3. The Belizean family and Joshua interpreted the explosion very differently.
4. Joshua had built up a high level of anxiety because it had been some time since he had seen his teacher.

The discussions of these alternative explanations begin on page 109.

30

A Foreign Guest

John, a teacher from Belize, traveled to the United States as part of a teacher exchange program. He was to stay in the home of Mr. and Mrs. Dalton, also teachers, in Eugene, Oregon. During the course of the visit, John was to experience American culture firsthand by living with the Dalton family. He had the responsibility of teaching about Belizean culture to small groups of teachers in the local community, and was considered very successful in this task by his American colleagues.

During the first few days, things seemed to be fairly comfortable for John and the Daltons. The excitement of being in such a new and different place kept John open-eyed and involved wherever he went. The Daltons, too, were thrilled to be hosting their first overseas guest. The initial excitement, however, soon wore off, especially for Mrs. Dalton. She seemed to become increasingly irritated and often complained to her husband about feeling like a servant. There was more food to prepare, extra laundry to do, day and evening outings to attend, and an additional person in an already small house as an extra burden. She began seeing herself as satisfying everyone's wishes but her own.

Her breaking point occurred midway through a breakfast she had prepared. John shoved an empty glass in front of Mrs. Dalton, and in a sharp tone, demanded, "More." With this, Mrs. Dalton refused to prepare any more meals; she vowed never to host a foreign guest again. If you were asked to help Mrs. Dalton work through this emotion, where would you focus?

1. Mrs. Dalton is not accustomed to having visitors in her home. She is reacting to the change in her routine.
2. John is acting as he feels a guest should act in an American home, allowing others to do most things for him.
3. John is treating Mrs. Dalton as he would many women in his home country.
4. John is assuming an attitude of superiority, feeling as if he is a high-level diplomatic representative of his country and therefore deserving of attention from all the Americans he meets.

The discussions of these alternative explanations begin on page 109.

31

Social Ease

Daureen was thrilled to have been asked by some of her new friends at school to attend a birthday party in honor of one of the girls' sisters. She had only recently arrived in Indonesia from the United States as part of a student exchange program, and she was excited to be meeting new friends.

When she arrived at the party, Daureen found many new things to experience. The food was certainly different from what she was used to, the drinks seemed to taste strange, and even the birthday greeting was done in a way she was not accustomed to. She was even aware that she was the only one dressed in typically Western clothes. This made her feel uneasy, as she had gone to some trouble to try to look her best—it did not seem right that she should feel so awkward. She did not seem to know how to act appropriately. She began feeling more and more uneasy as the night wore on.

Deciding that perhaps some food would help to relax her, Daureen approached a food table and began to help herself. Upon leaving the table, she inadvertently tripped on the leg of a chair and spilled her drink on the floor. Immediately, one of the girls nearby stooped down to begin mopping up the spill and everyone else in the room began laughing out loud. Daureen, uncertain of what to do next, quietly moved out of the way, with her head lowered in shame. She kept to herself for the remainder of the evening, hoping to avoid more trouble.

What is a good explanation of the reaction to the spilled drink in this incident?

1. Daureen had obviously been acting in an inappropriate manner all evening. The spilling of the drink was the straw that broke the camel's back, so to speak. Everyone simply found her actions amusing and could hold the laughter back no longer.

2. In Indonesia, laughter is often a means of dispersing tension.

3. Daureen began the evening wrong by not bringing a gift to the host. This immediately set the others against her, thus their reaction to her spilling the drink.

4. Daureen is experiencing a minor form of culture shock. The laughter was probably not caused by anything she did.

The discussions of these alternative explanations begin on page 110.

32

The Guest Meets the Maid

Robyn is an Australian currently working as an English teacher in Portugal. One of her students is a young doctor named Antonio, whom she finds very open and interesting, and she enjoys her lessons with him. Eventually, Antonio invites her to his home to have dinner and meet his family. When she arrives, Robyn is introduced to Antonio's wife, briefly meets the couple's two young children, and then is taken through to the dining room to commence dinner. She is surprised to find that the meal is brought out not by Antonio's wife but by a maid. Robyn comments that she did not think the family would need a maid in an apartment that to her seems quite small. As the maid is serving her, Robyn, to be pleasant, asks her questions about her family and how long she has been working for the family. The maid, however, seems reluctant to reply and becomes nervous. When, a little later, she accidentally drips some sauce on Robyn, Antonio speaks to her sharply and tells her to stay in the kitchen and his wife will serve the food. The rest of the meal is eaten in a strained atmosphere.

What is the cause of the tension between Robyn and her hosts?

1. Robyn should not have commented on the small size of the apartment.
2. The hosts are upset and embarrassed because the maid spilled sauce on Robyn.
3. Robyn should not have asked the maid questions about how long she had been working there because employment tenure is such a sensitive issue.
4. The hosts thought it very inappropriate for Robyn to converse socially with the maid.

The discussions of these alternative explanations begin on page 110.

33

Using the Local Language

Danny Johnson was assigned to a prospective Asian area (in a country undergoing technological development) to do a field site study of the region. Excited at the prospect of doing well on his first foreign project, he began to bone up on the language of the area. He had studied the language in college and had done very well. After he arrived in the country, he began immediately to talk to some of the local people to get a better idea of the area. Although Danny used mostly the host language, he noticed that the people would usually giggle and then answer him in English even if they only knew a little. He continued talking to various individuals about different aspects of the society. Often when Danny was trying to explain a relatively complex or intricate aspect of his interest, the people, in a smiling manner, would encourage him to use English. Even when Danny was confident that what he was saying was correct, people would laugh, grin, nod their heads, and then encourage him to continue. This left Danny very discouraged and confused as to whether or not people were really understanding him.

What is a good explanation of what was happening? Take into account as much information as possible in choosing your answer.

1. The people were offended that Danny thought they did not know any English, and wanted to prove their ability by speaking.
2. The people wanted to learn English, and so were trying to use conversations with Danny as opportunities to some authentic practice.
3. The people simply did not understand Danny's attempts at speaking their language.

4. The people thought that they were being polite and considerate of Danny by letting him use a language (English) more comfortable to him.

5. The people were reacting to a strange phenomenon, a foreigner adept in their language, but they were pleased even if they were not accustomed to such foreigners.

The discussions of these alternative explanations begin on page 111.

34

Invitation to a Social Gathering

Bart Rapson had brought his family to the Philippines on his job assignment for a multinational corporation. Although Bart and his wife were not particularly religious themselves, having largely abandoned the practice of their childhood Catholicism except for token church attendance at Christmas and Easter, they still felt that their children might benefit from church membership. They explained to friends that the church can give children a sense of belonging and can provide some moral and ethical guidance. Because the Philippines is largely a Catholic country, it was easy for Bart to place his 7-year-old daughter in a Sunday school class that would prepare her for her First Communion. As the actual day of the First Communion ceremony approached, Bart planned for an after-church party and invited colleagues from work and their families. One Filipino colleague, Manuel, to whom Bart felt especially close, kept putting off responding to Bart's invitation, saying neither yes nor no. Finally, Bart said, "My wife needs to know how many people to cook for." Still not giving a yes or no answer, Manuel later called and said that he would be going to another party that would be attended by other Filipinos. Manuel gave the names of the other Filipinos, mentioning that he regularly "partied" with them, but Bart did not recognize any names on this list. Manuel said that he would try to stop by sometime during Bart's party.

Bart was quite upset. He complained, "If this is supposedly a Catholic country, why would they not place a value on a First Communion party? Why would Manuel turn down a once-in-a-lifetime gathering, celebrating my daughter's First Communion, to go to a party with friends he admits to seeing all the time?" After the First Communion party, Bart was merely cordial to Manuel—there were no longer any indications of friendliness. Manuel was puzzled, but had no idea what the problem was. The director of the corporation for which Bart and Manuel worked, a sensitive individual, picked up the cues and realized that their relationship was strained.

If the company director asked you to intervene, on what would you focus your attention so as to have a good chance of improving the situation without making anyone overly defensive and thus uncommunicative?

1. The director's observation that Bart and Manuel's relationship was strained.
2. Bart's feelings concerning his Catholicism.
3. Bart's feelings that his wife's job of preparation was made more difficult because Manuel would not say whether he would come or not.
4. Manuel's relationship with his Filipino friends.

The discussions of these alternative explanations begin on page 112.

35

Rudeness Is in the Eye of the Beholder

Marcia, a deaf student at a Canadian university, began dating Jack, a hearing student. They were classmates in a social psychology course and had been on three dates over the past 2 months. One day in their social psychology class, the professor lectured on ethnocentrism. After the lecture, Marcia invited Jack to a party on Friday evening. Marcia mentioned that the people at the party would be mostly her friends, and that most of them were deaf.

When Jack and Marcia arrived at the party, they found that the partygoers were crowded together in a small room. It was difficult to move around the room without bumping into people. At one point, Marcia saw a friend she had not seen in about 6 months. She rushed across the room to her friend, and in so doing barged through the space between two people who were having a conversation in American Sign Language. Later, Jack asked Marcia, "Wasn't it rude to rush between those two people when you crossed the room to see your friend?" Marcia answered, "To use the professor's term from the recent lecture, I think you're being ethnocentric."

Are there aspects of culture involved in this difference of opinion between Jack and Marcia?

1. Marcia was indeed rude by the standards of both deaf and hearing culture.

2. If Jack had barged through the two people as Marcia had, he would have been labeled rude by most people at the party.

3. The reason for the misunderstanding centers on the behavior of the two deaf people who were communicating with each other, not Marcia's behavior.

4. Marcia was behaving appropriately according to the norms of deaf culture.

5. Jack's questioning of Marcia's behavior was based on the guidance of his cultural background.

The discussions of these alternative explanations begin on page 113.

36

The Soccer Game

Assigned to Great Britain as a manager of a division in a large multinational organization, Dave Mitchell from the United States was interested in doing well so as to have a solid set of achievements in his career development. As part of the settling in of his family, he decided to send his 10-year-old son Alan as a day pupil to a very exclusive local public school. (Of course, a public school in England is actually a private school, as the term *private* is used in the United States to refer to schooling, and its financial status is based on tuition payments from parents.)

Alan had begun to play soccer in the United States as part of a very well-run organization in Dave's hometown. Upon arriving in England, where some of the world's best soccer is played, Dave and Alan were naturally anxious to attend some games. Alan had become friendly with Derek, a British classmate at school, and Dave gave permission for Alan to ask Derek to a professional soccer game to be played in a nearby large city. Dave later called Derek's parents to make sure Derek could go and to arrange a time to pick Derek up. After the game, when Dave and Alan took Derek home, Derek's mother thanked them, but, as politely as possible, asked Dave not to extend to Derek any more invitations to soccer games. Dave was very puzzled by her request.

Why did Derek's mother ask Dave not to ask her son to any more soccer games?

1. Derek's mother felt that soccer was a sport for the lower classes.

2. The British in general do not support sporting events with their attendance.

3. Anti-Americanism is strong in Great Britain, and Derek's mother did not want her son associating with Americans.

4. The norms for using public transportation in Great Britain are so strong that Derek's mother was upset because Dave used his car.

The discussions of these alternative explanations begin on page 114.

Incident 8 (p. 68): Rationales for the Alternative Explanations

1. It may be true that introductions are important in Saudi Arabia, but this hardly seems to be the issue in this situation. The therapist is responsible for bathing Mr. Mohamed and helping him to use the restroom. There are much more important, delicate concerns in this incident than whether or not the therapist and patient were properly introduced. Please make another selection.

2. Given that Mr. Mohamed is partially paralyzed and almost certainly eager to regain control of his limbs, it is extremely unlikely that he does not understand the purpose and importance of physical therapy. Moreover, we are told that Sylvia explained to him her need for his cooperation. Please choose again.

3. This is the best response. It is unacceptable for an Arab man to be assisted in such personal, private tasks by a young woman not in his family. Mr. Mohamed, already frustrated and embarrassed by his paralysis, cannot stand that a woman who is a complete stranger has been sent to help him. As often happens in cross-cultural clashes, he reacts with an intense emotional response to this total violation of his cultural norms.

4. There is some truth to the first statement—Mr. Mohamed clearly prefers males to females—but with one addition: *in this particular context*. We cannot assume this to be true in any situation. If the supervisor had cross-cultural experience, she would have known that a young woman would not be the appropriate therapist for this patient, and she would have assigned a male therapist in the first place. There is a better response.

5. We have no reason to believe, based on the incident, that Sylvia is not a competent therapist. The conflict here clearly centers on the issue of gender. Sylvia's youth and relative inexperience may seem to have been additional factors in upsetting Mr. Mohamed, yet the supervisor hears no complaints about the new young male therapist assigned to the case. There is a better interpretation.

Incident 9 (p. 69): Rationales for the Alternative Explanations

1. It is possible that Jane was feeling paranoid. When one confronts new experiences and new behaviors without a frame of reference, it is common to

attach familiar attributions to them. Jane's assumption that Dinorah's physical closeness was sexually motivated, however, is not accurate. Please select another response.

2. There is a phenomenon called the queen bee syndrome in which women who are at the top find ways to keep other women from reaching the top also: The queen retains power by keeping others away. Although this is a possible explanation for the behavior described, it is doubtful that this fully explains this situation, given that Jane and Dinorah represent different firms. There is a better response.

3. This is the best response. Latin Americans usually stand closer to one another than do European Americans in the United States. Whereas the comfortable distance Jane would keep from others in conversation is about 18 inches, the comfortable distance for Dinorah and most Latin Americans is about 10-12 inches. Both Jane and Dinorah were trying to find their comfortable distance.

4. It is a common misconception that most Latin Americans are surrounded by an odor of garlic. There is no indication in the incident that this was the cause of Jane's actions. Please select a different response.

Incident 10 (p. 70): Rationales for the Alternative Explanations

1. This is the best answer. German students (European students in general) enjoy discussing politics and foreign policy and expect peers to be able to contribute to such discussions. A relatively frequent observation among European students is that American students overseas appear to be politically naive and ill informed. American students would do well to study current events before going overseas (e.g., carefully read the past 2 months of the *New York Times*) because they will almost surely be expected to comment on such issues. In fact, they may be asked to interpret fine points of foreign policy, seemingly at the level of detail demanded of a cabinet officer. In Betty's case, because she did not have much to say in the informal discussions, people did not think to ask her again to gatherings. The Germans may even have seen a lack of interest in their political discussions as a lack of interest in them personally.

2. Although there have been reports by Americans studying and living overseas that hosts seemed to bait them, this predicament is not so frequent as to be a good explanation for all or even most situations involving political discussions. Please choose again.

3. This answer reflects the sort of stereotyping that should not be accepted by sophisticated sojourners. It rarely is of much help to accept such overstated explanations—it is better to search for more specific explanations that take into account various aspects of the specific instance. In this case, relevant aspects of the specific instance are that one of the people is an American, it

involves informal student gatherings, and so forth. It should also be noted that levels of any personality trait that might be called authoritarianism are low among adolescents and young adults (Betty's likely college student colleagues) in Germany. Please choose again.

4. Although some Germans are anti-American, there is no evidence in this story that this is the case with Betty's colleagues. If they were anti-American, they might not have invited Betty to the four or five gatherings she did attend. Betty probably would have picked up anti-American feelings after the first two or three meetings if this were the best explanation. Please choose again.

Incident 11 (p. 71): Rationales for the Alternative Explanations

1. This is the best answer. The Chinese have a much more group-oriented culture than do Americans. It is fairly common for them to plan large club or organizational outings together. When they have an activity, it is rare that they would invite just one or two others. In contrast, David comes from a society in which people frequently prefers to do things individually or on a one-on-one basis.

2. It is most probable that the terrain was not what David was used to, but most hiking enthusiasts would see such a factor as a challenge rather than as a problem. It is doubtful that this would cause David's clear reaction of disappointment. Look for something else and choose again.

3. It is true that David will have less attention from Chen Li-men, but the reverse is also true. Chen Li-men, who wanted to practice his English, will have less interaction time with David. David, on the other hand, will have many opportunities to interact with the locals and to get a flavor of their way of thinking, just what he was hoping for. This is not a reasonable explanation of the situation. Please try again.

4. It may be fairly difficult to interact with those one does not know well, and even more so with those who already know each other. However, in this case most of the Chinese (including Chen Li-men) are eager to interact with a foreigner. David is also very eager to have some interaction. There is also the fact that David comes from a culture that is not known for its shyness, and although it could still be true that David is somewhat shy, there is nothing in the incident to indicate this. There is a more plausible answer; please choose again.

Incident 12 (p. 72): Rationales for the Alternative Explanations

1. This is a good answer. Sojourners often experience either a decrease or an increase in status. Increased status is often given to people from highly

industrialized countries who sojourn in less technologically developed societies. If he had stayed in the United States, 25-year-old Mark would not have been in a very high-status position. He would have been a part of a hierarchy, with many people above him. But in the Philippines (as in many other countries), he was given a lot of status because of his citizenship and education—all of this despite his age. Western know-how is still looked up to in many countries. Because he was given status, he was asked to many high-level parties, asked for his opinions on many important issues, and asked to lecture in universities. There is danger, however, that comes with the set of feelings that accompany a sudden change in status and power (here, power because of access to policy makers). It should also be remembered that most 25-year-olds do not have a great deal of experience with power, and Mark was ill prepared to handle the feelings accompanying status and power. David Kipnis (1976), who has done extensive research on reactions to gains in power, warns that four changes can accompany a set of experiences such as those Mark had: The individual may (a) seek more power for its own sake; (b) begin to degrade coworkers and take credit for their work; (c) become isolated from criticism, as no one likes to bring bad news to power holders; and (d) exaggerate his or her own self-importance.

2. There is no evidence of the low-cost housing project being poorly conceived, or that Mark discussed the project at parties. Please choose again.

3. Even though Mark was asked to give his opinion on a wide-ranging set of important projects, this does not mean that he was being considered for a higher position. High positions in the Philippines (as in many other countries) are held by nationals of the country. Please choose again.

4. The element in this choice concerning Mark's belief about the importance of keeping up high-level contacts could be true. However, Mark's motivation would most likely not include making a good impression on his coworkers. Please choose again.

Incident 13 (p. 73): Rationales for the Alternative Explanations

1. This is not the correct choice. Interestingly, however, John would not be considered the least polite person. He behaved the same way in Heather's presence as he would with any group of fellow students, and this should be taken into account. However, there is an additional behavior he could have called upon. Please choose again.

2. This is the correct answer according to the norms shared by many people with disabilities. Many disabled people can do a lot of things by themselves and do not always need helpers. They value the ability to do things for themselves. For instance, many people in such a situation would enjoy running their wheelchairs into the wastebasket and moving it out of the way themselves.

So Algea behaved in a polite manner simply by making eye contact with Heather. If Heather had wanted help, she could have asked for it after eye contact was made. As Heather did not take that opportunity, Algea could leave the classroom knowing that Heather felt she could take care of herself.

3. Our validation sample also suggested this as another viable alternative, and, given the rules of etiquette most people have learned, this would seem appropriate. But looked at from another perspective, according to norms shared by many people with disabilities, Bruce may, in fact, be the rudest person of the four. Bruce assumed that Heather needed help and then carried out his helping behavior without checking to see whether or not Heather wanted any assistance. This is considered rude, even patronizing and condescending, by many people with disabilities. Bruce should have found out whether or not Heather felt she needed help. Another explanation addresses this issue, so please select again.

4. This is not the correct answer, although Tiffany would not be considered the least polite person. She behaved in the same way she would with many students, with or without disabilities. She wanted Bruce's lecture notes, and so she waited for Bruce to finish what he was doing before she asked him if she could borrow the notes. To be considered "polite" according to the norms of many disabled individuals, she would have to engage in an additional behavior. Another alternative addresses this behavior. Please choose again.

Incident 14 (p. 74): Rationales for the Alternative Explanations

1. The norms for who one should meet first, a man or his wife, are not so strong in the United States as to provide a rule. The story says that Henry was introduced to the vice president. Given that it was Henry who was introduced by a third party, it was perfectly acceptable for Henry to then have a conversation with the vice president. Please choose again.

2. The norms for who one should meet at what time at a party are not so firm in the United States as to provide a rule that all should follow. Once someone introduced Henry to Mr. O'Neil a conversation could then quite reasonably and acceptably take place. Please choose again.

3. There is nothing in the story to suggest that Henry's English was inadequate. Please choose again.

4. This is the best answer. Henry was right in thinking that a good way to keep up a conversation is to choose topics in which the other person is interested, but he overdid the choice of topics. He reacted to the name of O'Neil, thought "Irish," and then brought up all he knew about Irish American culture. He had no evidence that Mr. O'Neil had any identification with Irish culture—many, many Americans have Irish names but have little or no interest in Irish

matters over and above those of any other country. In addition, Mr. O'Neil may have sensed that he was being categorized or stereotyped. He may have felt that he was being put in an "Irish category," and then subjected to all the stereotypical images of that category. Many people resent such a process. Sojourners have to be careful not to overuse stereotypes and must be careful about making decisions (in Henry's case, topics for conversation) based on stereotypes.

5. Actually, discussing business at social events is permissible. Usually, it is best to let the higher-status person (in this case, a highly placed representative of the American company) or host of the party be the first to discuss business matters, but once business is brought up, one can certainly keep up the conversation. Please choose again.

Incident 15 (p. 75): Rationales for the Alternative Explanations

1. There is no evidence in the story that Rosalita felt that Ronald and her friend would make a good pairing in the sense of male-female companionship. Even if there was this motivation in Rosalita's mind, there was a more immediate problem to which Rosalita was obviously reacting. Please choose again.

2. There is nothing in the story to indicate that Rosalita and Ronald were spending too much time together. Please choose again.

3. This choice comes close to one of the issues in the story. However, Rosalita probably did not feel that Ronald was making advances toward her—rather, the advances (if any) involved Ronald and Rosalita's friend. A direct translation of Ronald's comment is that he hoped the friend would not make advances toward him. Please choose again.

4. This is the best choice. In informal use of American English by native speakers, *hustle* can have at least two meanings. As he was the director of personnel for an important company, Ronald had undoubtedly been to many parties at which people asked him to use his influence to get them jobs. When he said, "I just hope I don't get hustled," he was using an informal English idiom to express his unwillingness to be "hustled for a job." As mentioned in the story, Ronald felt he could make such comments to Rosalita because he had a good relationship with her. However, *hustle* can also refer to making romantic or sexual advances toward a person. Rosalita must have thought that this was the meaning Ronald had in mind, and she was probably insulted that he felt her friend would do this. Rosalita must have felt that this went over the line, or beyond the acceptable level of candor, she and Ronald had established in their relationship. The general point is that sojourners have to be very careful with slang terms or idiomatic expressions because of the potential for misunderstanding. This is especially true of slang terms that can have more than one meaning, such as the term under consideration in this

story. Sojourners expect far too much when they feel they can use such terms and be well understood. In preparing talks for translation or simultaneous interpretation, sojourners are advised to delete such terms, because they are unlikely to have equivalents in other languages.

Incident 16 (p. 75): Rationales for the Alternative Explanations

1. In many instances, Americans may tend to think that exams are more important than friendships—at least for the time being—whereas Brazilians would place greater value on friendship. However, there is no indication that Tom was preparing for an exam. Please choose again.

2. There may be some truth to this. However, although most Americans may not keep their homes ready for visitors at all times, it was probably the unexpectedness of the visit that upset Tom the most. Please choose again.

3. This is the best explanation. Americans sometimes use rather vague statements as a signal to end a current discussion while at the same time encouraging the chance to meet again. Many do not really mean for such statements to be taken at face value—in this case, as an open invitation *really* to stop over at any time. American social life tends to be rather structured around work/school responsibilities, and therefore events are normally planned well in advance. The colloquialism "Drop in anytime" is not meant to be taken at face value. This is something the Nasciementos will slowly grow to understand.

4. There is no indication that Tom was insincere in his initial invitations. The present situation is strained because there is another factor at play. Please choose again.

Incident 17 (p. 77): Rationales for the Alternative Explanations

1. This is a rather simplistic viewpoint. Despite their lack of education, the rural Guatemalans were certainly sophisticated enough to comprehend Frank's rational arguments. However, they felt there were forces operating that made the logic of his argument irrelevant. There is a more thoughtful explanation. Please choose again.

2. Although this may seem plausible, Frank himself noticed the will and determination of the people to reconstruct their communities following disasters. Because of inadequate government assistance, most of this reconstruction was done on a self-help basis. There is a less political explanation. Please choose again.

3. There is little evidence for this in the story. If the Guatemalans could have seen some benefit in the programs, they would probably have been quite willing to accept aid. Please choose again.

4. This is the best response. Although Frank and the Guatemalans may have believed in the same God, cultural and historical influences have created divergent interpretations of the nature of the deity. European culture, through the pervasive influence of science, has become distinctly secularized, and this has led to a strong belief in humankind's technological mastery over nature and a greater self-determination than existed in medieval times. This belief tends to color all aspects of society, so that even Christians such as Frank who claim to accept the will of God still have a fundamental faith in their own self-will and less inclination to see God's hand in all that happens in the natural world. The Guatemalan Indians, on the other hand, have been little affected by these secular, technological influences and have a long, unbroken history of subjugation to the powers of god(s)—initially their Maya gods, more recently the Catholic, Christian God. Their culture has never really experienced or accepted forces (such as technology) that would seem to deflect the hand of God and so an intense religiosity continues to dominate their beliefs and actions.

Incident 18 (p. 77): Rationales for the Alternative Explanations

1. Although this may have been partially true in the past, it is rare now to encounter Samoans who are not used to handling money. Samoans generally go abroad with the main purpose of obtaining income, and Fua is probably sending a portion of his wages back to Samoa to his family (and this could be one reason he is often short of money). Moreover, this explanation does not account for Fua's lack of concern for future consequences. Please select again.

2. This is a somewhat stereotypical view of Samoans. Although young men or those not accustomed to alcohol may have occasional bouts of drunkenness, most refrain from constant drinking unless very depressed or alienated. Please select a different response.

3. This is the best response. The traditional Samoan has a strong regard for the social debts and obligations owed to family and friends. Because of the extensive social support network of the traditional society, Samoans can always depend on someone to assist them if a crisis or need occurs. Fua still trusts that such a system operates within his new environment and so depends on friends such as Bill to supply social (and financial) support as needed. Fua would expect Bill to come to him for help should the need arise on Bill's part. Bill should perhaps feel complimented that Fua regards him as part of his intimate and trusted social network.

4. This is probably not true. Samoans place a high value on fulfilling their obligations. Please choose again.

Incident 19 (p. 78): Rationales for the Alternative Explanations

1. There is no evidence in the incident to support this statement. A much stronger statement was made by Manuel that reflects the true concern. Please try again.
2. This is the best choice. Fred singled out a woman who was a member of a lower social class. Manuel, when considering people he would interact with and admire, did not even consider this woman because she was from such an obviously different level of society. In some societies social class and caste roots are often so firmly held that movement between levels is very difficult. Please see the essay on class and status in Chapter 12.
3. Although cultural preferences may influence choices in any number of areas, this is not the overriding issue here. Look more closely at the incident and try again.
4. There is no indication that the influence of alcohol is an overriding concern here. Please choose again.

Incident 20 (p. 79): Rationales for the Alternative Explanations

1. This is the most probable explanation. In Latin cultures the socialization of children (especially girls) is strictly controlled, and children learn early the value and necessity of conforming to social norms. Behavior that might be viewed in more individualistic (and less conforming) societies as simply adventurous is regarded in conformist societies with apprehension and as potentially disruptive of the close, interdependent social network. Rebelliousness and delinquency among the young are thus rare in such societies. The Mexican girls are much more conscious than Judy of the need to adhere strictly to social norms and expected behavior, and they fear dire consequences and shame if they do not. Sojourners should be aware of the social pressures to conform in such cultures and should not place hosts in situations where they are asked to go against social norms.
2. There is little indication that this is the case. The girls seem to accept Judy as part of their group, and although they may not be willing to take up her suggestions they do not resent them. There is a more probable explanation.
3. This seems unlikely. The girls are probably as interested in rock music as Judy is and would probably not see the need to fabricate excuses if they were not. There is a better explanation.
4. The girls are not as afraid of what might happen at the concert as they are of the consequences they might face if it is found out that they attended. There is a more probable explanation.

Incident 21 (p. 80): Rationales for the Alternative Explanations

1. Pacific Islanders are characteristically hospitable people. It is unlikely that they would behave in this manner. Please choose again.
2. This answer could be partially correct. Dave's feelings could be compounded by his reaction to being in a new and different place. Although his feelings are a part of the issue, 6 months is not an inordinate amount of time, so he is probably not due for a change. Please choose again.
3. Although the villagers occasionally saw tourists flaunting their money as they visited the village, it is doubtful that they put Dave in this category, especially after their long association with him. Please select another explanation.
4. This is the best answer. When one is finally accepted in a group, one is no longer considered different or in need of special attention. Those who enter new groups are often given increased attention in the initial stages, but as time wears on, the attention fades. This is what happened to Dave.

Incident 22 (p. 81): Rationales for the Alternative Explanations

1. This is the best answer. What may be acceptable (or even expected) behavior for children in one country may be offensive in another. American culture puts a great deal of emphasis on understanding the needs and wants of children. Whereas American children are often the center of attention and are encouraged to express their wants and desires, the opposite is true for children in Belize. The behavior of the Thomas children violated the Ushers' expectations and hence put the relationship in an uncomfortable position.
2. Appropriate conversation topics are often sensitive issues from culture to culture. What may be appropriate or assumed in one culture may be seen as offensive or presumptive in the next. Although this is an issue one should be cognizant of, it is not a major issue in the incident presented here. Please select another explanation.
3. Although in some countries reciprocity may be expected within a particular period of time, there is no mention of this rule in the incident. Please try again, focusing your choice on the information given.
4. Although the children expressed mild displeasure with the food, it is unlikely that the Ushers would place much value on their response (see explanation 1, above). Mr. and Mrs. Thomas made no complaints about the food. Please try again.

Incident 23 (p. 82): Rationales for the Alternative Explanations

1. This is the best answer. Jack was interpreting the woman's behavior based on experiences in his own culture, the middle-class urban United States. The

cues to which Jack responded were animated conversation, probably interpreted as flirtatiousness, matching and going beyond the level of personal information revealed, and touching. In some cultures, however, these cues do not carry the meaning that an invitation to go off alone should be forthcoming. Rather, such actions are considered proper social behavior. Gatherings of male sojourners around the world are filled with stories like this involving female reactions to what the males consider to be expected overtures. Please refer to the essay on roles in Chapter 12.

2. Although this is always a possibility, the rate of occurrence of teasing is no greater in the Philippines than in other countries. This does not provide a good explanation for the misunderstanding in this incident. Please choose again.

3. There is no evidence in the story that Jack has ambivalent feelings about his wife. The explanation that his wife is staying home so that their children do not have to leave school in midyear seems reasonable. This is often one reason men begin sojourns unaccompanied by their families. Please choose again.

4. In an ideal world, the friend would know that Jack might run into difficulties and would prepare Jack for them. In reality, however, this rarely happens. If Jack had asked his friend about potential difficulties, using cue words such as "male-female behavior at parties," which is one area where mistakes may potentially be made, the friend might have been able to tell him some important facts. But the friend cannot be faulted for not volunteering information, given that Jack asked no questions. Please choose again.

Incident 24 (p. 83): Rationales for the Alternative Explanations

1. This is the best response. What is considered an acceptable public display of affection varies considerably among cultures. In some Asian and Mediterranean countries, physical affection toward a person of the same sex is quite permissible, but public displays between persons of opposite sexes are not condoned. Zhiang thus probably found James's action very embarrassing and confusing, and, not knowing how to handle the situation, he left. It is always advisable to exercise discretion regarding physical affection while in foreign countries or in the presence of foreigners, unless one fully understands the codes of what is acceptable. Likewise, one should not be disturbed by displays of same-sex affection, which are quite common in many cultures.

2. It is possible Zhiang was a little offended by the couple's apparently ignoring his presence, and our validation sample found this very possible, but he probably would not show his displeasure so obviously. There is a stronger reason for his discomfort. Please choose again.

3. This does not seem very likely, as James was only causing a brief delaying. Please select another explanation.

4. This is possible but unlikely. If Zhiang had wanted to do this, he would probably have made some polite excuse to go ahead. There is a more direct reason for this sudden departure. Please choose again.

Incident 25 (p. 84): Rationales for the Alternative Explanations

1. This is not the case. There are very interesting syntactic structures in American Sign Language, but these can be demonstrated in conversations about many different topics. Please choose again.

2. This is the best choice. Deaf people often complain about interpreters, but they also realize that interpreters are necessary when they need to complete important communication tasks. Readers can appreciate the reason for the love-hate relationship if they put themselves in the position of a person needing a language interpreter. All of us are familiar with the process of carrying on a conversation with others who use our language. One person says something, another person says something that follows, and so forth. No one especially enjoys having to wait for a third person to tell the first two what is being communicated. Such a situation is irritating, and the negative feelings involved often are placed on the interpreter. One language interpreter we know well says, "We are necessary evils." That is, interpreters are often necessary, but because everyone prefers to communicate with others directly, there will often be negative feelings in deaf-hearing interactions. In addition, it is often difficult to find qualified interpreters who have expertise in certain areas. Assume a deaf student is taking an advanced course in organic chemistry. Not only must the interpreter be proficient in ASL, he or she must be competent in advanced-level organic chemistry. If he or she has no expertise in a given content area (e.g., chemistry, constitutional law, research methods), then the interpreter is able only to transfer collections of words from one language to another. Collections of words, of course, are not the same as communication based on understanding of the topic under discussion.

3. This is a possibility, and many in our validation sample chose this alternative. However, it does not answer the question posed at the end of the incident, concerning a general point widely shared among members of the deaf culture about which people planning careers in interpretation should know. On the other hand, this alternative does remind us of an important point. Recent negative experiences tend to stick in people's minds more often than do recent positive experiences. Because people will inevitably experience some negative events during their intercultural encounters, it is important that they not overemphasize these when making attributions about the behaviors of others (see the essay on attribution in Chapter 13).

4. There was no such inadvertent communication. John asked his deaf friends to discuss any topic of interest to them. The friends did just that, and nothing that John said directed their choice of topic.

Incident 26 (p. 85): Rationales for the Alternative Explanations

1. This is highly unlikely, because it is evident that Tamako did not know Jack before the orientation. There is also the fact that Tamako was very anxious to share her feelings with her cousin once she thought she had developed a romantic relationship. Please make another selection.

2. This is a typical overgeneralized stereotype of young American males. There is nothing in the incident to indicate that Jack was trying to take advantage of Tamako. The gestures mentioned indicate that he was being polite and perhaps friendly. We have no evidence by which to judge his motives. He may or may not have been planning to pursue the friendship. This is not sufficient as an answer. Please choose again.

3. This is the best answer. Tamako had been in the United States only briefly. In her own society, touch and casual interaction between members of the opposite sex are rare. Jack had been brought up in a culture (in the American South) that pays a lot of attention to such social graces and niceties as the polite gestures of opening doors, pulling out chairs, and assisting ladies with their coats or in maneuvering across hazardous areas. This came as a natural reflex to Jack and he probably thought very little of it. Tamako was not used to having such attention lavished on her by members of the opposite sex, and so she felt very flattered and sure that Jack was attracted to her. She misread the cultural cues. Sojourners from other countries often misunderstand the friendly gestures of Americans as aggressiveness, romantic intentions, or suspicious actions.

4. Yes, life in the United States is fast paced, but so is life in Tokyo. Although the social norms in Japan may restrict rapid development of personal relationships somewhat more than in the United States, there is no evidence to indicate that is what is happening here. That is too general an answer. Please take into consideration other factors in the incident and select again.

5. There is nothing to indicate that Tamako felt restricted or inhibited in her own society such that she would become uninhibited in the United States. This answer stereotypes life in Japan as participation in a restricted society, and such stereotypes are rarely helpful. Please choose again.

Incident 27 (p. 86): Rationales for the Alternative Explanations

1. This is the best choice. In Mediterranean and many other cultures there is a strong identification with the family and less concern for others outside of it (familism). Social bonds and activities are thus generally restricted to the extended family group, especially when the activities take place in the home. People are greatly defined by their roles within their families, which constitute a complex support network that becomes both self-supporting and exclusive.

Relationships with people such as neighbors or work colleagues are thus de-emphasized, and although friendships may develop, these friends are generally not invited to participate in family activities. Thus, although the neighbors do not dislike or seek to avoid contact with Chris and Margaret, they would feel very uneasy about inviting them into their homes or entering Chris and Margaret's home, considering they hardly know the women.

2. Although this may appear to be the case, it does not explain why the neighbors are reluctant to socialize. There is a more specific and helpful explanation. Please choose again.

3. There is little evidence for this in the story. The neighbors appear willing to chat with Chris and Margaret on an informal basis, but apparently do not wish to become more intimately involved. There is a more adequate explanation. Please choose again.

4. This seems unlikely, and if it were the case, the neighbors would probably shun or ignore Chris and Margaret when they run into them. Please choose again.

Incident 28 (p. 86): Rationales for the Alternative Explanations

1. Although Pitchit did not wish to confront Jack directly with his dissatisfaction, it was not fear that held him back. There is a more probable explanation. Please choose again.

2. To some extent, Pitchit probably was overwhelmed by Jack's behavior, but there were other more important factors influencing his unwillingness to complain. Please select another response.

3. Although Pitchit may have felt he should not complain, there is no indication in the story that he felt inferior to Jack in any way. There is a better response. Please choose again.

4. This is the best response. In Thai and many other Asian cultures, assertiveness is not highly valued; rather, it is seen as a potentially disruptive trait. Socialization in such cultures encourages a certain passivity, a willingness to tolerate or suffer discomforts or disturbances without complaint to a much greater degree than is manifested in Western cultures such as Jack's. Such passivity has its roots in both the religious (Buddhist) and environmental forces that have shaped Asian culture. Conversely, differing forces have influenced Western culture to regard assertiveness and willingness to stand up for one's rights as positive traits, and passivity and acceptance as signs of weakness. Pitchit probably expected Jack to have the sensitivity to realize his behavior could be disruptive, and when Jack showed no signs of changing he took the only option that seemed open to him—that of leaving the situation.

Incident 29 (p. 87): Rationales for the Alternative Explanations

1. This is not correct. The incident states that Joshua had adjusted rather well to this new environment. Please choose again.
2. The incident did not seem to affect the meal. The thought of being a "cultural teacher" is probably too abstract for a 12-year-old given the circumstances. Please choose again.
3. This is the best answer. The explosion, although not tremendously large, did frighten Joshua. Because the incident was taken lightly and he was in a new home, he had no opportunity to release his emotion. Such a scare would require a vent for the intense emotions it evoked. In the United States, such a vent would have occurred with Joshua's parents offering consolation and comfort. The Belizean family may have taken the incident lightly to avoid embarrassment to Joshua. Given the lack of a reaction from the family, Joshua did not show emotion himself. Controlling his emotions, however, did not eliminate his need to deal with them. Seeing a familiar face and having a few moments with his teacher gave Joshua the opportunity to allow these emotions to surface. The danger would be that someone would overinterpret this entire chain of events. No one is wrong in this situation: The family is not uncaring, nor is the child overly emotional. Please see the essay on attribution in Chapter 13.
4. Although Joshua's tears may have been due to his need to release anxiety, the teacher's behavior had little to do with causing them. The teacher made daily rounds to visit students and met regularly with them to discuss issues. There is a more immediate explanation; please select again.

Incident 30 (p. 88): Rationales for the Alternative Explanations

1. This is not the case. As the incident reads, John is the Daltons' first foreign visitor, not necessarily their first houseguest. Please select a different explanation.
2. Although our validation sample felt that this is a possible explanation, there is no indication in the incident that John has preconceived ideas of how a guest should act in an American home. In addition, "allowing others to do most things" is not a universal American norm. Some guests expect to pitch in and help when possible. However, this possibility is related to the preferred explanation in that both involve John's experiences with social roles. Please choose again.
3. This is the best answer. John obviously feels very much at home with the Daltons, as he is acting very similar to how he would act in his own home. Especially in his interactions with women, John is acting as his true self. Assuming a comfortable relationship (from his point of view) exists between him and Mrs. Dalton, he is at ease in his actions and requests. John is in fact

making his requests, although they are perceived as demands by Mrs. Dalton, in the same manner as he would in his own home. The relationship assumes role responsibilities; therefore, what Americans consider "politeness" is not expected. Please see the essay on roles in Chapter 12.

4. There is no evidence in the story to indicate that John expects attention typical of what a diplomat would receive. He is a teacher, well aware of his responsibilities and expectations while visiting the United States, as shown by the reactions of his colleagues at the school. Please choose again.

Incident 31 (p. 89): Rationales for the Alternative Explanations

1. Although Daureen did look and act differently from the others around her, this would not explain the apparent ridicule. Indonesians are characteristically accepting of most people. Please choose again.

2. This is the most correct answer. In Indonesia, laughter is one means of dispersing the tension that arises from embarrassing or otherwise difficult situations. It tells the person who is embarrassed or in other trouble that he or she is cared for and that others will help lessen his or her burden by sharing in it and lightening it. Even when a person talks about the death of a close friend or relative, others may laugh, again to help disperse the tears and lighten the burden.

3. Although in Indonesia it is appropriate to bring a gift to one's host, this is not what led to the behavior focused on here. Please choose again.

4. This answer, although quite possibly accurate to some extent, is not fully correct. Attributing individuals' responses to certain situations as general reactions to culture shock is not as helpful as understanding the exact reasons for their behavior. The laughter was triggered by the spilled drink, and the best answer focuses on the meaning of the laughter. Please choose again.

Incident 32 (p. 90): Rationales for the Alternative Explanations

1. It is unlikely that the hosts would have taken offense at such a remark, as they would appreciate that apartments are inevitably smaller than the houses in which Judy is accustomed to living. There is a more probable explanation.

2. This is a partial explanation. Although the hosts may have been a little embarrassed by such an accident, it is unlikely that it would cause Antonio to react as strongly as he did. There is a better explanation.

3. There is no indication in the story that such a question would cause embarrassment to the hosts. The specific issue is not a sensitive one. There is a more likely explanation.

4. This is the best explanation. In Portugal and many other countries, class distinctions are rigidly maintained despite modern egalitarian ideals. As such, servants are definitely of a lower social class, and it is regarded as very improper and embarrassing to include them in the general social conversation (thus acknowledging them as equals). Australia, by contrast, is a highly egalitarian society, and although people may work for others, they do not see themselves as inferior socially to their employers and would resent being treated as such. Judy probably feels very uncomfortable at being waited on in a domestic situation and tries to reduce this uneasiness by relating personally to the servant/maid. Sojourners should be aware of such class distinctions and not be too quick to condemn or deliberately flout them so as to embarrass hosts. Removal of such distinctions would in many cases completely disrupt social balance, and elimination of servants could create massive unemployment. Eradication of class distinctions, if seen as a social ideal, is something that can proceed only very gradually.

Incident 33 (p. 91): Rationales for the Alternative Explanations

1. In many cases, people in various countries do have the ability to speak English and welcome opportunities to use it or to show a native speaker that they have that ability. However, it is unlikely that they would take offense at a foreigner speaking their language. There is a better answer; please choose again.

2. This is partially correct. In most developing countries where people are trying to learn English, any speaker of that language, no matter how poor, is often a target for practice and authentic usage. However, this does not explain the cases in which Danny persisted in trying to speak the language and was met with giggles and more English. There is something more going on here. Please choose again.

3. In some cases, this explanation will contribute to an understanding of communication difficulties. Many times, English speakers study other languages at length and feel that they have pretty fair to good competency. However, when they find themselves in places where the languages they have studied are spoken, they are struck with a confusing state of affairs, because the local people actually cannot understand them. This can be caused by the native English speakers' poor accents or by their use of unnatural (or bookish) forms of the languages they are attempting to speak. This does not explain all the information presented in this incident, however. Please choose again.

4. This is also partially correct. The large majority of people in countries who also sometimes use English, or at least understand it, are aware of the awkward situations English speakers find themselves in when the general language used is not understandable to them. If they have the ability to use English they might do so in deference to an English speaker who is present.

However, Danny did display some knowledge of the people's language. Please choose again.

5. This is the best answer in light of all the data given. Foreigners do not often speak the "local" language. When they do, the people are surprised and do not know how to take it. In many cultures such as Asian ones, laughter or giggling is an outlet for expressing such awkwardness, but it also expresses delight that someone has invested the time in learning their mode of communication. Learning the language in an unfamiliar environment requires many hours of hard work and discipline, and it can at times be very tedious and unrewarding. Sojourners should be aware of this fact so that they can be prepared to learn to deal with it.

Incident 34 (p. 92): Rationales for the Alternative Explanations

1. This is the best choice. The assumption is that both Bart and Manuel would be interested and concerned that the director (both men's boss) had noticed a strain. This fact would be a good point to raise with both Manuel and Bart when introducing the problem to them. The fact that the observation was made by a third person, the boss, might also diminish the defensiveness that would be natural if Bart were directly challenged that he had a poor relationship with Manuel, or vice versa. Once the discussion starts, other facts might be brought in that are reflective of cultural differences. Americans often prefer knowing exactly how many will come to a party so as to have a good idea of how much food to prepare. Filipinos do not mind putting out the word that there will be a party and then preparing much more food than will probably be necessary; they are not upset that there is a lot of leftover food. Filipinos enjoy the company of familiar groups (see the essay on belonging in Chapter 11), and Manuel simply may have been in the mood for that type of gathering. For Filipinos, the baptism ceremony is a more important occasion (and opportunity for a party) than the First Communion. These and other cultural ideas could be covered. Without such direct communication on the issue in question (that the boss has noticed a problem), the relationship becomes susceptible to autistic hostility. This term, applicable to sojourns, refers to problems between people that arise because of cultural differences. One or both parties become upset, but because there is no communication to find out the reason, the problem continues and may intensify as the people become more and more uncomfortable with each other when their paths happen to cross. This discomfort may be interpreted as aloofness, intensifying the feelings of upset. The term *autistic* is used because the feelings are internal and are difficult to bring to the surface, because there is no communication between the parties. Please refer to the essay on emotional reactions during cross-cultural encounters in Chapter 11.

2. It would probably be of little use to examine Bart's religious feelings with him. The feelings are undoubtedly very complex, involving childhood experiences, and difficult for any but the best trained clinicians to identify. There is a more immediate issue that could be discussed with Bart. Please choose again.

3. This may be part of the reason for Bart's feelings, but challenging Bart with an issue specific to him would probably not be a good way to intervene. There is another choice that both addresses the immediate problem and does not automatically put either Manuel or Bart on the defensive. Please choose again.

4. Although this may be part of the reason for Manuel's choice of which party to attend, introducing the problem with a comment on Manuel's behavior might put him on the defensive. There is another choice that both addresses the immediate problem and makes neither Manuel nor Bart the sole object of attention. Please choose again.

Incident 35 (p. 93): Rationales for the Alternative Explanations

1. This is not the case. People in deaf culture would not label Marcia's behavior rude. Please choose again.

2. This is not a correct choice. If Jack had just barged through, the deaf people would have (a) not given the behavior a second thought, (b) concluded that Jack was deaf, or (c) concluded that he was a knowledgeable person. Please choose again.

3. This is not a correct choice. If the two people were standing or sitting opposite each other with a space between them, they were engaging in appropriate behavior. An interesting additional point is that signers need more space between them than do people using an oral language, because signers need enough space to use their hands and to see the total space (e.g., top of head, extended arms) used by their conversational partners. If signers stand at a comfortable distance (for them), there is the temptation for naive observers to conclude that they have a cool, unfriendly relationship.

4. This is one of two possible correct choices. According to the norms of deaf culture, the least intrusive way to get from one place to another in a very crowded room is to barge through people who are signing with each other. If a person moves quickly, he or she will not interfere with anyone's communication. It takes a person less than half a second to move between two signers—not enough time to interfere visually with the signers' interactions. If a person stops and does not barge through, on the other hand, this will interfere with the signers' conversation, because they will have to stop, acknowledge the third person, let him or her through, and then pick up their conversation. "Barging through" is an interesting example of a behavior that

is considered appropriate in one culture but rude in another. When Marcia used the word *ethnocentric,* then, she was making a reference to Jack's question, which was clearly based on the norms of his culture. Readers may want to search for the additional choice that represents Jack's viewpoint.

5. This is the second of two correct choices. According to Jack's cultural background, it is rude to walk between two people who are having a conversation. If a person cannot walk around the two people who are conversing (as is the case in this incident), good manners call for him or her to make eye contact with one of the communicators, apologize for the interruption, say something like "Can I please get by?" and carry out these steps with a pleasant tone of voice and facial expression. There is another choice that focuses on the cultural guidance provided by deaf culture, and readers may want to search for this additional piece of information.

Incident 36 (p. 94): Rationales for the Alternative Explanations

1. This is the best answer. In Great Britain, soccer is considered a sport followed by people from the lower classes. Derek's mother, obviously concerned with status, given that she sends her child to the same school as Alan, was not interested in having her child participate in a lower-class event. She probably did not refuse to allow Derek to accept the first invitation when Dave called because the matter had pretty much been settled between the two boys, but instead she made her feelings known when Dave dropped Derek off at home. Derek's mother may also have had safety on her mind, as "soccer hooligans," reportedly most often unemployed or working-class young men, have been known to disrupt soccer games through violent actions. Widely publicized tragedies in mid-1985 (in Bradford, England, and especially in Brussels, Belgium) led to the expulsion of England from international soccer competition. Many behaviors in many countries are influenced by class backgrounds and the class connotations of certain activities. For instance, if Derek had been invited to a rugby or tennis match, his mother would not have minded, because in Great Britain these sports are associated with the higher classes. Class is a difficult variable to see. Especially for Americans, who grow up with the belief that they belong to a relatively classless society, the influence of social class is hard to understand. Very few Americans would think to analyze this story in terms of the connotations of class vis-à-vis different sports. Please refer to the essay on class and status in Chapter 12.

2. The British do attend sporting events, but the particular types of sporting events (e.g., cricket, rugby, horse racing) they attend are significant. Please choose again.

3. Anti-Americanism is not so strong in Great Britain as to constitute a generally applicable answer to this story. Most Americans who have lived in Great

Britain report that, after an initial adjustment period, they had pleasant stays and were able to make friends with British people. Please choose again.

4. People may use public transportation, especially railroads, in Great Britain to a greater degree than in many American cities, but the norms for use are not so strong that this would constitute a good explanation. Please choose again.

5

SETTLING IN
AND MAKING ADJUSTMENTS

Often, and for a variety of reasons, people leave their homes and adjust to life in other communities. In addition to the typical difficulties accompanying any move from one place to another, sojourners face an extra burden brought about by the need to settle into very different cultures. Housing must be found, places where food can be obtained must be noted, hospitals must be located to prepare for an emergency, transportation must be arranged, and schools must be found for the children. No one of these problems is overwhelming, but the need to deal with all of them within a short period can cause fatigue and irritableness. Sojourners frequently confuse such short-term difficulties with long-term adjustment, or the successful accomplishment of goals for the entire sojourn. The former are the steps taken along the path toward accomplishment of the goals. Sojourners should take care not mix up the two concepts, or they may mistakenly label themselves as failures because of frustrations stemming from short-term difficulties.

37

The Gift Exchange

As a foreign student at the University of Wisconsin in Madison, Keiko Ihara was on a strict budget. She had all her tuition and books paid for by scholarships and grants and until recently was comfortably housed in the dormitory. Wanting to live in the community rather than in the dorm, she found a small apartment to share with a friend. Her college

116

friends, knowing of her monetary situation, offered to round up some of the necessary items for apartment living. Keiko politely declined, saying she could manage. Wanting to help out anyway, her friends found some old but still usable household appliances and furniture. Mary had an old desk that was in her garage, Ed had some chairs that had belonged to his uncle, and Joe and Marion had a few extra dishes. They cheerfully brought these items over to Keiko's apartment one day. Keiko seemed very embarrassed, but graciously accepted them and thanked her friends sincerely and profusely. The following week, Keiko presented them all with gifts. She gave Mary an ornate jewelry box, Ed a volume of woodcuts by a famous Japanese artist, and Joe and Marion a beautiful Japanese vase. All of the gifts were of considerable worth and value, much more than the old things her friends had donated to her. They all protested that she could not afford to give such elaborate gifts; they had really expected nothing in return, as the household items were not really being used and they would rather have her use them. Keiko, however, insisted that they take the gifts. In the end, they accepted the gifts, but they all felt uncomfortable as they knew Keiko really was sacrificing to give them.

How might you explain Keiko's reaction to the American college Good Samaritans?

1. Japanese are very independent, and Keiko really did not need their help.
2. Because their things were secondhand and old, Keiko did not really want them.
3. Keiko was really very grateful and felt obliged to return her friends' kindness.
4. The reason that Keiko was on such a tight budget in the first place was that she was too extravagant and often spent her money on foolish and impractical things.

The discussions of these alternative explanations begin on page 126.

38

Settling In

Following the exodus of the "boat people" from Vietnam in the mid-1970s, New Zealand, like many other countries, accepted large numbers of refugees. The first group of families were settled in the two main cities and tended to group together socially and geographically. Some government administrators in charge of resettlement felt this was hindering the immigrants' assimilation, by allowing small ghettos of refugees to develop. Consequently, the next wave of Vietnamese were dispersed throughout the country to small towns—in many cases only one or two families per town. However, when an evaluation of the resettlement program was carried out a year later by qualified independent evaluators, it was found that the separated families had poorer English skills and higher rates of health and adjustment problems and work absenteeism. The administrators were puzzled by these results and questioned the reliability of the evaluation.

How would you satisfactorily explain the results to the administrators? Try to get to the root of the problem.

1. The isolation of the separated families caused depression and consequent maladjustment.
2. The separated families were more closely attended to by their sponsors and social workers, and so their problems were made more obvious.
3. The separated families' loss of support groups led to their lesser ability to cope with the stresses of resettlement.
4. The second wave of immigrants had spent longer in refugee camps and had reduced resourcefulness and capacity to deal with the stresses of resettlement.

The discussions of these alternative explanations begin on page 126.

39

Auditing the Books

Richard, a consultant/auditor for an American-based international auditing company, has been sent to a city in Colombia to carry out an extensive audit for a Colombian firm having fiscal disputes with the Colombian government. He has been looking forward to the sojourn, especially as his wife Jane is accompanying him. Soon after arriving, Richard learns that the Colombian firm is really only seeking to use him as an apparently independent signatory to an audit document the firm is preparing and has no intention of really letting him go through the records. However, the firm promises to treat him well and provides Richard and his wife with excellent accommodations and a generous expense account, so Richard is not too unhappy about the situation. Meanwhile, his wife, who is a keen amateur potter, has managed to make contact with a local pottery school, where she is both studying local styles and teaching other potters some of her techniques. Despite his seemingly comfortable situation, as the weeks pass Richard grows increasingly irritable and complains constantly—about the weather, the dirtiness of the city, the corruptness of the Colombians, and other matters. He spends most of his time reading American magazines or drinking in a local bar and becomes very irritated about his wife's daily participation in pottery classes. This becomes a constant source of dispute between them and puts a severe strain on their relationship. What do you see as the underlying source of Richard's growing intolerance of the situation?

1. He is increasingly dissatisfied with having no worthwhile activity to occupy his time.

2. He doesn't like his wife being so involved with the locals, for whom he has little respect.

3. He believes the Colombian firm's behavior is morally wrong, and he is feeling increasingly guilty about his involvement.

4. He cannot adjust to the rather different living conditions of Colombia.

The discussions of these alternative explanations begin on page 127.

40

The Trip to the Doctor

Huang was the firstborn son of a well-to-do family in Hong Kong. He had done well in his undergraduate studies at the University of Hong Kong and had been accepted for graduate studies at a prestigious American university. He made his initial adjustment fairly well, finding housing and joining a supportive group of other students from Hong Kong who lived near his university. After a time, however, he began to be disappointed in his own work and was unhappy with life in America. He had become attracted to an American woman, but the relationship broke up because of personality differences. Although he was not failing any of his classes, he was by no means among the best students in his department as shown by both test scores and participation in class seminars. He began to experience some physical discomforts as well—

upset stomach, severe headaches, and lower back pain. Not wanting his friends from Hong Kong to learn about his problems, Huang went to the student health center for treatment of his ailments. The doctor at the health center prescribed acetaminophen with codeine. Huang began to take the pills, but the problems did not go away.

There is an issue in this story that is common to many sojourners, not just foreign students. What is this issue?

1. The doctor prescribed a placebo for Huang so that Huang would feel that he was getting help.

2. Huang came from an important family in Hong Kong and expected more deference in the United States from professors and fellow students.

3. The people from Hong Kong who formed Huang's support group in America were insensitive to his problems.

4. Huang experienced his personal problems in terms of physical symptoms, and the doctor prescribed for the physical symptoms.

5. Huang should have volunteered to take extra help classes at the university, such as noncredit courses in English as a second language, but his pride prevented him from doing so.

The discussions of these alternative explanations begin on page 128.

41

A Pacific Paradise?

Barbara had been teaching in Samoa for about 3 months when she became aware of an increasing uneasiness. She had made a remarkable adjustment at first, or so she thought. All the excitement when she arrived, the people who came to greet her, the peering faces as she set up her home, those interested in her work at the school, and the freedom with which people came through her home all made her feel welcome. All of this contact continued.

She was surprised at how well she took to the new foods, daily patterns, and change of activities, especially because this was her first real teaching job since she graduated from college. She was learning the local language at a reasonable rate. She felt respected in her school and was confident that she was well liked, both by her professional peers and by those in the community. People were always coming to her home. Everyone seemed to be looking out for her.

Everything seemed right, at least on the outside. Yet she was aware of becoming increasingly anxious, irritated, self-conscious, and, in a sense, paranoid, all without any apparent reason.

If Barbara asked you to help her sort her feelings out, on what main issue would you focus?

1. Barbara's reaction to the lack of privacy afforded her.
2. Barbara's disappointment that things did not shock her system upon her arrival. She felt as if some part of the adjustment process was not occurring as it was supposed to.
3. Barbara's latent reaction to having a routine job.
4. Barbara's lack of close friends.

The discussions of these alternative explanations begin on page 129.

42

Island Paradise: Two Experiences

Having lived most of his life in Hawaii, Robert had developed a negative image of Samoans. Long an ethnic group of significant numbers in Hawaii, Samoans had a reputation for aggressiveness; crime statistics for Samoans were high. Robert believed that Samoans were not at all sportsmanlike on the playing field, often using dirty tactics when losing, and that they frequently were the disciplinary problems in the schools. Robert himself had once been involved in a brawl with a Samoan who was 50 pounds heavier than him, and Robert had left the fight with a black eye and a swollen face.

At the age of 24, Robert graduated with a degree in teaching and found the job market in Hawaii to be poor. He and his wife were expecting a child, and as they had no savings, Robert could not afford to spend a great deal of time looking around for a position. In need of work, he interviewed for a teaching job in a rural village in Western Samoa and was offered the job. Although he was not particularly looking forward to living in Samoa, given his past feelings and experiences, the job paid well and he felt that he could save a great deal and then secure a more ideal position after his 2-year contract was up.

Arriving in the Western Samoan village, Robert was struck by the very rural qualities of village life compared with the urban settings in which he had observed Samoans in Hawaii. He was surprised to find that almost all the Samoans he met were cooperative, did not engage in overt aggression, were interested in their children's progress in school, and included Robert and his wife in their social gatherings. Robert's wife especially seemed to spend large amounts of time with Samoan women's groups, enjoying these experiences very much. Even with all these seemingly positive experiences, Robert was vaguely upset, reserved, and even had some mild physical problems, such as headaches, stomach aches, and diarrhea.

What psychological process, fairly common among sojourners, was Robert experiencing? Do not be satisfied with overly general explanations that are not specific enough to be of much help in explaining Robert's problem.

1. Robert was afraid that the seeming calm among the Samoans was just on the surface, and that there could be an explosion of aggression at any time.
2. Robert was getting used to the local sanitary conditions of the village, and until he did would likely have symptoms like headaches and diarrhea.
3. Robert was going through culture shock.
4. Robert was being confronted by his past prejudices and stereotypes and the anxiety resulting from this confrontation.
5. Robert was reacting to his wife's poor adjustment; her unresolved problems interfered with his own adjustment to Western Samoa.

The discussions of these alternative explanations begin on page 129.

43

Lengthening Her Sojourn

Susan had been teaching in an American school in Switzerland for a month when she learned that if she expected to remain in residence for longer than 3 months she must register her intent with the local officials. The following day on her way home from work, with passport in hand, she walked to the town hall to file the necessary papers. She was greeted by a man who introduced himself as Herr Schoch, the town registrar. He spoke some English, she some German. Presenting her passport, Susan stated that she intended to live in town for the remainder of the school year. Herr Schoch handed Susan a form and told her to come back the next day. He would keep her passport until a final decision was made. As best Susan could understand, the form she was given was to be completed by her employer.

When Susan returned the completed form to Herr Schoch the next day, he informed her that she would have to return again, this time with a letter from her landlord stating that he would accept her as a tenant for the required length of time. She would also have to bring a statement from her bank that showed how much money she had and a certified check for the amount of 1,000 Swiss francs, which would be kept as a deposit to be returned when she left the country.

Susan left the office growing more and more irritated by these demands. She did, however, do as instructed and returned the next day with all the necessary documents. Herr Schoch added this material to her file, still keeping her passport. "Only one request for tomorrow," Herr Schoch claimed: Susan was to report to the main police station for a security clearance. At this request she stormed out of the office, went to the nearest phone, and proceeded to telephone her school principal. Perhaps he could help.

If you were the principal, on what main issue would you focus your talk to help Susan overcome this situation?

1. Susan was bothered that she didn't have control of her passport, something all travelers should have at all times.
2. Susan was reacting to the red tape she was being put through.
3. Susan was upset because the time this was taking was making her fall behind in her work.
4. Herr Schoch resented having foreigners reside in his community and was doing all that he could to discourage Susan from remaining there.

The discussions of these alternative explanations begin on page 130.

44

The Reluctant Counselee

Alex recently received his counseling degree from the university and was immediately offered a position in the Community Counseling Center. This was a smooth transition for Alex, because he was already well known and respected in the university community. His primary responsibility was to provide support, guidance, and counseling for immigrants who were referred because they were having emotional and adjustment difficulties.

One of Alex's first clients was a Malaysian man, Quah, who had been in the United States for 4 months. Quah, who complained of poor energy and lack of concentration, was initially referred to the medical center by his social worker. Unable to find any physical cause for Quah's problems, and believing them to be of psychosomatic origin, the medical center sent him to the Community Counseling Center.

During his first interview with Alex, Quah was rather quiet and withdrawn, offering little about himself or the problems that were troubling him. Although Alex was quite accustomed to silences during counseling sessions, he became increasingly uncomfortable with Quah, who seemed to sit patiently, for extremely long periods of time, as though waiting for Alex to speak. Alex diagnosed Quah as suffering from anxiety and, judging that Quah did not understand the counseling process, launched into a long monologue about the process and how it helps people with problems. At the close of the session, Quah did not ask for any further counseling. After Quah left, Alex was surprised to realize that he knew very little about him; he really knew nothing of Quah's history or problems. Alex was disappointed in his skill as a counselor and began to have serious doubts about counseling clients who were culturally different from himself.

If you were asked to provide Alex with some insights into the situation that would help him better understand what was going on, what would you say?

1. Quah was so lonely and depressed that he was unable to respond to Alex's queries. He should probably have been sent to a hospital to undergo intense observation.

2. Alex misinterpreted Quah's silence as anxiety.

3. Quah was suffering from culture shock. Given sufficient time, his problems would simply go away.

4. Quah resented being sent to a counselor in the first place when he fully believed that he was suffering from a physical problem.

The discussions of these alternative explanations begin on page 131.

45

The Intense Discussion

Beatrice Riley, whose ancestors came from Ireland, was a longtime resident of Kansas who was well known in her community as a person who could be depended upon when volunteers were needed for various clubs and service organizations. She was especially active in an organization called Newcomers, which welcomed people who had recently moved to the community. Someone involved in the organization would take note when a person or family moved in, and an organizational representative would then visit the newcomers. Beatrice noticed, however, that Newcomers paid few visits to African Americans. She thought that it would be a good idea to address this issue, and so invited two African Americans, George Hodges and Lilian Burke, to a meeting of Newcomers to share their views. She did not know George and Lilian well, but she had heard from others that they were open and articulate people.

At the next Newcomers meeting, the two visitors were invited to give their viewpoint. Very quickly, they began to disagree with each other, expressing their differing views with great intensity. For example, George said, "One reason that there are few visits is that African Americans don't want them. Whites come to an African American neighborhood trying to welcome people, but they are patronizing and the newcomers don't like that at all. It is better if the whites just stay away!" Lilian responded, "George, as usual you have it wrong! The African Americans you are talking about have such a collection of chips on their shoulders that no white could ever be appreciated! We have to look at our own behavior sometimes and stop constantly blaming others!"

As the discussion continued along these lines, Beatrice tried to intervene. She said, "Perhaps we should all go home, calm down, and come back and discuss this at another time." George responded, "No, let Lilian have her say!" Lilian added, "There is no reason to wait for another time!"

Keeping in mind that there will always be individual differences among people who are members of the same culture, was there a cultural difference that the two African Americans possibly brought to the meeting that Beatrice arranged?

1. Compared with middle-class European Americans, African Americans are more comfortable expressing the intensity of their viewpoints to people who may disagree with those viewpoints.

2. Compared with African Americans who are members of the middle class, European Americans are more comfortable with open disagreements about controversial issues.

3. The set of behaviors expected of the person who calls a meeting (e.g., Beatrice) is noticeably different in African American culture compared with other cultures within the United States.

4. The topic, welcoming newcomers, brings up the issue of neighborhood integration and segregation, and this brings up intense feelings among African Americans.

5. The issue discussed at this meeting would have been more appropriately covered at gatherings organized by churches within African American communities.

The discussions of these alternative explanations begin on page 131.

Incident 37 (p. 116): Rationales for the Alternative Explanations

1. Although Japanese society is a very interdependent one, the Japanese themselves are taught to be very self-sufficient individuals. However, in this case it is evident from the context that Keiko did indeed need some items for her new home. Her friends were not being presumptuous, and Keiko was genuinely grateful for the items. There is a more suitable explanation. Please choose again.

2. One might think that acceptability was a factor in Keiko's receiving the items or declining them, because in Japanese culture old and used things are not acceptable gift items. The incident describes Keiko's need and her obvious gratitude, however, so this does not really explain the situation. Please choose again.

3. This is the best answer. Keiko really needed the items for her home, yet her socialization involved a very strict system of reciprocation. The Americans thought nothing of giving away several old items; they were glad to have the opportunity to put them to good use and probably did not think of them as gifts. On the other hand, Keiko was taught that one must not be in debt or owe favors to others; also, if possible, one must always outdo others in graciousness. In order to be proper, one must give gifts of equal or greater value than the gifts received. In this particular case, because the household items were so necessary to Keiko, they were valuable. It may also be the case that as Keiko was on a strict budget, she had no funds to purchase gifts and had to part with precious personal items.

4. There is nothing in the incident to imply that Keiko was unwise in her spending. Being on a tight budget is a common problem for college students. Please choose again.

Incident 38 (p. 117): Rationales for the Alternative Explanations

1. This is a partial explanation. Depression may have been a factor in some cases of maladjustment, but this explanation does not get to the root cause of what

variables in the isolation led to depression. There is another explanation. Please choose again.

2. This is plausible, but the evaluation was done systematically by independent researchers and so does not seem likely. Please try again.

3. This seems the most adequate explanation and is the one preferred by the evaluators upon reflection and reexamination of their data. For people settling in another culture, support from others of their own culture can be very important in the initial period. Culturally similar people can more easily recognize new immigrants' needs and can quickly establish mutual assistance networks that provide practical, social, and moral support on an informal and readily understandable basis. At a practical level, cooperative child care can allow immigrant parents to attend language classes and can reduce absenteeism once classes are under way. At the social level, immigrants who have access to others of their culture can see others who have overcome the same fears and problems they are facing, reducing their concern about their ability to adapt. There is some evidence that extensive interaction within such immigrant groups does not interfere with adjustment as contact and interaction with the host society are gradually increased, although in different roles and situations than occur among the immigrant group. This belonging to two cultural groups may thus (paradoxically) lead to better and more rapid adjustment to the new environment.

4. This is a plausible suggestion, but there is no mention of this in the story. In fact, a survey of the refugees' records showed that the mean time spent in camps was only slightly longer for the second group. There is another factor inherent in the present situation. Please try again.

Incident 39 (p. 118): Rationales for the Alternative Explanations

1. This is the best choice. Many sojourners find they cannot adjust to life in other countries unless they can find a niche or activity that is personally satisfying and is of value to others. Although Richard's presence is of value to the Colombians, he is effectively excluded from any real work or decisions and so has no worthwhile activity to occupy his time. He expresses his personal dissatisfaction through increasing irritability and feelings of alienation from the Colombians. His wife, by contrast, has a constant and absorbing activity and is quite content with her situation—which probably exacerbates Richard's feelings.

2. Although there is some suggestion that Richard does not like his wife's activities, this is only a contributing irritant to his overall situation. There is a more personal factor that is the root cause of his dissatisfaction. Please choose again.

3. Initially, Richard appeared quite willing to accept the situation, and there is no obvious indication of a change of mind. Perhaps the empty time Richard

has experienced has given him an opportunity to consider the heretofore unexamined moral concerns. There is another explanation that assists in understanding the incident. Please choose again.

4. This seems improbable, as he is living in quite comfortable conditions despite his disparaging comments about the country. His adjustment problems are caused by factors more specific to his sense of self-worth. Please choose again.

Incident 40 (p. 119): Rationales for the Alternative Explanations

1. Acetaminophen with codeine is not a placebo—it is a very powerful drug. Please choose again.

2. Although some foreign students expect deference because they are from high-status families, this has rarely been reported for students from Hong Kong. In any event, there is a much more immediate and obvious problem here that meets the criterion "common to many sojourners" specified in the question. Please choose again.

3. In an ideal world, Huang's support group would have understood the problem and intervened. However, members of such groups have their own lives to lead and cannot be expected to be attentive to one another to the degree that unexpressed problems are nevertheless communicated. The story mentions that Huang did not share his problems with his support group, so the group cannot be faulted for failing to intervene. Please choose again.

4. This is the best answer. People often have problems on their sojourns, but rather than coming to terms directly with the problems, they experience physical symptoms and then seek out help for those physical symptoms. Treating the symptoms, however, does not get at the root of the problems. Many host-country physicians miss this point when dealing with sojourners and react only to their physical symptoms, as did the doctor in this story. Such cases have now become common enough, however, that they are discussed as part of the training of young physicians, especially those who work on college and university campuses where there may be many foreign students. This problem, incidentally, has frequently been identified as common for foreign students coming to the United States from Asia, although it undoubtedly happens in all parts of the world whenever people are embarrassed to admit they are having personal problems in adjusting to another culture. One of the major purposes of this entire collection of materials, as we have mentioned, is to cover the normal range of issues experienced by virtually all sojourners. Clearly, a problem as common as this falls within that normal range, and should not be taken to be a sign of abnormality or weakness.

5. Extra classes may be of assistance, but there is a more immediate explanation here involving Huang's physical symptoms. Remember also the criterion in the question, "not just foreign students." Please choose again.

Incident 41 (p. 120): Rationales for the Alternative Explanations

1. This is the best answer. Although Barbara saw all the contacts she had, with people constantly watching her, as a sign of acceptance, it is very possible that she was reacting to a lack of privacy. Samoans typically include themselves in much of each others' lives and businesses. Houses have no walls, and so Barbara's standards of privacy, based on closed doors, are not workable in Samoa. Although this was a signal that Barbara has been accepted by the members of the community, it also opened the door (so to speak) to a lack of privacy to which she was not accustomed.

2. Although most sojourners expect to have some adjustment difficulties and Barbara did not report any, it is unlikely that she would have the feelings and react the way she is reported to as a result of this. Please select a different response.

3. Although this was Barbara's first real job, there is no indication in the incident that she was finding it difficult to adjust to her teaching. On the contrary, she felt quite confident in her work. Please select again.

4. Although a lack of close friends is often a critical factor in a person's satisfactory adjustment to a new culture and there is no mention of friends in the incident, Barbara would not be reporting the feelings mentioned in the story as a result of a lack of friends. Please relate her identified feelings to the possible choices and try again.

Incident 42 (p. 121): Rationales for the Alternative Explanations

1. This may be true in this specific case, given that Robert had experienced aggressiveness among Samoans in the past. However, it is not an explanation that answers the question posed at the end of the story: What psychological process, fairly common among sojourners, was Robert experiencing? Please choose again.

2. There is sometimes a period in which a person has to get accustomed to the local water, local waste disposal system, and the like. However, the question at the end of the story asks about a psychological process. Please choose again.

3. This is a frequently used term applied to cross-cultural experiences, and it has some explanatory value. However, it is very general in that it summarizes a whole collection of more specific feelings. Identifying these more specific feelings is always more useful than being satisfied with the general explanation of culture shock. Please choose again.

4. This is the best explanation. Robert found that his past feelings and opinions just do not seem to be applicable in rural Western Samoa. This caused him to feel anxiety, which in turn led to the psychosomatic symptoms of headaches

and diarrhea. The anxiety also resulted from Robert's new knowledge that his past feelings and opinions were wrong; such knowledge can also cause bodily distress. Attitude changes, however, do not take place quickly. As Robert has more and more new experiences, he will incorporate these into his thinking, but this will take place over time as new experiences are integrated with past ones. At the time of this incident, for instance, Robert was probably upset that his wife seemed to be having such a good time in the Samoan women's groups, because Robert still had (at best) ambivalent feelings about Samoans. Please refer to the essay on prejudice in Chapter 11.

5. There is no evidence that Robert's wife was making a poor adjustment. The incident specifically states that she enjoyed her experiences with the women's groups. Please choose again.

Incident 43 (p. 122): Rationales for the Alternative Explanations

1. People are often told to maintain control of their passports at all times, and our validation sample did indicate this as a possibility. Although Susan may have been concerned that she did not have hers, it is probably safe to assume that if she had needed to produce it for some other official purpose, she could have gotten it from the office. Problems with passports in Switzerland are not so common as to be part of warnings from experienced sojourners to newcomers. This is not a major issue here. Please try again.

2. This is the best answer. Accepting and abiding by another country's bureaucratic demands can be somewhat disturbing, especially if one is new to the country and not familiar with the demands usually placed on foreign residents. It is common in many countries for foreign nationals to be asked to register and to be put through experiences similar to Susan's. It is not uncommon to come away from this type of experience feeling belittled and humiliated. A suggested preparation or defense for such a situation might be to check with others who have been in the same position to see if, in fact, the demands being made are common. Being prepared to take multiple steps is also wise, because this will help one to avoid being frustrated by additional demands. It might also help to approach the situation with the acknowledgment that "you can't fight city hall."

3. There is no indication in the story that Susan was falling behind in her work. Please choose again.

4. There is no evidence in the story that Herr Schoch resented Susan. On the contrary, the Swiss are very fond of Americans and are usually pleased to open their communities to them. Herr Schoch is merely performing his role (which, by the way, the Swiss do very effectively and efficiently). Please select another explanation.

Incident 44 (p. 123): Rationales for the Alternative Explanations

1. Although there may be some truth to this, Quah's responses to Alex were not due to his loneliness. There is a more significant element at play here that is related to culture. Please select another explanation.

2. This is the correct explanation. Asians, in general, tend to wait somewhat longer than Westerners for others to finish speaking before they speak. This is especially true with authority figures, which Alex certainly represented to Quah. Alex compounded his mistake by expecting Quah to request another appointment. Quah would more naturally leave this decision up to Alex, the person in authority. Alex was not familiar with the extended silences common to Asian conversation and himself became quite nervous. His attempt to cover up his own anxiety by talking more meant that Quah never did have a chance to talk about himself.

3. Although people can and do suffer from the phenomenon called culture shock, it is such a general label as to not really offer much guidance to others. Be more specific in your judgment of the problem at hand, and select another explanation.

4. There may be some truth to this. It is not common for many people from countries where counseling is not an everyday practice, especially new immigrants, to seek out counseling as an approach to solving their problems. Asians in particular are not accustomed to discussing personal problems—precisely what American counselors seek to explore. Rather, they tend to explain many problems as physical ailments. Astute physicians and social workers who work closely with newly arrived immigrants should be quite accustomed to seeing psychological problems presented as physical issues. Their understanding of this phenomenon and effective communication about it to counseling staff would certainly be helpful. Although it may be the case that Quah's physical symptoms are psychological in origin, this probably does not explain his long silences. Please select another response.

Incident 45 (p. 124): Rationales for the Alternative Explanations

1. This is a good choice. Many African Americans are quite comfortable when they find themselves in conversations that involve intense disagreements. They view putting firm viewpoints forward as a sign of respect for others. In effect, they say, "Just tell me what you think—don't beat around the bush! Respect me for being able to understand your views, even when they disagree with mine. Then, I'll tell you what my views are, and I expect you to listen to them carefully and to show your respect for differing viewpoints." In contrast, European Americans often try to avoid intense disagreements and to find topics about which people can demonstrate agreement on at least a

few points. Thomas Kochman (1981), who has examined this difference, notes: "Blacks' capacity to deal with intense emotional outputs is relatively greater than that of Whites because Blacks have greater experience of being confronted with them. Reciprocally, this capacity also gives Blacks acting in response to their own feelings greater freedom to express them intensely, knowing that others have developed the capacity to receive them without becoming overwhelmed" (p. 204).

2. This is not a good choice. Compared with people from many other cultures, middle-class European Americans are not comfortable with open and intense disagreements. Please choose again.

3. There are no significant differences in the set of behaviors expected of people calling a meeting of the kind depicted in the incident. The one exception might be the people's familiarity with what can happen at the meeting. Please choose again.

4. Neighborhood integration and segregation are issues about which both African Americans and European Americans feel strongly, so this not the best choice. Please choose again.

5. Ministers and active members of churches indeed have played major roles in social movements and in the advancement of civil rights within African American communities. However, the issue discussed in this incident is not one that would be treated only in churches. It is the sort of issue that could be discussed appropriately in many public forums. Please choose again.

6

TOURIST EXPERIENCES

The term *tourist experiences* is used here to refer to those intercultural encounters reported by virtually all visitors to other countries. Shared by both tourists and long-term sojourners, these anecdotes concern such characters as taxi drivers, shopkeepers, restaurant workers, hotel desk clerks, and customs officials. The developers of these materials have wondered why taxi drivers play a part in so many sojourner anecdotes. Our suggestion is that taxi drivers are often the first representatives of the host country that tourists or sojourners meet. Arriving visitors are tired after their travels. They want to find their hotels or residences, and they need key information necessary for their survival (e.g., about money exchange, food, medical care). Taxi drivers are frequently the sources of new arrivals' necessary transportation and information, and if they are the slightest bit uncivil, sojourners (in a state of heightened arousal due to the excitement of their travel) are likely to react more intensely than they would to the same treatment in their own countries. The analysis of tourist experiences is important because these experiences are so commonly discussed among sojourners. Too often, sojourners relate their negative experiences to one another, and this may serve to reinforce negative images of various host countries. If the sophistication of sojourners' analyses of such experiences can be improved, the chances of their adjusting successfully to their new surroundings can be increased.

46

Too Hot—or Not Too Hot?

Stephanie Cohen, a native Californian, and her family had been living in western Europe for the past 2 years because of her husband's job

133

with a large construction company. There had been many adjustments to make, one of the greatest of which was learning to deal with extremes in climate. The family members eventually learned that they could remain comfortable if they adjusted to changes in the weather by adding or shedding layers of clothing. After 2 years in Europe, Stephanie's husband was transferred and the family moved to a Middle Eastern city that often received many tourists. There were also quite a few Americans living and working in that society. As it was hot and humid in the Middle East, many Euro-Americans touring the local attractions and shopping areas appeared in cool summer dresses and shorts. While visiting in the homes of neighboring wives, Stephanie also often wore shorts and other casual clothes. During these visits, Stephanie received recommendations on good places to shop. One day, as she was walking to the local marketplace in her shorts, a somewhat seedy-looking character grabbed her elbow and began saying amorous and lewd things to her. She shook herself free but was understandably upset and shaken.

If Stephanie came to you for advice, how would you explain what had happened?

1. Middle Eastern men are very aggressive; no woman should go out unaccompanied by a man.
2. The crime rate is very high in the Middle East, therefore Stephanie should be more careful.
3. Anti-American sentiment is rampant in that area, so Stephanie should choose another area in which to do her shopping.
4. Although shorts may be acceptable attire around the home and among some friends, many hosts feel that people who wear shorts in public have loose morals.

The discussions of these alternative explanations begin on page 143.

47

A Shopper's Delight?

Nancy Andrews, on a trip through Asia, was excited at the prospect of visiting a few of the Singaporean exchange students she had met in the United States. During their sojourn in the United States at her university, they had often commented on the high cost of clothing and other items compared with Singapore and other Asian cities. Nancy, an avid bargain hunter, was eager to do some shopping. Her friends had frequently described to her many of their colorful and elaborate customs and festivities, wishing there was some way that she could actually experience them. In preparation for her visit, she had read current articles about the progressive city/nation. In addition, several enthusiastic friends had given her the names of specific shops and sights to visit. When Nancy arrived, she was greeted heartily by her student friends, who hosted a dinner get-together for her that same evening. The next day, a couple of friends showed her some of the usual shopping areas and how to get around on the new transit system. In the street, she was jostled and pushed by hurrying passersby. In a shop she inquired about the price of an item (hoping the shopkeeper would decrease it) and was rudely met by a curt and loud reply that all prices were as marked. Sensing an embarrassing situation, her friends suggested that they go to another store. She found several items she liked, but found that prices were comparable to those in the United States. Her friends took her to some of the local places of interest, but Nancy found them overrun with tourists and artificial. She began to feel critical of her friends and annoyed with the city. She decided to go on to her next destination.

What would be a reasonable explanation of the factors involved in Nancy's visit?

1. The students had exaggerated their stories of their city and were not really sincere about their offer for her to visit them.
2. Nancy's preparation was not really adequate for her visit. She really did not know what she wanted to buy or see.
3. Nancy was not prepared for the actual situation, colored by the expectations she had built.
4. Nancy had inadvertently offended the people of the city by her questions.

The discussions of these alternative explanations begin on page 144.

48

A Chance Acquaintance

A Filipino couple were vacationing in England. While they were strolling along one of the main streets of London with a British acquaintance, they met another Filipino who had been residing in England for some time. He was a good friend from former times, whom they had not seen for several years. They greeted him warmly and effusively and carried on a conversation in a loud and animated fashion using their native tongue, as they were very excited by this chance meeting. After a while, their British friend became noticeably agitated, turning his head away and sighing. The Filipinos noted his reaction, looked at each other, and then recommenced their conversation, but in a quieter tone.

Why did the British man feel uncomfortable?

1. He did not want to be seen in the company of a group of foreigners.
2. He felt the Filipinos were indulging in an unnecessary and extravagant display of emotion in a public place.
3. He suspected the Filipinos were talking about him, as they were deliberately using a language he could not understand.
4. He felt the behavior of the Filipinos, in not formally introducing him or acknowledging him, was very ill-mannered.

The discussions of these alternative explanations begin on page 144.

49

Taken Into Custody on Drug Charges

Hans-Martin and Paul were traveling during the summer throughout Europe from their home in Scandinavia. Having seen many of the western European countries before, they directed their travels toward Greece and Turkey.

They met many other travelers from all over the world, especially North Americans, Israelis, Australians, and even some New Zealanders in the hostels they stayed in. It was not uncommon that they would be the center of attention, often being sought after regarding social activities and knowledge of the local customs and area given that they themselves were from the Continent. They also seemed more knowledgeable about drug use in Europe than were those from other parts of the world. Hans-Martin always had a small personal supply of marijuana that he was willing to share—something that was common among his friends back home.

Train travel from country to country was easy for Hans-Martin and Paul. They had both done it many times, moving with ease between borders and among the people. Between them, they spoke five languages. The trip to Turkey took them through countryside they had never seen before. It was quite beautiful scenery, and they found it very pleasant to watch the farms and small towns pass by the windows of the train as they swept along at a rather fast pace. Both were excited to see a country they had never seen before.

The train slowed as it approached the Turkish border, the sign that a routine Hans-Martin and Paul knew well was about to begin. As the train came to a stop, two border officials came through the train calling for passports. They had been through this many times before—having their passports checked, stating their destination, declaring goods they were carrying, and so on. Upon entering Hans-Martin's compartment and checking his passport, the officials signaled for him to open his bags. Finding a small bag of marijuana in the pocket of a pair of pants in the bag, the officials seized Hans-Martin and Paul, placed them under arrest, and took them to the local prison for questioning. Paul was set free, but Hans-Martin subsequently spent 18 months in prison.

What is the critical issue in this incident? Choose the alternative that provides a general rule all sojourners should know.

1. Border officials can take the law into their own hands and administer excessive punishment for seemingly small offenses.
2. Westerners are subject to being singled out for minor offenses in some countries.
3. Drugs are illegal throughout Asia and Europe.
4. What may be acceptable or a minor offense in one country may be a major offense in another.

The discussions of these alternative explanations begin on page 145.

50

The Immigration Officer

Felipe Cordova is a senior official in the Philippines Ministry of Communication. He is proud of the fact that he has been invited to the United States to attend an international conference and is excited at the prospect of his first trip there. Upon entering the United States, he has to pass through immigration and customs. The immigration officer subjects him to a long series of questions concerning how long he intends to stay, how much money he has, whether he intends to visit relatives, whether he understands the visa regulations, and so on. Felipe grows increasingly irritated by this questioning and finally refuses to answer any more queries. The officer then calls over a supervisor, who leads Felipe away to his office and spends considerable time verifying the authenticity of all Felipe's documents before finally allowing him to proceed. Felipe suffers all this with repressed indignation but swears to himself that he will never return to this uncivilized country.

How would you explain Felipe's obstinate and uncooperative attitude toward the immigration authorities?

1. He is fatigued and irritable because of the long plane trip.
2. He feels he is being singled out as a suspicious person and is insulted.
3. His expectations as to his status and treatment in the United States have been strongly violated.
4. He feels the officer's questioning is too personal and resents having to disclose such information.

The discussions of these alternative explanations begin on page 146.

51

They Are Talking About Me

Alan Burke had been in an Asian country for about 6 months and had begun work in an organization where 95% of the employees were citizens of the host country. Alan had worked all his life in his home country, New Zealand, and had done well in college-level foreign-language studies, including the language of his country of assignment. He was making good progress on the job and had been asked to give formal presentations on organization-related matters to the company as a whole. His language skills were good enough that he could do this in the hosts' own language.

Although he was pleased with his formal job progress, he was unhappy about informal contacts at work. He did not seem to be included in informal gatherings, such as during work breaks. Coworkers would sit around smiling and laughing and chatting, and Alan overheard his name mentioned often enough to become convinced that these informal groups were mostly talking about him. He became worried that they were talking negatively. He began to lose sleep, and this eventually was reflected in his lower productivity on the job.

If Alan asked you to help him sort out his feelings, what would you say to him? Focus on the issue that is almost certainly the case.

1. There is a natural tendency for sojourners to feel that they are being singled out for attention in hosts' conversations among themselves.
2. The coworkers should have been more sensitive and should have included Alan in their informal work breaks.
3. His coworkers were jealous of Alan's success, as shown by his being asked to address the company as a whole.
4. Alan's formal language studies in New Zealand did not include coverage of casual social conversations (language as it is used rather than language from a book), and so he was ill prepared to interact informally with people.

The discussions of these alternative explanations begin on page 146.

52

Spanish Vacation

Gustav and Bjorn are two young Swedish workers on holiday in the Costa del Sol, Spain. During their second week in Spain they enter a small cafe for a few beers and then decide to have something to eat. Gustav asks for steak, but is told by the waiter that there is none left—there is only chicken or seafood. Gustav irately tells the waiter to go out and buy some meat, as he wants steak. When the waiter objects and states that this is not possible, Gustav angrily begins to berate the waiter in Swedish. An English tourist intervenes and suggests the young men go to another cafe just down the street. Bjorn persuades Gustav to leave and apologizes to the waiter and the Englishman, saying that Gustav does not usually behave like this—at home he is quiet and reserved.

Which alternative best explains Gustav's rude and atypical behavior?

1. He is not used to alcohol, and his behavior is the result of drunkenness.
2. Swedes are often demanding and aggressive when contradicted.
3. The waiter's attitude was unhelpful and hostile and so Gustav has a perfect right to be upset.
4. Gustav feels no compulsion to control his feelings of irritation as he does not really care how those around him view his behavior.

The discussions of these alternative explanations begin on page 147.

53

Trip to the Public Market

Jane Jefferson, an Australian who had recently arrived in a Central American country on a job assignment for a multinational organization, wanted to see something of the local culture. She went to the public market and stopped at one stall and looked at some dresses, chatting with the owner of the stall in her high school-level Spanish. Upon leaving the stall without buying anything, the owner seemed to shout at Jane in an unpleasant tone. Jane began to develop negative feelings about her entire job assignment and about the country.

What is a good analysis of Jane's negative feelings?

1. Jane's company should never have sent a person to Central America whose Spanish was only high school level.
2. Jane was the target of prejudice, possibly of jealousy, on the part of the stall owner.
3. Jane damaged a dress, and this was the reason for the owner's anger.
4. The owner of the stall was having a bad day, and this was the cause of his anger.
5. Jane was overreacting to a very vivid, personal, but probably atypical event.

The discussions of these alternative explanations begin on page 148.

54

The Shopper and the Vendor

Brian Shige, an American of Chinese-Japanese heritage, was visiting in Singapore from Hawaii. In shopping around, trying to buy some fruit and souvenirs, he was trying out a few local words he had learned from the tour guide. He noticed many people staring at him as he walked along in the marketplace. As he was bargaining with a vendor, the vendor asked, "You from Filipine?" "No," Brian replied, "I'm from Hawaii!" "Oh, Hawaii, you Hawaiian!" the vendor commented, very pleased with himself. "No, I'm Chinese-Japanese," said Brian.

"Oh? You Chinese?" repeated the vendor in a questioning manner.

"No! Actually I'm Chinese-Japanese, my mother is Chinese and my father is Japanese!" replied Brian, beginning to be irritated.

"Oh! You Japanese!" the vendor stated definitely. Frustrated, Brian shrugged his shoulders and walked off without getting the fruit he was looking at.

What best explains this situation?

1. The vendor did not understand much English, and so did not really understand what Brian was saying.
2. The vendor was tired of visitors haggling over his wares and was trying to tease Brian.
3. The vendor was trying to find out more information from Brian to see if he was rich so he could charge him more for the fruit.
4. The vendor was not used to mixed races, and because Brian had familiar features, the vender identified him with some of the local people.

The discussions of these alternative explanations begin on page 148.

55

A Political Debate?

Sharlene and Qing-yu were discussing an assignment for their political science class, looking at the differences in policies held by various countries. They decided it would be easier to talk about their own countries first and then compare them. As Sharlene was expounding upon the international policies of the United States, Qing-yu asked her about an aspect that she thought illogical and did not quite understand. Sharlene agreed that it did not make any sense, and then began stating several other such policies, as well as her criticisms of them. Qing-yu was very surprised, but made no comment. Later, as Qing-yu was explaining several Chinese policies, Sharlene interrupted with a comment and proceeded to list her objections to and criticisms of several other related policies. Qing-yu became quite defensive and upset and finally refused to continue any further discussion.

How would you help explain Qing-yu's behavior?

1. Qing-yu really did not understand much about politics and was confused by Sharlene's train of thought.
2. Qing-yu felt that Sharlene was attacking her personally.
3. Qing-yu did not like being interrupted and felt that Sharlene was being very rude.

4. Qing-yu had a much more ethnocentric view of her country's policies than Sharlene had of U.S. policies, and thus was offended.

The discussions of these alternative explanations begin on page 149.

56

Am I That Different?

Susan was a rather tall, blonde Canadian who had just arrived in Mexico City to spend a month doing historical research at the Museum of Fine Arts. She was excited about the trip although she had some feelings of trepidation, as this was the first time she had traveled to anywhere besides the United States and her spoken Spanish was very poor. From the moment she first stepped out on the bustling streets of the city her feelings of apprehension were confirmed and then intensified. She continually felt all eyes upon her, sensing her differences, and believed that passersby were talking about her in phrases she could only half comprehend. She tried shutting all this out but it became impossible—the stares, the whispers, the suggestive leers of the men were too overwhelming. She hated having to go out in public and took taxis to the museum every day even though she could not really afford it. At night she stayed in her small and rather depressing boardinghouse room, feeling trapped and persecuted. She was extremely relieved when her month was up and she could return to Canada.

How would you help Susan sort out her feelings about her experience?

1. Explain that Mexicans are by nature very curious about foreigners and meant no harm.
2. Suggest that she should have been more assertive and stared them down.
3. Explain that her feelings of persecution were largely just a figment of her overly vivid imagination.
4. Suggest that she was probably being overly self-conscious as to the amount of attention she was getting.

The discussions of these alternative explanations begin on page 150.

57

Breakfast at the Cafe

Gunnar and Ingrid are a Swedish couple on their first trip to southern Europe. They have just arrived in Spain and on their first day they discover a little cafe near their hotel with friendly service and good coffee. The next morning, they return to the cafe for breakfast, sit outside in the warm morning sun, and enjoy an excellent breakfast of coffee and croissants. However, when they are presented with the bill, Gunnar notices that it is almost double what they paid the day before for exactly the same items. Angrily, he calls the waiter over and accuses him of overcharging. The waiter tries to explain in broken English that they are sitting in a different place and so must pay more, but Gunnar does not believe this explanation and eventually slams down his money and leaves, feeling extremely resentful that tourists have to suffer such exploitative practices.

What advice would you give this Swedish couple in dealing with such situations? Choose the alternative that has the best chance of reducing their indignation.

1. The waiter could well be in the right, and it would be better to establish the facts clearly before making hasty judgment on his actions.
2. Such practices are very common in many countries, and it is less stressful simply to try to accept them.
3. The couple would do better to refuse to pay or to call the police in such situations.
4. The couple should try not to take it too personally; they should see themselves as playing the role of tourists, who are often regarded as fair game.

The discussions of these alternative explanations begin on page 150.

Incident 46 (p. 133): Rationales for the Alternative Explanations

1. Although in many Middle Eastern countries it is not acceptable for women to go about by themselves by tradition, in more modern times this is rather impractical and most have adopted certain exceptions (going to market, for instance). There were also many other tourists in this place, who often tend to roam about by themselves. Though the Middle Eastern male could be

classified as aggressive, this is stereotypical information that is not very helpful. There is a better answer.

2. Because this was a tourist-populated area, we could consider this answer, but there was nothing to indicate that the man was committing a crime. He seemed to mistake Stephanie for someone who might be open to his overtures. Please choose again.

3. As Stephanie had recently moved, perhaps she may have wandered into an area that could be dangerous. However, it is more likely that she was in an area recommended to her, as mentioned in the story. Please choose again.

4. This is the best answer. As Stephanie had felt comfortable in other situations in the country, she may have assumed that her old customs were also acceptable. Wearing shorts in California and in some parts of Europe has no meaning other than that the person is trying to keep cool. In many Asian and Middle Eastern countries, however, it is understood as a sign of immorality.

Incident 47 (p. 134): Rationales for the Alternative Explanations

1. Sojourning students often have exaggerated views of their own fair homelands. However, her friends were delighted to see Nancy, and had not idly extended an invitation. The fact that they hosted a dinner in her honor also disproves any lack of real interest. There is more going on here. Please choose again.

2. In spite of the often confusing data available, the fact that Nancy read current articles would lead one to believe that she had a good idea of what she wanted to do. She also had personal cultural guides to help her decipher many of the confusing signals. Although Nancy's preparation may not have been altogether adequate, she did have a good idea from the preparation she had. There is a better explanation.

3. This is the best explanation. Because of the many helpful suggestions of well-meaning friends and the many stories she heard from the Singaporean students, Nancy had unrealistic expectations. When these expectations were not met, disappointment set in. This is common among sojourners, who must eventually come to grips with the fact that all of their expectations cannot be met.

4. There is nothing to indicate that she may have offended anyone. The shopkeeper may have appeared offended in some way but this is not certain. In any case, that does not explain Nancy's attitude. Look for something more in the incident.

Incident 48 (p. 135): Rationales for the Alternative Explanations

1. Although many British people may feel uncomfortable in the presence of people who speak different languages or who behave in different ways, this

seems unlikely here as the man was already accompanying the Filipino couple along the main streets. Please make another choice.

2. The behavior of his companions may have caused the British man some discomfort, and our validation sample did indicate this possibility. But as he himself was expressing strong emotion about the incident, there are probably other factors involved in his reaction. Please select again.

3. Although there is a tendency for people to feel that they are being talked about when others speak a language they do not understand in their presence, there is no indication that this was the case here. The Filipino couple were friends of the British man, and as he was accompanying them it is doubtful that he would suspect them of this. Please make another selection.

4. This is a good explanation. The British try to preserve formality and social graces even in moments of strong emotion, and so it may have been difficult for this man to accept the Filipinos' ignoring him (even temporarily) and failing to introduce him to their friend. It may also have been difficult for him to appreciate the depth of emotion felt by the Filipinos that would cause them to become oblivious to his presence and to use their own language to express their feelings adequately. In situations like this that involve a multitude of unfamiliar cues, sojourners are apt to react strongly upon seeing a familiar face or familiar cultural cue. When this occurs they often become oblivious to their surroundings, including persons they may be with, and this can be interpreted as rudeness. This is a phenomenon of which sojourners should be aware.

Incident 49 (p. 136): Rationales for the Alternative Explanations

1. There is no evidence in the incident to suggest that the border officials were doing anything out of their jurisdiction. Please select another explanation.

2. Although it is plausible that this may occur in any number of countries, especially depending upon world events at the time, there is no indication in the incident that this was of concern here. One needs to be cautious of the possibility of a double standard regarding locally acceptable behavior and that actually stated in the law. However, there is a better reason that relates to a general rule all sojourners should know. Please choose again.

3. Although drugs are illegal in many countries of the world, and obviously in Turkey, there is an issue here that is more critical and worthy of attention. Please select again.

4. Although drug use may be a minor (if any) offense in some countries, it is a much more major offense in others (Turkey especially). Hans-Martin came from a culture where drug use goes relatively unnoticed. His ease and freedom with marijuana use at home does not mean that he need not respect the laws of other countries he visits, hence the arrest. This is the correct choice.

Incident 50 (p. 137): Rationales for the Alternative Explanations

1. Felipe's fatigue may contribute toward his irritation, but this is not the primary cause of his negative reactions. Please select another explanation.

2. Our validation sample found this to be a probable alternative, but it is not a complete explanation. Although Felipe is insulted by the questioning, and there is always a tendency for a person to feel singled out in such situations, there is an explanation that more fully accounts for his indignation. Please choose again.

3. This is the best explanation. Felipe has a high-status position in his own country and feels that he is coming to the United States as an invited and honored guest. As such, he expects his path through bureaucracy and formalities to be smooth and unhindered. When he finds that he is treated like any other common traveler or as a poor Filipino immigrant, his expectations as to his status are strongly violated and he feels both outraged and humiliated. Travelers should be careful not to be too set in their expectations about their treatment or the conditions in foreign countries, as such preconceptions can cause undue stress when they are not met.

4. Although Felipe resents having to give the information, there is no indication that his irritation results from feelings of intrusion on his privacy. There is a better response. Please try again.

Incident 51 (p. 138): Rationales for the Alternative Explanations

1. This is the best answer. Sojourners, all of whom go through some degree of culture shock, are naturally anxious about their relationships with hosts. Most want to make a good impression and most want to be well remembered after they return to their own countries. But it should be kept in mind that a sojourner is a unique event—with 95% host nationals in an organization, as in this case, outsiders are noticeably different and will be the focus of hosts' curiosity and informal conversations. Sojourners should be advised that they will be the focus of others' conversations, but that they should not overinterpret this fact. They should not conclude that hosts are always talking ill of them, are talking about them all the time, or are calling special meetings to talk about them. Such feelings are rarely warranted.

2. Although this is perhaps true, it is not the best answer to help Alan sort out his feelings. People are comfortable with the familiar in their informal chats, and the presence of an outsider (Alan) would make them less comfortable and would make the work breaks more formal. People like to be with their in-groups during informal chats, and although this may lead to exclusion of newcomers and outsiders, informal groupings of people who are similar is a natural tendency. Please choose again.

3. This is a possibility, and unfortunately one about which sojourners should be careful. However, it does not happen in all Asian countries with such frequency that it can be considered a general principle, especially if Alan is modest about his accomplishments (braggarts are rarely liked; this is true of most places, including Alan's home country). Although the possibility of jealousy is a topic that Alan might well discuss with experienced sojourners he respects, there is another answer that meets the criterion. Please choose again.

4. The content of what is taught in college-level language classes varies widely. Some instructors, realizing that the criticism that students once left classes "talking like books" was valid, now regularly introduce material on informal conversational styles in their course work. Thus Alan could well have had a good deal of exposure to informal conversational styles. For instance, language instructors sometimes invite foreign students to come to their classes and engage in informal chats with students. Although this is a good answer, there is another one that sheds additional light on the issue. Please choose again.

Incident 52 (p. 139): Rationales for the Alternative Explanations

1. This is probably not the correct response. Gustav only had a few beers and most Swedish males are quite accustomed to alcohol. Please choose again.

2. This is a rather stereotypical depiction of the Germanic personality and does not explain the apparent change in Gustav's character. Such stereotypical explanations are rarely helpful in thinking about cross-cultural experiences. There is a more thoughtful explanation. Please choose again.

3. Gustav may quite well have sensed some hostility in the waiter's attitude, but this does not explain his overreaction and atypical aggression. There is little evidence of any hostility from the waiter. There is a further factor in the situation that more adequately accounts for Gustav's behavior. Please select another response.

4. This is the most probable explanation. Back home in Sweden, Gustav's reserved manner is probably conditioned mainly by fear of censure from family or the community in which he lives and that he respects. Once outside of these censors Gustav (and sojourners in general) feel much less bound to their homelands' accepted standards of behavior. To some extent Gustav feels anonymous or deindividuated with respect to his normal social group. Having no fear of damaging his reputation or upsetting those he respects, he feels less compulsion to control emotions he would normally repress and becomes indifferent to and fails to recognize the local (Spanish) standards of behavior.

Incident 53 (p. 140): Rationales for the Alternative Explanations

1. Although it may be true that no multinational organization should send out representatives who have a poor command of the local language, the fact remains that they often do. Language fluency probably contributed to the problem, but there is a better explanation. Please choose again.

2. This is possible. Visitors from highly industrialized countries, where the average standard of living is high, sometimes report that they are the targets of jealousy when they go abroad. But it is rarely true that all or even most people in any given culture display such jealousy, and there is no evidence in this story that the stall owner felt this way. Please choose again.

3. The story says that Jane only looked at the dresses, and so this answer is unlikely. Please choose again.

4. This is a possibility, and is the sort of thought Jane should explore before coming up with a more general conclusion about the country and the people as a whole. There is another explanation that involves Jane's thinking. Please choose again.

5. This is the best explanation. There is a strong tendency to react to vivid events that involve a person in a very direct way. The fact that Jane herself was the target of what seemed like anger is a much stronger influence than less vivid, perhaps dull, information. For instance, Jane might have read in a well-researched survey report that most representatives of multinational organizations find this country a pleasure to live in and its citizens cooperative. This written report would be much less important in her mind than this one negative event in which she was directly involved. Given that Jane was a recent arrival and was still getting settled, the negative event probably was even more influential in her thinking. Sojourners would be well advised to ask themselves in such situations, "Am I overinterpreting a vivid, colorful event in which I was directly involved? Is there other information I should seek out before coming to a conclusion?"

Incident 54 (p. 140): Rationales for the Alternative Explanations

1. Although the vendor's English may not have been standard, he was able to carry on his business with tourists and others. He was already communicating enough to elicit correct answers from Brian. There is a better explanation.

2. In many Asian countries, haggling or bargaining is quite acceptable. The vendor may not like the extent to which some visitors push the system, but it is his business to participate in the system. Some vendors may decide to give some visitors a hard time, but there are other factors involved here. There is a more reasonable explanation.

3. In many bargain-system countries the vendors often try to discern how much a person is able and willing to pay for an item and charge that amount. However, the questions this vendor was asking, even though they had to do with Brian's background and family, were more related to other factors. There is a better explanation.

4. This is the best response. In many Asian countries, although a broad mix of nationalities and peoples is often present, there is still very little intermarrying and there are large distinctions among peoples. The vendor was trying to place Brian in a category that was familiar to him. Please see the essay on categorization in Chapter 13.

Incident 55 (p. 141): Rationales for the Alternative Explanations

1. Because Qing-yu and Sharlene were in the political science class together, we can assume that they were academically on the same level. Even if this were not so, most Chinese scholars who are studying abroad are very versed in their country's policies and politics. There is nothing in the incident to indicate that Sharlene confused Qing-yu. Please choose again.

2. Often when others speak about things that reflect a part of us (certainly in terms of country or nationality) we take it personally, even though it is not meant to be so. Although Qing-yu may have felt somewhat personally berated, Sharlene's comments pertained to political policies and views and should not have been taken personally. This is a partial explanation, but there is a better answer. Please choose again.

3. No one likes to be interrupted, but it does not appear that Sharlene did this in a rude fashion or that she cut off Qing-yu's opinion; she seems to have made more of an interjection. There was another factor offending Qing-yu. Please choose again.

4. This is the best answer. In many Asian countries the citizens have much more nationalistic worldviews than are found in Western countries. They not only think very highly of their own countries, they also reserve the right to criticize them in their own limited way. That is, they will not allow others to find fault with their beloved homelands, which in their understanding cannot be compared with other countries. It is not that they do not have realistic views of their countries; rather, with respect to the rest of the world, their viewpoints may be colored. The Chinese in particular have long held a viewpoint of superiority. In recent times this has diminished somewhat, but China still maintains a high degree of respect and loyalty from its citizens. Qing-yu, raised with these sorts of ideas, found it hard to believe that Sharlene criticized her own country, but found it intolerable that she openly criticized Qing-yu's, especially given that her country is one as great as China. Sharlene, in contrast, has been educated to question and analyze, to consider both negative

and positive aspects of a question. Most countries cultivate some degree of ethnocentric thinking in their citizens, so most people have a tendency to think of their own homelands as wonderful. However, certain countries tolerate criticism and varying opinions to a greater degree than do others.

Incident 56 (p. 142): Rationales for the Alternative Explanations

1. This may be some consolation, and our validation sample found this possible, but it would probably not be very convincing to Susan. There is a factor involving Susan's reaction to the attention she received that has more validity. Please choose again.

2. This would have taken a lot of dogged will and would have been dangerous in that it would have been regarded as rude, strange, or inviting attention from males. There are more useful suggestions. Please choose again.

3. Although there may be some elements of truth in this, it obliges Susan to accept that there was something wrong with her. There is a more acceptable explanation that applies to many foreigners. Please choose again.

4. This is the best explanation. Although individuals have different degrees of sensitivity to feeling themselves the focus of attention or being made to feel different, many sojourners find they develop heightened self-consciousness in their initial experiences abroad. For most, these feelings gradually lessen, but some are unable to ignore them and they consequently become intensified and lead to exaggerated reactions concerning the attention they are being given or their perceived degree of difference. As a tall blonde in a city of predominantly short, dark people, Susan would undoubtedly stand out, but it is unlikely that most would pay her more than a passing glance or appreciative stare. Her sense of apprehension or furtiveness stemming from her self-consciousness was just as likely to have caught people's attention and could have made personal interaction with the Mexicans strained. If sojourners can be persuaded that such feelings are not unnatural, that indeed they are a relatively harmless result of the situation in which they find themselves, they may accept and gradually lose this heightened awareness.

Incident 57 (p. 143): Rationales for the Alternative Explanations

1. This is the best choice. Although overcharging of tourists is not an uncommon practice, it is more the exception than the rule. If Gunnar and Ingrid had been more patient and willing to suspend judgment until they ascertained clearly what had happened, they would have found that the waiter was indeed in the right—it is quite common to charge more for service to tables outside of the

cafe than inside or at the bar. Overly quick assessment can often distort a relatively trivial misunderstanding.

2. This can be the safest way to deal with such incidents, and our validation sample found this possible. This would not, however, reduce the couple's indignation very much. There is a better response that sheds more light on the issue; please choose again.

3. This could lead to a lot of embarrassment if they were not correct. It is better first to try to establish all the facts impartially and calmly. Other advice would be preferable. Please choose again.

4. This may help to decrease some of their indignation, but does not really contribute toward any respect for the locals. Further advice is needed. Please choose again.

7

THE WORKPLACE

Various types of work assignments bring people into contact with other cultures. The physical appearance of the workplace is very often similar regardless of its location. People can generally find some familiar artifacts in classrooms, office buildings, embassies, farms, and factories. Because of these familiar aspects, people sometimes feel that the behaviors that take place in these locations will also be similar. But just a few days' experience usually brings a confrontation with real cultural differences concerning such matters as punctuality, control over resources, decision making, sex roles, or relations with colleagues. Because many people identify the success of their entire sojourns with success in their work, they should be aware of the wide range of culturally influenced issues they will encounter in the workplace.

58

The Proposal Process

Called to a staff meeting by his principal, Stan Brown from New Zealand reread materials on a mathematics curriculum development project that he wished to see incorporated into the high school at which he taught. Stan had been teaching in the Philippines for 2 years and was enjoying his sojourn at an international school in Manila that attracted not only Filipino students but also students from many other countries whose parents worked in the Philippines.

Jose, who had developed a close relationship with Stan, was also asked to the meeting. The principal asked Stan to review his proposal, the substance of which was already known to the others at the meeting.

The proposal went through without very much modification and it was agreed that the school would take the next step toward possible eventual implementation. As this had taken less time than expected, the principal asked Jose to say a few words about another curriculum development project on which he (Jose) was working. Again, most of the people at the meeting knew of this project. Jose gave an outline of his thinking, and Stan then asked some difficult questions that forced Jose to think quickly on his feet and to defend some of his earlier assumptions. The principal called an end to the meeting, and Jose then told Stan that he could not meet Stan for dinner as earlier planned. Stan was puzzled by Jose's cancellation, because Jose seemed upset when informing Stan of his wish not to meet for dinner.

Of these four alternatives, which provides the greatest insight into the reasons for Jose's cancellation of the dinner appointment?

1. Jose wanted to go to a library to get more information so as to better defend his proposal in the future.

2. Jose was jealous that Stan's proposal had passed on to the next step toward implementation without very much modification.

3. Jose felt that Stan withdrew his friendship at the meeting.

4. The principal asked Jose to sharpen up his thinking about his proposal.

The discussions of these alternative explanations begin on page 172.

59

Going to Language Class

Having graduated from college third in his class, Ron Moore had several options for the direction of his career. He selected a position with a large international construction company. He was excited about a long-term assignment in a developing country that could eventually lead to a promotion. He would have the experience of being a part of establishing several projects and then would have the chance of heading them up in terms of operations, depending on the evaluation of the project director. Ron was placed in a planning and consulting capacity. The first few months went well, and Ron's suggestions were instrumental in drawing the plans together. However, as construction began, the project director suggested that Ron go to a language school so that later he could help in the supervision and direction of the local workers and because such education would be useful to his future needs should he be placed in charge of the whole operation. Ron, too, saw the wisdom of knowing the language, and so enrolled for a full-time course. The first 2 weeks were great, and Ron enjoyed the challenge; by the fourth week, however, his enthusiasm waned. He regularly checked in with the project director, who merely inquired about his progress. Ron tried to offer comments about various projects that he might assist in, but the director thought that Ron's capability in the language was more important. By the sixth week, Ron was very discouraged, although his language teachers were visibly impressed with his progress and apparent ease with the language. He became increasingly dissatisfied with the whole project and finally requested to be transferred back to the Stateside office.

How would you explain Ron's dissatisfaction?

1. The job was just beyond Ron's capabilities.
2. The language was too hard for Ron.
3. Ron was experiencing some frustration at not being able to accomplish something that had tangible results.
4. The project director viewed Ron as competition for the position that he himself wanted and was trying to make life more difficult for him.

The discussions of these alternative explanations begin on page 173.

60

A Development Project

Having recently overseen the completion of the project that originally brought him to Africa, Matt was proud of the 3 years he had spent in Nigeria. He was able to acquire excellent materials for the sewage treatment system of which he was in charge. It was functioning well and was an important point of interest for various officials who visited Nigeria to report on development progress. Nigerian officials also pointed with pride to the sewage treatment system. Matt returned to Canada, the country whose technical assistance program sent him to Nigeria, with a promotion and a reputation for getting things done.

However, 5 years later, the sewage treatment system was not functioning well. Parts had rusted, and no one seemed able to replace worn-out parts and otherwise look after system maintenance. Officials in Nigeria, when asked to speak about successful and unsuccessful development projects, stopped mentioning the sewage treatment system. Further, hosts did not report favorable retrospective feelings about Matt's 3-year assignment in Nigeria.

What was the source of the problem with the sewage treatment system?

1. Matt was not able to use the best materials available. Eventually, these materials wore out.

2. Matt had not trained Nigerians in the skills necessary to carry on work at the sewage treatment system.

3. The hosts resented the development assistance from Canada because this put Nigeria in the embarrassing role of being the recipient of aid from outside.

4. Matt was careless in the details of construction, so what looked like a model sewage treatment system had many problems visible only to other construction engineers given unlimited rights of inspection.

The discussions of these alternative explanations begin on page 174.

61

Business or Pleasure?

Tom Bancroft, the top salesman in his midwestern U.S. area, was asked to head up a presentation of his office equipment firm to a Latin American company. He had set up an appointment for the day he arrived, and even began explaining some of his objectives to the marketing representative who was sent to meet his plane. However, it seemed that the representative was always changing the subject; he persisted in asking a lot of personal questions about Tom, his family, and his interests. Tom was later informed that the meeting had been arranged for several days later, and his hosts hoped that he would be able to relax a little first and recover from his journey, perhaps see some sights and enjoy the country's hospitality. Tom responded by saying that he was quite fit and prepared to give a presentation that day, if possible. The representative seemed a little taken aback at this, but said he would discuss it with his superiors. Eventually they agreed to meet with Tom, but at the subsequent meeting, after a bit of chat and some preliminaries, they suggested that as he might be tired they could continue the next day after he had some time to recover. During the next few days, Tom noticed that though they had said they wanted to discuss details of his presentation, they seemed to spend an inordinate amount of time on inconsequential activities. This began to annoy Tom, as he thought that the deal could have been closed several days ago. He just did not know what they were driving at.

How would you help Tom view the situation?

1. The company was trying to check on Tom and his firm by finding out more information.
2. Latin Americans are not used to working hard and just wanted to relax more.
3. The Latin American company was not really interested in the products of Tom's company and was just putting him off.
4. Tom, from his American perspective, was concerned with getting the job done, whereas the representatives of the Latin American company approached the situation from a different perspective: They were interested in building a relationship with Tom and his company.

The discussions of these alternative explanations begin on page 174.

62

A Manager's Dilemma

Ned Schwartz, the manager of a large factory operation in Canada, had been transferred to an operation of the same size in a Central American branch, as its production had always been low. Ned had a reputation for getting things done, but from the start, he had a hard time. Government regulations in his new country made procuring needed materials difficult. Communication from his site to headquarters was slow and often garbled. Even Ned's personal work habits had to be changed. He was used to working late and inspecting the plant after most of the workers had gone home, but strict military rule imposed curfew hours over such installations as Ned's. In Canada there were organizations to protest such unreasonable restrictions, but superiors here said there was nothing one could do. Ned became increasingly depressed and ineffective. He finally asked to be sent back to his original operation.

What can help explain Ned's situation?

1. The job was not really appropriate for Ned because the difficulties were too great.
2. Ned found himself in a situation where he had relatively little control over matters.
3. Operations in Third World countries are impossible to bring to maximization, given the resources available.
4. Ned did not have the proper local support. If he had been nicer to local authorities and workers, they would have offered him more cooperation.

The discussions of these alternative explanations begin on page 175.

63

Who's in Charge?

The president of Janice Tani's firm asked her, as chief executive of the marketing division, and her staff (three male M.B.A.s) to set up and close an important contract with a Japanese firm. The president thought his choice especially good, as Janice (a Japanese American from California) knew the industry well and could also speak Japanese.

As she and her staff were being introduced to representatives of the Japanese company, Janice noticed a quizzical look on Mr. Yamamoto's face and heard him repeat "chief executive" to his assistant in an unsure manner. After Janice had presented the merits of the strategy in Japanese, referring to notes provided by her staff, she asked Mr. Yamamoto what he thought. He responded by saying that he needed to discuss some things further with the head of her department. Janice explained that was why she was there. Smiling, Mr. Yamamoto replied that she had done an especially good job of explaining, but that he wanted to talk things over with the person in charge. Beginning to become frustrated, Janice stated that she had authority for her company. Mr. Yamamoto glanced at his assistant, still smiling, and arranged to meet with Janice at another time.

Why did Mr. Yamamoto keep asking Janice about the executive in charge?

1. He did not really believe that she was actually telling the truth about who she was.
2. He had never heard the term *executive* before and did not understand the meaning of *chief executive*.

3. He had never personally dealt with a woman in Janice's position, and her language ability caused him to think of her in another capacity.
4. He really did not like her presentation and did not want to deal with her firm.
5. He was attracted to her and wanted to meet with her alone.

The discussions of these alternative explanations begin on page 175.

64

Engineering a Decision

M. Legrand is a French engineer who works for a Japanese company in France. One day, the company's general manager, Mr. Tanaka, calls M. Legrand into his office to discuss a new project in the Middle East. Mr. Tanaka tells him that the company is very pleased with his dedicated work and would like him to act as chief engineer for the project. It will mean 2 to 3 years away from home, but his family will be able to accompany him and there will be considerable personal financial benefits to the position—and, of course, he will be performing a valuable service to the company. M. Legrand thanks Mr. Tanaka for his confidence in him, but says that he will have to discuss it with his wife before deciding. Two days later, he returns and tells Mr. Tanaka that both he and his wife do not like the thought of leaving France, and so he does not want to accept the position. Mr. Tanaka says nothing but is somewhat dumbfounded by the decision.

Why is Mr. Tanaka so bewildered by M. Legrand's decision?

1. He believes it is foolish for M. Legrand to refuse all the financial benefits that go with the position.
2. He cannot accept that M. Legrand should take any notice of his wife's opinion in the matter.
3. He believes M. Legrand is possibly trying to bluff him into offering greater incentives to accept the offer.
4. He feels it is not appropriate for M. Legrand to place his personal inclinations above those of his role as an employee of the company.

The discussions of these alternative explanations begin on page 176.

65

Can I Extend My Stay?

Dr. Hong was a visiting professor from Korea at a large American university participating in a 6-month sabbatical-type program funded by an international organization. He was doing research, lecturing, reading, and in general seemed to be having a successful sojourn. Dr. Hong also interacted well with the local coordinator of the international program under which Dr. Hong's grant was administered, a professor named Dr. Brown. Dr. Hong and Dr. Brown met frequently to discuss matters of mutual interest and also attended each other's public lectures. Dr. Brown was quite well known in his field, the author of several well-received and frequently cited books. He had worked previously with many international visitors.

Toward the end of the fifth month of his stay, Dr. Hong visited Dr. Brown in the latter's office. Dr. Hong explained that he wanted to stay longer in the United States and asked Dr. Brown to arrange for a grant that would allow him to stay an additional year. Dr. Brown answered by explaining the difficulties of the funding process and the administrative difficulties involved in extending grants. Dr. Hong left the meeting obviously disappointed. During the last month of Dr. Hong's originally agreed-upon 6-month sabbatical, he was noticeably cool toward Dr. Brown, did not seek him out to discuss issues, and did not attend his lectures.

What is the issue here, strongly colored by cultural differences, that is the cause of the strained relationship?

1. Dr. Hong felt that Dr. Brown had the authority to grant additional funds for a longer stay in the United States.

2. Dr. Brown felt that Dr. Hong was being selfish in asking for additional funds, because additional funds for Hong necessarily meant no funds for some other international visitor.

3. Dr. Brown felt that Dr. Hong was making friendship dependent on his (Brown's) ability to find funding.

4. Dr. Hong did not want to return to Korea, and instead wanted to resettle in the United States.

The discussions of these alternative explanations begin on page 177.

66

Opening a Medical Office

Dr. Tom McDivern, a physician from New York City, was offered a 2-year assignment to practice medicine in a growing urban center in Saudi Arabia. Many of the residents in the area he was assigned to were recent immigrants from the much smaller outlying rural areas. Because Western medicine was relatively unknown to many of these people, one of Dr. McDivern's main responsibilities was to introduce himself and his services to those in the community. A meeting at a local school was organized for that specific purpose. Many people turned out, and Tom's presentation went well. Some local residents also presented their experiences with Western medicine so that others could understand the value of using his services. Some of Tom's office staff were also present to make appointments for those interested in seeing him when his doors opened a week later. The meeting was an obvious success; his opening day was booked solid.

When that day finally arrived, Tom was anxious to greet his first patients. Thirty minutes had passed, however, and neither of his first two patients had arrived. Tom began to worry about the future of his practice as he wondered where his patients were.

What was the major cause of Tom's worries?

1. Although in Tom's mind and by his standards his presentation was a success, people actually only made appointments so as not to hurt his feelings. They really had no intention of using his services, as modern medicine is so foreign to their past experiences.

2. Given the time lag between sign-up and the actual day of their appointments, people had time to rethink their decisions. They had just changed their minds.

3. Views concerning units of time differ between Arabs and Americans. Whereas Tom believed his patients were very late, the Arab patients could still arrive and consider themselves to be on time.

4. Tom's patients were seeing their own traditional healers from their own culture; after that, they could go on to see the new doctor.

The discussions of these alternative explanations begin on page 178.

67

Skillful at Getting Grants

Herb Evans was very knowledgeable about the nature of funding sources in the United States and was known as a good "grantsman"—someone very skillful at writing up proposals, making contacts, and getting organizations to give him money to support the programs he designed. Herb was also known as a person of integrity, one who would not alter or slant the findings of his research projects to please sponsoring agencies (or to avoid their wrath).

Herb knew that certain money was "clean": that certain sponsoring organizations attached no strings to their funding, encouraged honest research, and put no pressures on researchers. One such organization was the Center for Defense Studies, housed in Washington, D.C. Its mandate was to provide information useful for the defense of the United States, and in fulfilling that mandate it funded a wide variety of research projects. Herb approached this organization with a proposal involving the training of diplomats in conflict negotiation, arguing that having a number of trained people in different parts of the world who are skillful in conflict negotiation would mean that they could be called upon quickly in a crisis so that problems could be nipped in the bud and not grow into matters necessitating military intervention. Herb proposed that such conflict-negotiation training take place in a number of Southeast Asian countries (e.g., Indonesia, Malaysia, Singapore) and that it be carried out with promising mid-career diplomats who have a high probability of being tomorrow's leaders.

Herb's proposal was funded and he made travel plans for an Asian trip in order to introduce his program. Malaysia was Herb's first stop, but he did not find much enthusiasm for his proposal among embassies that would have to cooperate by freeing up the time of their mid-career people so that they could participate in the training. Herb had done a great deal of work in the United States on topics comparatively as important (e.g., school desegregation, training of the hard-core unemployed), and he was surprised that his proposal for conflict negotiation training was not well received.

Can you see a reason in the story for Herb's problem?

1. People in Southeast Asia did not separate Herb's work from his funding source.

2. In work involving Indonesia, Malaysia, and Singapore, Indonesia should always be the first stop.

3. Officials in Southeast Asia who might have helped Herb do not like people who can be labeled "grantsmen."

4. Officials in Southeast Asia really resent American money coming into their countries for any reason.

The discussions of these alternative explanations begin on page 178.

68

The Shinto Priest

The U.S. branch of a Japanese manufacturing company had been operating successfully for some years, but in recent months a series of seemingly unrelated incidents had caused concern. First, there was a rash of accidents in the plant itself, then one of the Japanese executive's children died of a rare illness and another executive's car caught fire, severely burning him. Rumors of a jinx on the company began to spread among the employees, and morale lowered. Consequently, the management called a meeting of the executives to decide how to react to the situation. The American managers suggested that all safety and quality control procedures be reviewed so as to reassure the workers that their welfare was taken seriously. The Japanese managers, however, held that this had already been done; they felt that other forces were at work. They wished to bring in a Shinto priest to bless the company and protect it against evil spirits—this was the only course of action that would reassure them. The Americans were reluctant to adopt such an action and preferred the idea of seeking suggestions from the employees. The meeting ended in disagreement.

What was the underlying reason for the disagreement between the American and Japanese managers?

1. Many of the American managers were probably Christians and objected to Shinto rituals being performed on company property.

2. The Americans regarded the Japanese proposal as based in mere superstition.

3. The Japanese were unwilling to admit that their safety procedures were at fault and sought to blame other forces.

4. The Japanese managers did not like the idea of calling for employee suggestions as this would undermine their authority.

The discussions of these alternative explanations begin on page 179.

69

Was Somebody Saying No?

Dr. Xuang Xi, who worked at an important economic planning institute in Beijing, was on a study tour of the United States when he contacted Dr. Ronald Hastings, who was affiliated with a similar organization in New York City. Hastings, the author of several well-received books, was a high-status economist and considered a leading authority in the field of economic forecasting based on microeconomic predictors. Dr. Xi invited Dr. Hastings to come to China for 2 months to give seminars on microeconomic variables in forecasting, with special attention to using data sets available in China. Dr. Hastings responded, "I'm interested, but I have to check the invitation with the administrators here in this [American] organization. The organization just received a grant that frees me from any teaching responsibilities for 3 years, and that's great because I can devote full time to research and writing. But I don't know the details of what that grant allows, for instance, time away from New York to go to China as well as a more teaching-oriented than research-oriented 2 months in China. So I'll check with the administrators here to get their approval." Dr. Hastings then ended his meeting with Dr. Xi, thinking that it had gone well. However, Dr. Hastings never heard again from Dr. Xi.

What cultural difference in the way people negotiate with each other could be involved in this incident?

1. Dr. Hastings was trying to be polite in communicating the message, "No, I don't want to go to China."

2. Dr. Xi thought that Dr. Hastings was trying to be polite in communicating the message, "No."

3. Dr. Hastings wanted to return to the activity that gives the highest status in his profession, teaching, but did not want to tell this to Dr. Xi directly.

4. Dr. Xi thought that Dr. Hastings could make his own decisions about what he does with his time.

5. Dr. Xi wanted to meet Dr. Hastings because of the networking value of interacting with such a high-status person, but had no intention of following through with the China trip plans.

The discussions of these alternative explanations begin on page 180.

70

Transmitting Information on Transmission Systems

"Adjustment to Japan has been much easier than I thought it would be," Ted Owens told his wife about a year after their move from the United States. Ted had been sent by an automobile company in Detroit to see if he could establish production facilities for transmission systems that would be built in Japan and imported into the United States. Having been told that negotiations take a long time in Japan, he was not disappointed that it had taken a year for a major meeting to be set up with his key Japanese counterparts. But the Japanese had studied the proposal and were ready to discuss it this morning, and Ted was excited as he left for work. At the meeting, people discussed matters that were already in the written proposal that had been circulated beforehand. Suddenly, it occurred to Ted that there was an aspect of quality control inspection that he had left out of the proposal. He knew that the Japanese should know of this concern because it was important to the long-range success of the project. Ted asked the senior person at the meeting if he could speak, apologized for not having already introduced the quality control concern he was about to raise, and then went into his addition to the proposal. His presentation was met with silence, and the meeting was later adjourned without a decision having been made on the whole manufacture-importation program. Because Ted thought that a decision would be made that day, he was puzzled.

What was the reason for Ted's difficulty?

1. Ted had brought up quality control, an issue about which the Japanese are very proud. The Japanese thought that Ted was questioning their commitment to quality control.

2. Ted had brought up an issue on which there had not been prior discussion among the people somehow involved in that specific issue.

3. Ted had asked the senior person about speaking; in actuality, there was a younger person present who was in charge and Ted should have deferred to that person.

4. Expecting a decision in a year was still unrealistic. Ted should have been more patient.

The discussions of these alternative explanations begin on page 181.

71

Learning the Ropes

Helen Connor had been working in a Japanese company involved in marketing cameras for 2 years and was well respected by her colleagues. In fact, she was so respected that she often was asked to work with new employees of the firm as these younger employees learned the ropes. Recently, one young employee, Hideo Tanaka, was assigned to develop a marketing scheme for a new model of camera. He worked quite hard on it, but the scheme was not accepted by his superiors because of industrywide economic conditions. Helen and Hideo happened to be working at desks near each other when company executives transmitted the news of the scheme's nonacceptance. Hideo said very little at that point. That evening, however, Helen and Hideo happened to be at the same bar. Hideo had been drinking, and he vigorously criticized his superiors at work. Helen concluded that Hideo was a very aggressive Japanese male and that she would have difficulty working with him again in the future.

Which alternative provides an accurate statement about Helen's conclusion?

1. Helen was making an inappropriate judgment about Hideo's traits based on behavior that she observed.

2. Because decorum in public is highly valued in Japan, Helen reasonably concluded that Hideo's vigorous criticism in the bar marked him as a difficult coworker.

3. Company executives had failed to tell Helen and Hideo about economic conditions, and consequently Helen should be upset with the executives, not Hideo.

4. Helen felt that Hideo was attacking her personally.

The discussions of these alternative explanations begin on page 182.

72

Are There Ethical Issues Involved?

Jack Williams and Herb Edwards had come to Shanghai to discuss a joint venture with a Chinese electronics firm. Jack and Herb had been struck by the number of Americans who owned personal pagers, and they thought that they could compete in the American market given low labor costs in China. They also had in the backs of their minds that personal pagers might be attractive to consumers in China.

Jack and Herb met with executives and engineers in a large electronics firm. Many meetings were scheduled, and Jack and Herb conscientiously gave presentations on their ideas at all the meetings. At about the seventh meeting, Herb noticed that different engineers seemed to be attending the meetings. At about this same time, Jack noticed that the questions from the Chinese engineers were becoming more and more technical, and that the Americans found it difficult to answer them without giving away trade secrets. After the twelfth meeting, Jack and Herb went out for a drink. Herb said, "I realize that the books with titles such as *Guide to Doing Business in China* say that the Chinese schedule meetings to gain specialized information about technology, but this is getting ridiculous. I should think that scheduling all these meetings would go against their ethical code. How do they sleep at night?"

If you were asked to help Herb deal with his frustration, what might you say to him?

1. The engineers who began attending at about the seventh meeting needed to catch up on the basics of the technology with their colleagues who had attended since the first meeting.

2. Herb was incorrect: The Chinese were looking for something else besides specialized information on the technology surrounding the manufacture of personal pagers.

3. The Chinese were setting aside any guilt they were experiencing in their quest for advanced technological information.

4. The Chinese did not view their behavior as unethical, and they might point out that there were aspects of Jack's and Herb's behavior that could be looked at as ethically troublesome.

5. The Chinese were trying to continue negotiations with Herb and Jack as they weighed the men's proposal against those of other companies interested in doing business in China.

The discussions of these alternative explanations begin on page 183.

73

Selling Abroad

Mark is a salesman recently promoted to the international division of a U.S. company. He has been sent on a month-long tour of the company's European clients and is eager to prove himself in this new phase of his career. His schedule looks hectic, but this does not worry him, as he is accustomed to constant traveling on business in the United States and its accompanying social demands. The first few weeks of his European trip go well. He throws himself enthusiastically into the business and social activities expected of him and appears to get on well with clients. However, by the third week (and the fifth country) Mark begins to exhibit increasing apathy toward his work and his environment. He excuses himself from social invitations, seems far less sharp in business negotiations, and also finds that he has little interest in seeing the sights of countries he had always dreamed about visiting. Upon his return to the United States, reports of his lackluster performance filter back to the division office and his boss becomes convinced Mark should be transferred back to the domestic division.

How would you explain Mark's poor performance to his boss?

1. Mark has no real empathy for foreigners and finds dealing with large numbers of them too tiresome and stressful.
2. The constant changes in Mark's environment gradually dulled his senses and overwhelmed his ability to respond.
3. Mark's excessive social activities of the first few weeks caught up with him and caused prolonged physical exhaustion.
4. Mark developed strong homesickness and so became depressed.

The discussions of these alternative explanations begin on page 184.

74

The Quiet Participant

Machmud had recently been promoted to a position of authority and was asked to represent his company and Indonesia's needs at the head office in Butte, Montana. His relationships with fellow workers seemed cordial but rather formal from his perspective. He was invited to attend many policy and planning sessions with other company officials, where he often sat rather quietly as others generated ideas and engaged in conversation. The time finally came when the direction the company was to take in Indonesia was to be discussed. A meeting was called to which Machmud was invited. As the meeting was drawing to a close after almost 2 hours of discussion, Machmud, almost apologetically, offered a suggestion—his first contribution to any meeting. Almost immediately, John Stewart, a local vice president, said, "Why did you wait so long to contribute? We needed your comments all along." Machmud felt that Stewart's reply was harsh.

How would you best explain this incident? Focus on a specific cultural difference in Machmud's experience compared with the experience of the Americans in Butte.

1. It is common in Indonesia for decisions to take a long time to be made. Machmud was expecting much more discussion before the company adopted a new policy. When suddenly faced with the realization that his thoughts had not been heard, he let them be known at the last minute.

2. Machmud did not want to stand out as an individual and therefore he did not make his contribution earlier.

3. Machmud was overwhelmed by new policies, procedures, people, and customs, and was not able to function appropriately within this new context.

4. Machmud was not confident with his use of the English language, and therefore was reluctant to participate.

The discussions of these alternative explanations begin on page 185.

75

A Demanding Job

Melinda was beginning her twelfth month as foreign student adviser in a large midwestern U.S. university. The transition from working as a successful inner-city social worker to that of counselor/advocate for a growing foreign student population was exciting. She had many different responsibilities at this new job: handling of visa requests and problems; orientation of all new students to life in the United States and on an American college campus; counseling students who were facing adjustment problems, loneliness, homesickness, academic difficulties, and social problems; advising professors concerning the problems they faced in teaching a new type of student; and arranging and chaperoning a variety of social get-togethers, outings, and community education programs. Although she was compensated with an occasional free day for all her extra time put in, Melinda and her half-time student worker were always busy. There seemed never to be a dull moment with all the crises and activities that had to be dealt with.

Lately, however, things seemed to be wearing on Melinda. She was emotionally tired and often irritable over seemingly trivial things. She would frequently just take an extra day and stay at home, doing nothing in particular, merely relaxing and collecting her energy. She strongly considered leaving her position.

If you were approached by Melinda and asked to help her sort out her situation, what would be the central area of your focus?

1. Melinda was probably not comfortable working with culturally different people.

2. As with all new jobs, the initial excitement was followed by the realities of doing the day-to-day work. Melinda was probably entering this phase and would soon pull out of it.

3. The time demands of the position were probably too erratic for her.

4. Melinda was probably experiencing counselor burnout and was in need of emotional support herself.

The discussions of these alternative explanations begin on page 185.

76

Quoth the Raven, "Nevermore"

Carl was pleased that he was invited to a company party shortly after he began his assignment to Japan. Desiring to experience the Japanese culture as much as he could, he was happy to learn that about 90% of his coworkers were hosts, as were the vast majority of senior managers. At the party, everyone was expected to entertain. Even the senior managers got up to sing little songs or to tell jokes. Carl recited part of Edgar Allan Poe's poem "The Raven" in a mock serious tone. After the party, Carl was asked to go along with a group of Japanese to one of their favorite bars, where he was introduced to some women who worked there.

Carl thought that he would enjoy his sojourn. People seemed so informal and cooperative, not like the rather stodgy, stuffy people he had read about before coming to Japan. At a meeting shortly after the party, Carl found himself in the same room as several of the coworkers and senior managers who had been at the party and who had contributed to the merriment of the evening with their songs and stories. One of the senior managers mentioned to Carl how much he had enjoyed "The Raven," which he had been exposed to in school. Keeping this informality in mind, Carl used the meeting as an opportunity to present a proposal for an aspect of company policy that he had been developing ever since his arrival in Japan. When Carl brought up his proposal, however, he was met with a wall of silence. After the meeting, Carl was noticeably not made part of the typical series of informal exchanges in which people engage as they leave a meeting.

What was Carl's mistake?

1. The raven is a sacred symbol in Japan and Carl made a major blunder in reciting Poe's poem at the party. The senior manager mentioned the poem only to get Carl to think about the whole matter.

2. Carl should not have contributed to the entertainment in any way. This is to be done only by the Japanese—guests should not entertain.

3. At the bar, Carl had been too friendly with one of the girls who worked there, and this girl was a special friend of a senior manager.

4. Not knowing the Japanese language as well as he should, Carl did not pick up the cues concerning when people were being informal. He was speaking informally when the situation called for formal conversation and vice versa.

5. Carl thought that the informality he observed at the party would also be part of the meeting at work.

The discussions of these alternative explanations begin on page 186.

77

Shaping Up the Office

Ronald, an ambitious young executive, had been sent to take over the sales branch of his American company in São Paulo, Brazil. He spent a few weeks learning routines with the departing manager and was somewhat disturbed by the informality and lack of discipline that seemed to characterize the office. People seemed to indulge in excessive socializing, conversations seemed to deal more with personal than business matters, and no one seemed to keep to their set schedules. Once he had formally taken over, he resolved to do something about this general slackness and called the staff together for a general meeting. He told them bluntly that work rates and schedules would have to be adhered to and that he hoped a more businesslike atmosphere would prevail. Over the next few months he concentrated on improving office efficiency, offering higher bonuses and incentives to those who worked well and private warnings to those who did not. By the end of the first quarter he felt he had considerably improved the situation and was therefore somewhat surprised to find sales figures had significantly dropped since his takeover.

What reason would you give to Ronald for this drop in sales?

1. He had probably lowered office morale.
2. The salesmen probably resented his management style and were deliberately trying to make him look bad.
3. The salesmen would probably have responded better to a more participative approach to the problems.
4. Key Brazilian workers lost face through Ronald's actions.

The discussions of these alternative explanations begin on page 187.

78

The Sick Secretary

Todd works for an American company in Korea. Sometimes he wonders why he ever accepted a position overseas—there seems to be so much that he just doesn't understand. One incident in particular occurred the previous Friday when his secretary, Chungmin, made a mistake and forgot to type a letter. Todd considered this a small error, but made sure to mention it when he saw her during lunch in the company cafeteria. Ever since then, Chungmin has been acting a bit strange and distant. When she walks out of his office, she closes the door more loudly than usual. She will not even look him in the eye, and she has been acting very moody. She even took a few days of sick leave, which she has not done in many years. Todd has no idea how to understand her behavior. Perhaps she really is ill or feels a bit overworked.

When Chungmin returns to work the following Wednesday, Todd calls her into his office. "Is there a problem?" he asks. "Because if there is, we need to talk about it. It's affecting your performance. Is something wrong? Why don't you tell me, it's okay."

At this, Chungmin looks quite distressed. She admits the problem has something to do with her mistake the previous Friday, and Todd explains that it was no big deal. "Forget it," he says, feeling satisfied with himself for working this out. "In the future, just make sure to tell me if something is wrong." But over the next few weeks, Chungmin takes 6 more sick days and does not speak to Todd once.

Paying close attention to the details of the story, how can you best interpret these events?

1. Todd is using American managerial techniques for a Korean workplace. He should pay more attention to his staff's feelings and actions.

2. Chungmin should not have become so upset over what her boss considers a minor error. He would have forgotten the whole episode.

3. Todd should never have scolded Chungmin for her mistake in public. This is considered very rude behavior in Korea.

4. Chungmin and Todd have different expectations about how to communicate and resolve problems.

The discussions of these alternative explanations begin on page 188.

Incident 58 (p. 152): Rationales for the Alternative Explanations

1. It is possible that Jose wanted to improve his proposal, but this does not mean that he would have to go to the library right away, thus breaking his previous engagement for the evening. Certainly the library trip could wait until the next day. Please choose again.

2. Jealousy is always a possible reaction whenever one person has success, but this does not constitute such a general reaction in the Philippines as to provide a good explanation here. In addition, as Stan's proposal was well known among the people at the meeting because of prior communications among the principal, Stan, and the rest of the people, Jose probably had known for some time that the proposal would be approved for its next step toward implementation. Please choose again.

3. This is the best answer. In his own country, New Zealand, Stan is familiar with the fact that a person can be both a friend and a critic who makes

constructive suggestions (this ability to be a friend and critic is in general true of English-speaking countries). In fact, if Stan did *not* make constructive suggestions that in the long run would improve a friend's proposal, that friend could criticize Stan for not helping out when he could. In the Philippines, the roles of friend and critic are differentiated, or separate. The same person cannot easily be both a friend and a critic who makes suggestions about the friend's work, at least in public. People in the Philippines have a set of expectations about what a friend is, and Stan's behavior violated these expectations. It is possible that if Stan had made his suggestions in private, when the principal and the rest of the school staff were absent, Jose might not have felt so bad. Even then, however, Stan would want to be sure that he was making his suggestions in a style acceptable in the Philippines (and, in general, Southeast Asia). That style would include saying a number of good things about the proposal, being much more indirect than he would in his own country, and keeping the tone of the meeting light, with jokes and anecdotes.

4. It is possible that the principal would eventually ask Jose to improve his proposal, but it would be rude to do so right after the meeting, necessitating an immediate trip to the library. The principal would rather pick a later moment, after the unpleasantness of the present meeting have faded. The principal seems very sensitive to local norms, for instance, in only calling for discussion of proposals with which all meeting-goers are familiar. Please choose again.

Incident 59 (p. 153): Rationales for the Alternative Explanations

1. Although the nature of the job may have been more difficult than an ordinary Stateside job, Ron was handpicked because of his class standing and other accomplishments. Given that the incident further states that Ron had been very instrumental in the initial plans, this does not fit as an explanation. Please choose again.

2. Language is a factor that often discourages sojourners. However, in spite of the fact that Ron himself may have felt he was making no progress, his teachers were very pleased and even impressed with how he was doing. This is not sufficient to explain his attitude. Please choose again.

3. This is the best answer. As his presence at the top of his class indicates, Ron was accustomed to being very competitive and achieving a great deal. He also comes from a society where there is a high value on such achievement. Although Ron made substantial contributions to the project, the area he was now working on, language, yields very low measurable results at first. He was suffering because his need for high achievement was not being gratified.

4. Although there may have been some feelings about Ron being in a position to head up the new operation, there is no real indication from the incident that

the project director was acting negatively toward him. This is not an acceptable answer. Please choose again.

Incident 60 (p. 154): Rationales for the Alternative Explanations

1. The story specifically says that Matt was able to acquire excellent materials. Just because materials wear out, this does not mean they were inadequate. Maintenance, including the replacement of worn-out parts, is part of the long-range success of any construction project. Please choose again.
2. This is the best answer. Matt may have done an excellent job in supervising construction of the system, but he did not transfer his skills to his Nigerian hosts, especially skills concerning maintenance. Research coming out of the Canadian International Development Agency has shown that transfer of skills is one of the major components of the long-range success of technical assistance advisers. Hosts are sensitive to this problem. In their own judgments concerning good versus poor sojourners, they incorporate observations of who (e.g., Matt) makes sure or does not make sure that hosts learn technical skills that allow them to maintain the current project and construction of others. The conclusion from this research is that excellent training and experience in engineering are not enough. Technical assistance advisers must also have enough human relations skills, and cultural knowledge, to be able to develop procedures by which hosts learn engineering skills from them.
3. Although occasionally this is a problem, it is not widespread enough to constitute an answer as to why the sewage treatment system became nonfunctioning. The reasoning behind choosing this explanation would be that host resentment could be expected to cause purposeful sabotage. But the story indicates that the Nigerians were proud of the project. They would not be expected to sabotage something they valued, even if they were not completely happy with its source. Please choose again.
4. There is no evidence to suggest this is the case. Matt was known to be a good engineer and was proud of his work, and from all accounts when he returned to Canada he left behind an excellent piece of construction. Just because the system developed problems, it does not mean that the original construction was poor. Careful maintenance is necessary for the smooth functioning of any complex project. Please choose again.

Incident 61 (p. 155): Rationales for the Alternative Explanations

1. There are more efficient and accurate ways to find out such kinds of information about a company. This explanation is rather unlikely. Please choose again.

2. This is a typical overgeneralized stereotype of Latins. Although they do enjoy leisure activities in their culture, they are also hard workers. Please choose again.

3. There is no evidence to support this. It is doubtful that they would waste so much time and money on Tom just to be kind while refusing him. There is a more reasonable answer. Please choose again.

4. This is the best answer. Much of American culture is concerned with efficiency and time. Although other cultures are also concerned about these things, Americans have a tendency to stress getting the job done, with emphasis on the end product rather than on the means or the process of getting it done. In the Latin culture, although product is important, there is equal concern about personal relationships.

Incident 62 (p. 156): Rationales for the Alternative Explanations

1. Ned had already proved that he could handle a big factory—that was why he was sent to Central America in the first place. This is an unsatisfactory answer. Please choose again.

2. This is the best answer. Ned came from a culture where he had substantial control over his own life and also the lives of many others. He was placed in a situation where he was able to have relatively little personal control, and he simply did not know how to handle this.

3. Although operations in Third World countries often have limited resources, they can and have been brought to reasonable levels of production. There is a better response. Please choose again.

4. There is nothing in the story to indicate that Ned did not have the support of the local people. Chances are that because this was a local plant, it provided much needed work for many in the area and indeed did have local support. Please select a better response.

Incident 63 (p. 157): Rationales for the Alternative Explanations

1. Although Mr. Yamamoto may have thought of Janice as the secretary or the interpreter, she was introduced as the chief executive and there would be no reason for her to lie about her position. There is a more correct alternative. Please choose again.

2. There is a possibility that Mr. Yamamoto may have never heard the term *executive* before, but there would be people functioning in that capacity even in his own organization. His assistant would have been sure to explain the term if there were any doubts. There is a better response. Please try again.

3. This is the best response. Generally, in Asia, although women are found in all strata in the working world, very few, especially in Japan, are in positions where they have a great deal of authority over men. There are more cases where they would be working quite closely with someone with that authority but not possess the actual authority themselves. The fact that Janice was using Japanese and many of her assistants were not also added to the confusion of her role.

4. This could be a possibility. Asians are very sensitive about making others feel uncomfortable and may have thought that a direct comment of displeasure would be too embarrassing. However, as this was the first presentation and Janice did ask for comments, some negotiating would be expected and would not seem out of order. If refusal was on their minds, they probably would have directed their comments more toward the products than toward questions about the person in charge. There is a more appropriate answer. Please choose again.

5. This is highly unlikely. As women in authoritative positions are rather rare in the Japanese system, the Japanese male tends to think of women in certain roles. However, in this situation it is not likely that Mr. Yamamoto would try to make romantic overtures. He may try a more direct approach at a more appropriate time, but this is not a likely explanation for what went on in this business meeting. Please choose again.

Incident 64 (p.158): Rationales for the Alternative Explanations

1. There is little evidence for this in the story. Although the financial benefits are relevant, to Mr. Tanaka they are probably a minor consideration in the situation. Please choose another explanation.

2. It is quite probable that, coming from male-dominant Japanese society, Mr. Tanaka does think it odd that M. Legrand should mention his wife's opinion. However, the decision not to go to the Middle East also appears to be M. Legrand's personal inclination, so this does not fully account for Mr. Tanaka's bewilderment. There is another explanation. Please choose again.

3. It is unlikely that Mr. Tanaka would consider this. There are factors far removed from personal gain dominating his concern. Please choose again.

4. This is the most likely explanation. In Japanese and many other collectivist societies, a person is defined much more as a collection of roles (parent, employee, servant, official) than by his or her individual identity. As such, fulfilling these roles to the best of one's ability is regarded as more important than one's personal inclinations. Thus Mr. Tanaka would understand M. Legrand's responsibility as a company employee to be to accept the position, whether or not he is personally happy about the idea. M. Legrand's refusal is thus bewildering and makes Mr. Tanaka think that his belief in M. Legrand's dedication has been completely misplaced. M. Legrand, however, comes

from a culture where individual freedoms are highly valued and so exercises his right to refuse the offer with little compunction. The cultural conflict thus resides in different strengths of values applied to the roles occupied by a person in the culture.

Incident 65 (p. 159): Rationales for the Alternative Explanations

1. This is the best answer. Because Dr. Brown was a high-status scholar in the United States, Dr. Hong thought that Brown had control (or at least very strong influence) over large amounts of money. This is sometimes the case in Asia—high-status scholars may have major influence in funding, perhaps by a well-placed telephone call, the right word dropped during a conversation, or subtle reminders of past favors that now demand reciprocity. But in the United States, procedures for grants specifically and funding in general are highly competitive and are designed to be removed from the influence of powerful and high-status individuals. People wanting grants have to apply long in advance of their preferred starting dates. Grants are reviewed by independent committees whose members are rarely known to the persons making applications. All any one individual, such as Dr. Brown, can do is introduce a grant seeker such as Dr. Hong to the procedures and write one of the needed recommendation letters. For Dr. Brown to promise more to Dr. Hong could well be seen as unethical. Dr. Hong undoubtedly was working with expectations from his experience in Korea—that a high-status individual could intervene with great effect. When Dr. Brown did not do this, Hong interpreted Brown's behavior as rejection. Although Dr. Brown might have done a better job explaining these facts to Dr. Hong, he was faced with a difficult task. Because of the normal mild paranoia that sojourners feel (see the essay on emotional experiences in Chapter 11), it was likely that Dr. Hong would see Dr. Brown's actions as personally directed at him.

2. Although possible, this is not the most probable reason for the difficulty. It is mentioned in the incident that Dr. Brown had worked with many international visitors. A large number of such visitors want to extend grants—the United States is a very attractive place for Asian professors on sabbatical because Asians very frequently have heavier teaching loads and fewer research facilities than do professors in the United States. Dr. Brown would be accustomed to people wanting to extend their grants. As he had known many visitors, he would also be familiar with the rather single-minded goals that sojourners develop when they are emotionally aroused. In this case, Dr. Hong's arousal would be due to the normal pressures of cross-cultural adjustment plus his desire to stay longer in the United States. Please choose again.

3. Although possible, this is not the most probable reason. Because Dr. Brown had worked with many international visitors, he would be familiar with the

desire of many to extend grants (see the rationale for choice 2, above). Dr. Brown would be accustomed to the disappointment people feel when their goals of obtaining longer grant periods are blocked. Please choose again.

4. This might seem to be the case, even though there is no direct evidence in the story, given that most people know academics from other countries who have settled in the United States. Actually, Dr. Hong could have every intention of returning to Korea. Research shows that people from other countries often spend a great deal of time in highly industrialized nations such as the United States, but that they do this as part of their career development, the ultimate goal of which is to spend the great majority of their adult, productive years in their own countries. Some sojourners obtain their advanced degrees in the United States and then continue their sojourns by taking jobs for as much as 5 years, but after their combined graduate study-job experience periods, they return to their own countries. In Dr. Hong's case, he may simply have discovered that he could accomplish much more in his area of interest if he could extend his grant. Please choose again.

Incident 66 (p. 160): Rationales for the Alternative Explanations

1. It is unlikely that people would sign up solely to mollify a newcomer's feelings. There is a better explanation. Please select again.

2. If there is a considerable time lag between when a person makes a decision and when he or she acts upon it, it is possible that the person may change his or her mind. However, there is no indication in the incident to support this explanation. Please select another response.

3. This is the best answer. Units of time reference differ markedly between Arab and American cultures. To an American, the major unit of time is 5 minutes, and 15 minutes is a significant period of time. To an urban Arab, the unit of time that corresponds to the American 5-minute block is 15 minutes. Thus when an Arab is 30 minutes late (by the clock), according to Arab standards he or she is not late by any significant amount, as 30 minutes in Arab culture corresponds to an interval of only 10 minutes. Tom's patients were not yet very late from their perspective, and could still arrive.

4. Although the patients may have been seeing their own traditional healers, they would not necessarily do so in the strict sequence suggested by this alternative. There is a more precise explanation. Please choose again.

Incident 67 (p. 161): Rationales for the Alternative Explanations

1. This is the best explanation. Herb may have been convinced that his proposal has a clean funding source that will apply no pressures and pull no strings.

However, this does not mean that people in the countries he approached interpreted the situation the same way. Herb probably said to himself, "I do good work. If the Center for Defense Studies wants to support my work, that's fine. My accepting money from the center does not mean that I agree with all that they say." Herb could separate himself and his project to some extent from his funding source. However, such a separation is not made in many parts of the world. Officials in many countries who could help with research projects want to know about researchers' funding sources and make attributions based on those sources. Because Herb's funding came from a Defense Department (read "military") source, officials were very wary. Remembering other projects involving American military intervention in Southeast Asia in recent history, they were not anxious to become involved in anything resembling military work. Problems such as those faced by Herb are so widespread that even researchers with funding from the National Science Foundation or the National Institute for Mental Health are frequently seen in many countries as operatives for the Central Intelligence Agency and as using CIA money. The general rule is that people cannot easily separate themselves from their sources of support, whether those be private or public agencies, multinational organizations, or government bureaus.

2. The order of countries makes no difference here. If officials in the other two countries thought that Indonesia was always visited first in such cases, they would be upset. Please choose again.

3. There is nothing about a good grantsman to which Southeast Asians would object over and above the category of "researcher," which will be covered in another incident. In fact, a person able to bring money into a country is welcome, as long as the project is one that is approved by high-level officials. Please choose again.

4. Officials in Southeast Asia have no objections to American money as long as it is for projects they approve and feel will be of benefit to their countries. Please choose again.

Incident 68 (p. 162): Rationales for the Alternative Explanations

1. Although many of the managers who were Christians may have felt uneasy about such practices, there is no indication in the story that this was the principal motive behind their reluctance to concur with the Japanese managers' proposal. There is a more likely explanation. Please try again.

2. This is the most probable explanation. Western societies are strongly secular and tend to view any regard for supernatural forces or spirits as mere superstition. Thus the American managers viewed the Japanese proposal as ineffective and unlikely to reassure the workforce. To the Japanese, however, the series of events had no obvious rational explanation, and they thus saw

more irrational or supernatural forces at work that somehow must be control-led. Whether the Americans were willing to accept such beliefs or not, they should still have recognized that the Shinto blessing could well reassure the Japanese workers and help restore morale. Moreover, in dismissing rituals and behaviors of other cultures as superstition, Westerners often fail to recognize the extent to which superstition persists in their own societies—from avoiding having thirteenth floors in hotels to keeping lucky charms and reading daily horoscopes. Such actions, although trivial, have no rational basis. Superstition exists to varying degrees in all cultures.

3. The Japanese are generally very concerned with correct procedures, and these managers would probably be quite willing to review the procedures if they felt they could possibly be at fault. Moreover, this explanation does not take into account that some of the incidents happened outside of the workplace. There is a more appropriate explanation. Please try again.

4. This seems unlikely, as Japanese management practices usually encourage em-ployee participation where appropriate. The Japanese managers probably had no strong objections to the Americans' proposal; rather, they saw it as unlikely to bring any solution to the problem. There is a better explanation for the disagree-ment as to the course of action. Please select another explanation.

Incident 69 (p. 163): Rationales for the Alternative Explanations

1. Although this is always a possibility (appealing to a vague bureaucratic authority as an excuse for not doing something), Dr. Hastings was not using a widely accepted American style of saying no. And keep in mind that he was surprised that there was no follow-up communication from Dr. Xi. Please choose another explanation.

2. This is one of two good answers. From Dr. Xi's point of view, Dr. Hastings may have been saying no, but in a polite way. When Dr. Xi heard Dr. Hastings talking about administrative burdens that needed to be faced, he may have thought, "Dr. Hastings is trying to be polite and to communicate in an indirect manner by pointing to all the administrators who will eventually say no." This explanation becomes even clearer when combined with another that also contributes to a fuller understanding of the incident. Please look for this other good answer.

3. Actually, and perhaps unfortunately, in the United States teaching is not the activity that leads to high status in the development of careers such as that of Dr. Hastings. Research and extensive writing lead to greater prestige than does teaching. Please choose again.

4. This is one of two good answers. From Dr. Xi's point of view, someone with the very high status of Dr. Hastings should be able to make his or her own

decisions about the use of time. A person of such high status should not have to receive permission from a set of administrators. This is one benefit of high status (from Dr. Xi's point of view)—a certain amount of removal from petty bureaucracies. This is especially true (again, from Dr. Xi's viewpoint) given that Dr. Hastings is from a country where people have a great deal of freedom. How can people be free if they have to clear their time with petty bureaucracies? From Dr. Hastings's point of view, on the other hand, there were many legal restrictions on how the grant money he had access to could be spent, and he indeed did have to check with administrators before making any commitments. When Dr. Hastings talked about administrators, however, Dr. Xi heard a different message. Another explanation deals with this message. Please look for this alternative.

5. There are always individuals who abuse visits to other countries and make promises they cannot possibly fulfill. However, this is not so common among Chinese as to be considered part of Chinese culture. In addition, if Dr. Xi knew about the value of networking in the United States (as implied in the wording of this alternative), he knew that he would damage his networking position if he became known as a person who does not follow through on promises. Please choose another alternative.

Incident 70 (p. 164): Rationales for the Alternative Explanations

1. Although the Japanese are very proud of their success in the area of quality control, it is not automatic that they would be upset if an issue concerning quality control were raised. If well handled, it would be an opportunity for the Japanese to make a good presentation. Providing a time to discuss quality control might well help the progress of a proposal. The key is the phrase "if well handled." Please choose again.

2. This is the best answer. The big cultural mistake on Ted's part was in his method of introducing the new issue about quality control. In Japan (and, in general, Southeast Asia) people do not like surprises at meetings. Most information sharing and introduction of new ideas takes place in one-on-one meetings between the parties involved in the decisions to be made. After all corrections, modifications, and additions are made in these interactions, an addition to a proposal can be put on the agenda of a later meeting at which all the people involved in the project will be present. By that time, everyone in the meeting will have had extensive opportunities to study the addition to the proposal and no one will be embarrassed by an aspect of the proposal that might affect his or her responsibilities but about which he or she is unprepared to comment.

3. Even if this was the case, the Japanese would probably have sensed that Ted was being polite in deferring to the senior person. Attempts to be polite, even

if they do not exactly meet the norms in a given situation, are often taken as indications of goodwill. There is a better answer that focuses on a mistake Ted made in style rather than in the exact substance of his remarks. Please choose again.

4. It does take a long time to develop new business ventures and production-export-import projects, but the Japanese have become accustomed to working with Americans and have made some concessions to American sensitivity to time. The project involving Ted seemed to be proceeding reasonably well in a realistic time frame (expectations of completion in 3 months would be the sort of mistake American companies have made in the past). Ted made a mistake at the meeting discussed in the story. Please choose again.

Incident 71 (p. 165): Rationales for the Alternative Explanations

1. This is the best answer. When we observe the behavior of others, we commonly make the mistake of drawing conclusions about those persons' traits or qualities. Here, Helen's judgments (or attributions) are that Hideo is aggressive and hard to work with. When making such attributions, we often fail to take into account the immediate factors in a situation that could influence the observed behavior, such as the frustration of hearing bad news. Interestingly, if Helen had been asked to interpret her own behavior had she gotten angry, she would undoubtedly have said something like, "Well, wouldn't you be angry if a plan you had worked hard on ended up being rejected?" In addition, in Japan, vigorous behavior in a bar is an acceptable outlet; people are not supposed to make permanent conclusions about others based on those persons' bar behaviors. But in analyzing the behavior of others, we often fail to take into account the immediate factors of the situation or social context. This error—making trait judgments about others without taking situational factors into account—has been called the *fundamental attribution error*. It is probably especially prevalent in cross-cultural encounters because sojourners observe so many behaviors that are new and different from what they are accustomed to. When working across cultures, individuals often make more attributions about people and events than they would in their own countries. Even though Helen had been in Japan for 2 years, she was still encountering new experiences that demanded judgments or attributions from her.

2. Certainly a common observation about Japan is that decorum is highly valued, but Japanese people do become angry and upset. Rather than jumping to a conclusion, it is usually better to go beyond the common observation (in this case the frequently noted value placed on proper decorum) and analyze in more detail the specific instance. If a person has been exposed only to the common observation, he or she is ill prepared for behaviors (which will

inevitably be encountered on a long sojourn) that are at odds with the general observation. An important point is that, in Japan, vigorous behavior in bars is an acceptable outlet. Japanese hosts tell us that one should not draw permanent conclusions about individuals based on their bar behavior. Please choose again.

3. If they are capable professionals, Helen and Hideo should have known about industrywide conditions. Although Hideo might have been expected to take those conditions into account before reacting to the nonacceptance of his plan, a highly abstract and nonimmediate element such as "industrywide conditions" will rarely wipe out the frustration of seeing hard work lead to no visible reward. Please choose again.

4. This could be part of the interpretation. People have a strong tendency, upon seeing the negative behaviors of others, to wonder if they are somehow involved. Because Helen had been working with Hideo, such feelings on her part would be natural. During cross-cultural experiences, this tendency is probably stronger. Because Helen and Hideo had not worked together for a long time and were still learning things about each other, Helen was not able to interpret all of Hideo's actions readily. As she was not intimately knowledgeable about Japanese culture after 2 years, she could have been motivated to wonder even more if she somehow was personally involved. Because of this felt personal involvement, any of Helen's final conclusions would be intensified. There is another explanation that focuses on a mistake Helen could have been making in her thinking. Please choose again.

Incident 72 (p. 165): Rationales for the Alternative Explanations

1. This is probably not accurate, and there are cultural reasons. In China, if one engineer in a company knows some technological material, he or she would be expected to share it with others. This would reflect the cooperation possible in a well-run company within a collectivist culture. An engineer who keeps technological knowledge to him- or herself would be known as an uncooperative fellow worker. The engineers at the seventh meeting, then, would have learned from others about the material presented at the first six meetings. Please choose again.

2. In selecting this alternative, you may be on the right track, because the Chinese may have had another agenda in requesting so many meetings. However, they were interested in using the meetings to learn advanced technological material concerning pagers. Please choose again.

3. You may be on the right track in selecting this alternative, but it is incorrect to say that the Chinese were setting aside guilt, for a very simple reason: They did not feel any guilt in scheduling so many meetings so that they could be exposed to advanced technology. It may be helpful to ask, What might people

from other cultures think about Herb's and Jack's ethical standards? Please choose again.

4. This is a correct alternative. The Chinese wanted to learn advanced technology and did not see any ethical difficulties in scheduling multiple meetings and asking pointed questions meant to discover advanced knowledge among businesspeople who are proposing joint ventures. They might have said, "This is just good business practice—to learn from others with advanced technology." They might also have pointed out, "We feel that our practice is good business just as people from the United States (and many other parts of the world) feel that it is good practice to do business in China because of low labor costs." The Chinese might also have asked how Herb and Jack could sleep at night given the wages they proposed paying to Chinese workers, compared with the wages they would have had to pay American workers. You may also want to search for a second correct alternative.

5. This is a strong possibility. The Chinese may have been maintaining contact with Herb and Jack while also negotiating with other companies. Scheduling meetings with these two Americans allowed the Chinese to keep up interactions (and to keep the two in China) while negotiations with other companies proceeded. In addition, the Chinese may well have used technical information learned from Herb and Jack to negotiate more effectively with these other companies. Such practices are viewed negatively by Americans, and businesspeople such as Herb and Jack might accuse those who use them of "stringing us along" or "taking advantage of our willingness to discuss technology." However, scheduling meetings to learn about technology and using the newly gained knowledge during negotiations with other companies are accepted business practices in China, and businesspeople from other nations considering joint ventures with the Chinese should know about these practices.

Incident 73 (p. 167): Rationales for the Alternative Explanations

1. There is no indication that this is the case; Mark appears to relate well to the people he deals with in the first weeks. There is a better response; please choose again.

2. This is the most probable explanation. Although Mark is used to constant traveling, this is only within the United States, where the people and places he encounters have a sameness about them wherever he is. In Europe, he is continually forced to confront and attempt to adapt to quite different behaviors, languages, and surroundings, which necessitates continual alertness and relearning of expected responses. Too much of this can rapidly become mentally exhausting, and apathy, tiredness, and partial withdrawal may result. Those going abroad (especially for the first time) should attempt to limit their contacts to just one or two cultures so as to provide some familiarity and

predictability in their environments. Constant change creates continual arousal, which can be maintained only for a limited period.

3. Although our validation sample suggested that this is a possibility, Mark is probably used to such a program while traveling in the United States. The physical exhaustion he exhibits probably has a less direct and more psychological origin. Please select another response.

4. This answer is not entirely correct. Although Mark is quite used to being away from home, he is not used to being away from his own culture and so probably would develop some degree of homesickness for the United States. However, the reason for his indifference and tiredness has more complex origins than just missing home. Please choose again.

Incident 74 (p. 167): Rationales for the Alternative Explanations

1. This is a good answer and the one selected as most probable by our validation sample. Although it is often a stereotype that in many developing nations it takes longer to complete some tasks, in the United States also many decisions are reached only after a long time. In fact, Machmud had been exposed to a sufficient number of meetings to know about technical or structural matters such as time. However, he may not have been in the United States long enough to assimilate behavior reflecting a deep cultural difference. Such a cultural difference is present, and another alternative reflects this.

2. This is the response that best reflects culturally determined behavioral differences. In Indonesia, the group often comes before any action of the individual. Machmud was acting as one would in a meeting in his home country. Rather than stand out as an idea person seeking attention, an individual may present suggestions quickly toward the close of a meeting, with the hope that little attention will be paid to him or her. It is important that a leader understand the group dynamics and decision-making processes of the cultures represented in a group to benefit fully from all possible input and to prevent misunderstandings.

3. Although Machmud may have had difficult moments adjusting to his new environment, there is no indication that this was the cause of his behavior. Please select again.

4. There is no indication in the story that this was a problem. The fact that Machmud had been invited to many such meetings excludes the possibility that his language ability was poor. There is a better explanation. Please choose again.

Incident 75 (p. 168): Rationales for the Alternative Explanations

1. Although working with culturally different people places particular demands on the individual, this is probably not the case here. Melinda had successfully

completed a position as an inner-city social worker, which would probably have provided her ample opportunity to interact with culturally different people. There is a better answer. Please try again.

2. This could be part of the explanation. Although it may be true that many people hit a low period after experiencing the realities rather than the romance of a new job, this would probably have occurred before the twelfth month. In Melinda's case, other factors were at play. Please try again.

3. The work was not erratic—it was demanding all the time, according to the incident. There is a more pressing issue here. Please try again.

4. This is the best answer. Counselor burnout often results when a person faces too many emotional demands and has no avenues available through which to restore his or her own emotional balance. Melinda was responding constantly to highly emotional people—those having problems or crises that need to be addressed. She was expected to listen and be empathic and patient with everyone while receiving a tremendous amount of negative feedback. Although this negative feedback may not have been directed at her personally, she often shared the burden with her students. Because she worked in essentially a one-person office (a half-time student worker probably could not offer much emotional support), she had nobody with whom she could discuss her needs.

Incident 76 (p. 169): Rationales for the Alternative Explanations

1. There was no reason Carl should not have recited part of "The Raven." Although there are particular symbols in different cultures that people should know about and avoid making the targets of humor, this was not a problem here. Please choose again.

2. It is quite proper for guests to contribute if they wish. Most often, such a contribution would be taken as a compliment by the Japanese, because the visitor is participating in one of their activities. Please choose again.

3. Although one should always be careful about which (if any) woman is attached to what man (and vice versa), there is no indication that this was a problem here. Please choose again.

4. This is correct to some extent and in some situations. Although language competence always plays a part in interpreting cues so that proper, acceptable behaviors can be found, there is no indication here that language competence versus incompetence played a major part in the story. The mistake Carl made may be noticeable to both people who speak Japanese and those who do not. There is more at issue here. Please choose again.

5. This is the best answer. Carl thought that the informality he experienced at the party would not be differentiated from informality at the company

meeting. In reality, there is a sharp distinction. Senior managers can be very informal, even silly, at parties, but they expect respect and adherence to accepted procedures at company meetings during the workday. Carl probably made a trait attribution of "informal" from his observations at the party. Sojourners have a strong tendency to make trait attributions and not to take situational factors into account. Here, the situational distinction is the party versus the company meeting. Analysis of this story according to both differentiation and trait-situation attribution shows that the sophisticated sojourner must gather information that goes beyond first impressions to make responses considered proper and acceptable by hosts. Please refer to the essay on attribution in Chapter 13.

Incident 77 (p. 170): Rationales for the Alternative Explanations

1. This is the best response. Although Ronald believed his actions would increase morale and sense of purpose, he probably brought about the opposite state of affairs. Ronald's North American business training emphasized action, efficiency, and organization as prerequisites of success and motivation as coming from the lure of financial gain. In many other cultures, however, such factors assume lesser importance. Work is not viewed as the center of life, and time spent in personal interaction ("being" with others) is regarded as important, positive, and essential in the development of group feeling and morale. Whereas Ronald probably "worked hard and played hard," the Brazilians saw not so sharp a differentiation between the two and thus regarded rigid schedules and rules with suspicion. All Ronald's efficiency drive did was decrease overt social interaction and lower office morale, which was reflected in the salesmen's poorer performance. They did not see potential financial gains as sufficient compensation to offset the disturbance of their social orientation.

2. Although some may have resented his management practices rather than his style, it is unlikely that they would deliberately lower their sales to get at Ronald as this would hurt them as much as him. (Salesmen generally work on partial commission or on an incentive basis.) There is a more straightforward explanation. Please choose again.

3. Business management in Latin American companies is generally still fairly traditional, and employees are accustomed to and respect a clear distinction between top management and the workforce. There is another explanation that better reflects the reason for the decline in sales. Please choose again.

4. Although loss of face is always a potential problem whenever a manager has to make changes, this is not the best explanation here. The story mentions that Ronald gave warnings about what he considered poor performance in the privacy of his office; it does not mention that anyone in particular was singled out for public criticism. Please choose again.

Incident 78 (p. 171): Rationales for the Alternative Explanations

1. This alternative explains part of the problem. That Todd is using American managerial techniques means two things: (a) He is counting on Chungmin to come to him and complain if she has a problem, and (b) he will rely on verbal communication, or "talking it out," to solve the problem. If Todd were to pay more attention to his staff's feelings and behaviors, he would realize that these two techniques for resolving conflicts do not work well in Korea. In fact, what Chungmin's behavior should tell him is that the Korean system is almost the opposite. Unlike in the United States, where the responsibility for reporting a problem rests with the complainant, in Korea the other person is supposed to pick up from the complainant's nonverbal cues that something is wrong. Moreover, in Korea, verbal communication is seen as a last resort. If the problem must actually be talked about, then it is extremely serious. As a manager in Korea working with a Korean staff, if Todd wants to accomplish his goals, he should realize these differences and start behaving as a Korean boss would. There is a more complete explanation, however. Please choose again.

2. Although, from Todd's perspective, and even in Chungmin's eyes, the mistake seems minor, Chungmin is reacting to the context in which the reprimand took place. She would not have become upset if Todd had simply mentioned the error to her in his office. However, the fact that he mentioned it during lunch, in a public forum, resulted in a loss of face for Chungmin. As a result, she can hardly forget about it. There is a more complete explanation, however. Please choose again.

3. This response explains part of the misunderstanding. Although from Todd's point of view he just casually mentioned the mistake during lunch, from Chungmin's point of view Todd scolded her in public and therefore made her lose face in front of her colleagues. The context in which he scolded her, then, and not his supposedly casual mentioning of the error, is the real reason for her complaint. There is a more complete explanation, however. Please choose again.

4. This is the best response because it explains both issues involved in the incident: how (and more specifically, in what context) to communicate a problem and how it may be resolved. Todd's original mistake was mentioning the error to Chungmin at lunch. Chungmin considers this very rude, as it embarrassed her in front of her colleagues. No matter how small an error, this public scolding made her look very bad. Chungmin has lost face and has become upset with Todd for his thoughtlessness. Later on, the second problem developed when Todd failed to respond to Chungmin's cues indicating she was upset. They used two different styles of conflict resolution. In the United States, it would be Chungmin's, and not Todd's, responsibility to voice the

problem. In Korea, a female secretary would never complain to her boss that he did something rude and "wrong" according to Korean culture. On the contrary, it is the boss's responsibility to figure out, based on nonverbal cues, that his worker has a complaint and then to resolve the conflict without verbal communication. Todd, however, tells Chungmin to talk to him if she has a problem. Chungmin is not accustomed to this style of conflict resolution, which she views as a last resort. Thus if Todd wants to run a successful business in Korea, he needs to adapt not only in how he communicates a problem, but also in how he resolves conflicts.

8

THE FAMILY

When a family leaves its home and settles into a new area, the breadwinner is usually the center of attention. He or she may receive preparation, may be able to ask questions of experienced colleagues in the workplace, may be the recipient of positive attention from hosts, and, in the case of immigrants, may receive extra support from social service agencies (e.g., job training and placement). The problems of other family members may be neglected in the excitement of settling into the new home, and unresolved problems may appear in more severe form at a later date. These problems can become so serious as to threaten the successful adjustment of the family breadwinner. A frequent reason for the premature termination of a cross-cultural assignment, for instance, is the inadequate adjustment of the spouse. Children's lack of success at school, or failures in developing new friendships, can also cause difficulties for the entire family. Attention should be given to finding niches for all family members—activities in which they receive a sense of personal satisfaction as well as the respect of others. Niches may take the form of volunteer activities, participation in religious groups, and membership in various clubs, team sports, or informal support networks.

79

Bringing Him Home to Dad

Scott, an American living in Iran, was introduced to Nazilah, an Iranian woman, by a mutual friend. As time went on, Scott and Nazilah began seeing each other socially, going to movies, nightclubs, and parties together. After a few weeks, Nazilah suggested that Scott meet her parents, as they were interested in knowing who he was. Scott arrived at Nazilah's home on the evening previously decided upon. Formal introductions were made, and almost immediately, Nazilah's family began questioning Scott about his presence in Iran, his background, and his family, immediate and extended. After Scott had answered a number of questions, Nazilah's father came out with a very direct and specific request. He wanted to know when Scott was going to tell him when he planned to marry Nazilah and where they expected to live. Scott responded that marriage was not being considered at that time because he and Nazilah had known each other for only a short period of time. The father, obviously upset by Scott's response, asked Scott to leave and never to see his daughter again. Scott left in disbelief. If you were to help Scott with this situation, on what issue would you focus?

1. The father wished Nazilah to marry an American. When this obviously was not about to happen, the father wished the relationship to end.

2. The father felt insulted because Scott had not already married Nazilah.

3. Nazilah's father was adhering to traditional practices regarding courtship, whereas Nazilah was attempting to live according to more modern roles.

4. By bringing Scott to her home, Nazilah was hoping to coerce him into a proposal.

The discussions of these alternative explanations begin on page 194.

80

The Delay

It may not have been love at first sight, but the romantic relationship between Junko and Robert had developed quickly. Robert was a 25-year-old businessman on assignment to Tokyo to develop joint ventures in the electronics industry. Junko was a language interpreter who had accompanied Robert, early in his sojourn, when he had been asked to give a public presentation about his company. After the speech, Robert had asked Junko out to dinner, and the romance proceeded from that point.

After they had been dating for about 6 months, Junko (who originally had come to Tokyo from a rural community 300 miles away) wanted Robert to meet her parents. Although not overjoyed at the idea, remembering clumsy meetings with parents of college girlfriends in the United States, Robert was culturally sensitive enough to realize that Junko had to show respect to her parents by introducing him to them. The couple traveled by train to Junko's home community and were entertained by her parents. Robert thought the visit went well, even though the parents asked him a large number of questions about himself. About 3 months later, Junko and Robert discussed the possibility of marriage. Again, Robert realized that Junko would have to discuss the matter with her family. Junko called her parents, informed them of her plans, and asked for their approval. The parents did not agree right away, but promised to call Junko back as soon as possible. Weeks passed, with no call from the parents.

What was the most likely reason for the delay?

1. Junko's parents were checking into Robert's family background.

2. The telephone system is poor in Japan and Junko's parents would have had a hard time making a call from their rural community.

3. Junko had been seeing Robert in Tokyo without a chaperon.

4. Junko had an unmarried older sister, and this sister had to be married before Junko would be allowed to become engaged.

The discussions of these alternative explanations begin on page 194.

81

Problems at Home

Dennis Zale, a management consultant with a large international financial institution, was transferred to Zurich, Switzerland, for a planned 2-year stay. Although he and his family had traveled extensively, they had never lived overseas for any extended period of time. They were all quite excited about the move.

Dennis's company handled most of the arrangements for the transfer and provided Dennis with 2 weeks of extensive language and cross-cultural training. The company also arranged for the moving of the family's household furniture and personal belongings, found them a suitable apartment, arranged for the lease of an automobile, enrolled the two children (David and Peter, ages 14 and 10) in a nearby international school, and even arranged to have the family dog transported to Switzerland.

The move went well—everything arrived intact and when expected. After a few weeks of adjustment, Dennis found that things at work were running quite smoothly; in fact, he was quite pleased with his accomplishments on the job. As time progressed, however, he became increasingly short-tempered and moody, both at home and on the job. Things at home were changing, and he seemed unable to control them. He often argued with his wife, who complained of missing her friends from home and of being bored. She was also upset that she could not seem to manage her home as she used to. The right foods were not available, and she could barely understand the directions for preparing the food she did buy. The children, too, were having a hard time. They were doing poorly in school, and on more than one occasion, Mrs. Zale was called in because David was involved in fighting with classmates. What is the most plausible cause of the above difficulties?

1. Mrs. Zale probably did not have the right personality for overseas living.
2. These problems were merely extensions of preexisting conditions in the family.
3. There was a lack of attention and preparation for the move given to Mrs. Zale and the children.
4. Many of the problems the family experienced were caused by David, the oldest child, who was just entering adolescence and causing problems for all.

The discussions of these alternative explanations begin on page 195.

82

The Mother-in-Law's Visit

Mrs. Reyes, a Filipino, was visiting her daughter Wilma, who had been living with her American husband, Tom, in Los Angeles for some 10 years. It was her first trip to the United States and she seemed intent on seeing everything; she insisted that Wilma and Tom accompany her in her sightseeing, upsetting their work routines considerably. After a few days, Mrs. Reyes told them that she would like to extend her stay for 3 more weeks, and that she was writing to ask that her other children fly to the United States and also join them. Upon learning this, Tom became very uncomfortable and tried to suggest tactfully that it would be very difficult for him and Wilma to put up the whole family and provide for their needs. Wilma said nothing, seeming to support Tom. Mrs. Reyes appeared to accept the situation, but a few days later suddenly cut short her stay and returned to the Philippines. Tom was very confused by her impulsive behavior. Why did Mrs. Reyes leave so hurriedly for the Philippines?

1. Filipinos are unpredictable people, and she just changed her mind because of some other plans.

2. She was hurt by her son-in-law's attitude, which she considered inhospitable and disrespectful.

3. She sensed that Tom felt she was imposing and, feeling a little guilty, decided it was better that she not prolong her stay.

4. She felt she could not cope with the pressures and very different lifestyle of Los Angeles.

The discussions of these alternative explanations begin on page 196.

Incident 79 (p. 190): Rationales for the Alternative Explanations

1. Although it is a wish of some fathers in some developing nations to have their children marry foreign nationals, therefore enabling them to leave their countries, there is no evidence in the story to support this statement. Please choose again.

2. Nazilah's father was behaving according to traditional norms, but such norms do not include the expectation that Scott should already have married Nazilah. Please select again.

3. This is the best answer. In Iran, as in many other Middle Eastern countries, traditional customs dictate that it is not considered proper for a single woman to see a man socially without the approval of her father. Nazilah, by seeing Scott as she had been doing recently, before a meeting with her parents, was attempting to step beyond the traditional culture. Her father was obviously opposed to her modern desires.

4. There is no evidence in the incident to support this statement. The relationship seems to be progressing to the satisfaction of both Scott and Nazilah. Please choose again.

Incident 80 (p. 191): Rationales for the Alternative Explanations

1. This is the best choice. In Japan, as in many countries, family ties and family obligations are very important, as are feelings about class and status. Junko's

parents realized that they would be incurring obligations to Robert and Robert's family if they agreed to the marriage. They felt that their daughter would not be marrying only an individual; she would be marrying into a group (Robert's family). Consequently, they wanted to learn as much as possible about the nature of that group. Knowledge about Robert would not be enough. Robert would probably be upset at hearing this, and might say something like, "It's me Junko is marrying. What do my relatives have to do with it?" This difference also reflects the individual/collective theme that has been examined in several incidents. Further, people at any level of society are proud of their status and do not want to see that status threatened. Thus they would be careful about giving approval to a marriage that may involve links to people of lower status or to people from a lower social class. Carefulness about incurring obligations to an "inappropriate" group through marriage has led to the establishment of agencies in Japan that examine the backgrounds of potential marriage partners. For a fee, such an agency will do an investigation and report back to the interested party (for example, a parent). If Junko's parents did this, it would be one reason for the delay; it would take time for the agency to find out about Robert's family in the United States.

2. This is most unlikely. The telephone system in Japan is excellent. Please choose again.

3. There is not a system of chaperoning in Japan as there is in Latin American countries. Traditionally, matchmakers or go-betweens may have arranged marriages, but so many marriages in Japan now take place without the use of these people that Junko's parents could not be surprised that she met Robert on her own. Japanese people from rural areas are aware of societal changes and the fast pace of life in Tokyo. Junko's parents must have realized that their daughter would be meeting men, one of whom she might marry. Please choose again.

4. Traditionally, Japanese parents may have preferred that their eldest daughters be married before any of the younger daughters could become engaged, but there is no sister mentioned in the incident, and so this is not the best choice. Even if there were a sister, the custom of insisting on her marriage first is currently not so strong as to provide the most likely reason specified in the question at the end of the incident. Please choose again.

Incident 81 (p. 192): Rationales for the Alternative Explanations

1. There is no evidence in the incident to support this statement. Mrs. Zale complained about and reacted to events in a manner similar to that of many people when they are first adjusting to a new environment. There is a more plausible explanation for the family's condition. Please try again.

2. There is no indication that the family unit was undergoing intense stress prior to the move to Switzerland. Please limit your response to events as evident in the story and try again.

3. This is the correct response. Although companies may spend a considerable amount of time and effort in preparing their employees for overseas experiences, they often offer little, if any, preparation for the employees' family members. A critical factor for satisfactory family adjustment is the understanding that all family members will experience the changes associated with a move; further, they must adapt to a new environment that is in many ways much different from that of the employee. Children adjusting to new schools in foreign countries must contend with new languages, different peers and peer influences and demands, different recreational outlets, new neighborhood designs, and the like. Spouses attempting to set up new homes must also contend with new languages, new places to shop, unfamiliar goods, and new foods, and they often lose their established social support groups and recreational outlets. These changes should all be anticipated and planned for.

4. Although David is at a very vulnerable age and is experiencing problems in school, it is doubtful that he is the cause of all the family disturbances. Rather, he is probably reacting to the same conditions that are affecting his mother. Please select another explanation.

Incident 82 (p. 193): Rationales for the Alternative Explanations

1. This is most unlikely. After all, Mrs. Reyes, from all indications, was quite keen on staying longer. Besides, a Filipino mother would not usually leave hurriedly; traditionally, leave-taking involves lengthy ritual farewells (*despedidas*). Please choose again.

2. This is the best answer. When a Filipino mother visits one of her children, she expects to receive that child's attention and concern. She would expect equal devotion from a son-in-law, who should love all persons close to his wife. Mrs. Reyes was hurt by Tom, whom she thought very cold, disrespectful, and inhospitable. She felt Tom's lack of attention and reluctance to accommodate the whole family was a rejection of her and an indication of ingratitude toward her role as a mother.

3. This is close, but not the best answer. Even if Mrs. Reyes hardly knew Tom, she would expect him to go out of his way to please her. She may have sensed Tom's attitude, but she would not feel guilty in any way. Please choose again.

4. Mrs. Reyes may have felt uncomfortable or overwhelmed, but still, this would not be a legitimate reason for her to leave. As long as she felt welcomed and secure within her daughter's house, she would not mind having to adjust to the different lifestyle. There is in fact no indication that she was having problems coping with the new setting. Please choose again.

9

EDUCATION AND SCHOOLING

People living and working across cultures often take part in various types of educational activities, even though they do not label their efforts as such. By working with host colleagues, they frequently transfer skills so that hosts can follow through on jointly developed activities after the sojourners return home. In fact, this point has become well enough known that it provides the basis of advice to newly assigned people: Seek out opportunities to transfer your skills to hosts; if you do so, you will leave behind something of value after your sojourn is over. Hosts appreciate the efforts involved in skills transfer and remember most favorably those sojourners who give attention to this issue.

Schools, of course, are places where formal efforts are made to introduce new learning opportunities. Teachers new to a given area are often surprised that students do not seem to learn as quickly as they had expected or in a manner familiar to them; their carefully prepared lessons seem to have no impact. Teachers must themselves learn to be flexible so that they can redesign their lesson plans to take advantage of the ways their students typically learn new material in their everyday lives. Several of the incidents in this chapter, as well as the essay on learning styles in Chapter 13, suggest how this goal might be accomplished.

83

The Assessment of His Efforts

Tal was an African student from Gambia who had recently begun a postgraduate business administration course at a British university. It was the first time he had been to a foreign country, but having won a

Gambian scholarship to attend the university he was quite confident of his ability to do well. He applied himself enthusiastically to his studies and felt he had few difficulties with the material presented. However, when he received the first assessments of his papers and contributions to tutorials, he was disconcerted to find they were not very favorable. He was told that although his ideas were "interesting," he did not keep to the topic, brought in too many irrelevancies, and did not present his arguments in a logical manner. Tal was puzzled by this, as his work seemed logical and relevant to him, so he sought advice from Tony, one of his British classmates. Tony showed him some of his own papers that had been given good grades, but this only increased Tal's confusion, because Tony's work seemed to Tal to be insubstantial and dull.

How would you help explain to Tal's professors the origins of his confusion as to what is expected of him?

1. The Gambian and British modes of thinking and communicating are very different.
2. Tal probably did not have the intellectual capability to tackle a postgraduate course.
3. Tal's Gambian education did not prepare him for the more rigorous British educational system.
4. Tal was probably going through a confusing settling-in period, and with time would produce more organized work.

The discussions of these alternative explanations begin on page 219.

84

A Secretary's Work Is Never Easy

Mrs. Jane Simpson enjoyed her job as a department secretary in a large, well-respected university in the United States. She enjoyed trying to be helpful to students as they worked their way through department and university regulations on their way toward earning their bachelor's, master's, and doctoral degrees. One day, a student from India entered the department office and began demanding attention to his various problems with his visa, low course grades, and his thesis adviser. He never said "please" or "thank you," talked in a tone of voice reminiscent of a superior talking to subordinates, and gave orders to Mrs. Simpson. Mrs. Simpson became angry at such treatment; she counted slowly to

10, but her anger did not subside. She went to see the department chairperson to see if someone else could work with this student in the future.
How would you help Mrs. Simpson sort out her feelings about this incident?

1. Visa problems are uncommon, and so the Indian student was very upset because there were no well-established procedures to deal with his problem.
2. Mrs. Simpson was not being attacked personally; rather, she was being attacked because of her role.
3. Foreign students are often some of the best students in university departments, and so this student from India was upset that he was getting low grades.
4. Foreign students frequently (or at least often enough to be memorable from university administrators' points of view) run into problems involving charges of plagiarizing the work of others. This was the reason for the student's frustration and anger.

The discussions of these alternative explanations begin on page 220.

85

Who Gains Entry?

The Intramural Office employs student workers in a variety of roles. The workers perform many duties, among which are to check the validity of identification of those entering the gym, to sell daily passes, to serve as resource persons for guests, to assist in providing a safe and secure environment, and to provide first aid when needed. Their main responsibilities are to check student identification cards and to sell passes. There is a sign posted that clearly states the requirements for entry into the gym, and the employee on duty is specifically told to check the ID of each person entering the building.

One Saturday afternoon, two female employees, Alice, an African American, and Joanna, a European American, were working at the back entrance when two white males entered the building. Immediately behind them, two black males followed. One of the white males did not have his ID with him. Alice, however, knew that he was in one of her classes, so she let him in.

When the two black men approached, they were asked to show their IDs. One of them was unable to produce valid identification, and Joanna told him that he would not be allowed in the gym. At hearing this, he became angry and started arguing with both women, demanding that they explain why they had let someone in before him who did not have ID either. Insisting the incident was racially motivated, the individual who had been denied entrance took his friend's ID card and threw it at Joanna, opening a small cut beneath her eye. When Alice and Joanna discussed this incident with another person at a later time, they said they had smelled alcohol on the man's breath.

What insights might you offer that would help explain what seems to be going on?

1. The requirements for entry were not clear. Perhaps a double standard or selective entry was at play here.
2. The individual was correct in his judgment; the incident was racially motivated and Joanna should be reprimanded.
3. Without full knowledge of what had transpired beforehand, the man who was denied entrance may possibly have misjudged Joanna's behavior.
4. The individual had a chip on his shoulder and would have probably argued with Joanna anyway, especially as he had been drinking.

The discussions of these alternative explanations begin on page 221.

86

The New ESL Teacher

After 2 years of travel throughout Asia and Europe and a year of study and preparation in a master's program in English as a second language (ESL), George felt quite confident. Although he had not had any real classroom experience, he had taught English informally to a Malaysian student he met while traveling, had studied all the latest approaches to teaching English, was keen to employ an intercultural dimension in his teaching, and was quite eager to get to know as many international students coming to the United States as he could. He was, not surprisingly, excited to be offered his first position at a nearby university to teach in a special ESL summer program for a group of visiting Japanese students. He eagerly prepared for his upcoming teaching assignment.

The first day of class arrived. George had found out earlier that the majority of his students would be business majors, because the importance of English for business purposes had become quite evident. From the very first day, even though he had learned a bit of Japanese during his earlier travels, George made sure to only use English in class to communicate and to teach his students. He tried to be as friendly as he could and to maintain interaction with his students. It puzzled him that when he approached a student with a question, the student inevitably looked down at his or her textbook and would not give an answer to the question he asked. This behavior continued down the line, with each student maintaining an embarrassed silence. The students were not the only ones embarrassed by the silence—George was also in a quandary. He did not know how to manage the situation. He decided to sit next to one of his students in order to communicate better. To his dismay, he noticed after he tried this that more and more students started sitting at the back of the classroom rather than filling the chairs up front.

Things finally flared up when George asked a particular student to summarize the points made in the previous class. What he had neglected to notice was that the student he chose had been absent the previous day. As a result, the student maintained a long and uncomfortable silence. George had had enough. He told the student to look at him directly and tell him if she knew the material. After this confrontation, most of the students stopped coming to class.

What insights might you offer George that would help him better understand what was going on?

1. Japanese students revere and respect elderly teachers. There was not enough of an age gap between George and his students.

2. In Japanese custom, in order to gain full respect, it is necessary to greet people in the Japanese language. Because George made a point of using only English, he never really gained the respect of his students.

3. George's style of teaching was in direct conflict with the manner in which Japanese students learn.

4. George was struggling because he was a new teacher. The situation would certainly improve as he gained experience and confidence.

The discussions of these alternative explanations begin on page 222.

87

Informal Gatherings of People

After a year in the United States, Fumio, from Japan, seemed to be adjusting well to his graduate-level studies. He had cordial relations with his professors, interacted frequently with other graduate students at midday coffee breaks, and was content with his housing arrangements in the graduate student dormitory. Fumio's statistical knowledge was so good that professors recommended that certain American students should consult him for help in this area. He seemed to be excluded, however, from at least one type of activity in which many of the other American graduate students participated—the informal gathering of students at the local pub (bar) at about 5:00 on Friday afternoons. People did not stop and invite him to these gatherings. As he was not invited, Fumio felt uncomfortable about simply showing up at the pub. He wondered if the lack of an invitation should be interpreted as a sign that he was doing something wrong—that he was offending the American students in some way.

What is a good explanation for Fumio's not being invited to join the others at the pub?

1. The Americans were rude in not inviting Fumio, a guest in their country.

2. The pub gatherings were meant to be an activity in which people who were very familiar with each other (an in-group) could relax on a very informal basis.

3. Japanese rarely drink beer. Realizing this, the Americans did not invite Fumio.

4. The Americans did not invite Fumio because they resented the fact that Fumio knew more statistics than they did; having to ask Fumio for help made them feel inferior.

5. Such pub gatherings on Friday afternoons are largely based on pairings of specific males with specific females. Because Fumio had no girlfriend, he was not invited.

The discussions of these alternative explanations begin on page 222.

88

From Providence to San Francisco

Joao was a teenager from Providence, Rhode Island, who had been sent to live for 2 years in San Francisco with his aunt and uncle. This was the first time that Joao had been away from his own family, which was strongly united and felt a deep pride in their Portuguese heritage. Joao's family had emigrated from Portugal when he was a child. The high school in San Francisco that Joao began attending was one that included students from a variety of ethnic and cultural groups. Joao knew that the school had a good reputation as being a place where students from different backgrounds got along well together, so he did not worry about the fact that he would be the only Portuguese person in the student body. He looked forward to attending the new school.

During Joao's first week in the school, he discovered that several members of the faculty viewed him as belonging to a group of students who spoke Spanish. A few teachers greeted him in Spanish; one said Joao might like to join a club mainly for Central American students. Joao felt resentful at being thought of as from anywhere other than Portugal. During his second week, a teacher gave Joao a notice to take home to his uncle; it was in Spanish. Joao startled the teacher by loudly protesting, "Please try to remember, *I'm Portuguese!*"

If Joao asked someone for advice, which of the following would be the most helpful?

1. "Joao, you probably didn't realize this, but you must have felt resentment at being sent to San Francisco to live with your aunt and uncle. Your sense of unity with your family in Providence was very strong and, deep down, you probably hated to leave it."

2. "Joao, you had been attending schools in Providence, where many other students were native Portuguese, just like you. The idea of going to a school with students from other ethnic and cultural groups—but no Portuguese—must have deeply disturbed you."

3. "Joao, you probably were deeply upset about being identified as a member of an ethnic or cultural group other than your own. You felt proud to be a native Portuguese, so you just couldn't adjust to being viewed as a Spanish speaker from Mexico or Central America."

4. "Joao, your parents in Providence kept you under tight discipline, so you never had to learn any self-discipline. It was inevitable that on this first

experience living away from your parents, you would do something to embarrass yourself."

The discussions of these alternative explanations begin on page 223.

89

Problems With Teaching Her Students

Jan Albert had met Amanda Adams shortly after her arrival in China on her assignment as a teacher of English. Even though they had not known each other before, Jan and Amanda were both from the southern United States and so had some common experiences to share. Amanda was also an English teacher, and she was enjoying her sojourn. Jan began to have problems in her teaching—she was not making the progress that she had thought she would. She went to Amanda and complained, "The students do not work very hard; they don't do their homework. They don't ask questions, and I can't make corrections in my lessons based on their feedback. How can anyone with any standards enjoy teaching here? How can you, Amanda, sit there and accept your paycheck with a clear conscience?"

Which of the following is most likely true of Jan's outburst?

1. Jan was venting her aggression on a convenient target, Amanda.
2. Jan was justified in her feelings about her students, and her reaction was reasonable.
3. Jan was not a very good teacher and was reacting to a realization of this fact.
4. There were not enough outlets in Jan's life so that she could discharge her frustrations in a constructive or at least neutral way.

The discussions of these alternative explanations begin on page 224.

90

Careful Preparation of Lectures

Robert felt extremely fortunate to have been invited to spend 4 weeks on the island of Kauai in Hawaii training four groups of young farmworkers (average age of 20 years) for 1 week each in the use and maintenance of some new farm machinery they had just purchased. This would be the first time he would have the opportunity to combine his undergraduate training as a teacher with his graduate work as an agricultural engineer, the field in which he was currently employed.

Recalling the many hours he had spent in his instructional resource lab, Robert made certain he had the most explicit diagrams of the machinery (both internal and external views) and extensive diagrams explaining the use of the machines and maintenance of their parts. He was especially pleased with the diagrams he had made that explained possible problems and actions one should take when a problem occurs. These media, combined with his extensive lecture notes, company operating manuals, films, books, and audio materials, would assure a most successful program.

Much to his surprise, Robert found his teaching experience to be an extreme struggle, for both himself and his students. The first day of each week-long session seemed to go well, but the remaining four seemed long and drawn out. The students often complained that they did not understand what he was trying to teach them. They were restless, talkative, and seemingly uninterested in what Robert had to offer. This really confused Robert, as he had assumed they would be eager to learn the use of these machines, which would ultimately improve their crop yield.

If you were asked to assist Robert with his problem, where would you focus?

1. Robert's students were much older than those he had initially been trained to teach. They should have been taught according to adult learning theory.

2. Robert ignored the fact that most of his students spoke Hawaiian English (commonly called Pidgin). He should have incorporated this into his presentation.

3. Hawaiian Americans are not as successful with learning from books and papers as they are with other methods, and prefer hands-on training with real objects over instruction from diagrams.

4. The students resented Robert's imposing his new technology on them and did not want this new machinery interfering with the methods to which they were accustomed.

The discussions of these alternative explanations begin on page 225.

91

Teaching Third Grade

Marie had recently moved to Honolulu from Oakland, California, with her husband, who was transferred with the U.S. military. She felt quite fortunate to have obtained a position teaching third grade in an elementary school in the Honolulu area, especially after hearing how difficult the job market was. She felt confident that her 3 years' experience in a multicultural classroom back in California was the factor that placed her in front of the other candidates.

Wanting to start the year off right, she prepared her classroom so that it was bright and inviting, had an ample supply of supplementary learning materials, set up individualized learning centers throughout the room, and prepared posters and checklists to make student achievement and advances visible to all.

During the first weeks of the school year, Marie stressed to her students that the classroom was a place of learning and demonstrated that she believed all should and could succeed by providing rewards, recognition, and extra activities for each individual child as he or she completed homework and various class assignments. All had equal opportunities to perform successfully and to display their accomplishments.

When the first grading period came to an end, it was brought to her attention that a significantly higher percentage of children of Japanese and Caucasian heritage than Native Hawaiian children were receiving awards and achieving high grades. She was told by her principal to treat all the children equally.

If you were Marie, where would you focus your attention?

1. More attempts to individualize instruction and to reward each Native Hawaiian child would have led to greater success.
2. Native Hawaiian children do not perform well for individual recognition; rather, they work for group rewards.
3. Children throughout Hawaii have had a great deal of contact with Japanese teachers and therefore have difficulty in adapting their learning styles to a Caucasian teacher.
4. Native Hawaiian children, like children in many ethnic minority groups, suffer from cultural deprivation and are therefore more apt to fail in school settings.

The discussions of these alternative explanations begin on page 226.

92

Making Friends

John entered the third-grade class at Central Elementary School in October after being home-schooled. This was his first real experience in school; aside from his interactions with others in his community of Jehovah's Witnesses, he had not had much contact with other children. John's parents told the school officials that they had taught him at home in the early years so he could develop a strong foundation in reading before he entered the public school.

On the first day of school, John eagerly joined the other children in all kinds of activities, including a game of touch football during recess. He appeared to enjoy the game, as well as playing with the other children. Likewise, the other children seemed to enjoy John's participation. John seemed particularly fond of Sam, another student in his class.

After recess, Sam brought out some cupcakes his mother had baked for him to share as a birthday treat with the others in his class. He gave John a cupcake, but John returned it, saying that he did not want it. Sam took the treat back, but seemed rather upset at having been refused. He could not understand why John, who had been so friendly on the playground, became cold and refused his treat on Sam's special day.

How might you help Sam understand this situation better?

1. John felt uncomfortable taking food from someone he did not know very well.
2. John's beliefs did not allow him to celebrate birthdays in the same way as most children in the class.
3. John really was not sure that he wanted to remain friends with Sam. By accepting the treat he felt he was obligating himself to Sam.
4. John's mother was overly concerned with the kinds of food he ate and did not want him to have excessive amounts of sugar during the day.

The discussions of these alternative explanations begin on page 227.

93

The Feelings and Conversations of a Sojourner

Ramon Garcia from Venezuela was making satisfactory progress at a graduate school in the United States, although he did have a complaint that faculty members did not consult him on matters relevant to South America about which they spoke in their lectures. Other people in the department to whom he felt close included Jan Adams, an attractive woman who, according to common knowledge around the department, had recently broken up with a long-term boyfriend. Both Ramon and Jan took courses from Professor Smith. Although Professor Smith was happily married, it was also common knowledge around the department that his wife had been away for the past 4 months taking care of her ill mother.

One evening, Professor Smith and Jan happened to finish up their work in the department at about 6:00. Professor Smith left the building through the main door and happened to see Jan leaving through the same exit. Wanting a simple meal and feeling that Jan might want the same, Professor Smith suggested that he and Jan eat together at the student union cafeteria. Jan agreed.

Ramon happened to be eating at the cafeteria when he saw Professor Smith and Jan leave the food line with their trays. They noticed Ramon at his table, acknowledged his presence, but found another table. Ramon wondered, "Why does Jan get more personal attention from Professor Smith than I do? Is she a better student than I? Am I doing something wrong?"

The next morning, Ramon happened to see the department chairperson in the computer lab because both were working on statistical analyses at the same time. While waiting for output from the computer, Ramon and the chairperson began to discuss departmental matters as they affect graduate students. Ramon then brought up his observations of the previous evening in the cafeteria, and repeated his question as to whether or not Professor Smith was giving him enough attention.

Upon receiving his computer output, the chairperson went back to his department office, called Professor Smith, and asked him to come to the office immediately for a discussion.

What was the most probable topic of the conversation between the chairperson and Professor Smith?

1. Professor Smith's lack of attention to Ramon's progress in graduate school.
2. Professor Smith's meeting with Jan Adams the previous evening.
3. The chairperson's recommendations for better procedures at the computer center.
4. The health of Professor Smith's mother-in-law.

The discussions of these alternative explanations begin on page 227.

94

Oh! So Proper!

The English class that Martha Anderson is helping to teach is going very well. The Vietnamese, Cambodian, and Central American students seem to enjoy one another and are adjusting to each other well. The men and women frequently help one another. Having had very little exposure to other cultures, Martha is amazed at their ease of interaction and often asks the other instructor about the different behaviors she observes in the classroom. The students are all very polite to each other even when they do not seem to be able to understand each other. They are also especially polite when they are talking to her or to the other instructor, always addressing them in very formal polite titles.

Martha would like to develop relationships with some of the students and to make them feel more at home. In one particular instance, as she talks in private with Vien Thuy Ng, she asks him to call her by her first name, saying, "My name is Martha; please call me Martha!" Vien responds by acknowledging that he does indeed know her name, but, "Would it not be good to call you by your proper title?" She persists, saying that is too formal and that they can just be good friends and go by first names. Vien just smiles and nods, but he does not return to the English class the next week.

What could explain what happened here?

1. Vien Thuy Ng thought that Martha was too aggressive and forward to him, as women do not talk to men.
2. Martha should not have singled out one individual person. Vien did not like being singled out.
3. The English class was too complicated for Vien and he did not really know what was going on.
4. Martha violated a rather intricate system of hierarchy that exists in Southeast Asian countries.

The discussions of these alternative explanations begin on page 228.

95

Failing to Appear at the Appointed Time

Mariko, who had recently arrived from Japan, was a student at a large U.S. university. Although at first apprehensive, she had become accustomed to the different routines and lifestyle of the United States and was doing quite well in her courses. She had become quite good friends with one of her classmates, Linda, and the two often had lunch together. One afternoon, the professor in a class the two women took together asked for two volunteers to come in early the next morning to help code some research data. Linda volunteered and suggested that Mariko might also be willing. Mariko replied hesitantly that she did not think her English was good enough for her to do it and that it would be better to ask for another volunteer. Linda said that Mariko would be quite capable and told the professor that she and Mariko would do the work. The next day, Mariko failed to turn up and Linda was obliged to do all the work herself. The next time she saw Mariko she asked her rather coldly what had happened to her. Mariko apologized and said that she had had to study for an exam that day and did not really feel capable of doing the work. Linda exasperatedly asked her why she had not said so clearly at the time Linda committed them to do it. Mariko just looked down and said nothing.

How would you explain Mariko's failure to state explicitly her intentions not to come?

1. Mariko did not really understand what was asked of her and did not want to show her lack of comprehension in front of the class.
2. Mariko felt it wrong to give a direct refusal to the professor.
3. Mariko probably forgot or confused the time but was too embarrassed to admit her silly mistake.
4. Mariko resented Linda's publicly volunteering her without asking her first.

The discussions of these alternative explanations begin on page 228.

96

Participation in a Seminar

Michael, who comes from an extended family in Nigeria whose members enjoy a great deal of contact, was very proud upon receiving a letter informing him that he had been selected for a fellowship that would allow him to pursue graduate studies in the United States. His family members made his award a major topic of conversation. Upon his arrival in the United States, he attended an orientation program with

50 other students. He later began his graduate student seminars, where attendance ranged from 10 in specialized courses to 30 in courses required of all first-year graduate students. The professors, working under a norm widely accepted in the United States, treated students equally in the classes, giving special attention when students came to the professors' offices with individualized questions. Michael felt that his contributions during seminars were not given sufficient attention and follow-up by the rest of the class. After a few months in the United States, he was not enjoying his sojourn and was not doing particularly well in his classes.

If Michael came to you to try to sort out the reasons for his feelings, what issue would you raise?

1. Michael did not have a good predeparture orientation to the United States while still in Nigeria.
2. The professors should have sensed that Michael was upset and should have made efforts to call Michael into their offices to discuss matters.
3. Michael had not been exposed to an educational system in Nigeria that was good enough to prepare him for advanced study in the United States.
4. Michael was reacting to a loss in status.

The discussions of these alternative explanations begin on page 229.

97

The Eager Teacher

Upon graduating college with a degree in English education with a Spanish minor, Rick Meyers accepted a position teaching English in a fairly large and progressive coeducational school in Merida, Mexico, capital city of the state of Yucatan. He had met the language director earlier that year while on a spring recess tour of Mexico and felt quite comfortable with him.

Eager to start the new school year off right, Rick spent a considerable amount of time in preparation of lessons and materials and in extra-help sessions with students. It seemed as if he was always doing something school related, often spending his lunch hour, free periods, and after-school hours with small groups of students.

Although his relationships with the students were growing, after the first few weeks, Rick noticed that his fellow teachers seemed cold and removed. He was seldom invited to after-school and weekend get-togethers or sought out during free times at school. Not sure what to make of this, Rick kept more and more to himself, feeling increasingly lonely and rejected.

What is the major issue of concern for Rick?

1. It is not common or acceptable for teachers in Mexico to show so much personal attention to students.
2. Rick has not spent the requisite amount of social time with his fellow workers.
3. The other teachers were resentful, as most of the students saw Rick as someone special and paid him particular attention.
4. Rick expected to be perceived as an expert. When this was not the case, he was disappointed that his talents were not utilized by all.

The discussions of these alternative explanations begin on page 230.

98

Special Educational Needs

Qin Yu had fully intended to return to China to continue teaching physics at her university after completing her doctoral studies in the United States. But, as is common for many international students, her sentiments and situations changed, and, fortunately for her, so did the job market. Qin Yu was able to obtain a teaching position in a large midwestern university.

Some years later, Qin Yu married a man in a similar situation and began to raise a family, a true Chinese American family that would honor both the couple's Chinese traditions and those of their new homeland. Their second child, a daughter named Yung Soon (affectionately called Sue by her American neighbors and others who knew her), was born with Down's syndrome. At 5 years of age, Sue began to attend a school for children with developmental disabilities. Both teachers and aides found Sue to be cheerful, affectionate, and eager to interact with those around her.

In the course of their daily routine, the aides spent much time playing with Sue and teaching her simple vocabulary and daily living skills. One aide in particular taught Sue to fold her hands together and bow slightly while repeating, "Ahh-so!" Sue received so much reinforcement for this behavior that she would repeat it whenever she saw her aides or upon meeting someone new. She continued to repeat this behavior at home, especially when new guests arrived, completely infuriating her parents. No matter what Qin Yu or her husband did, Sue continued this behavior.

After a few weeks, Qin Yu furiously approached the teachers, aides, and administrators at Sue's school and demanded that they stop this behavior and that they desist from teaching her daughter any more such repulsive behaviors. Two weeks went by and Sue's behavior did not change. Feeling she had no other recourse, Qin Yu pulled Sue out of the school and refused to take her back.

What underlying issue is the cause of Qin Yu's anger and subsequent behavior?

1. Qin Yu had heard a great deal about parent-teacher collaboration in American schools and was upset that her desires and needs had not been responded to adequately.

2. Saying "ahh-so" is a stereotype many Americans have of the Japanese. Qin Yu was offended at being considered Japanese.

3. Qin Yu thought the aides were mocking Sue and her family by making her learn and repeat such a simple phrase.

4. Qin Yu was experiencing classic symptoms of a "Supermom." She was overworked, overstressed, and obviously taking on too many demands. The fast-paced American lifestyle was just not suitable for her.

The discussions of these alternative explanations begin on page 231.

99

Interpreting for the Hard of Hearing

Jill was a hardworking university student who worked 20 hours a week as an oral interpreter for deaf and hard-of-hearing students. She became fascinated with this work after taking a sign-language course. She later received training from Julie, a middle-aged woman who had lost her hearing in her early 20s. Because of her own hearing loss, Julie was able to help her trainees understand the importance of their work.

Julie explained that the functions of an interpreter are to transliterate what is being said to the client, to work with the client at a comfortable distance, and to act as the client's voice as the need arises. For lip-readers, this means enunciating and repeating every word very clearly as it is said to the client, without voice, and with as little lag time as possible. Jill was taught to use a variety of methods, including sign language and gestures, to help in interpreting information, while being sensitive to nonverbal cues from the client.

Jill's first client was a young man named Ted, who was enrolled in a lecture-based computer science class held in a hall that accommodated 150 students. The professor relied heavily on overhead transparencies to illustrate his points. Ted insisted on sitting in the back of the room. Jill sat on a chair next to him, so that Ted could read her lips and also see the transparencies. Jill cleverly used the reflections of the transparencies in the windows behind Ted to help explain the information. She used gestures, words, and sign language to keep up with the pace of the lecturer.

Because Ted failed to keep his appointment to meet with Jill and get acquainted before their work in the class began, she never realized that he did not want anyone else to know that he was hard of hearing. He quickly became very displeased with Jill's use of her hands in relaying information and insisted that she stop. Her only recourse was to sit on her hands and mouth the words to convey the instructor's lesson. Jill felt that certain material was being left out, and that she was not doing her job adequately.

What was the source of Jill's frustration?

1. Jill was concerned that she would lose her position, as her trainer was very specific about the skills that were to be used in oral interpretation.
2. Jill was torn between using as many methods as possible to interpret for Ted and simple transliterating (mouthing the words) to convey the information and thus leaving out part of the material.
3. Ted did not seem to be cooperating with the program's policies, including meeting with the interpreter beforehand to establish the parameters of the working relationship.
4. Jill was experiencing the burnout that comes with working in such a highly emotionally charged position.

The discussions of these alternative explanations begin on page 231.

100

The Local Gang

Pedro is a 13-year-old immigrant Filipino who arrived in Hawaii just 2 months ago. He is sent to a high school where there are a lot of other

Filipinos, both immigrant and local-born. On the first day of classes, not knowing anybody and wanting to make friends, Pedro approaches a group of Filipino boys, all of whom were born in Hawaii. Pedro is dressed in a polo shirt and black bell-bottom pants. The local group members are all wearing plain T-shirts and faded jeans. Pedro starts a conversation with the usual Filipino greeting of "Kumusta?" One of the local group members responds in English, and the conversation goes on with Pedro speaking in broken English with a Filipino accent and a lot of Filipino words in between. Pedro also notices that the boys keep looking at him from head to foot and talking to each other frequently in a type of English (local Pidgin) that he has never heard before, thus excluding him from the conversation. This makes it difficult for him to be part of the group. He is also surprised that the boys, although Filipinos, do not really understand the Filipino language, except for two or three words. Slowly, the boys leave, one by one, until Pedro is by himself.

The following day, Pedro approaches the group again, but notices that they are ignoring him. Finally, one of the group says to Pedro, "Hey, brah, ovah dah, Flips from P.I., yeah? Go join'em, yeah?" (Hey, brother, over there are some Filipinos from the Philippines. Go and join them, okay?) Pedro feels very hurt and upset.

Why does the local group reject Pedro's efforts to be part of the group?

1. The boys feel that Pedro should not be part of the group because he is an immigrant Filipino and not a local-born one.

2. They consider Pedro's clothing to be strange and unfashionable (they consider bell-bottoms to be definitely outdated), and they do not want to be seen in public with him.

3. Pedro does not speak the same language as the local group, and they feel that they cannot really communicate with him.

4. The boys in the group, like many preadolescents, frequently have difficulty accepting new members.

The discussions of these alternative explanations begin on page 232.

101

Office Hours

Karl had recently joined the faculty at a prestigious university in the United States, after earning his doctorate and teaching for many years in the former East Germany. He had been quite happy that things had changed in the two Germanys and that he now had greater freedoms to study and teach in other countries. He was excited about this upcoming opportunity, as it would enable him to work closely with colleagues and students in his area of interest. He was especially looking forward to the opportunity to interact with American students on a one-to-one basis and to discuss ideas in depth during office hours as he had been accustomed to doing with his students in Germany.

A month into his teaching, Karl's enthusiasm began to wane. He had prepared quite detailed lectures and had chosen what he thought were adequate textbooks to supplement his course. He had become quite bothered, however, by two unanticipated occurrences. First, despite his enthusiasm for the material, his students never asked questions or engaged in dialogue in class. Rather, they seemed quite content simply to record everything in their notebooks in a passive manner. But what really was confusing was that many of the students seemed to show up during his office hours, wanting to discuss rather basic material he had already presented in class. Karl wondered why these students were wasting his time with such trivialities. Office hours should be for serious issues. Why did the students not ask these questions in class?

If Karl came to you with this question, what would you suggest?

1. The students considered interrupting the professor during class to be impolite and discourteous.

2. The students were afraid of asking "stupid" questions in front of their peers.

3. The students felt they must review their class notes before speaking alone with the professor, so they could speak intelligently.

4. The students felt that it was important for their final grades for the professor to know them individually.

The discussions of these alternative explanations begin on page 232.

102

Rosita's Homeroom Teacher

Rosita is a fifth-grade student who immigrated with her family to the United States from Mexico approximately 2 years ago. She seems to speak English rather well and to complete her schoolwork with few problems. She is, however, reading several years below her grade level and performs rather poorly on standardized tests of academic achievement. Rosita's homeroom teacher, Mrs. Jones, cannot understand why Rosita's comprehension is so poor, especially as she has arranged for Rosita to go to the bilingual lab for instructional support once a week. Mrs. Jones can offer only two explanations for the discrepancy she observes. Either Mrs. Lopez, the bilingual teacher, has been doing some of Rosita's homework for her or Rosita is in need of a referral to the special education department for help with a possible learning disability or to explore other cognitive deficiencies.

What is the best explanation for why Rosita's academic performance does not seem to be congruent with her verbal skills?

1. Being Hispanic also, the bilingual teacher is overly sympathetic to Rosita and has, in fact, sometimes done Rosita's homework for her.

2. It is not uncommon for students whose first language is not English to be able to understand English on a very literal level, but not comprehend the subtleties and complexities of the language when reading independently.

3. Minority students relate better to teachers who share their same ethnic backgrounds or racial identities. Rosita performs well for Mrs. Lopez because they are both Hispanic.

4. Research has shown that large numbers of students in certain minority groups display an above-average incidence of being either learning disabled or mentally retarded.

The discussions of these alternative explanations begin on page 233.

103

The Unpopular Professor

Dr. Fazio, a recent immigrant from southern Italy, is a respected, well-published professor at an American university. Despite his illustrious position and acknowledged expertise in the field of Italian literature, his classes repeatedly receive unfavorable ratings, especially from female students. Clara Smith, the dean of students, decides to investigate this situation. After conducting many interviews with students in Dr. Fazio's classes, she begins to notice a pattern. Several of the females complain that Dr. Fazio stands too close when discussing things with them, makes offensive sexual innuendoes, and even, on occasion, blows in their ears. They do not want to report him, however, because they know of his power and status in the academic community. Dean Smith makes up her mind to speak with Dr. Fazio. She arrives at his office the next morning. After some pleasant chitchat about the weather, she brings up the subject of Dr. Fazio's alleged sexual advances. She explains that many women students feel violated and threatened by his behavior. Dr. Fazio laughs and explains that physical closeness and sexual banter are an accepted part of Italian culture. His students should not take offense at his behavior. On the contrary, they should relax and try to enjoy his compliments. He is merely behaving as any "real" Italian man would.

For someone in Dean Smith's position, what would be the appropriate response to Dr. Fazio's explanations?

1. As his behavior is a part of his culture, Dr. Fazio should not be expected to change. He should be allowed to continue as before.

2. Dr. Fazio should warn students at the beginning of the semester of his cultural background and its influence on his classroom behavior.

3. Female students should be advised not to take Dr. Fazio's class.

4. Dean Smith should fire Dr. Fazio immediately and should be wary when male Italian professors come to the school in the future.

5. Dr. Fazio must discontinue his behaviors, even if he says this would be going against his culture's norms.

The discussions of these alternative explanations begin on page 234.

104

Silence and Talkativeness

Deborah Franklin had just completed her student teaching assignment in a small town in California. Her husband was offered a good job in the electronics industry in Los Angeles, and the couple decided that it would be best for their family to move there. Deborah and her husband packed up their belongings (largely comprising gifts from their recent wedding), rented a truck, and drove the freeways into Los Angeles. After about a week of job searching, Deborah was offered a job teaching ninth-grade social studies; she was to replace a woman who had suddenly become ill.

One day, Deborah planned a lesson based on the question, "In the entire history of America, who have been some influential men and women?" Even though she had never been able to generate much class discussion, she thought that many of her students could offer their opinions and that lively classroom interactions would occur. However, Deborah found that only a few students offered their opinions, and most of these were the Anglo students. Disappointed but not discouraged, she tried to think of ways to encourage more class discussion in the future.

Walking across a nearby playground about an hour after school the next day, Deborah observed a number of the African American students playing with both Anglos and Hispanics. There were no other teachers or adults nearby. Some of the African Americans at the playground were students in her social studies class. She overheard them arguing about the prominence of various people in both the athletic and the entertainment industries. The African Americans were especially articulate and witty in putting their opinions forward. Deborah asked herself, "Why are the African Americans so verbal on the playground but not in my classroom?"

If Deborah asked this question of you, what would you say?

1. The African Americans are more comfortable using their verbal skills on the playground than they are in the classroom.

2. Verbal skills are not particularly highly valued within the African American community.

3. African Americans are less familiar than members of other cultural groups with Deborah's classroom topic, "influential men and women."

4. African Americans are more sensitive to the mix of cultural groups in the classroom than they are on the playground.

The discussions of these alternative explanations begin on page 235.

Incident 83 (p. 197): Rationales for the Alternative Explanations

1. This is the best explanation. In many cultures (such as African or Arab), communication takes place through associations. Everything that is associated with a phenomenon or idea is considered relevant in thinking about or communicating the concept. Such communication may be highly indirect, and reasoning may be more intuitive than analytic or deductive. Most Western cultures, by contrast, are strongly abstractive; that is, they communicate in

more abstract but directly relevant terms and arrive at conclusions through step-by-step deductions or logically derived inductions (at least in the academic world). Tal's presentations are highly associative, as this is the way one would demonstrate knowledge of a subject as well as intellectual ability within his culture. The more restrained, abstractive thinking demanded by his professors probably seems bare or even simplistic to him; recall that Tal was not impressed by Tony's papers. With practice, Tal would probably be quite capable of adapting his communicative style more closely to that of the British (at least in his formal, academic work). Both Tal and his professors must first be made aware of where the differences lie in order to eradicate the confusions.

2. There is often a tendency to attribute poor performance of others to their lack of ability, without first considering what situational factors could be influencing their performance. Tal was a top student in his own country and so would be expected to perform at least adequately. There would seem, therefore, to be other factors hindering his performance. Please reconsider your answer and choose again.

3. Although this is true to the extent that Tal's Gambian education did not adequately prepare him for the British system, it is not because Gambian education is less rigorous or demanding; it is simply different. There is a more specific explanation. Please choose again.

4. Although it is possible that initial uncertainties or stresses in Tal's life may have affected his work, there is no indication in the story that this was the case. There was a deeper reason for his confusion. A general explanation concerning confusion due to settling in and culture shock is rarely helpful. Please choose again.

Incident 84 (p. 198). Rationales for the Alternative Explanations

1. Actually, visa problems are frequent on large American university campuses, and there are well-established ways of dealing with such problems. If Mrs. Simpson could not deal with them directly, she would be able to refer the student to people who could help, such as the foreign student adviser's office. Please choose again.

2. This is the best answer. Mrs. Simpson was playing a role that could have been played by any of a hundred people. It was the body in the department secretary's chair to whom the student was complaining, not Mrs. Simpson personally. Although, admittedly, this is easier to point out than to internalize, people working with Mrs. Simpson should remind her that there is nothing personal in such encounters, unpleasant as they are. Many cross-cultural encounters are based on roles that could be filled by any of hundreds of people, but there is still a strong tendency to interpret negative instances personally. Perhaps the reason is that Mrs. Simpson quite reasonably feels,

"We are doing a lot for these foreign students who are guests in our country. Why don't they behave like cordial guests?" Because some do not behave cordially, the natural tendency is for hosts to feel they are personally involved—Mrs. Simpson felt that she herself was the target of this student's frustration, not simply her role as department secretary. Another role aspect of this incident is that Indians from wealthy families often have had servants. An unfortunate fact is that often only wealthy families can afford to send sons and daughters overseas for their schooling, as scholarships are not easily available and are highly competitive. These wealthy students may adopt role-based behaviors in their interactions with others, taking on the role of superior when interacting with those they perceive to be fulfilling servantlike roles (as Mrs. Simpson was perceived by this student in her role of secretary). This is a big problem in cross-cultural encounters—figuring out which behaviors directed toward one are role-based and which should be interpreted personally. The concept of role-based behaviors is one every sojourner should have in mind when traveling abroad.

3. Although some foreign students are very able scholars, on the whole they rarely have the reputation of being the best students on American campuses. Please choose again.

4. Although it is true that foreign students sometimes run into plagiarism problems, there is no evidence in this story that this was the case or that plagiarism was somehow involved. Please choose again.

Incident 85 (p. 199). Rationales for the Alternative Explanations

1. After having observed a similar situation resolved differently immediately before, it is unlikely that anyone would accept such behavior directed at him- or herself. It is possible that the students were observing the women employees and assumed there was a two-tiered system of categorization at play—into obvious in-groups and out-groups. However, the rules for entry were clearly posted for all to see. Please select a response that better explains the situation.

2. Although it is often a quick and easy explanation, there is really no indication in the incident that racism was involved. Please select another response.

3. This is the best explanation. This is a classic case of ambiguity and misattribution. There was a high degree of ambiguity in this situation—not all the details were known by all the parties involved, yet quick judgments were made. The second pair of males did not have all the details of the previous situation and understandably expected to be treated as they had seen the first men treated. They did not know what had gone on in Alice's mind when she made her judgment and allowed the first man without ID to enter; they only witnessed the behavior. It is easy to see how they made the misattributions or misjudgments they did. Nonetheless, this does not excuse Alice's and Joanna's behavior; it merely sets it in a context that can be understood.

4. There is no indication in the incident that anybody had a chip on his shoulder. In addition, the allegation of drinking may just be that—an allegation. Here, too, there is no indication that alcohol is the root cause of the problem. Please choose again.

Incident 86 (p. 200). Rationales for the Alternative Explanations

1. It is true that Japanese students revere and respect elderly teachers, but Japanese students tend to revere and respect any and all teachers. The title *sensei,* given to teachers, is a sign of honor and respect. George would most probably have been afforded all the respect coming to any teacher by Japanese students—certainly far more respect than would be given by most American students. Please select an alternative explanation.

2. It is true that there may be certain customs for greeting that are important to the maintenance of interpersonal relationships. However, these students came to the United States with the express intention of learning English in an American context. There is no indication in the story that George's use of English only was the problem. Please select an alternative explanation.

3. This explanation provides the most insight into this situation. In George's classroom there were many instances where instructional style and learning style seemed to be in conflict. George's attempts at friendliness and informality would have been rather uncomfortable for students accustomed to a more formal, structured relationship between teacher and student. In addition, in Japan, where group conformity is strongly encouraged, a teacher would rarely single individual students out from the group. Students thus singled out would become quite uncomfortable, which would explain George's students' reluctance to return to class. On another level, this incident demonstrates how many people who are well-traveled believe they know how to be effective when working intimately with those from other cultures; George's problems clearly suggest that this is not always the case.

4. It is true that George was a new teacher and was probably learning to adapt all that he had learned in school to the real world of teaching. However, in this case, without attending to the cultural differences in learning and teaching style, it was unlikely things would change. There is a better explanation for the problems George experienced. Please choose again.

Incident 87 (p. 202): Rationales for the Alternative Explanations

1. In an ideal world, people would be extremely sensitive to each other and make sure of invitations to participate in such gatherings, but people's busy schedules mean that social niceties are not always followed to the ultimate level. It

is doubtful that the Americans wanted to be rude, and the nature of Friday afternoon gatherings is such that the Americans might have felt that Fumio would have been uncomfortable if he actually participated. Please choose again.

2. This is the best answer. There are often activities within a culture that are meant for a certain in-group, a number of people very familiar with each other and with whom everyone feels comfortable. The purpose of the gatherings is relaxation: People tell jokes based on shared experiences in the culture and generally relieve tension after a busy week. They do not have to try to impress each other, because they already are familiar with the group's members. Fumio would have interfered slightly with these purposes: He would not have been able to understand the points of the jokes, he was not well enough known to everyone to contribute to the relaxed atmosphere, and so on. Good questions for a sojourner to ask him- or herself in Fumio's situation would be, "Are there activities in which only in-group members regularly participate? How often do these include sojourners, even those sojourners in a country for more than 2 or 3 years? If there are such activities, is it realistic for me to be insulted if I am not included?"

3. The Japanese make some of the finest beer in the world, and many enjoy its consumption. Please choose again.

4. Although jealousy toward a colleague who is doing well is always a possibility, ill feelings of American graduate students toward those from other countries are not common enough to constitute a likely explanation here. Just because the Americans asked for help does not mean that they were resentful of the help received. Please choose again.

5. Friday afternoon gatherings of this type are not necessarily (or even frequently) based on specific pairings of males and females. The fact that Fumio had no girlfriend is irrelevant here. Please choose again.

Incident 88 (p. 203): Rationales for the Alternative Explanations

1. This may contain an element of truth, but there is no information in the incident to support this interpretation. The story actually says that Joao "looked forward to attending the new school." Another suggestion is much better than this one. Please choose again.

2. To some extent, this may be true. However, the schools in Providence include students from many ethnic and cultural groups. Joao would have been accustomed to going to school with students from different backgrounds. There is a better explanation. Please choose again.

3. This is the best alternative. The story suggests that Joao's family "felt a deep pride in their Portuguese heritage." While going to school in Providence, Joao

had other native Portuguese students with whom to share his ethnic pride. It is highly likely that the students at his high school in Providence included people from non-Portuguese backgrounds, but their presence might have helped Joao become even more strongly aware of his contrasting identity as a native Portuguese. When Joao entered the school in San Francisco, he probably had no difficulty becoming accustomed to the presence of students from a variety of backgrounds. But it was difficult for him to be the only native Portuguese in that school. It was even more difficult for him to be identified by some of the teachers as a member of a non-Portuguese group. Because he felt strongly Portuguese, their viewing him as a Central American confused Joao. His rude comment to the teacher probably resulted from his confusion. The teachers meant to be helpful to Joao, of course. They probably thought of him as coming from one of the Spanish-speaking countries to the South because they needed to fit him into one of the ethnic/cultural categories already familiar in the school as well as to them. As the Portuguese language is quite similar to Spanish (so that Joao did understand people when they addressed him in Spanish), they found it convenient to categorize him along with other Spanish-speaking students.

4. This may be true for some young people when they are away from home for the first time, but there is nothing in the incident to support the interpretation that Joao inevitably would do something to embarrass himself. Please select an alternative response.

Incident 89 (p. 204): Rationales for the Alternative Explanations

1. This is the best answer. Feelings of culture shock in general and frustrations with their jobs in particular can make sojourners tense and angry. Because they do not understand these feelings very well (as they are not able to analyze the exact reasons for them, given their unfamiliarity with the local culture), sojourners do not know what to do with them. A fairly frequent response is for them to lash out at convenient targets who do not have much authority over them. (Obviously, it is unwise to lash out at authority figures.) In many cases, this may be a good friend who is only trying to help as best he or she can. Unfortunately, the target can also be a professional in cross-cultural contact, such as a foreign student adviser at a college or university or a member of the personnel office in a multinational organization assigned to help sojourners adjust. Neither foreign student advisers nor personnel officers, despite their visibility, have much authority, so they are convenient targets for sojourner frustration. Being the target of such frustration too frequently leads to burnout and to premature departure from the profession of working with sojourners. As with other aspects of the cross-cultural experience discussed throughout these materials, lashing out due to frustration has to be examined as an expected part of a sojourn, not as an anomaly.

2. Even if Jan's feelings about her students were justified, it would not seem reasonable for her to direct her outburst at Amanda, who seems to be a genuinely good friend. Please choose again.

3. There is no evidence that Jan was a bad teacher. She appeared to be very concerned with doing a good job and seemed to have prepared lessons. She could only be considered bad if her outburst was indicative of a poorly qualified person. But such outbursts, although not pleasant to people who are their targets, are fairly frequent on sojourns. Thus it is best to examine the totality of the experience and the context in addition to focusing on the individual. Please choose again.

4. Although our validation sample found this a strong possibility, there is no evidence that describes either the presence or the absence of outlets in Jan's life in China. The validation sample members obviously felt, from their own past experiences, that outlets are sometimes hard to find on sojourns. As a footnote, psychologists are in disagreement about the use of outlets for frustration and aggression even if they are readily available. Some psychologists argue that even if outlets are available, they do not drain off unwanted frustration and aggression. Rather, because the draining-off process is pleasurable, the use of outlets reinforces the expression of frustration. This draining-off procedure can be pleasurable even if the expression is not positive or prosocial (e.g., kicking one's dog is not positive, but it can be pleasurable). Because the draining off is pleasurable, people will seek out other opportunities for the expression of frustration, not all of which can be positive. Please choose another explanation.

Incident 90 (p. 204): Rationales for the Alternative Explanations

1. Although there is an increasing body of knowledge and literature emerging that focuses on the adult learner that teachers should utilize when planning instruction for adults, the students in this incident were not that much older than the typical high school student. These young farmworkers would not require these kinds of modifications. Please select a different explanation.

2. Although these students probably all spoke Pidgin, they also understood and regularly spoke Standard English. This is not a critical factor here. Please select a different explanation.

3. This is the best explanation. It has been found that Hawaiian Americans (as well as people in many other cultures without long experience with written language) typically teach each other, and therefore learn, in context rather than out of context. Although Robert's professional training as well as his own educational experience have stressed out-of-context learning (through books, films, and so on) that would be applied at a later time, many people learn more and become more involved and motivated when taught in an

in-context situation. An out-of-the-classroom hands-on approach would probably have facilitated Robert's students' learning process.

4. On the contrary, these people had purchased the machinery and had requested Robert's presence. Please try again.

Incident 91 (p. 206): Rationales for the Alternative Explanations

1. This is not the best answer. Native Hawaiian children actually perform better in school when allowed to work in groups, rather than individually. They are socialized into the family in such a way that they are recognized for helping to maintain the group's needs. The individualized learning center approach does not allow for small groups to work, and thus would be in conflict with their socialization history. Please select another explanation.

2. This is the best explanation. The Hawaiian family socializes children to support the group, rather than encourages members to stand out individually. This is true in many cultures throughout the world that value the group collectivity more than single individuals' needs. Group reinforcement is typically a more powerful motivator in such cultures. In this incident, the individual recognition of having his or her name somehow recorded was not something valued by the Hawaiian child; rather, it was shunned. The Hawaiian children, then, may not have been motivated to achieve the intended goals. Team or group formation and recognition would be better motivators for Native Hawaiian children.

3. It is true that among Hawaiian teachers there is greater representation of Japanese than of other ethnic groups. However, most public school teacher traits are similar, whether the teachers are Japanese American, mainland American, or otherwise. The fact that Marie was not representative of the majority of teachers is not a critical issue in this case. Please select another explanation.

4. Believing that an individual is culturally deprived or culturally deficient in some manner assumes that one group has a cultural or genetic superiority over another. This view should not be taken, as it is unfounded and unproductive when used as the basis for change programs. Rather, a culturally different point of view should be adopted. The problem here lies at the interface of two cultures, that of the Native Hawaiian child's home upbringing and socialization and that of the school, which may make demands and have expectations quite different from each other. The child then is the loser as he or she attempts to respond to school stimuli with behaviors he or she has learned at home. Although there is a conflict of cultures in this incident, it is not the result of a cultural deficit or deprivation. There is a better explanation. Please try again.

Incident 92 (p. 207): Rationales for the Alternative Explanations

1. Although many children are told not to accept food from strangers, this probably does not apply in this situation. Please choose again.
2. This is the best explanation. Jehovah's Witnesses do not celebrate holidays and other events in the same way those in the majority do. Birthdays, for example, as well as national holidays, are not celebrated. Although this may create some confusion and hurt feelings initially, children and teachers, can become sensitive and understanding about such differences and make appropriate modifications.
3. There is no indication in the incident that John felt he would have an obligation to Sam if he accepted the treat. Please select an alternative explanation.
4. Although it is increasingly the case that children bring a diversity of eating habits into the classroom, there is no indication that this is so here. Please select an alternative explanation.

Incident 93 (p. 207): Rationales for the Alternative Explanations

1. Although this could be of concern to the chair, it is doubtful that he would call Professor Smith in immediately to discuss the matter. In addition, the amount of time a given professor spends with a given student is a matter normally governed by academic freedom, meaning that the chair would have to be very careful about introducing the matter with a professor. If this was the chairperson's concern, he would probably have chosen a convenient moment when he and Smith happened to be together for some other reason, such as at a cocktail party. Then he might mention the matter quietly and indirectly. Please choose again.
2. This is the best answer. The issue of sexual harassment is a very sensitive one on American campuses. The question is, How much individual attention can a professor give to a student of the opposite sex without it causing embarrassment to and pressure on the student? The thought that could go through the student's mind is, "If I say no to this informal dinner invitation, is this going to affect my professional relationship with this professor?" Rather than put any student in such a quandary, some schools have instituted informal standards that discourage any one-on-one informal meetings outside the department between professors and students of the opposite sex. The problem in this case would have been lessened if the professor and Jan had joined Ramon rather than sat at a separate table. Then the gathering would have been one of several students with a professor, which is considered okay. It may seem as if the chair was overreacting, but there have been enough charges of sexual harassment at American schools, involving hours and hours of administrators' time, that he probably wanted to make sure he averted

a potential problem. (As the American saying goes, A stitch in time saves nine.) The chair did not want such a problem in his department, because he would then have to mediate charges and countercharges and perhaps even deal with police and attorneys.

3. This is not the sort of problem the chair would make an issue in a meeting he called so abruptly. He might bring it up at another time, such as at the computer users' committee, but he would not call Professor Smith and request his immediate presence for such a discussion. Please choose again.

4. Although the chair may have wanted to ask after the health of Professor Smith's mother-in-law, as it was common knowledge she was ill, there was no reason for him to call for an immediate meeting to do so. Please choose again.

Incident 94 (p. 209): Rationales for the Alternative Explanations

1. In many Southeast Asian countries the roles of women may be restricted in some ways, including in how women may approach men. However, this class is in the United States and there are some students from other countries as well as the instructors interacting together. That the class is mixed and the students seem to get along fairly well suggests this is really not the reason for Vien's disappearance from the class. There is a better explanation. Please select again.

2. It is true that individuals from Asian societies do not like to be singled out. However, in this instance, this minor correction could not be considered a singling out. Martha was talking with Vien alone, so there would be no great embarrassment involved. There is more going on. Please select again.

3. This conclusion can hardly be drawn, as the scenario states that all seemed to be going well in the class. Please select again.

4. This is the best answer. Southeast Asians have a very intricate system of status hierarchy, which Martha violated by trying to downplay her role or perceived status. Her attempt to convince Vien to address her by her first name may not have been the total cause for Vien's not wanting to return, however. Probably if she had just suggested it and then left it open for Vien to choose he may have felt more comfortable, but her persistence in the matter forced Vien into a situation where he had to relinquish a value that affected his whole worldview or lifestyle.

Incident 95 (p. 209): Rationales for the Alternative Explanations

1. This seems unlikely, as it is stated that she was doing well in her classes, so her comprehension was probably quite reasonable. Moreover, if she was

confused she would probably have asked Linda to explain. Please choose another explanation.

2. This is the best explanation. In many cultures it is considered rude to give a direct rejection or refusal. Hesitancy and ambiguity are used to convey reluctance and so to avoid embarrassment to either party. Linda, however, failed to perceive this and so regarded Mariko's actions as basically dishonest or deceptive. To Mariko, however, honesty is of lesser value than the preservation of dignity in interpersonal interactions. Thus one of the main sources of cultural conflict in this situation concerns the differing weights attached to honesty. Whereas many Western cultures view the direct and honest statement of intentions or opinions as a very positive trait, others regard such behavior more ambivalently, or even as discourtesy. When one is uncertain of the cultural "rules," discretion and tact are always advisable.

3. This is possible, but it is likely that Mariko would have admitted such a mistake and offered profuse apologies. There is a more probable explanation. Please choose again.

4. Although she may have been a little disturbed at having her name proffered without being asked, she probably would not have resented it. Although she did not want to do the task, she was probably flattered by Linda's confidence in her. There is a more precise explanation. Please choose again.

Incident 96 (p. 210): Rationales for the Alternative Explanations

1. It may be true that Michael did not have access to a good predeparture program, but this answer does not directly address Michael's feelings. Undoubtedly, attention should be given to better orientation programs, but given that good orientation programs are still the exception rather than the rule, people who work with sojourners must deal with people who have infrequently had opportunities to work through their feelings concerning cross-cultural experiences. There is a better explanation. Please choose again.

2. In an ideal world, the professors would have been prepared for Michael's reactions and would have been willing to do something about them. In actuality, however, professors rarely take it upon themselves to intervene in the lives of foreign students unless they are directly requested to do so. Even then, lack of training on the professors' parts in helping sojourners sort out their feelings means that (at best) referrals to the foreign student adviser's office will be forthcoming. Please choose again.

3. There is no evidence that the educational system in Nigeria did not prepare Michael for advanced study. In many countries, the educational systems are very hierarchical, with few students going on from high school (or its equivalent) to the limited number of places available in college or university.

The few students who do go to college are most often very able, and as the governments have relatively few colleges to support, the ones that exist are good. Please choose again.

4. This is the best explanation. In Nigeria, being a graduate student is a high-status position. Michael is looked up to, given deference, is the pride of his family, and so forth. In the United States, being a graduate student is not a particularly high-status position. Graduate students are not given much deference, if any. On many U.S. campuses, much younger students, if they happen to be football players, are given much more status than graduate students. Michael may have been expecting special attention from authorities in his introduction to the United States, not placement in a general orientation with 50 others. He may have expected a special introduction in his seminars, such as, "We look forward to the contributions of the expert from Nigeria." But such singling out for attention is rare for foreign students in the United States. Loss of status can cause feelings of mild depression and annoyance. In good orientation programs, this is the sort of fact that can be introduced with role plays and/or thorough discussions. Administrators of programs designed to help sojourners should communicate that trainees should not feel personally discriminated against when they meet the status loss that accompanies many sojourns.

Incident 97 (p. 211): Rationales for the Alternative Explanations

1. Our validation sample suggested this as a possibility, but one of the authors' firsthand experiences demonstrate otherwise. Especially in the larger and more progressive schools in Mexico, contact between teachers and students is quite frequent and in many ways expected, as it helps to build the sense of belonging or inclusion that is critical for many to experience educational success. Please choose again.

2. This is the best answer. Although skillful in his teaching and quite successful on the job, Rick's participation with other staff had been minimal. In many places, the degree to which one socializes with others is of critical importance. Most Americans want to perform their tasks efficiently and well, but they should remember, especially when interacting cross-culturally, that they need to pay attention also to social norms and expectations with colleagues to ensure success in the workplace.

3. There is no indication in the story that the students were responding to anything more than Rick's genuine offers of time and assistance. There is a better explanation. Please try again.

4. Although this may result in problems for some people in some situations, there is no indication that this was an issue for Rick. There is a better answer. Please choose again.

Incident 98 (p. 212): Rationales for the Alternative Explanations

1. Although it is true that increasingly parents and teachers are working in collaboration, there does not seem to be any indication in the story that this was the issue. Please select another alternative.

2. This is the best explanation. Too often, well-meaning Americans (and others), having little frequent interaction with those from distant shores, simply lump together many people who look similar into one large category. Such is the basis of stereotypes—people's need to simplify the world around them by putting those elements with seemingly similar characteristics into the same categories. In this situation, not only were the teachers and aides putting Japanese and Chinese into the same category, they were displaying their ignorance of the historical animosities between the two countries that would prohibit such linkage. Qin Yu was extremely upset about her daughter's being taught to repeat a characteristically Japanese phrase, something unheard of in China.

3. There is no indication that this was the case here. Qin Yu was apparently quite understanding of her daughter's developmental needs. Please select another alternative.

4. There is no indication in the incident that Qin Yu was taking on too much responsibility or was overworked. Please choose another explanation.

Incident 99 (p. 213): Rationales for the Alternative Explanations

1. Jill may very well have been concerned that she could lose her job. However, she needed to remember that although the trainer expected her to use as many skills as possible in her work, she also was expected to be sensitive to the needs of the specific client and her or his preferred mode of communication. Another explanation more adequately addresses the situation. Please choose again.

2. This is the best explanation. Jill has been trained to use as many methods as possible to communicate with her client so that he could learn most effectively. She was concerned that she would not be able to provide Ted with direct access to the flow of conversation in the lecture at a fast enough pace using only transliteration. Ted, therefore, might not do as well in class as possible.

3. This may be true to some extent. In some instances, individuals may not wish others to know that they are hard of hearing. Although there have been major strides taken in deaf pride, including the crowning of 1994's Miss America, there are still some who would prefer not to be known as having impaired hearing. However, there is a better explanation for the frustration Jill felt. Please choose again.

4. Jill may have been working in a highly stressful and demanding position, but there is no indication in the incident that she was experiencing burnout. Please select another response.

Incident 100 (p. 214): Rationales for the Alternative Explanations

1. This is the best explanation. There are underlying conflicts between local-born Filipinos and immigrant Filipinos in Hawaii that have led to segregation of the two groups on school grounds. The conflict can be traced historically to the plantation experience of early Filipino immigrant workers in Hawaii, who were stereotyped negatively by other peoples in Hawaii. In an effort to be accepted and to assimilate into the dominant group of a culture, local-born first- and second-generation immigrants often downplay their cultural origins and heritage and may seek to differentiate themselves from recently arrived immigrants. They see themselves as full citizens of the country to which they or their parents immigrated and may resent being identified by their cultural origins. Newly arrived immigrants usually fail to appreciate this attitude and are confused by the lack of cultural identification of the local-born group.

2. Preadolescents are very susceptible to peer pressure and often strive to be like everyone else. To them, anyone who appears different may be unacceptable. This answer is partially correct, but there is a better explanation for the group's behavior. Try again.

3. Pedro's strong Filipino accent as he speaks English is very hard to follow. Besides, he uses Filipino words that the group does not understand. However, the reason for their rejection goes beyond differences in language and communication difficulties. There is a better explanation than this that goes to the core of the problem. Please choose again.

4. Preadolescent boys and girls are moving from childhood to adulthood and may be experiencing identity crises. They choose friends and close their societies by rejecting outsiders. This explanation is thus partially correct, but it is incomplete. Please look for an explanation that takes into account the fact that all of the people involved are from the Philippines or are of Filipino ancestry.

Incident 101 (p. 215): Rationales for the Alternative Explanations

1. Although this may be true in classrooms in some countries, it is not the case in the United States. Indeed, intellectual curiosity is valued by professors and is taken to be an indication of a serious student. Please select an alternative explanation.

2. Many students experience a certain amount of hesitancy before posing a question within a group setting, especially when the classroom environment

is competitive. Although this response could partially explain the students' behavior in this situation, it does not hold true for all students or for the majority of American classrooms. Most American instructors try hard to create classroom environments that welcome questions and interaction. Please select an alternative explanation.

3. This is quite logical and reasonable at an individual level, but the issue here concerns group behavior. Please select an alternative explanation.

4. This is the best explanation. Americans place a great value on individuality. Often, students feel "lost in the system" or that they are little more than numbers. In response, many try hard to counterbalance those feelings by actively seeking opportunities to meet with instructors to establish some type of personal rapport. Among students who are new to a university or to an academic discipline, deep and intellectually stimulating questions are not yet the norm. Therefore, common ground can best be sought only with available information. Beyond this, students may also have the selfish hope that any rapport they can establish with a teacher will result in better final grades. Foreign instructors in the United States must be prepared for their office hours to be filled with these types of issues.

Incident 102 (p. 216): Rationales for the Alternative Explanations

1. There is no evidence to support this statement. What may be true is that Rosita receives explanations from Mrs. Lopez in Spanish, which allows her to comprehend the task better and, in turn, to perform better. This, however, is not the correct response. There is a better explanation for the apparent differences in Rosita's academic success. Please choose again.

2. Based on the information presented in the incident, this is the best explanation. Bilingual students, especially very early in their experience, generally develop two levels of competency when learning to use the dominant language. Many learn to speak a second language and to understand it on a very literal level within a relatively short period of time—as little as a year. However, for students to understand fully and comprehend the subtleties of a language and to be able to use it in the manner expected in schools, 5 to 7 years of instruction and practice may be required. Rosita speaks English well enough to converse with Mrs. Jones and her peers, but probably does not understand the more complex use of language that is required for academic success.

3. Many students from Latino backgrounds need to develop personal relationships with teachers before they are able to achieve maximum benefit from instruction. It is probably easier for Rosita to build rapport with Mrs. Lopez, but that does not mean that Rosita cannot do the same with Mrs. Jones. Although this answer is partially correct, there is another choice that more fully explains the situation. Please choose again.

4. This is incorrect. What is true is that it is not uncommon for students of Latino or African American heritage to be classified as learning disabled or mentally retarded at rates higher than their representation in the general population. Many teachers refer Latino and other children of color to such programs more frequently than they do students who are from the dominant culture. This may be explained in a number of ways—it may be a result of racial discrimination and prejudice on the part of teachers, or of teachers' inability to meet the linguistic needs of some students, or of the presence of bias in the various forms of assessment in common use in classrooms today. Although perhaps true in certain contexts, it is not the best explanation for this situation. Please choose again.

Incident 103 (p. 217): Rationales for the Alternative Explanations

1. This is not a valid response. In the first place, although standing closer to people (spatial orientation) may be a part of Italian culture, blowing into the ears of students is not. Moreover, even if all of Dr. Fazio's actions were accepted by his culture, he should still discontinue these behaviors if they make his students feel uncomfortable. In fact, Dr. Fazio could be legally prosecuted for harassment at many American universities. There are some situations in which, despite people's cultural backgrounds, they simply must change their behaviors or risk getting into trouble with the law. Please select another response.

2. Although warning students about his behavior might make them more pre-pared, it would not make them comfortable with his actions, and therefore cannot be the only solution to this situation. Because he can be legally prosecuted for harassment, Dr. Fazio must change his behaviors. He might want to offer this warning, however, in conjunction with an attempt to modify his behaviors. Significant changes in behavior, especially learning to stand further away from people, require time and practice. If students feel comfort-able enough to tell him when they do not like his behaviors, they may help Dr. Fazio to change. Please choose again.

3. By advising women not to take the course, the dean would deprive them of an opportunity open to men. If women feel uncomfortable with Dr. Fazio's behavior, it is he, not they, who should be advised to change. There is a better response.

4. Because Dr. Fazio's behaviors are somewhat rooted in his cultural back-ground, the dean should first give him a warning that he needs to change. If he then continues to harass his female students, such behavior would probably be grounds for termination of employment. (Although, as one member of the validation sample pointed out, the dean of students herself would never fire a professor.) Moreover, Dean Smith does not need to be wary of all Italian

men in the future. Although closer physical proximity to others is a part of Italian culture, blowing in students' ears is not. The dean should not expect that all Italians will harass their female students just because Dr. Fazio does.

5. This is the best response. Socialization into the culture in which we grow up plays a central role in who we are and how we behave. Nevertheless, the dean should not completely excuse Dr. Fazio's behavior. He can change his habit of standing "too close" by American standards. In addition, blowing in students' ears is not part of Italian culture. Even if it were, Dr. Fazio would still have to change. At times, one has no choice but to change behaviors, no matter how difficult that may be, or risk legal prosecution. Dr. Fazio's offensive behavior is more of an individual than a cultural difference, however. Closer spatial orientation is a part of Italian culture, but blowing in ears is not. He is almost certainly aware both of what he is doing when he makes sexual innuendoes and blows in students' ears (harassing students) and the effect he is having on his students (many women feel uncomfortable). Culture should not, and cannot, be used as an excuse for inappropriate sexual behavior.

Incident 104 (p. 218): Rationales for the Alternative Explanations

1. This is a good choice. There are a number of factors in the classroom that may inhibit people from different backgrounds. They may not feel comfortable using dialects different from those of their teachers or members of the dominant culture (in this case, Anglos). African American students may not want to cooperate with an Anglo teacher through their class discussion if this is seen as distancing themselves from African American peers. In the case of Deborah's particular classroom discussion question, the African American students may have felt that she wanted to hear a list of influential Anglos (e.g., George Washington, Thomas Jefferson) and would not have approved of their nominees (e.g., Harriet Tubman, Malcolm X). On the playground, on the other hand, the African American students were not in the presence of a possibly judgmental teacher. They could also use the sort of clever language that reinforces their ethnic identity while arguing with members of other ethnic groups. Verbal skills are highly valued in African American culture, and the playground was a place Deborah's students could demonstrate their skills. The challenge for concerned teachers like Deborah is to encourage otherwise reluctant students to use their verbal skills in the classroom. She might ask other teachers if they have had success doing this. One approach we have found successful is to ask students to form small groups and to come up with contributions to the general discussion in collaboration with others in their groups. Then, representatives of the groups report back to the entire class. Many students are more comfortable making contributions in small groups of four or five people than they are in speaking to a large class.

2. This is not a good choice. Verbal skills are highly valued in African American culture. African Americans, however, are very sensitive to the social contexts in which they might demonstrate their skills. Please choose again.

3. This is not likely to be true. African Americans are as knowledgeable about people they consider important and influential as are members of any American ethnic group. They may believe that members of other groups would not come up with the same lists, but they certainly have their own nominees. Please choose again.

4. This is possibly true. The African American students may have felt that Deborah and the Anglo students were controlling the classroom. The African Americans may have believed their contributions would not be welcome if they felt that the classroom was being run according to Anglo norms. Deborah, of course, needs to be sensitive to this possibility and must communicate through both verbal and nonverbal behaviors that she welcomes the contributions of the African American students even if these reflect differences in both style and content. She must realize that there is every probability that, in a classroom exercise such as this one, the African American and Anglo-American students would not come up with similar lists of influential Americans. In addition, it must be kept in mind that playground behavior and classroom behavior involve a number of contextual differences. The incident states that the African Americans were highly verbal on the playground in the presence of Anglo-Americans. On the playground, it must be kept in mind, people select themselves concerning their participation. The African Americans could have been very comfortable with the particular Anglos who were voluntarily on the playground. Perhaps they knew members of this select Anglo group well enough that they were comfortable voicing their opinions (just as all of us are more comfortable voicing our opinions with people we know). In the classroom, on the other hand, people find themselves in the company of other ethnic group members whether they want to or not. There is another choice that also assists with an understanding of this incident; readers may want to select another alternative.

10

RETURNING HOME

Even with all the difficult issues sojourners face, and that form the bases of the incidents covered to this point, they generally have fond memories of their cross-cultural experiences. One reason for this is that most successfully overcome these difficulties and thus internalize images of themselves as successful individuals who can face difficult problems. After their successful experiences, they are naturally satisfied with their efforts and consequently give a great deal of attention to their lives in their host countries. By this time, they are probably known as old hands who can assist in the orientation of new people entering similar situations. Their expertise is respected and their hints for successful adjustment are sought by others. But these people often have another hurdle to face, especially if they have been living in countries other than their own: their return to their own cultures. The return home often causes more upheaval than the demands of the initial cross-cultural adjustment, in part because the problems that arise are so often unforeseen. Most people simply do not envision any possibility that they will have difficulties in their own cultures, which they know so well.

105

Lessons in English?

Masayo had just returned to Japan and had begun looking for a job after a long period abroad studying at an American university. Both her English and her Japanese were excellent. After she had been job hunting unsuccessfully for a month, her mother called her and asked if she would be interested in giving English lessons to the daughter of one of the mother's friends, Mrs. Osaki. Masayo agreed, but said she would have to discuss the matter directly with Mrs. Osaki. Masayo's mother informed Mrs. Osaki, who then phoned Masayo. In initial conversation, Mrs. Osaki insisted upon establishing the exact amount that Masayo would charge for the lessons. Masayo was reluctant to say anything definite before meeting the student, but, because of Mrs. Osaki's persistence, eventually quoted a rough figure. Mrs. Osaki then promised to call back again after discussing the matter with her daughter. When she called the following week, Masayo tried to arrange a schedule for the lessons, but Mrs. Osaki told her that her daughter was ill and had been hospitalized.

In the succeeding month, Masayo had several more phone conversations with Mrs. Osaki but failed to gain any clear indication of whether the lessons were to be given or not. After a time, Mrs. Osaki stopped contacting Masayo, although the two occasionally saw each other when visiting Masayo's mother. At those times Masayo was very tempted to bring up the topic of the English lessons but somehow felt hesitant to do so. She felt very ambivalent about the whole situation—confused and frustrated by what she regarded as insincere behavior on Mrs. Osaki's part, yet conscious that she really did not know how to handle the situation.

Why did Mrs. Osaki not give Masayo a clear indication that she did not wish the lessons to proceed? Focus on a cultural difference between what Masayo would have learned in the United States and what she would have experienced in Japan.

1. Mrs. Osaki did not have any intention of having her daughter take the English lessons from the beginning. She was just trying to be nice to Masayo's mother.

2. Mrs. Osaki felt that the cost of the lessons was too high; she hoped that if she kept postponing the decision, Masayo might lower the fee.

3. Mrs. Osaki was jealous of Masayo. Her daughter was the same age as Masayo but hardly spoke any English, and she did not like the idea of her daughter taking lessons from someone the same age simply because that person was a returnee.

4. Mrs. Osaki did not think the arrangement was going to work out. By mentioning her daughter's illness and failing to give a clear answer, she was giving Masayo the message that the lessons were not going to proceed.

The discussions of these alternative explanations begin on page 243.

106

A Tricky Situation

[This is the same incident as the one immediately preceding, but with a different question and alternate explanations.]

Masayo had just returned to Japan and had begun looking for a job after a long period abroad studying at an American university. Both her English and her Japanese were excellent. After she had been job hunting unsuccessfully for a month, her mother called her and asked if she would be interested in giving English lessons to the daughter of one of the mother's friends, Mrs. Osaki. Masayo agreed, but said she would have to discuss the matter directly with Mrs. Osaki. Masayo's mother informed Mrs. Osaki, who then phoned Masayo. In initial conversation, Mrs. Osaki insisted upon establishing the exact amount that Masayo would charge for the lessons. Masayo was reluctant to say anything definite before meeting the student, but, because of Mrs. Osaki's persistence, eventually quoted a rough figure. Mrs. Osaki then promised to call back again after discussing the matter with her daughter. When she called the following week, Masayo tried to arrange a schedule for the lessons, but Mrs. Osaki told her that her daughter was ill and had been hospitalized.

In the succeeding month, Masayo had several more phone conversations with Mrs. Osaki but failed to gain any clear indication of whether the lessons were to be given or not. After a time, Mrs. Osaki stopped contacting Masayo, although the two occasionally saw each other when visiting Masayo's mother. At those times Masayo was very tempted to bring up the topic of the English lessons but somehow felt hesitant to do so. She felt very ambivalent about the whole situation—confused and frustrated by what she regarded as insincere behavior on Mrs. Osaki's part, yet conscious that she really did not know how to handle the situation.

Why did Masayo feel hesitant about asking Mrs. Osaki for clarification of the situation?

1. Masayo felt that her Japanese was not good enough for her to communicate with Mrs. Osaki.
2. Masayo really did not need the money, and so did not feel she needed to push for a decision about the lessons.
3. Masayo somehow sensed that she should not ask, but did not fully understand her feelings.

4. Masayo thought her mother was likely to clarify the situation voluntarily, which would make any further interaction with Mrs. Osaki unnecessary.

The discussions of these alternative explanations begin on page 244.

107

Back Home in Japan

A 28-year-old Japanese mechanic was assigned to work in Libya as an assistant manager in the service division of an automobile dealership. In Japan he was a technician and active in the union organization, with the responsibility for looking after younger subordinates in their personal activities. After a 6-month technical training program, he was sent to Libya. Because he was the only Japanese employee in Libya, he did not receive any cultural briefing or assistance. Nevertheless, he developed new management skills and expected to receive a higher position after returning to Japan.

At the end of 2 years, he returned to Japan and was assigned a position similar to the one he had held prior to his sojourn in Libya, but in a new department. He did not resume an active role in the union. One year after his return, he married a woman who also worked at the company. He did not mention his marriage to his superior or to any of his colleagues. Later, his department head, who had learned of the young man's marriage from his supervisor, asked the young man why he had not mentioned his marriage. The employee apologized for not saying anything, but, upon leaving the department head's office, he commented to himself that his personal life was nobody else's business and he resented the inquiry.

Why was the department head concerned that the employee had not mentioned his marriage? Several of the following explanations are close to adequate, but only one incorporates all of the elements important to this case.

1. The department head was upset that the supervisor and department head were not invited to the wedding.
2. The department head acted like a father to his employees and wanted to know everything about his subordinates that may affect their job performance. He felt that a marriage may have an impact upon the employee's work.
3. The department head wished the employee would feel that he had become part of the group family, and conform by changing his general behavior.

4. The department head knew the woman the employee had married and was upset that she had married this particular individual.

The discussions of these alternative explanations begin on page 245.

108

After Exhilaration at the Airport

Bob Fisher had checked out the last of his luggage filled with intricate souvenirs and mementos of the 3 years he had spent in East Africa developing the personnel department of a large industrial company. He had spent his time with a local counterpart, training employees and developing a system for use in the expanding city of Nairobi. He had enjoyed his work and had learned about many customs and new modes of doing things. He was anxious to communicate the new techniques he had learned to some of his colleagues back home. In addition, he had experienced many things that he wanted to share with his friends.

Upon his arrival home, he was greeted by his family and several close friends. They all rushed to greet him, overwhelmed him with questions, and then whisked him off and began filling him in on all that had taken place in the 3 years he was gone. After the first 2 hours, however, no one asked him any questions about his experiences in Nairobi. Even later, when several of his friends stopped by and they went out for a drink, Bob felt uncomfortable and lost in their conversation about goings-on in the local community. When his friends did occasionally ask about his sojourn, he noticed that no one paid much attention to his answers and that they often soon changed the subject. He felt miserable and wished he had not returned home. He interpreted his friends' actions as lack of interest in his experiences abroad.

How could you help interpret the situation?

1. Bob's friends were not really that glad to see him return.
2. Bob was monopolizing the conversation with his stories, so his friends changed the subject to give others a chance.
3. Bob was disoriented and misinterpreted his friends' actions as lack of interest in the details of his sojourn.
4. Bob's expectations concerning his return home were not being met.

The discussions of these alternative explanations begin on page 245.

109

Coming Back Home

Becky Engle had been home in Colorado for 2 months, and she often found herself thinking of her time in the Philippines and wishing she were there. This confused her, as when she was there she had longed to be at home. She had despised the hot sticky weather in the Philippines and dreamed of the snows of the Rockies. The foods that the Filipino people ate she thought strange and untasty. She had often yearned for the fresh vegetables and salads of her native home in Boulder. There were countless things she had perpetually gone over that had annoyed her in the Philippines—the dirty air, the transportation system, the plumbing, and more. Now she was home, but the things she had missed about home while in the Philippines did not seem so important. What was more, she felt odd and out of place somehow and longed for the things that had been familiar to her during her 3 years in the Philippines.

How could you help explain to Becky what was going on? Focus on her current feelings and take into account as much information as possible.

1. Becky was going through a period of readjustment and felt that although things should seem familiar, they were not.
2. Things in the Philippines were not as bad as Becky had imagined them, and she was just realizing that.
3. Becky was missing some of her friends in the Philippines. This is normal—she would get over it in a few months.
4. Becky had changed so much during her stay in the Philippines that she no longer fit into her own society.

The discussions of these alternative explanations begin on page 246.

110

Not Accepted by Her Peers

Tomoko recently returned to Japan after spending 4 years in the United States with her family (her father having been sent by his company). She recommenced her schooling at a local junior high. Initially, she was very pleased to be back home; she had been fascinated by American life, but was always conscious that she never really belonged. After a few weeks back at school, however, she began having doubts about Japan. She complained constantly about how dull and repetitive the lessons seemed. The only class she enjoyed was English (because of her fluency), but even there the teacher never asked her questions or asked her to read to the class. Moreover, her classmates seemed very cold and not easily befriended. They ridiculed her American clothes and mannerisms and her accent when she spoke Japanese. She felt unable to join in conversations, as they usually talked about topics unfamiliar to her and none seemed interested in hearing about her American experiences. After a while, she became more and more withdrawn and her teachers complained about her lack of attention and dedication to her work.

What reason(s) would you give to Tomoko for her apparent ostracism by her classmates and teachers?

1. They were envious of her American style and ability to speak English.
2. They probably thought her behavior was just showing off.
3. They were intolerant of anybody who seemed to deviate from the fairly rigid norms of behavior and appearance.
4. They were offended because she criticized the school and the teachers.

The discussions of these alternative explanations begin on page 247.

Incident 105 (p. 237): Rationales for the Alternative Explanations

1. Although Mrs. Osaki might have been trying to be nice to Masayo's mother, she would not go to the extent of inquiring from Masayo's mother as well as making several phone calls to Masayo directly. Please choose again.

2. This technique of "bargaining," although very common in some Arab, South American, and Asian countries, is usually not used by Japanese in their everyday transactions. If Mrs. Osaki felt that the cost was too high, she would have found another way to let Masayo know, probably through her mother. Please choose again.

3. Jealousy of Japanese who have been raised abroad can be observed among some people whose educational goals are very high. In recent times there have been changes in educational policies that enable Japanese students educated overseas to be considered in a more lenient manner for entrance to high schools and colleges, which may lead to envy or resentment. But Mrs. Osaki is a friend of Masayo's mother. Even though she might have had such feelings, she would not show them in a way that would hurt the relationship. Also,

there is an explanation that more directly addresses the question posed concerning a cultural difference. Please choose again.

4. This is the best answer. The cultural conflict here is between the commonly accepted Japanese behavioral norms exhibited by Mrs. Osaki and those held by some Japanese who have been exposed to, and have acquired, more American norms, as Masayo had. In situations where some kind of rejection or refusal must be given (when a person must say no), usually it is not conveyed directly. A series of maybes and perhapses followed by information about some unchangeable condition (e.g., illness) can be taken as signs of a courteous and polite no. This could be interpreted as insincerity by non-Japanese, who may say that Japanese do not honestly say what they mean. But sojourners should appreciate the efforts made by Japanese to avoid embarrassing situations (especially in close, interpersonal relations) by stating such refusals in an ambiguous and indirect manner. Many cultures convey meanings and decisions through such indirect, subtle behaviors, and sojourners should be cautious in making assumptions about situations that have some degree of ambiguity about them—there may well be subtle cues that sojourners have missed. When in doubt, sojourners should seek advice from others with sound knowledge of the culture.

Incident 106 (p. 239): Rationales for the Alternative Explanations

1. This is a stereotype held by many people in Japan with regard to Japanese raised abroad. The story mentions that Masayo's Japanese was quite good. This is not the best explanation. Please choose again.

2. The story mentions that Masayo was out of work for a month, which indicates that she probably did need the money from the lessons. Please choose again.

3. This is the most likely explanation. Masayo felt that it was somehow not acceptable to ask Mrs. Osaki directly (her Japanese upbringing), but at the same time, she had learned to speak and deal directly with people in the United States. She thus found herself caught in an ambiguous situation that led to frustration and hesitancy to act. Further, there was probably no one around to point out these cultural differences to Masayo; her fellow Japanese would probably not think to point out basic cultural norms to her. This lack of understanding added to her ambiguous feelings. Sojourners often find themselves in similarly ambiguous situations because of their incomplete knowledge of the host culture or because host culture behavior is contrary to their normal responses or expected behavior. Where possible, sojourners should avoid drawing hasty conclusions and should seek the advice of individuals who have more intimate knowledge of the host culture. Sojourners have to be very active in their search for such knowledge, however, because hosts rarely volunteer information on their own initiative.

4. This is not likely. The mother probably interpreted Mrs. Osaki's behavior correctly, thereby assessing the situation as "no English lessons for Masayo to teach," but she may not have realized the necessity to teach her daughter why this was so. In many cases where a younger member of a family learns the cultural norms of another system, parents often neglect (or may not even realize the necessity for) their need to interpret and reteach the cultural rules. Family members rarely think to clarify possible ambiguities brought on by differences between the culture of birth and the culture in which a person sojourns. There is a more precise reason. Please choose again.

Incident 107 (p. 240): Rationales for the Alternative Explanations

1. Most supervisory personnel and department heads might be embarrassed about not being invited to an employee's wedding. However, the group identity in Japan goes much deeper than just embarrassment. Review the information again to make a better choice.

2. This is a good answer. The department head may, at times, have needed to know much of what was going on in his workers' lives, but this feeling may not have been a simple paternalistic attitude on his part. Reread the scenario for additional information that will shed light on another possible answer.

3. This is a good answer. The department head knew that for group harmony to exist, conformity by all employees must be valued. The department head was not being critical of the employee's attitude but was concerned for his welfare. He did not understand the impact the assignment in Libya had on the employee's attitude or actions. The department head did not mean to be uncaring, however. He felt concerned about the employee's relation to his work group and to the organization as a whole. He was concerned that the employee did not seem to be involved in the "family." Harmony with and participation in the group is highly valued, being deeply rooted in tradition. In addition to this alternative, there is another explanation that provides insights into the incident.

4. Although this might occur, it is highly unlikely the department head would express to the employee any direct feelings regarding the situation. Furthermore, there is nothing in the incident to support this answer. Try again.

Incident 108 (p. 241): Rationales for the Alternative Explanations

1. This seems highly unlikely. Even though friendships may wane somewhat over the years, a number of Bob's friends showed up to greet him at the airport. This is a gesture that is not necessary even among good friends, and it would indicate that they were indeed very glad to see Bob. This is not the best answer; please choose again.

2. It is true that having a lot to share and not seeing one's friends for a long period of time may tend to move one to monopolize the conversation when in their presence again. However, there is nothing in the incident to indicate Bob did this. There is more going on here. Please choose again.

3. Yes, it is fairly evident that Bob was disoriented and was not understanding all that he was being bombarded with. This often happens with sojourners who have been away for sufficient time to develop identity with or understanding of other cultures (see Incident 106). Although that was undoubtedly happening here, Bob was not misinterpreting his friends' behavior. They really were not interested in the details of his experiences abroad. There is more going on here. Please choose again.

4. This is the best answer. Bob expected his friends to be interested in hearing about Nairobi. Because he had been so involved, he felt that others close to him would also be interested in the details of his sojourn, which had so deeply affected him. But his friends back home had been involved in their own communities, and that is what they wanted to talk about. Almost all sojourners, upon returning home, complain that "no one wants to see my pictures and slides." Thus the problem Bob faces is one of unmet expectations.

Incident 109 (p. 242): Rationales for the Alternative Explanations

1. This is the best explanation. Whenever there is change, we must make adjustments. One of the most problematic aspects of sojourns is the fact that sojourners often fail to realize that they will have some difficulties readjusting to their original societies. This is especially true when a sojourn has been lengthy. Sojourners often spend a great deal of time and energy preparing for the initial changes and shocks of living in "foreign" or different societies, but presume that their return to their original starting places will not require any adjustments. They fail to acknowledge that the adjustments they made to their host societies left them changed persons, and now they must make certain other readjustments to fit into the original mold once again. It is strange to think that things that should seem familiar and comforting may actually make a returning sojourner uncomfortable. The fact is that sojourners change. They are still part of their original cultural environments, but now have the addition of factors from other environments, which may or may not clash with the original. This readjustment to original environments is referred to as *reentry shock*. This may be compounded by the fact that when we are faced with unfamiliar things, we tend to idealize old familiar things that are not available to us. Becky was indeed suffering from reentry shock.

2. It is true that when things are not familiar, people tend to overemphasize or even to exaggerate factors out of proper perspective. The discomforting factors in Becky's experience were real, however, and though they may have

been somewhat exaggerated in her mind at the time of the experience and may have diminished in significance now, this does not explain why Becky felt odd or uncomfortable in her own hometown. There is much more going on here, and another alternative offers a better explanation. Please choose again.

3. When one has formed friendships and they are disrupted by distance, some feelings of despondency are indeed normal. No doubt Becky was experiencing this to some degree. Although these feelings may make Becky wish she was back in the Philippines, this does not explain her attitude toward her present surroundings. There is more to her feelings than this; please choose again.

4. Yes, undeniably Becky has changed. A 3-year sojourn will have made some sort of impact, as Becky had worked through many adjustments and learning processes. Undoubtedly, some of those changes would conflict with her original environment. However, it is very unlikely that Becky would have changed so much as to be unable to readjust to the United States. This is not the best answer. Please choose again.

Incident 110 (p. 242): Rationales for the Alternative Explanations

1. Although this may have applied to some of her classmates, it seems unlikely that all would react in such a manner. There is a more adequate explanation. Please choose again.

2. Although this may have been the case, and our validation sample cited it as a possibility, it would not seem a sufficient reason for her complete exclusion from the social groups. If it were only a matter of their belief that she was showing off, they might have made fun of her but would still probably have included her in some activities. There is a more complete explanation. Please choose again.

3. This is the best response. Many cultures are quite intolerant of members who appear to deviate too far from the behavioral norms of the majority, and this intolerance is often exhibited in ridicule or exclusion of offending members from existing social groups. Although foreigners may be treated quite tolerantly, as they cannot be expected to know any better, those belonging to the society who do not conform may be regarded as somewhat exhibitionist, pretentious, disrespectful, or even dangerous for exhibiting behaviors that may seem quite trivial to the persons being judged. Teenagers are especially concerned with conformity (among their peers, at least), and Tomoko's fellow students probably regarded her with very mixed feelings. Her teachers were probably very anxious to downplay her differences and so did not call attention to her in class. Such reactions are stronger in some societies (such as Japan) than in others, but sojourners should realize that experiences of this

type are common for many when they return to their home cultures. For children, such experiences can be particularly traumatic; they need to be counseled as to the reasons for their ostracism and perhaps coached to eliminate offending behaviors. Teachers working with returnee children also need to be made aware of the potential for problems and encouraged to develop more empathy for their plight.

4. Although this may be one reason they regarded Tomoko with hostility or apprehension, and our validation sample cited it as such, it would not seem to be an adequate explanation for her total exclusion by her classmates. There is a fuller explanation. Please choose again.

11

PEOPLE'S INTENSE FEELINGS

Most people are aware that they will be faced with unfamiliar customs when they interact with people from other cultures. They may also be aware that they will engage in novel behaviors in such activities as greeting others, eating, and participating in another culture's religious services. Most people are relatively unprepared, however, for the impacts such encounters will have on their inner feelings—their anxieties, emotions, prejudices, and sense of belonging (Bond, 1994). Collectively, psychologists call these reactions *affective experiences*. In everyday language, these are the intense feelings brought about during intercultural encounters and sojourns (Moghaddam, Ditto, & Taylor, 1990).

Anxiety among sojourners stems from their need to make decisions in other cultures despite imperfect knowledge. The appropriateness of various emotions, such as happiness, fear, and anger, may be less clear than in their own cultures. One factor contributing to emotional responses is the set of cues available to a person. If an individual is at a party where everyone is laughing and having a good time, for instance, he or she will incorporate this cue into his or her own reactions. But just what constitutes "happy" behavior may differ from culture to culture. Such problems can affect sojourners' interpersonal relations with hosts and, consequently, can interfere with their desire and ability to belong or to feel at home (Yoshida, 1994). In the absence of good relations with hosts, past prejudices that sojourners are trying to shed may play a more active role than is desirable (Devine & Zuwerink, 1994).

No set of written materials can nullify the intense feelings people will experience during extensive intercultural interactions. However, it is possible for sojourners to gain a greater understanding of typical affective reactions, and they can use such knowledge to lessen the difficulties brought about by their emotional upheavals.

249

ANXIETY

Many of the incidents and explanations offered in the preceding chapters point to the differences sojourners and others working or living across cultures will encounter. Acceptance into and rejection from groups will occur for unclear reasons, an individual's status may increase or decrease from the level to which he or she has become accustomed, and the behaviors associated with various roles will cause confusion. These and other differences will lead individuals to think about their behavior and to decide about the changes they need to make to maximize the probability of achieving their goals. Such thinking will be much more frequent than when the individuals are in their own groups, because they "know" how to behave in the familiar surroundings where they have had years and years of experience. All of this thought about unfamiliar events, and about necessary changes, will inevitably result in ventures into the unknown. In turn, dealing with the unknown invariably results in anxiety.

Anxiety is an unpleasant feeling involving discomfort concerning some object or event. Individuals have a strong desire to avoid behaviors that will bring about any encounters with objects or events that are the cause of such discomfort (Byrne & Kelley, 1981; Stephan & Stephan, 1992). Fear is similar to anxiety, with the major difference centering on the focus of the discomfort. With fear, the focus is very specific—for example, fear may focus on the high places that a group of tourists will encounter during a scheduled trip to the mountains. With anxiety, the focus is more vague, less defined, and consequently uncertain and sometimes amorphous. A person can be anxious about an upcoming sojourn, for instance, without being able to specify the exact reasons.

Symptoms of Anxiety

A useful way of looking at the symptoms of anxiety is to examine a major instrument used to measure the phenomenon, the Taylor Manifest Anxiety Scale (Taylor, 1953). If people are anxious, they report such psychological symptoms as the following:

1. I work under a great deal of tension.
2. I worry quite a bit over possible misfortunes.
3. I frequently find myself worrying about something.

4. I have been afraid of things or people that I know could not hurt me.
5. I certainly feel useless at times.

Anxious people also report such bodily (somatic) complaints as nausea, headaches, pounding heart, diarrhea, dry mouth, fitful sleep, nightmares, shortness of breath, perspiration, constipation, stomach trouble, and more crying than normal.

Anxiety is a better term than *fear* for people's feelings during cross-cultural encounters, because exact knowledge of what is causing the unpleasant emotions is rarely available (Anderson, 1994). Rather, people are aware that they are upset but cannot explain why. In their own culture, or when with a number of people from their group, people might be able to verbalize their reasons for anxiety, such as rejection by a friend or uncertainty about the fate of their suggestions for improvement in the workplace. Verbalizations of the reasons for one's feelings and careful thinking about the possible behaviors that will best meet the demands one faces can reduce the unpleasant emotional reactions that accompany anxiety (Janis & Mann, 1977). When one is living and working across cultures, however, the reasons for one's feelings are often unclear, as are the positive actions one might take to reduce anxiety (Gudykunst, 1994). Billy Davis (1972), who grew up in a family of migrant farmworkers, speaks of the irrelevance of testing in school for children who do not share many of the experiences expected by most classroom teachers. Through his words, one can almost feel the anxiety and frustration he felt as a child in the classroom:

> No expert in measurement knows better than I the wishful thinking inherent in the concept of culture-free testing. I have sat with cold, damp hands, holding my breath, hoping the teacher would not call on me. . . . We never had a private bathroom, or a kitchen sink, or an oven. I never owned a tricycle, bicycle, or pets (stray dogs are a separate category). We did not "go on vacations," "have company," "take lessons," or "pack luggage." . . . For years I owned no hairbrush, toothbrush, nail file, or pajamas. I could go on. In short, the ordinary middle class world was strange to me and its terms frightened me.

One way of coping with high levels of anxiety is to avoid the very situations that elicit feelings of discomfort. The feelings Davis expresses may help explain why so many young people feel isolated in the school setting and why they may subsequently drop out of school. When people feel anxious, they also lose the opportunity they need to learn about others and thus become more effective in their own intercultural interactions.

Another frequently ineffective response to a high level of anxiety is to ignore the psychological feelings (such as those listed above) and focus only on the somatic symptoms. Many people who react in this way will visit medical doctors and seek medication (Mullavey-O'Byrne, 1994a), and physicians, many of whom are not cognizant of the normal anxieties faced by people taking part in cross-cultural encounters, will all too frequently prescribe pills and potions for them. Consequently, the individuals never deal directly with the anxieties stemming from their intercultural experiences.

Mild Paranoia

There are a number of consequences of the fact that people experience anxieties in cross-cultural encounters. The reasons for most of these anxieties are vague, and, too frequently, the anxieties are not dealt with effectively (Draguns, 1990; Manson, 1994). One consequence is that the anxious individual will spend a great deal of time brooding over his or her feelings, often coming up with inexact or incorrect conclusions. One incorrect conclusion such a person may reach is that others are plotting to make life difficult for him or her. He or she may have frequent thoughts such as, "These people are always talking about me! They are purposely trying to make me unhappy." This conclusion probably results from a combination of normal anxiety and the fact that people in the host culture do frequently have conversations concerning sojourners—but their comments are not always negative. People crossing cultures must realize that in many ways they are unique and that they add something different to the lives of their hosts. Such differences may include physical characteristics, such as height, hair color, and skin color; speaking accents; knowledge based on education in special areas of expertise; and psychological characteristics such as gregariousness or aloofness. Given these differences, sojourners often are the focus of conversations. This is a fact that is difficult for many to accept, because in their own cultures they may not have had the experience of being discussed by others. They should not, however, combine this fact with their anxious feelings such that they reach the incorrect conclusion that others are "out to get them." Such paranoia will do them no good; it will only lead to avoidance of others and, consequently, the loss of opportunities to discover information that would lessen the paranoia.

Burnout

When the anxieties stemming from cross-cultural contact occur over a long period, the phenomenon known as burnout can result. Burnout is marked by emotional exhaustion that results in the loss of sympathy for those in a person's immediate environment (Maslach, 1978; Schaufeli & Janczur, 1994). Further, burned-out individuals feel unappreciated and begin to degrade other people with whom they have contact. For sojourners, for instance, this may mean that hosts become the targets of unsympathetic feelings and negative judgments. Another cause of burnout among sojourners, in addition to long-term anxiety, is the lack of control they frequently encounter. They often begin their work with high expectations: They will be good teachers, technical assistance advisers, social service providers, or businesspeople. But reality often interferes with their expectations, and they may soon learn that they do not have as much control over goal attainment as they would in their own cultural contexts. It is hard to be a good teacher if one has inadequate or nonexistent materials for students. It is difficult for technical assistance advisers to exercise control over project management when they are dependent on others for the hiring of a competent workforce. It is difficult to provide social services to people who have been angry at the system for so long that they see the well-intentioned provider as merely another representative of an uncaring bureaucracy. It is disturbing for businesspeople working in cultures other than their own to discover that decisions are made in unfamiliar ways. All of these examples involve a loss of control and a subsequent feeling of helplessness.

One way to help people who are about to undertake work across cultures is to encourage them to set realistic goals and to benefit from the experiences of others who have gone through similar difficulties. Indeed, one of the major goals behind the development of the cross-cultural training materials presented in this volume is to encourage people to learn from the experiences of others. A sojourner, for example, may feel as if he or she is the only one who has unfulfilled expectations, who feels helpless and anxious, or who harbors negative feelings about hosts, when, in actuality, virtually all sojourners go through periods during which these feelings overwhelm them. Communicating to people that they are not alone in their feelings is a major contribution to their well-being (Bhawuk, 1990).

Deindividuation

So far, we have presented anxiety as a negative phenomenon. As it is discussed in everyday language, a focus on the negative aspects of anxiety

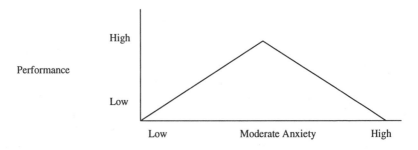

Figure 11.1. Consequences of Anxiety

is common. But anxiety has a positive side as well. For instance, students *should* be moderately anxious about an upcoming test so that they will be motivated to study. Sojourners should be somewhat anxious about their upcoming trips so that they will be motivated to prepare themselves. Anxiety becomes a problem when it is so intense as to be debilitating. A frequently cited theoretical concept in psychology is that anxiety improves performance (e.g., on a test or in completing a task) when it is of moderate intensity (Byrne & Kelley, 1981). Very low or very high levels of anxiety, however, interfere with performance. When anxiety is too low, people do not care enough to perform well; when anxiety is very high, its somatic and psychological consequences make concentration on the task at hand extremely difficult. Figure 11.1 summarizes the consequences of differing levels of anxiety.

Moderate levels of anxiety, then, encourage people to seek out appropriate behaviors so that they can achieve their goals. The cross-cultural encounter, however, can interfere with moderate levels of anxiety. One reason for normal, healthy anxiety is the desire to make a good impression on particular others whom one respects. But when an individual is on a sojourn, for instance, and often in other intercultural settings as well, such people are frequently absent. The respected others are not available to approve socially desirable behaviors and to raise their eyebrows when norms are violated. Consequently, sojourners may occasionally engage in negative behaviors they would not even consider in their own cultures. The well-mannered banker may shout at a waiter in another country; the foreign student may skip out of exams; the researcher may forget guidelines such as consultation with human subject review committees.

Deindividuation is a term that has been applied to people who engage in atypical behaviors when normal social sanctions are removed. Zimbardo

(1970; Zimbardo & Leippe, 1991), who developed the concept, has done research in a number of social settings to demonstrate the explanatory power of deindividuation. In one such demonstration, Zimbardo's research team abandoned cars in big cities and in smaller communities. The cars in the cities were stripped in a very short period of time; the cars in the smaller communities went untouched. Zimbardo describes cities as more deindividuating than small towns, because people in cities are likely to encounter many others with whom they have no relationships. Because of this lack of relationships, individuals are relatively unconcerned about others observing them in the act of breaking a norm. In contrast, a would-be vandal in a small community would risk being seen by a familiar other: perhaps the minister, a teacher, or the lady down the street. Triandis (1977) comments about the relationship between increased urbanization and antisocial behavior: "Industrialized society tends to create more and more settings in which people become deindividuated, and hence there is increasing aggression" (p. 82).

Application to the Culture Assimilator Incidents

Because people in cross-cultural encounters want to explain the reasons for their anxiety, they search their current environments for convenient explanations. In this search, they inevitably focus on hosts, because there are so many of them compared with people from their own backgrounds. Attributing the cause of anxiety to hosts leads to mild paranoia: "It's those people who are looking at me all the time." This mild paranoia is at the root of the problem in two of the incidents presented in this volume. In Incident 51 ("They Are Talking About Me"), Alan seemed to overhear his name being mentioned during hosts' conversations. He was probably right, but he should not have overinterpreted this fact. Given that, as indicated in the incident, he belonged to a very small minority group in the host organization, Alan indeed stood out and was naturally the focus of people's attention. Becoming upset at such an inevitability serves no positive function. In Incident 56 ("Am I That Different?"), Susan also felt that she was the object of special attention. The reason was her physical characteristics: She was a tall blonde in a land of dark-haired people. It is unwise for sojourners to overreact to the stares of others, especially, as Susan did, to the point of avoiding hosts altogether.

Onewayin which sojourners deal with the problems stemming from anxiety is to seek out medication for physical symptoms. In Incident 40

("The Trip to the Doctor"), Huang, a foreign student at an American university, had a number of personal setbacks but did not want to deal with their psychological basis. Instead, he emphasized his physical symptoms—perhaps he experienced these as real, or perhaps he believed them a convenient excuse to seek help without losing face. Foreign students engage in such behavior so often that it has become a well-known phenomenon among specialists (e.g., counselors, advisers) who work with sojourners. A term frequently used by these specialists is *somaticizing the problem.*

The feeling of overstimulation on a sojourn is a frequent reaction, because so much is new, so much seems possible, and so many opportunities for exploration seem available. But overstimulation can dull the senses. One of the developers of these materials is an amateur musician who enjoys talking to professionals about life on the road. One told him, "I left the road. It was very exciting, but one only wants so much excitement in life. It's also nice to settle down to a quiet existence."

Overstimulation is a problem illustrated in Incident 73 ("Selling Abroad"). Mark begins his tour of European companies with enthusiasm, but the excitement wanes after about 3 weeks. He sees so much on the trip, and meets so many people, that he cannot possibly remain excited and fresh on each new stop. The resulting fatigue causes him to perform his work poorly. In Incident 75 ("A Demanding Job"), Melinda never seemed to experience a dull moment in her job as foreign student adviser—and that was the problem. She never had a chance to renew her energy or to seek out emotional outlets for *her* problems because she was spending so much time with other people's difficulties. Burnout resulted, and Melinda considered resigning from her job. The wise administrator makes sure that people like Melinda have various emotional supports in the form of free time, supportive coworkers, and feedback on successes. An administrator might also put limits on the number of projects overeager newcomers undertake, realizing that unbridled enthusiasm can eventually result in burnout.

Another anxiety-related possibility people may face is that some of their behavior will be deindividuated. When people are no longer in the presence of respected others, they may engage in unpleasant behaviors because those others are unable to apply social sanctions. In Incident 52 ("Spanish Vacation"), Gustav is rude to a waiter while vacationing in Spain. His friend Bjorn informs anonymous but embarrassed onlookers that Gustav never behaves like this. Bjorn is telling the truth as he understands Gustav's behavior—Gustav does not behave like this in his home country, where he knows that onlookers would express their displeasure.

Absence from familiar surroundings can also lead to a loss of respect, because status is assigned by others with whom an individual has an established identity. As an English wit once wrote, a naked man has no status. Similarly, a strange sojourner has no status in the host country. In new surroundings, people familiar with an individual's background and experiences are not present to remind everyone of the individual's status. The anxiety resulting from status loss, combined with anonymity with respect to familiar people, can lead to deindividuated behavior. This combination of factors is present in the second example incident presented in Chapter 2. Jack Edwards, a highly respected professional, traveled to a conference in another country at which he was not well known by others. Put another way, his good reputation did not precede him. Bothered by this status loss, and absent from familiar faces, he lashed out at a defenseless conference participant. Intervention by concerned outsiders would have been difficult in this case, because Jack would have been unlikely to admit that his behavior was a result of status loss and deindividuation. Some success in this area has been achieved through preventive measures. Experienced conference administrators who are aware of the problems under discussion here can make efforts to ensure that all participants are paid a great deal of respect and attention, so that feelings of status loss are unlikely to surface.

EMOTIONAL EXPERIENCES
AND DISCONFIRMED EXPECTATIONS

When sojourners are asked to discuss the most memorable events of their sojourns, they most often bring up incidents involving intense emotions. Further, the incidents they discuss are more often negative than positive. People seem more able to bring forth memories of disappointment, anger, fear, and frustration than of happiness and contentment. Still, most sojourners remain enthusiastic about their sojourns and frequently recommend that more people should have the experience of living and working in other cultures. Researchers have documented positive changes among sojourners, such as declines in authoritarianism and increases in world-mindedness (Hansel, 1988; Kagitçibasi, 1978). There is a seeming paradox here: Sojourners gain positive outcomes from, and are enthusiastic about, their sojourns, but they also recall many negative incidents from their time in other cultures. There are several reasons for this interesting set of facts. One is that negative events seem to stick in people's minds more than positive ones. Most people expect good things to happen to them, and when anything deviates from this expectation, it has significant impact and is consequently memorable. Another reason is that people experience feelings of success in overcoming negative incidents, and so sojourners add to their self-images new perceptions of themselves as people who can solve problems.

An important task for people who work with sojourners as well as others interacting across cultures is to understand the nature of the often unexpected negative emotional experiences they will have, so as to help prevent those experiences from becoming debilitating (Anderson, 1994; Brislin, 1993; Gudykunst, 1994). Although it is impossible to prevent sojourners' negative experiences—as it is impossible (and perhaps not even desirable) to eliminate the experience of culture shock—the long-term effects of those experiences can be minimized. If sojourners are informed about what to expect, and can keep their emotions from becoming overly intense, they can attain the positive benefits of cross-cultural interaction with minimal emotional anguish. The relation between emotional response and performance is similar to the relation between anxiety and behavior, as discussed in the previous essay. A moderate amount of emotion is preferable to either too little or too much. Sojourners and others interacting across cultures *will* experience strong emotional reactions. If they have access to supportive people who can help them to interpret their responses and can assist them in viewing emotional reactions as learning opportunities, then their entire experiences will be more beneficial for the people involved.

Somatic Changes

When people have intense emotional reactions, such as anger or fear, a number of things occur in their bodies: (a) their blood pressure and heart rate increase, (b) their breathing becomes rapid, (c) their blood sugar level increases to provide more energy, (d) muscles become tense, (e) they become easily irritated by any other noxious stimulus (unrelated to the stimulus that caused the initial emotional reaction), (f) they may perspire more or experience a cold sweat, and (g) they may feel queasiness in their stomachs, sometimes called butterflies (Hilgard, Atkinson, & Atkinson, 1975). These somatic changes undoubtedly help to explain why emotional experiences are so memorable. Because these changes are relatively infrequent, they are well remembered when they do occur. One influential theoretical proposition is that people want to know why they feel as they do whenever these intense somatic changes occur (Epstein, 1994; Schachter & Singer, 1962). Thus, upon experiencing such feelings, people search their environments for explanations. In the case of sojourners or others interacting across cultures, such searches can lead to mistaken conclusions. In a person's own cultural context, there are convenient, familiar explanations for somatic changes, given that the individual would have memories of other times during which he or she had similar feelings. But often there is no such set of familiar explanations in a cross-cultural context. Consequently, sojourners may either make incorrect attributions or find themselves unable to explain their feelings. Either possibility can lead to even more problems, as people react to the mistakes or to the frustration brought on by the lack of available explanations.

Disconfirmed Expectations

One explanation for many emotional reactions, often unrecognized, is the confusion caused by disconfirmed expectations. People generally want to do well in the various capacities in which they work and interact; they want to be good teachers, businesspeople, social workers, researchers. When they encounter difficulties, they often react emotionally, but not simply because of the difficulties themselves; rather, their reactions stem from the contrast between their expectations and their actual achievement of those expectations (Rogers & Ward, 1993; Singer, 1993). The concept of the contrast effect in psychology (Helson, 1964) centers on the difference between expectation and reality. If a person has a strong expectation, then he or she sees any deviation from it is as greater than it really is. For instance, assume that a graduate student from Africa expects to be given a reasonable amount of deference at an American university (as in Incident 96, "Participation in a Seminar"), but instead is given the same treatment as everyone else. From an objective standpoint, the African student is not the target of discrimination, because everyone is being treated the same way. But because the student expected deference, he sees the deviation from that expectation as more discriminatory than it actually is. As another example, imagine a social worker who assumes that the services she is about to provide a client will be welcomed and highly appreciated. She is likely to be disappointed in these expectations, however, because it is not unusual for social workers to be greeted by new clients with reserve, mistrust, and apprehension (Mullavey-O'Byrne, 1994b). As these examples illustrate, individuals may experience strong emotional reactions when there is incongruence between their expectations and reality. In most, if not all, of the critical incidents in this collection, which are reflective of many kinds of intercultural encounters, disconfirmed expectations play an important role.

Frustration is a major component of people's emotional reactions to disconfirmed expectations. Frustration involves feelings of intense discomfort stemming from the blockage of paths toward goals. Upon completion of 4 intense years of college-level language study, for instance, a person will find it frustrating to discover that he or she cannot carry on a conversation with hosts. Frustration, in turn, often leads to aggressive behavior as people try to vent their negative feelings. Stories of angry sojourners, for instance, which can be found in virtually all countries, often originate in the experiences of people who want something, find that it is unavailable, become frustrated, and ultimately become aggressive toward a convenient target (Pedersen, 1993). Too often, the convenient target is an unsuspecting host.

One way of coping with the frustrations that arise from disconfirmed expectations is to create an intervention between the frustrating stimulus and the emotional response. This can be done in a variety of ways. Deep breathing, meditation, heavy exercise, pleasurable activities, and the substitution of positive for negative thoughts have all been suggested. "Positive thought substitution" can be especially useful during cross-cultural encounters (Meichenbaum, 1977; see also Adler & Matthews, 1994). When people are in danger of becoming overly upset, they can either heighten or lessen their emotional responses by the thoughts they create. The thought, "Those people are out to get me," will undoubtedly heighten any unpleasant emotional arousal. On the other hand, thoughts such as, "Is this really all that important?" will often diminish negative feelings. Other multipurpose positive thoughts are "This may be tough now, but it will make a good story afterward" and "Perhaps this behavior is occurring for reasons I don't completely understand right now."

Because the lowering of a person's expectations may reduce the amount of stress he or she subsequently encounters (Brislin & Yoshida, 1994b), one goal of good cross-cultural training might be to help sojourners develop realistic, or perhaps even somewhat pessimistic, expectations about their upcoming experiences. Two of the major goals of the set of training materials presented in this volume are (a) to give people information about cross-cultural encounters (e.g., attributions, in-groups and out-groups, status and power) that will allow them to engage in thought processes that will help neutralize their potentially negative emotional reactions and (b) to provide a vocabulary that will enable them to be more specific in the questions they ask of others.

Application to the Culture Assimilator Incidents

Sojourners usually consider their cross-cultural experiences to be among the most important in their lives, and they want to share their new knowledge, feelings, and excitement with others. Upon returning home, sojourners expect that their families and friends will be just as excited and will want to participate vicariously by listening to all their stories about overseas life. But friends and family members are rarely as interested as the sojourners themselves, and consequently sojourners often run up against another major, even shocking, disconfirmed expectation. In Incident 108 ("After Exhilaration at the Airport"), Bob Fisher had exactly this sort of disappointment. Specialists in cross-cultural training often organize "reorientation seminars" for people returning to their own cultures (Brislin & Pedersen, 1976; Rogers & Ward, 1993). One of the themes in such programs is that lack of interest on the part of family and friends is very common. A sojourner should not feel that he or she is being treated in a unique way if others are indifferent to the stories of his or her experience.

Sojourners, however, can never completely dismiss from their minds the fact that people are not interested. The reactions of others will always cause sojourners to think about themselves. This is undoubtedly the case in Incident 109 ("Coming Back Home"). In addition to the unexpected reactions she received from others, Becky Engle felt out of place. Sojourners perceive their sojourns as extremely influential, and such important events cause changes in people. Sojourners will feel somewhat uncomfortable upon returning home until they integrate their new knowledge and feelings with their goals for life in their own societies. It may take 2 years or more for returnees to feel comfortable again in their own countries.

Another difference between expectation and reality can be seen in Incident 29 ("Pizza for Dinner"). Joshua had agreed to cook dinner for his host family. As in all youth exchange programs, everyone was trying to make others feel at ease, and all were doing what they could to make the sojourn a success. Given these very reasonable and laudable goals, any difficulties became magnified, experienced as more severe than they really were. There was a problem with the gas stove that should have been given the 5 minutes of attention it deserved, but because everyone involved was trying to make others feel comfortable, the matter was labeled a major cultural faux pas and was not discussed for fear of embarrassing Joshua. In other words, a stitch was not applied immediately in order to save nine later. Joshua later expressed his pent-up emotions when his teacher stopped by the house for a visit. Seeing Joshua's intense emotional state, the teacher probably concluded that something far more serious had happened than was really the case.

The expression of pent-up emotions also plays a role in Incident 89 ("Problems With Teaching Her Students"). Jan was having difficulties with her teaching assignment, and her problems were due in part to her high expectations. When students did not make as much progress as Jan had hoped, she became frustrated. In turn, the frustration led to aggression against a convenient target. To deal with this problem, there has to be an intervention of some kind between the feelings of frustration and the aggressive behavior. Such an intervention is the key to Incident 34 ("Invitation to a Social Gathering"). Bart was upset with Manuel, and the director of the company where both men worked realized this fact. The question at the end of the incident mentions the intervention. Any intervention that singled out the attitudes of Bart or of Manuel would place either or both of them on the defensive. The best way to intervene in such a situation is to focus on a neutral statement of the problem so that the statement will take the place of emotion-arousing thoughts. Neutral statements in Bart and Manuel's case would not concern topics such as Bart's religion or Manuel's interpersonal relationships. Rather, it would be best to focus on the fact that the company director had noted that there was a problem. With this out in the open, Bart, Manuel, and the intervener could develop ways to alleviate the problem. In this way, the problem, rather than any individual's behavior, becomes the focus of attention.

In Incident 25 ("Do I Really Want to Study This?"), John Solomon found himself in an ambiguous situation with regard to his chosen major area of study. John, who had decided to study American Sign Language and become an interpreter for the deaf, was surprised when he witnessed his deaf friends complaining about their interpreters. John had assumed that all of his efforts at interpreting would always be appreciated. What he did not understand was that the presence of an interpreter often makes deaf individuals feel somewhat awkward. John, and all sign-language interpreters, may be viewed, in a sense, as a necessary evil. Deaf people need interpreters' skills in order to understand effectively all that they may encounter in the hearing world. At the same time, however, they may not wish to feel dependent upon others. This situation presents a tug-of-war between loyalty and need on the one hand and resentment and desire for avoidance on the other. John discovered that he would have to come to grips with this reality if he was to be successful in his chosen career.

In a related incident (Incident 99, "Interpreting for the Hard of Hearing"), another interpreter for the deaf, Jill, became quite frustrated when Ted, her client, refused to allow her to use her hands in relaying information. Jill's training included practice in a variety of methods, including sign language and gestures, to help interpret information for deaf and hard-of-hearing students. Ted, however, did not wish to draw attention to himself, and asked Jill merely to mouth the words so that he could lip-read. This came as a surprise to Jill, and she worried that Ted was missing pertinent information. She subsequently began to feel that she was not doing her job in an adequate manner.

BELONGING

Humans are inherently social beings—the desire to experience union with others, to belong, is rooted in the conditions that characterize the social and biological evolution of our species (Bowlby, 1988; Epstein, 1994). For many, the fear of being excluded or becoming outcasts is greater than that of dying. Anthropologists have noted that in many societies, being cast out, not death, has been considered the ultimate punishment. In effect, such banishment means death, because the cast-out individual no longer exists as far as the group is concerned—he or she does not belong to the human universe.

We must of necessity belong to various social groups, some involuntary—such as family, race, and social class—and others voluntary (to varying degrees)—such as political, religious, and community groups and groups based on personal interests. As we proceed through life, the nature and number of our affiliations change, but we learn early on to become dependent on their support and existence. Our affiliative tendencies are consequently reinforced and strengthened. Such tendencies are affected by a host of complex variables, and so vary among individuals and across cultures, but, in the normal pattern of events, networks of relationships with others are a major aspect of human experience.

Sociologists and psychologists have advanced many theories regarding these affiliative tendencies and the rewards of belonging. A sociologist, Weiss, has proposed that there is a basic set of six provisions fulfilled by social relationships, and that the relationships tend to become specialized as to their provisions; that is, different needs are met by different social networks (in Peplau & Perlman, 1982). These provisions Weiss categorizes as (a) social integration (i.e., a feeling of shared concerns and activities), which is commonly provided by family and/or friends; (b) attachment (i.e., a sense of security and commitment), which most often comes from a romantic partner or from the family; (c) sense of reliable alliance (i.e., assurance of continuing assistance), commonly met by the family; (d) reassurance of worth, predominantly provided by coworkers or colleagues; (e) guidance, which may be offered by mentors, teachers, or older kin; and (f) opportunity for nurturance, provided by offspring or other dependents (if any).

These provisions conform to some degree with social psychologists' theories concerning why people seek to affiliate with others (e.g., Berscheid, 1994; Fiske, 1991; Wrightsman & Deaux, 1981). Some, for example, see affiliation as a kind of social exchange; that is, social communication is regarded as a trade of social commodities, with individuals belonging to particular networks or groups to satisfy certain socially mediated goals. These goals may include an emotional, expressive function (in which individuals seek to release or air feelings by talking to others), self-clarification (i.e., talking or being with others so as to increase understanding and to reduce uncertainty), and social validation (i.e., seeking out others to find support or confirmation for one's actions and beliefs). Other psychologists have suggested that affiliation with others represents a reward in itself— social relations are seen as a class of reinforcement, with the kind and amount of contact individuals seek with others being a product of their personal reinforcement history. It can perhaps be accepted, then, that at the center of human affiliative behavior (or behavior based in the need to belong) lies concerns for self-confirmation, attention, emotional release, esteem, and security that help to provide stability and order as well as structure and meaning to our lives.

As mentioned before, people belong to a range of social groups and networks, some transient, some permanent. A few of these groups may be characterized by a high degree of intimacy (e.g., family, close friends) and are fundamental to the development of personal values, attitudes, and emotions. Other, more secondary, groupings may be governed by less personal contact and more formal rules (such as work and community groups and groups based on personal interests) but may prove important in providing niches, roles, or identities for individuals within the social fabric. The needs fulfilled by the various groups may, of course, overlap, and their relative importance may alter markedly with situational or personality changes. Psychologists have shown, for example, that situations that create anxiety cause individuals to seek out others for help in interpreting reactions and for social support and validation. It thus becomes critically important for individuals working across cultures to be able to find people with whom they are comfortable and with whom they can interact on a rather close or intimate level.

We thus find meaning and security in life through belonging to various networks of relationships. If we are excluded from these networks or our contacts with them are markedly reduced or altered in some manner, we may have various negative responses: feelings of loneliness and alienation, loss of self-esteem, decreased sense of direction or purpose in life. Social relationships may be deficient in either quality or quantity, or both, but it is usually the quality of relationships that most affects the individual. For example, a number of shallow acquaintances can seldom compensate for the loss of an intimate relationship, which may result in profound feelings of loneliness. What amounts to a deficiency is also, of course, very much subjective and will vary enormously across individuals and across cultures. Adult European Americans, for example, tend to accept separation from their parents and siblings more readily than Latinos, who generally carry strong attachments to their families throughout their lives (Marin & Marin, 1991).

Deficiencies in relationships do not result only from physical or social isolation—they can also stem from failure to exercise appropriate social skills in relating to others, and the isolation resulting from such social incompetence can be just as profound as that arising from physical separation. In the cross-cultural context, the possibility of isolation is particularly salient, as individuals may often lack the essential social and linguistic skills to communicate effectively and/or to develop intimate relationships with members of another culture. Whatever the cause, the feelings aroused by social isolation tend to be similar; psychologists have noted that those suffering deficiencies in relationships may be characterized as more negative, rejecting, self-absorbed, and self-deprecating, and less responsive, than individuals with satisfactory relationships. One could say they are not themselves, because their selves have been distorted or disoriented through their lack of belonging.

The complexity of the many functions provided by social groups and the effects of partial or temporary isolation from key groups can be seen in the following example. Jane was an English student studying romance languages at a British university. As part of an exchange program, she had been given the chance to spend the summer with an Italian family in a small provincial town in Italy. She had only just begun studying Italian, but felt this complete immersion in the culture would be the quickest way to progress. Jane had not been abroad before, but she was a very open and sociable person—always willing to lend a sympathetic ear to a friend with a problem or to discuss her own problems with friends or family members. The first few weeks in Italy passed quickly; Jane liked the family she was staying with and seemed to settle in well. Her very limited Italian prevented her from having anything beyond elementary exchanges of pleasantries with people, but her cheery manner made her popular with the locals. By the end of the first month, however, Jane began to become moody and irritable. At times she was very withdrawn, and she lost interest in her Italian studies. In her letters home, she constantly declared how much she missed everyone, and she became very bitter if she did not receive a letter from a certain friend or family member (with whom she had always been close) for more than a week. She wanted very much to cut short her stay and return home.

Recall that one of the primary attributes of people who are well-adjusted in an intercultural context is that they have developed the ability to develop and maintain interpersonal relationships. It is precisely this aspect that was critical to Jane at this time in her experience. Jane seemed to be a confident and sociable person, yet once she was separated from her primary support groups her personality gradually changed and she became uncharacteristically moody and withdrawn. Although Jane still had plenty of company, the quality of her relationships had changed. A deficiency of intimacy existed, and this led to a lack of social integration, loss of attachment and security, and increasing uncertainty about the worth of what she was doing. The roles or functions fulfilled by her previous close, intimate relationships could probably have been served by the development of other intimate friendships if she were simply moving within her own culture. For instance, if she were leaving home to attend college, the relationship roles that had been filled by family members could largely be filled through the development of new close friendships. However, in the Italian context, Jane did not have sufficient language or social skills as yet to be able to form such relationships, and her gradually increasing negativeness only exacerbated the situation, thus making it more unlikely that she would develop these badly needed relationships. If Jane had been aware of what was happening and why, she may have been better able to accept the problem and thus stay in Italy long enough to develop the skills necessary to form new relationships and so regain her sense of belonging.

Sojourners and others interacting across cultures are particularly susceptible to strong emotional responses in relation to their need to belong.

It should be evident to the reader that many of the 18 themes examined in this volume are interrelated; for example, it is clear that an individual's anxiety would be likely to increase in a situation that threatens his or her sense of belonging.

Application to the Culture Assimilator Incidents

Referring again to the example above of Jane's stay in Italy: One of the functions fulfilled by Jane's intimate groups back home was that of allowing the release of emotions within an accepting and understanding environment. In the more impersonal groupings with which she was affiliated during her time in Italy, this function was somewhat repressed and led to tension and frustration. This phenomenon is also portrayed in Incidents 29 ("Pizza for Dinner") and 48 ("A Chance Acquaintance"). In the former, Joshua suffered fright and anxiety from the small explosion, but he did not feel secure or confident enough to express his emotions within the family with which he was temporarily affiliated. He was reluctant to betray (and release) his true emotions and did not receive any cues from the family that it was appropriate to do so. His anxiety persisted, however, and the appearance of a familiar face and secure presence (his teacher) restored his sense of belonging and sparked an emotional release. In Incident 48, the Filipinos reacted similarly to the unexpected appearance of a familiar cue within the relatively restrained and repressive context of the British culture, which failed to provide for their needs for expression and social validation.

In Incident 39 ("Auditing the Books"), Richard has the presence of his wife to fulfill the needs that intimate relationships provide, but he is suffering a gradual loss of self-esteem and identity because he has no social group to provide validation and respect from others as well as a sense of participation, of belonging to the world around him. Doing important work that is recognized as valuable by others often fulfills an individual's need for respect, and Richard finds himself in a job where he is not expected to make a real contribution. This leads to his increasing dissatisfaction with and hostility toward his environment and those around him.

Incident 38 ("Settling In") exhibits the importance of primary, intimate support groups, which often can come only from the same culture—in this case, from fellow immigrants. (However, in some cases well-established immigrants may view newly arrived immigrants as threats, embarrassments, or both—see Incident 100, "The Local Gang.") Fellow immigrants ideally provide the social integration, attachment, sense of reliable alliance, and social clarifications necessary for newly arrived immigrants to bridge the (quite lengthy) period of adjustment (Rogler, 1994). Ideally, fellow immigrants provide such social support until some of these functions can be fulfilled by members or groups within the host culture, once newer immigrants develop the necessary social and language skills.

Awareness of the functions fulfilled by different social groups, and the potential effects of their absence or deficiency, is thus important in efforts to assist those who are interacting across cultures.

AMBIGUITY

In *Webster's Third New International Dictionary* (1966), *ambiguity* is defined as follows:

(1) the condition of admitting to two or more meanings, of being understood in more than one way, or of referring to two or more things at the same time. (2) looseness of signification or reference; uncertainty of meaning or significance of a position in relation to something or somebody else; mystery or mysteriousness arising especially from a vague knowledge or understanding. (3) the intellectual or emotional interplay or tension resulting from the opposition or contraposing of apparently incompatible or contradictory elements or levels of meaning.

All people have been required at one time or another to make decisions regarding situations about which they were not quite clear. Most circumstances in life have elements of ambivalence or ambiguity in them. In any given situation, organizations and individuals have to deal with factors over which they may not have complete (if any) control (Adler, 1992; Ball & McCulloch, 1993; March & Olsen, 1980). One of the main causes of ambiguity is a lack of clarity or reference. This occurs when the feedback available makes several interpretations possible. An ambiguous statement is one that has two or more possible meanings. But at the same time, "the meanings of an ambiguous expression are mutually exclusive in the context, in the sense that if one applies, the other cannot apply, and vice-versa" (Rimmon, 1977, p. 17). For example, consider a conversation between two people who are exchanging opinions and discussing appropriate behaviors regarding an upcoming trip to another country. One says to the other, "Understanding is required of the visitor." This sentence could be taken to mean either that people of the host country need to be more understanding of the visitor or that the visitor needs to understand something more about the host country. It is ambiguous because it is unclear whether the visitor is giving or receiving understanding. Although either could be true, both meanings cannot operate at the same time and communicate the speaker's intent.

Brislin and Yoshida (1994b) describe how the manner in which people are socialized in one culture subsequently may lead to ambiguity later in life when people cross cultures. Children learn what is, as well as what is not, considered appropriate and effective behavior as they are socialized within any particular culture. Part of the difficulty of growing up stems from the fact that many of a culture's norms are learned by trial and error. Once people have reached adulthood, they have become quite fluent in what is expected and are able to function smoothly within their culture's parameters. Brislin and Yoshida liken this process to that of learning the particular functions certain keys represent on a keyboard for a particular word-processing program. When people find themselves in new and different cultural settings, they are faced with what on the outside appear to be familiar surroundings, but the functions of the elements of those surroundings may be somewhat different from what they have come to know. Life and work situations that used to be quite predictable suddenly becomes ambiguous, unpredictable, and confusing.

One of the major conflicts an individual in a cross-cultural context faces in terms of ambiguity is that of having insufficient information or experience to make judgments. Sometimes individuals are aware of the spectrum of choices and simply cannot make selections; more often, however, they have no clue as to what the various possibilities might be, though they know they must make choices. When a person encounters an ambiguous expression, he or she must choose among the possible meanings, even though he or she may not have sufficient information to do so. If a person must make an important decision and yet lacks the relevant information to base it on, stress, frustration, and misunderstandings often result (Triandis, Kurowski, Tecktiel, & Chan, 1993). Individual stress is greatest where information or presuppositions are most incomplete or seemingly inconsistent. To overcome this stress, individuals must make conscious or preconscious guesses to provide the appropriate context or judgmental standards. Thus people frequently fill in information, usually from their own familiar and potentially inaccurate frames of reference, without realizing they have done so.

In cross-cultural situations, people are often operating with less information than usual, yet are still required to make decisions (Pruegger &

Rogers, 1994; Witte, 1993). This can be both confusing and frustrating. An individual can alleviate a great deal of stress by cultivating an open mind concerning divergent or unfamiliar meanings. Because in many such situations no guidelines are available, it is advisable for sojourners to suspend judgment or refrain from making attributions until they can obtain as much information as possible. It is also helpful to develop patience and an attitude of openness.

A second kind of ambiguity that individuals face in cross-cultural contexts occurs when they are confronted by situations that are somewhat familiar, but that carry different significance or consequences from those that apply in their own culture. Often in such cases individuals are unaware of what appropriate responses would be. The complexity of this is compounded by factors in the host culture that may be unfamiliar to outsiders. The various domains of politics, religion, family, and social structure all play influential roles. Adding to the confusion is the fact that even within a given society or culture, expected responses may vary from situation to situation and from individual to individual. The individual, then, must think about issues in terms of many dimensions, should be open to change even when all aspects of the situation seem perfectly clear, should be patient in dealing with others, and should take a broad point of view (Brislin, 1981, 1993).

Another form of ambiguity can occur when an individual has many associations or predetermined conceptions. In ambiguous instances, there is a salient expectation factor. That is, people tend to see what they expect to see when faced with vagueness or ambiguity; they may believe they have found the target of their expectations, even if it is not actually present (Triandis et al., 1993). This expectation factor differs from individual to individual, depending on the person's past experiences and on the present situation. For instance, sojourners wanting to be accepted by hosts and anxious about host reactions might overinterpret casual remarks. In the United States, for example, comments such as "We must get together soon and have a cup of coffee" and "Come on over anytime" are often used as part of attempts to close conversations. These are often just casual remarks and not real invitations; however, if a visitor is desirous of developing relationships, he or she might misinterpret them and push to set an actual time and place for another meeting when none was really intended. He or she may even show up at a host's home unannounced, causing the host to feel embarrassed and to feel that the visitor is a bit pushy (see Incident 16, "New Friends").

Those with very well established and explicit value systems may have a hard time accepting the idea that certain behaviors and situations may have different meanings and consequences. Thus they may have inappropriate or perhaps even damaging expectations. Sojourners would be wise to take some time to examine their own personal value systems and worldviews and to become aware of what some of their expectations might be. They may then be able to adjust their expectations if they seem unreasonable in terms of a new and different environment. (We have also examined these issues in the essay above on emotional experiences and disconfirmed expectations.)

Coping with ambiguity is difficult, but there are ways to deal with it beyond passive acceptance and a futile worldview. To accomplish this, some understanding is required on the part of the individual. The trait of tolerance for ambiguity has been identified as one of the key characteristics necessary for any individual who hopes to adjust successfully to an intercultural context. A tolerance for ambiguity includes the ability to think clearly about problems and issues even though one does not know all the facts and probable outcomes of one's decisions. "A person who has this trait realizes that, especially with respect to important problems, decisions cannot be made which will address all ramifications and please everyone" (Brislin, 1981, p. 55). Individuals can develop and cultivate this trait by consciously trying to broaden their worldviews (Gudykunst, 1994; Gudykunst, Wiseman, & Hammer, 1977). They should keep open and inquisitive minds, and should realize that there are valid points of view different from their own. Living with ambiguity can be very uncomfortable, but it can also be an enriching experience.

Application to the Culture Assimilator Incidents

Incidents 31 and 85 present ambiguous situations where the information the persons involved needed to make decisions was incomplete or lacking. They could readily entertain a diversity of interpretations, and at the same time could see no clues on which to base appropriate choices. In Incident 85 ("Who Gains Entry?"), the man who was denied entry was involved in a quite ambiguous situation. Although the person who entered the gymnasium before him also did not have the required identification card, it was not made clear that the attendant had admitted him because she knew him. It is easy to see how the man denied entry might have misinterpreted the situation and subsequently responded in an inappropriate manner. In Incident 31 ("Social Ease"), Daureen was confronted with a seemingly familiar occasion—a birthday party. She found herself, however, in the uncomfortable position of not understanding her hosts' reactions to her behavior. Operating on beliefs formed from her previous experiences, she had no clues to help her discern what appropriate and socially skilled behavior might be. In her confusion, Daureen concluded erroneously that the laughter of the others at the party was directed at her personally. This increases her frustration and feelings of disorientation. People who find themselves in such ambiguous situations should avoid drawing conclusions too quickly. Rather, they should seek out explanations for what they have witnessed or should consult with resource people who have more intimate knowledge of the host culture. Sojourners, particularly, should keep in mind that cross-cultural interactions often operate on value systems that are not known to them, and this frequently leads to confusion. They would be wise to recognize this factor, and thus not let confusion lead to further frustration. Sojourners should be encouraged to cultivate openness and patience, qualities that help people to cope with ambiguous situations.

Related to the variations in value systems is the problem presented in Incident 46 ("Too Hot—or Not Too Hot?"), where the circumstances seemed familiar enough, but the appropriate responses were not ones to which the people involved were accustomed. Rather, they were based on differing value hierarchies. In the incident, Stephanie applied a familiar customary response to the stimulus of being too hot: She donned shorts. In her new environment, however, this was not an appropriate action, and the subsequent reaction from the host society confused her (and potentially could have harmed her). The wearing of shorts in the host culture had other connotations attached to it that in turn stimulated further unpleasant reactions. Sojourners should be mindful that customs or behavior acceptable in their own countries may have different meanings or consequences in others. They should try to investigate the possible repercussions of their actions *before* acting.

Incidents 47, 50, and 105 deal with the relationship between expectation and ambiguity. When faced with ambiguous situations, people tend to find what they expect to find. If their expectations are not met, disappointment results. Tolerance for ambiguity in such a situation means that people must be willing to go beyond their predetermined expectations and be open to new experiences. In Incident 47 ("A Shopper's Delight?"), Nancy's expectations of her experience had been so predetermined that when the actual situation occurred she became very disappointed and her reaction was characterized by negativeness. Sojourners should be careful not to allow their expectations to be so high as to be unrealistic. In Incident 50 ("The Immigration Officer"), Felipe also becomes disillusioned, because his expectations concerning his status and subsequent treatment are strongly violated. To avoid undue stress, sojourners should be wary of establishing expectations based upon preconceptions that may be erroneous. They would be wise to examine carefully whatever expectations they may have so as to adjust them readily if the need arises. Part of people's expectations should also be to consider that things will not be as they seem and that an extra measure of patience and openness may be required. In some cases, tolerance will mean seeing ambiguity from the point of view of the hosts.

Consider Incident 50 again. This situation is very ambiguous for the customs inspector as well. He does not know of the significance of Felipe's status (or how one from Felipe's country would treat someone of high status). The customs inspector does not know anything about Felipe's immigration plans, or how many presents someone from Felipe's country must bring for his friends, and so forth. The customs agent's way of coping with ambiguity may be to treat everyone (high or low status) in a standard manner. If Felipe were to consider this fact, he would not feel that he is the target of discrimination. Considering this aspect again, let's look at Incident 105 ("Lessons in English?"). Masayo's conflict and confusion stemmed from the fact that her expectations of how Mrs. Osaki should respond to her were not fulfilled. Having been exposed to American values, Masayo had incorporated some of them into her own personal system. She made a judgment and concluded that Mrs. Osaki was not sincere. Mrs. Osaki, on the other hand, was operating according to another value hierarchy and did not wish to offend Masayo or her family. She had no idea how one might make a refusal in the American culture and was puzzled by Masayo's "half-American" behavior. She did know that Masayo and her family had been in Japan for many years and so chose to operate in a way that was most familiar to herself. If sojourners would consider the fact that their hosts may also be placed in ambiguous situations by their presence, perhaps it would be easier for them to be patient and to take the time and extra effort needed to investigate and clarify ambiguous situations and develop tolerance.

PREJUDICE AND ETHNOCENTRISM

A basic fact about human nature, probably a result of our evolutionary history, is that people need to surround themselves with others who provide social acceptance and help in times of need (Fiske, 1991). (See also the essay on the in-group/out-group distinction in Chapter 13.) One conse-quence of this is that people invest large amounts of time and energy in learning the norms of the groups to which they want to belong, as well as learning proper ways of behaving in large numbers of social settings. Given this investment, people come to believe that the behaviors they practice are good and that behaviors practiced by other groups are either not as good or, in some cases, bad. People's judgments about the behavior of out-group members based on learned concepts of good and bad are the basis of ethnocentrism and prejudice (Allport, 1954). Ethnocentrism is the making of judgments based on the standards of one's own ethnic or cultural group and applying those standards in judging others, who may be from different cultural backgrounds. It is useful to break the term down into its component parts: *Ethno* is from a root word referring to racial, ethnic, or cultural groupings; *centrism* is from the root word *center*. Ethnocentric persons hold views that are own-group centered; they make judgments about other groups based on the perspective of their own, and believe those judgments to be reasonable and appropriate.

When people make judgments that are harsh, unkind, or discriminatory toward out-group members and that involve rejection such that the emotions of anger, disgust, and/or desire to avoid contact are felt, these judgments are called *prejudiced*. Further, use of the term *prejudice* connotes a lack of thought or care given to the making of judgments. Again, it is useful to break down the term: *Pre* means beforehand; *judice* comes from the same root as *judge*. Thus prejudice is a form of prejudgment, or judging based on no particular knowledge, without any previous thought or concern.[1]

The Functions of Prejudice

A good way to understand the nature of prejudice is to examine its functions or uses (Brislin, 1993; Katz, 1960). The basic assumption behind a functional analysis is that if psychological phenomena did not have uses for people, they would disappear. For example, fear encourages people to prepare for danger; pain makes people aware of injury, so that they do not injure themselves further.

Prejudice serves at least four functions. The first is the *utilitarian* or *adjustment* function. People need to adjust to a complex world. If holding certain prejudiced attitudes helps them to adjust, then they will maintain those attitudes. For example, the belief that members of a certain ethnic out-group cannot hold responsible jobs means that there will be less competition for those jobs (Jones, 1989). Among sojourners, this problem has been analyzed by Kidder (1977), who has noted that some people maintain colonial attitudes by viewing locals as fit only for the roles of servant or subordinate. The *ego-defensive* function of prejudice is to protect people's views of themselves. If some individuals want to think of themselves as good businesspeople even though they are not particularly successful, they may view those in another and more successful group as cheaters or schemers. This attitude protects the individuals' self-image and does not necessitate examination of their reasons for failure in the business world. Prejudice is also ego defensive in that it protects a positive view of one's in-group. People learn to value highly the viewpoints put forth by their in-group, and it is easier to reject out-groups than it is to admit that they may have their own worthwhile standards and points of view.

The *value-expressive* function of prejudice is to project or demonstrate the individual's self-image. For example, if people believe themselves to be standing up for the one true God through their religious attitudes, then other groups must be incorrect in some way. If one's in-group has attained creature comforts through the use of valued high technology, then one may see out-group members who have no knowledge of this technology as backward. The value-expressive function of prejudice can complement the ego-defensive function. The former projects or shows an image to the world, whereas the latter protects that image through attitudes that shift the blame for difficulties to others.

The *knowledge* function of prejudice involves the way information is learned and organized. Some prejudiced attitudes serve to provide knowledge about the world as seen by the in-group (Tzeng & Jackson, 1994), such as the knowledge that certain out-group members are not desirable business partners or romantic companions. Such attitudes help people make decisions when faced with choices in the business world or in their personal lives. (We discuss the important topic of how people in various cultures acquire and use knowledge in other essays, such as those on categorization, differentiation, and learning styles.) An important point for understanding prejudiced attitudes is that the acquisition of knowledge requires time and energy. Given this investment, people have a natural tendency to see others who have not acquired the same knowledge as undereducated or ignorant. Another important point is that, when interacting in other cultures, at least in the international context, sojourners will almost always be placed in the category of out-group members, although often the exact reasons may be unclear. The reasons for such placement will differ from culture to culture, and many of these reasons will be unfamiliar and thus strange to sojourners. If sojourners make an effort to understand the reasons, they may be able to behave in ways that will minimize the negative consequences of their out-group placement. There is a close relationship between the knowledge function and the adjustment function of prejudice. The former involves the facts and information that people in the in-group think should be known and understood. The latter involves the use of that information in making actual decisions. Returning to the above example of knowledge about the business world and friends of the opposite sex, there can be severe consequences for those who violate expectations based in this shared knowledge. People can be expelled from their in-group for entering into relationships with the wrong business associates or marriage partners.

Application to the Culture Assimilator Incidents

In Incident 42 ("Island Paradise: Two Experiences"), all four of the functions of prejudice were involved in Robert's reactions to Samoa. Robert had previously experienced bad relations with Samoans in Hawaii (knowledge function), which had led to his avoiding Samoans so as to circumvent trouble (adjustment function). Undoubtedly, he felt that his own ethnic group was much wiser when it came to settling disputes (value-expressive function), and he felt that Samoans were entirely to blame for all the difficulties he had encountered (ego-defensive function). Financial circumstances, however, forced him to move to Samoa. There, his previous prejudices simply did not work and did not help him in his adjustment. He found, instead, that Samoans could be very pleasant people when seen on their own terms and in their own cultural setting. Prejudice itself is an emotional reaction. Coming to terms with one's past prejudices, and discovering that they no longer work, is an emotional experience that many sojourners encounter.

Confronting one's prejudices can yield benefits. In the 1940s, Red Barber was the radio broadcaster for the Brooklyn Dodgers baseball team. Raised in the American South, he had been socialized into a set of very prejudicial attitudes toward blacks. The Dodgers' management decided to integrate baseball by bringing in the first black player, Jackie Robinson. At first, Barber threatened to quit his job rather than broadcast for a team with a black man on its roster. Talked out of his decision, Barber later came to view working with Robinson as a "cleansing experience" during which he grew as a person and overcame the prejudices of his childhood (Tygiel, 1983).

Understanding the nature of ethnocentrism is important in analyzing Incident 55 ("A Political Debate?"). Qing-yu, from mainland China, had been socialized to believe in the superiority of her political system and had not been encouraged, in her formal education, to analyze seriously the positive and negative aspects of other systems. Her point of view was ethnocentric; she judged other political systems from the perspective of only a limited set of familiar concepts. Sharlene, on the other hand, had been exposed to an educational philosophy that encouraged the study of other systems and the analysis of good and bad points according to a variety of standards. Consequently, Sharlene was much better prepared than Qing-yu to engage in serious discussion in which both parties try to learn rather than simply defend their own cultures' policies. In general, sojourners from highly industrialized nations often find that hosts in less technologically developed societies are very sensitive to having "negative" aspects of their countries pointed out to them.

A number of incidents that are discussed in other essays also bring out points involving prejudiced attitudes. In Incident 50 ("The Immigration Officer"), Felipe feels that he has been singled out for special attention and has been treated in a prejudiced manner. The officer, on the other hand, is trying to do his job as best he can. All sojourners will encounter episodes during which they feel they are the targets of prejudice, but looking beneath the surface of the encounter may yield a more innocuous explanation. In Incident 110 ("Not Accepted by Her Peers"), Tomoko felt she was being treated badly. She undoubtedly had been the target of prejudice in that her peers were not tolerant of her because she deviated from very rigid norms. Tomoko had studied abroad for several years and so had not had as much exposure to Japanese norms as her peers. In some countries, including Japan, special schools are now being established to help integrate returning students into their own cultures and to reduce the stress of readjustment.

Two incidents bring up reasons for prejudice, or placement in an out-group category, that may have been unfamiliar to the sojourners involved. In Incident 36 ("The Soccer Game"), Dave was sojourning in Great Britain and was surprised to find that he encountered difficulties in trying to help his son develop friendships with hosts. Dave took his son, Alan, and Alan's British friend to a soccer game, failing to recognize that different cultures view the same activity in different ways. In Great Britain, soccer is considered a sport for the working class, and upper-middle-class parents may frown on their children's involvement. The British boy's parents may also have been concerned about safety, because gangs of hooligans, reportedly composed of working-class people, make a point of disrupting soccer games. The reason for the problem Dave encountered, prejudice involving social class, may be relatively unfamiliar to Americans, who usually associate prejudice with ethnic and racial differences. In Incident 67 ("Skillful at Getting Grants"), Herb was puzzled by the lack of acceptance of his project. The reason for the difficulty was that Herb had been placed in an out-group and denied the possibility of cooperation from colleagues because of his funding source. This reason for out-group placement is far less common in the United States than in other countries, and so Herb was puzzled. If he could have discovered the reason for his rejection, he might have been able to challenge the preconceptions of his colleagues in the host country and encourage them to cooperate. But unless he learned the exact reason for his hosts' judgment, he could not effectively appeal any decision.

For sojourners, then, a key to obtaining goals is to learn the reasons for hosts' decisions and then make appropriate changes in their own behavior. Sometimes these changes will lead people to behave quite differently from the ways they learned were appropriate in their own cultures (Bhawuk & Brislin, 1992). In Incident 68 ("The Shinto Priest"), the Americans viewed the act of bringing in a priest to solve an industrial problem as silly. The Japanese viewed such an intervention as necessary. Disaster was likely to occur unless the Americans found out the reason for the Japanese recommendation and learned to understand the host point of view regarding the industrial problem.

NOTE

1. Some prejudices may be viewed as positive, as when sojourners believe that everything about their host culture is good. This can lead to problems, however, when these positive prejudices are disconfirmed by the inevitable negative behaviors that all sojourners encounter. We address in this essay the more frequent use of the term *prejudice,* with its negative connotations.

12

KNOWLEDGE AREAS

Education, both formal and informal, is a long and arduous process. People must invest a great deal of time and energy to learn enough to achieve their goals in their own cultures. Great effort is expended in learning to speak and to write one's native language well, to discover what is needed to complete important tasks, and to learn to interact effectively with others at society's various status levels. Because people have intense investments in their knowledge, they find it upsetting to discover that some others believe educated people should possess quite different knowledge. Put another way, people learn the "facts" necessary to meet their desired goals in their own cultures, and they find it very upsetting to discover that members of other cultures have different views concerning the "facts."

People working across cultures frequently report "war stories" based on confrontations between what one person considers knowledge and someone else considers ignorance. Certain topic areas seem to be brought up again and again in these stories:

1. interpretation of knowledge about what are considered good and poor efforts at work;
2. the manner in which people orient themselves in time and space;
3. verbal and nonverbal communication, as well as the process of language learning;
4. the behaviors associated with different roles (e.g., boss, father, student);
5. when the individual person is emphasized in contrast to when the group is the focus of attention;
6. rituals and superstitions;
7. where people fit into a society's hierarchy (sometimes called the pecking order); and

8. values concerning such basic concepts as politics, aesthetics, economics, and religion.

Collectively, we call these topics *knowledge areas*. Sojourners who have some understanding of these areas are better equipped than those who do not to make decisions regarding many everyday behaviors.

WORK

It has been suggested that people experience disorientation when they enter new workplaces that is comparable to the beginnings of an experience in a new culture (Handy, 1976). Both of these processes can be problematic because of the lack of congruence between people's prior socialization and the day-to-day demands of the new environment. For instance, people socialized to interact cooperatively with peers will become disoriented if they go to work in organizations where rewards are distributed individual-istically (Graen & Wakabayashi, 1994) and on a competitive basis (e.g., salespeople on commission). Because the workplace occupies such a large part of most people's time, and given that the majority of those using these training materials will most likely encounter many of their cross-cultural interactions in conjunction with their work, we give special consideration here to the dynamics of the workplace (Adler, 1992; Dowling, Schuler, & Welch, 1994; Erez, 1994).

One characteristic of the workplace is that it affords a common ground for many different kinds of people to come together. Unlike in most marriage arrangements and most social and recreational interactions, individuals do not generally have control over the selection of individuals with whom they must work. A variety of interpersonal and intrapersonal differences are, therefore, expected to occur. In addition, the context of the workplace creates its own culture. Deal and Kennedy (1982) identify five elements that come together to create a corporate culture: (a) the business environment, determined by the types of products bought and sold, competitors, customers, technologies, and government influences; (b) values, which define success for employees as well as establish standards of success; (c) heroes, or individuals who illustrate the corporate values through their particular deeds; (d) rites and rituals, or the specific rules that are followed within the organization, including degree of formality and rules for meetings; and (e) the cultural network, consisting of the informal communication that takes place within the organization.

In the cross-cultural setting, individuals bring with them particular ways of interacting and particular expectations of others that may be quite different from the behaviors and beliefs of others in the organization. For instance, for people of many Latin American and Asian countries, work and social relationships are closely intertwined (elements d and e in Deal & Kennedy's list). A considerable amount of emphasis and expectations may be placed on socializing with fellow workers during and after the workday (Graen & Wakabayashi, 1994).

A potential problem arises when European Americans, who are generally relatively task oriented, go to work in more socially oriented societies. European Americans often bring to work situations in other contexts the behaviors they would expect to manifest at their home offices: precision, diligence, punctuality—a hardworking, nose-to-the-grindstone, Protestant work ethic. To others who may define work as a combination of job-related activities and social relations, European American workers may appear dogmatic, oppressive, pushy, and cold—characteristics diametrically opposed to those expected in their own setting (Hofstede, 1991). Working style and individual interactive style are critical factors that must be identified and understood if workers from two cultures are to interact effectively. The skills that benefit European Americans in their home culture (precision, perseverance, task completion, punctuality), and that are often the focus of peer admiration and rewards through promotion, may be a hindrance in more socially oriented societies.

As patterns of interaction and artifacts that make life easier in a particular environmental setting emerge from individual cultures, so organizations take on particular characteristics that differentiate them from others and help to define their uniqueness. Handy (1976) identifies a variety of factors in the organizational setting that may vary from culture to culture. These characteristics, which should be addressed, include the way in which work should be organized; the manner in which authority should be exercised; the amount of planning that should be done and the time perspective applied to work; how rewards, reinforcements, and controls should be carried out; the degree to which conformity and initiative should be expected; the degree to which the individual feels she or he can control the situation; and the physical setting of the work environment.

Hofstede (1980, 1991), in his landmark study of cultural differences among more than 116,000 IBM employees working in more than 50 countries and speaking 20 different languages, found large cross-cultural differences with regard to worker values in four areas:

1. *Power distance.* This refers to the amount of preferred psychological distance between workers and managers. Countries with a high score on instruments that measure power distance are those where authority is concentrated among a relatively small number of managers. The Philippines, Mexico, Venezuela, and India are examples of countries with high power indexes. New Zealand, Israel, Austria, and Denmark are relatively low on this dimension.

2. *Uncertainty avoidance.* This includes the perceived freedom to break company rules, the frequency of stress on the job, and the perceived length of an employee's stay with a certain company. Generally speaking, the higher the uncertainty avoidance level, the lower the willingness to take risks.

3. *Individualism.* This refers to the amount of freedom people have in making decisions related to their work.

4. *Masculinity-femininity.* This refers to goals *traditionally* preferred by males (advancement, earnings, training, and up-to-dateness) in highly industrialized countries and goals *traditionally* preferred by females (friendly atmosphere, position security, good physical conditions, good relations). (We emphasize *traditionally* here because women are increasingly demanding equal opportunities for good salaries and advancement in many countries.)

Hofstede and Bond (1988; see also Hofstede, 1991; Wang, 1994) later added a fifth dimension they call *Confucian dynamism,* developed to help explain the tremendous economic growth recently experienced by the "five dragons" of Japan, South Korea, Hong Kong, Taiwan, and Singapore. Characteristic of countries that rank high in Confucian dynamism is the importance of understanding and respecting unequal relationships, such as those between parent and child, teacher and student, and manager and subordinate. Such relationships seem to be marked by mutual obligations—"seniors" are expected to provide guidance and to look out for the interests and development of "juniors." Other characteristics of Confucian dynamism include a high value on hard work and perseverance, and a concern for the future.

An area of special concern confronting both managers and subordinates centers on the issue of decision-making style. Although many European Americans are comfortable with, and have come to expect, a democratic and participative decision-making process in the workplace, whereby many individuals have input into decisions, other cultural systems may not offer this luxury. Those countries where a value is placed on high power distance (to use Hofstede's term) tend to defer decisions solely to the individual in authority.

Potential problems exist for both sides. The worker who expects to be consulted when decisions are being made may find him- or herself feeling rejected, with lowered self-esteem, when in a work setting that does not encourage employee participation. In a similar manner, tensions may arise between a European American superior who expects input from others and a host subordinate who can only comfortably accept a directive from a superior. A close look at the decision-making styles and expectations of all parties is necessary for good cross-cultural adjustments in the workplace (Erez, 1994; Triandis, Kurowski, & Gelfand, 1994).

Application to the Culture Assimilator Incidents

The importance of socializing and building relationships with work associates is reflected in Incidents 61, 77, and 97. In Incident 61 ("Business or Pleasure?"), Tom's insistence on getting the job done was met with resistance by his Latin American hosts, who found it essential to develop a personal relationship with colleagues in business ventures. In Incident 77 ("Shaping Up the Office"), Ronald was surprised when office morale declined after he made special efforts to change procedures and to increase productivity. A close analysis of his actions, however, shows that his application of American business techniques overlooked an important need of his Latin American employees—the need for a certain amount of workplace socializing. The lack of attention paid to Rick by his fellow teachers in Incident 97 ("The Eager Teacher") was, likewise, due to their orientation to the importance of socializing and relationship building, which was different from Rick's. While concentrating on doing an exceptional teaching job, Rick overlooked the necessity of spending time with his fellow teachers.

Incidents 70 and 74 are concerned with group dynamics and procedures regarding decision making. In Incident 70 ("Transmitting Information on Transmission Systems"), Ted's meeting with the Japanese company did not result in the positive decision that he had originally expected. The reason for this was that Ted violated customary decision-making patterns by introducing a topic for discussion that had not been previously addressed with individual members of the firm. Here, an understanding and sensitivity to cultural differences concerning how decisions are made is essential.

Machmud, in Incident 74 ("The Quiet Participant"), was confronted by John for not fully participating in discussions regarding company decisions. The decision-making styles of John, an American, and Machmud, an Indonesian, differed greatly. In many Asian countries—in general, in countries where the collectivity is valued over the individual—individuals may resist appearing different or standing out from the crowd. This was the reason Machmud was hesitant to participate in the decision-making process. Being confronted by a sudden lack of control on the job is the issue at hand in Incident 62 ("A Manager's Dilemma"). Ned Schwartz, who came from a North American company where he had considerable control, was suddenly faced with lack of cooperation, inefficiency, and large numbers of government regulations. This lack of control led to depression and his subsequent request to return home.

An issue of increasing importance regarding the training of personnel in developing countries centers on what remains behind after the experts depart. In Incident 60 ("A Development Project"), although Matt oversaw the development of a model sewage treatment plant in Nigeria, it began to fail soon after his departure. The primary reason for this failure was the lack of attention paid to education and training programs for host country workers, so they would be able to repair and maintain the system. Transfer of skills is, in some cases, more important than the mere provision of material support. The effective sojourner encourages hosts to develop a sense of ownership for the projects or ideas to which the sojourner contributes. Hosts are most likely to look after innovations in which they have an extensive personal investment.

At issue in Incident 72 ("Are There Ethical Issues Involved?"), are questions related to acceptable business practices. The Chinese want to learn about advanced technology, and they see nothing wrong in scheduling multiple meetings and asking pointed questions meant to discover advanced knowledge among businesspeople who are proposing joint ventures. What may be thought to be a common approach and understanding toward joint work projects may, in fact, be considerably different and should be investigated and understood before two parties begin collaborative work.

Finally, in Incident 59 ("Going to Language Class"), Ron became increasingly dissatisfied with his overseas transfer because his need for achievement and recognition, which had been satisfied in college, was not easily fulfilled by his full-time language studies. Language learning is often slow, and Ron found few immediate rewards in his studies compared with his prior contributions to an important construction project. Good administrators are aware of the potential difficulties that high-need achievers like Ron might face when they must attend language classes full-time. They might meet periodically with such workers to reiterate the need for good language skills, the importance of their presence in the classroom, and the company's appreciation of their efforts.

TIME AND SPACE

The issues of time perspective and spatial orientation stand out as classic examples of culturally determined behavior patterns that give rise to confusing, and often unsettling, experiences (Hall, 1959, 1966, 1983). Concepts of time, except for certain circadian rhythms of the body, are not innate to the human species. Likewise, relatively little of our physical world is bound by any regularity, except perhaps in defining the year and the day. Yet our Western world seems, at times, to revolve entirely around the clock (Kim, 1994).

To Europeans and European Americans, *time* primarily refers to the duration between two points. In everyday conversation, the word *time* is used most frequently with reference to the present and the future. Plans are made for the relatively immediate future, and deadlines and appointments are taken quite seriously. The working unit of time for European Americans is the 5-minute block; any amount of time smaller than that is not considered very important. Thus an individual can typically be 2 or 3 minutes late for a meeting without apologizing. After 5 minutes, he or she is expected to offer a brief apology. If the individual is 15 minutes late—a block of time representing three significant units—he or she is expected to make a lengthy, sincere apology, and perhaps may even be expected to make a phone call to the waiting party to explain the delay. Other cultures, however, do not place the same emphasis on time and punctuality as do most Europeans and European Americans. To the Arab, a historical perspective is important. Arab culture has a 6,000-year history, and many Arabs will address the historical aspects of a situation before addressing the current issue. The working unit of time for many Arabs is also a much larger block than that of European Americans—about 15 minutes.

Many ethnic conflicts that are ongoing today have their roots in events that took place centuries ago. Such conflicts are often puzzling to people whose cultural guidance is to "forget past feelings and examine what is possible for the future."

To the Hopi Indians, time consists of a series of events. It is not fixed or measured; rather, it is expressed or experienced with regard to changes in the environment (such as the maturation of corn or the growth of livestock). Thus, in Hopi culture, there is no fixed time in which something must be completed.

It is evident that references to time and adherence to timetables are culturally determined patterns of behavior. Take, for example, an executive visiting a Latin American branch of his New York firm. Assuming that a

10:00 a.m. appointment that had been set for weeks with the local supervisor would be honored, our executive arrives precisely on time, perhaps even a few minutes early. To his dismay, the meeting does not commence when expected. In fact, the supervisor is not in his office, has not yet arrived at work, and has not contacted his secretary regarding the appointment or his expected arrival time. What should our executive do? He could just sit, for who knows how long, awaiting the arrival of the supervisor (no doubt with his level of annoyance and anger rising every minute). He could leave after waiting an appropriate length of time (but, as we have already seen, what may be considered an appropriate length of time varies, and our unknowledgeable executive does not have this important piece of information). Alternatively, he might misdirect his anger toward the secretary or demand to see the supervisor's superior (assuming there is one). In any case, it is the executive who, because he has assumed (or wished) that things are the same everywhere, will probably act out of place. What should he do? Given that the working time blocks for these individuals are different, it is very possible that the meeting will still take place; the supervisor is not late by his own standards. The executive could use the time available to him to develop a good interpersonal relationship with the secretary or other people in the office, because the qualities of such relationships will aid him in cutting through much red tape in Latin America.

This more relaxed attitude toward time demands is evident in many cultures and has given rise to such expressions as "Hawaiian time" in Hawaii, "rubber time" in Malaysia, and CPT ("colored people's time") in the mainland United States. In the Philippines, "Stateside time" is mentioned as a reminder that people should arrive promptly for a given event. Deaf people often spend large amounts of time saying good-bye to one another, which may interfere with their keeping any prearranged appointments they may have made (Moore & Levitan, 1993; Siple, 1994). One reason for this is that interpersonal relations among the deaf are very important, and so they want to spend as much time as possible with others who use their language. Those sojourning in countries other than their own, as well as those interacting interculturally within a given country, would do well to understand time references from the point of view of those with whom they interact, in order to prevent any embarrassing moments and personal anxieties. They might also check with experienced people from their own cultures or with someone from the host society to find out what to expect.

Spatial Orientation

The way people orient themselves in space with regard to others is also culturally determined (Dolphin, 1988; Hall, 1966). Humans are territorial creatures, as are many other animals, and we share a tendency to feel threatened or attacked when our personal space is encroached upon. We are not, in fact, much different from the many species of birds that, when perched upon a telephone wire, space themselves equidistant from one another. It is easy to cause havoc among a flock of seagulls, for instance, by spreading morsels of bread among them. As they unwillingly violate each others' individual spaces, the frequency of pecking and squabbles increases. Witness, too, what happens among European Americans on an elevator when it stops to pick up another passenger. The occupants shift around to redistribute the space between them and thus maximize their distance from each other. (There is also a cultural distance maintained by silence; it is uncomfortably quiet for most when riding on a crowded elevator.)

The comfortable distances people keep between themselves remain rather constant among members of a given culture, but comfortable distances differ among cultural groups (as they do among intimate friends and relatives). For instance, Latin Americans typically keep much less distance between themselves during casual conversation than do European Americans. The close distance comfortably maintained between Latin Americans typically evokes hostile or sexual feelings in northern Europeans and European Americans; care should be taken to avoid misinterpretation of such culturally influenced differences.

Likewise, it is not uncommon for European Americans to refer to some people as pushy or distant and cold (all adjectives with negative connotations in this context). Think for a moment of the problems that might arise given these labels and the fact that distances between people are based in cultural preferences. For instance, the Latin American who reduces the distance between herself and another when engaged in conversation, out of habit and comfort, may be labeled pushy because her actions have been misinterpreted. The spaces maintained between individuals are usually not reflections of aggressive or pushy personalities (or of cold and distant ones, should a larger comfortable distance be maintained); rather, they are culturally determined. There are some cultures whose norms call for large distances between people (Siple, 1994). For example, the deaf stand or sit relatively far apart so that they can see each other when they are signing (signs typically occur from about 6 inches above the head to the waist, and occasionally beyond those boundaries). If people communicating in sign stand too close to each other, they will not be able to see all the signs made by their conversational partners. A careless observer might make the attribution that such people feel cool and distant toward one another.

Application to the Culture Assimilator Incidents

A case in point with reference to time and adherence to timeliness is presented in Incident 66 ("Opening a Medical Office"). Tom was anxiously awaiting his new patients, who were late for their appointments according to Tom's perspective. But the unit of time that Tom was comfortable working with was quite different from that of his Arab patients. Although the patients appeared to be 30 minutes late (and they *were* by the clock), it was still likely that they would arrive, given their own acceptable time frame.

The issue of personal distance is taken up in Incident 9 ("The Final Advance"). In this incident, both Jane and Dinorah attempted to maintain their comfortable distances. As Dinorah moved closer, Jane responded by moving away, and thus the two moved constantly across the floor. Jane finally felt threatened and left this uncomfortable situation.

Incident 24 ("A Kiss Away") takes the issue of personal distance one step further and explores cultural differences regarding displays of affection in public places. Although in some countries public displays of affection are commonplace, in others they are not. More confusing for some is the fact that in some countries (particularly in some Asian and Mediterranean ones), displays of affection between persons of the same sex are acceptable, but those between persons of different sexes are not condoned. Sojourners are advised to use discretion in this area until they thoroughly understand the local customs.

Incident 103 ("The Unpopular Professor") considers the issue of spatial orientation and sexual harassment. In this case, Dr. Fazio consistently maintains too close an interpersonal distance between himself and his students, thus causing tremendous anxiety on the part of his female students. This case illustrates the fact that even if a person's socialization in a given culture demands such close proximity, when he or she is living and working in another setting it may be best to adopt local norms. Such is what Dr. Fazio's dean recommends.

Incident 41 ("A Pacific Paradise?") brings forth the issue of public versus private space. In Barbara's case, she was reacting adversely to a lack of privacy, something she was accustomed to having back home. Yet although this privacy was not available to her in her home in Samoa, the community at large was showing their acceptance of her by treating her no differently than they would one of their own. Arabs typically take this one step further. In Arab culture, what is public space is considered to be open to the public, and what a European American might consider the personal space around him or her may be "violated" by an Arab if it is in a public space. For instance, if one person is standing in a certain spot and a second person wants to stand there, the second person would think nothing of making the first person so uncomfortable that he or she will leave, thus freeing the space for the second person to take over.

VIEWING COMMUNICATION IN A CROSS-CULTURAL CONTEXT

Human beings, no matter where they are found, are constantly expressing themselves, using both verbal and nonverbal language. People use verbal as well as nonverbal expression to communicate feelings, intentions, personality, and needs—in essence, their subjective culture (Burgoon, Buller, & Woodall, 1989; Keating, 1994). Individuals also use verbal and nonverbal expression to link themselves to others, usually communicating with those with whom they share a mutual understanding of meanings (Kochman, 1981; Moore & Levitan, 1993). Sometimes the meanings may have slightly different significance attached to them; sometimes the meanings are so disparate that there is a great deal of confusion; and sometimes the differences are extremely subtle and act solely on the nonverbal level (Singelis, 1994). Within any community, the majority use the same modes of communication; thus we tend to take our own language for granted. In crossing over from one society or culture to another, one of the most obvious aspects with which people must cope is communication differences.

One of the reasons communication differences appear so obvious is that much of our everyday maneuvering is accomplished through the use of language. The sojourner confronted by language differences but lacking ability in the host language must learn to carry out the normal daily activities by communicating through other means. For instance, the busy mother who needs to provide for her hungry family goes out to shop for food. In her own society, she probably uses familiar shopping areas; in a new area within her own country, she may depend on street signs or ask directions of someone. However, in a place where a different language is used to communicate, this mother may have to depend on sign language, gestures, or drawings for information. When she finally gets to an area that sells the items she is searching for, instead of being able to tell the shopkeepers what she wants, she again has to depend on pointing or describing with gestures or drawings. The stress of such a predicament is apt to lead to discouragement and/or depression and can affect one's whole mental outlook. Everyday, simple activities may suddenly become very complex. Some of this is due to the fact that familiar and mastered rules and modes of communication have changed and are sometimes unknown, as in the example cited earlier of learning to use a new word-processing program—the keyboard remains the same, but the functions of the various keys have become different. If sojourners are prepared to expect such difficulties, it may conceivably lessen their impact and thus the overall stress of adjustment. Sojourners in particular, but also anybody working and living in cultural settings other than their own, must accept the fact that they will go through an awkward learning stage, and inherent in this process are the uncomfortable feelings of clumsiness and failure. Such discomfort often inhibits and threatens people, as it affects their self-worth and self-esteem. If sojourners are able to realize that learning is a process and that their uncomfortable and helpless emotions are relatively normal and transitory, this may hasten their adjustment and improve the whole learning environment, and thus the learning process.

Another aspect of language is that it not only encompasses a person's self-esteem but also inculcates the broader perspective of a person's or society's customs and values system. This perspective on language—referred to as the Sapir-Whorf hypothesis (Whorf, 1956)—is of major importance. Language learning can greatly enhance and deepen sojourners' understanding of their experiences, by allowing them greater insight into and improving their adaptation to their new environments. Take, for example, the sojourner in the South Sea Islands who discovers that the people there have not one word for coconut but numerous words, depending on the function or state of the particular part of the coconut indicated (see the essay on differentiation in Chapter 13). Understanding this allows the sojourner to see that, in this society, the coconut plays a very important role in the people's lives. The same would hold true for someone visiting in Japan, where there are numerous ways of referring to rice. Sojourners might be stimulated by such insights based in language to reflect on aspects of their own societies that are revealed in language—do they have many terms to refer to such things as automobiles, politics, or economics? Such reflection on the part of sojourners may lead them to greater understanding of their own cultures as well.

There are also many pitfalls involved in learning a new language. For instance, an individual may eagerly learn how to say a word or phrase familiar in his or her own language and think to use it in the same fashion in the new environment. However, in this new situation, there may be social mores or other significant meanings attached to such phrases of which he or she is unaware, and this may lead to misunderstandings. People who make such mistakes in language use should try to remember that learning is difficult and that such faux pas may often occur. The key is to be alert to such problems and to learn from them (Brislin & Yoshida, 1994b).

In crossing communication barriers, one often finds words, phrases, actions, and concepts that are not common in one's own system, and vice versa. Learning to use these new meanings (or lack of meanings) correctly can be difficult. Individuals should be forewarned about using phrases that have multiple meanings. Although such phrases may be readily understood in their own societies, their use may have disastrous effects in another society if hearers choose a meaning that was not intended. This often happens with phrases governed by sociolinguistic-type rules, such as when an American says, "Well, I've got to go. See you later." The phrase "see you later" is governed by a leave-taking rule known to other Americans. This does not necessarily mean that the speaker will in fact see the other person later; it is merely a parting formula. Speakers of other languages have frequently accused Americans of being insincere because of the use of such expressions. Those interacting across cultures should use such colloquialisms and slang terms carefully; in some cases, it would be best to avoid them altogether (Freimanis, 1994).

Language learning can and should be a very rewarding process, as long as one remembers to take a learner's attitude and to be cautious in the use of new learning. One should also keep in mind that failure is part of learning and, as such, should not be taken too seriously. Moreover, members of the host culture often greatly appreciate sojourners' efforts to handle their language and communication style, however clumsily. If time demands prevent intensive language study, sojourners should make a point of learning about 100 common phrases in the host language. Such efforts show concern and interest in the host culture and open many doors for further learning, adding to the total value of the intercultural experience. The converse is also true—not knowing the language limits the interaction one can have in a new culture. More important, a language is more than a related set of vocabulary phrases and rules—it represents the worldview of the people who speak it, and as such reflects important concepts and modes of thinking. In this light, it is important to note that an individual's attitude toward the host language will affect his or her attitude toward the host people and culture as well (Lambert, 1972). However, as Brislin and Yoshida (1994b) caution, the sojourner should take care not to concentrate on learning a language to the exclusion of learning about the culture (not an unheard-of approach in some training efforts). In such a situation, a person can become a "fluent fool"—he or she may speak the language rather well, yet still be culturally ignorant. Because of his or her language skills, others may assume such a person is culturally fluent as well, and so when a cross-cultural misunderstanding occurs, the hosts may blame it on the person's personality rather than on his or her well-meaning ignorance.

Application to the Culture Assimilator Incidents

Two excellent examples of the problems caused by using colloquialisms are present in Incidents 15 ("Party Problems") and 16 ("New Friends"). In Incident 15, Ronald mistakenly assumed that the many familiar cues about his good relationship with Rosalita meant that he would be understood. He used the colloquial phrase "getting hustled" to mean being manipulated or coerced into doing something. Although the phrase does carry that meaning in English, it also has an additional meaning that has sexual connotations. Although Ronald and Rosalita may have had a good understanding of one another, the circumstances in which he used the expression made for a very ambiguous interpretation. Those interacting across cultures would be wise to avoid using expressions that may have multiple meanings. In Incident 16, the Nasciementos interpreted the Johnsons' parting statement, "Drop in anytime," in a literal manner. As we have noted, such statements are a common part of leave-taking behavior known to other Americans. When they are taken literally, as in this incident, the resulting situations can be embarrassing for all involved.

A great part of language learning involves coping with one's inadequacy in the language. Incidents 33 and 59 focus on this issue. In Incident 59 ("Going to Language Class"), Ron had problems in accepting his role in the country. Being accustomed to high personal achievement, which was greatly reduced by his inadequacy in the local language, he found himself in a discouraging situation. Often while people are in the process of learning it is difficult for them to see the actual progress and accomplishments they are making. Sojourners should remember that language learning is a slow process, and that it is unwise for them to set unrealistic goals. In Incident 33 ("Using the Local Language"), Danny was inhibited by the host people's reactions to his efforts in learning the language. Although there may be a number of reasons for any given response, sojourners should remember that hosts' responses of pleasure may be entirely different from their own. In light of the fact that relatively few sojourners take the time and effort required to learn their hosts' language, hosts are apt to be surprised (though delighted) when they do, and may not know how to respond at all. The sojourner's learning attitude is what is important, and it communicates a great deal of care and interest to the hosts.

Both language learners in the incidents discussed above, Ron and Danny, were probably upset by the inevitable instances in which they were misunderstood. Even in their own familiar communities, people are apt to become irate at the thought of being misrepresented or misunderstood, and this reaction is likely to be more intense in an unfamiliar setting. Again, sojourners should keep in mind that learning is a stressful experience that is often sprinkled with failures. With this in mind, they may find it somewhat easier to keep from making erroneous attributions about hosts' responses or motivations. It is also helpful to remember that sometimes, even though sojourners work hard and put out great effort, their hosts will simply not understand the utterances that sojourners may produce. It is important for sojourners to keep trying.

Critical to the issue of language learning is the length of time required to become competent in a second language. This is the key issue in Incident 102 ("Rosita's Homeroom Teacher"). Especially evident in schools is the fact that people are generally able to develop linguistic fluency sufficient to allow them to function in everyday affairs quite readily. This is often referred to as *context-embedded language* (Cummins, 1981); that is, language use is richly supported by the context in which it occurs. It is relatively easy (as among children playing, for instance) to use many context clues from the surrounding environment to assist one's communication competence. However, the language often used in classroom settings is *context-reduced language*. The language used in teaching the distinction between long and short vowels, for instance, is far more complex than playground language and demands a considerable degree of abstract thought. In the incident, Rosita was able to communicate quite readily, and effectively, with children in her daily interactions. Such a degree of linguistic fluency can often be mastered within 1 or 2 years. Mastery of the more complex demands of language, on the level needed for success in the classroom, for instance, may require 5 to 7 years of study. This helped to explain the discrepancy in language mastery observed by Rosita's teacher.

Incident 13 ("The Helpful Classmate") explored communication between able-bodied and disabled individuals. Nonverbal behavior of a person with disabilities is often misinterpreted and viewed as inappropriate by those without disabilities. In a similar manner, the behavior of an able-bodied individual may signal discomfort, confusion, or rejection to a person with disabilities. An unintended cycle of confusion and miscommunication can build up as the behavior of one constrains the behavior of the other. According to the norms shared by many people with disabilities, Algea was the person in Incident 13 who was most polite and accepting of Heather's disability. Many disabled people can do many things by themselves and do not always need or want helpers. Like able-bodied people, people with disabilities also have abilities, and most value their independence. In the situation outlined in the incident, Algea made eye contact with Heather. If Heather had wanted help, she had the opportunity to ask for it after this eye contact had been made. As she did not take this opportunity, Algea left the classroom, knowing that Heather felt she could take care of herself.

Incident 35 ("Rudeness Is in the Eye of the Beholder") explores issues of communication between hearing and hard-of-hearing individuals. At issue in the incident is the appropriateness of moving between two individuals who are signing. According to the norms of deaf culture, the least intrusive way to get from one place to another in a very crowded room where sign conversations are being carried on is to move quickly through people who are signing with each other. If the person crossing the room moves quickly, he or she will not interfere with anyone's communication. If he or she stops to ask permission to move between the signers and does not simply move right through, he or she interferes with their conversation, as they will have to stop, acknowledge the person, let him or her through, and then pick up their conversation. Thus "barging through" is an interesting example of a behavior that is considered appropriate in one culture but rude in another.

Issues concerning extended silence in communication are at the core of Incident 44 ("The Reluctant Counselee"). Quah, a recent Malaysian immigrant, communicated with others from a framework different from that of his counselor. Asians in general tend to wait somewhat longer than Americans for others to finish speaking before they then follow. This is especially true with authority figures, of which Alex, the counselor, was certainly one. Alex was not familiar with such extended silences and became quite nervous. His attempt to cover up his own anxiety by talking more meant that Quah never did have a chance to talk about himself. Unfamiliar with the general "rules" of counseling, Quah left the session without asking for a second appointment. Alex, too, left the session rather frustrated, and he began to question his own abilities as a counselor.

Incident 45 ("The Intense Discussion") explores intensity of verbal communication as it is openly expressed. Many African Americans are quite comfortable when they find themselves in conversations that involve intense disagreements. In contrast, European Americans tend to avoid intense disagreements and to find topics about which people can demonstrate agreement on at least a few points. African Americans tend to operate from the standpoint that putting firm viewpoints forward demonstrates a sign of respect for others. In effect, they say, "Just tell me what you think—don't beat around the bush! Respect me for being able to understand your views, even when they disagree with mine. Then I'll tell you what my views are, and I expect you to listen to them carefully and to show your respect for differing viewpoints." The intensity of many verbal exchanges among African Americans is often misinterpreted by outsiders as anger or hostility.

Related to this issue is Incident 104 ("Silence and Talkativeness"). Deborah, the new teacher, was somewhat confused by the apparent ease and ability of her African American students in discussing and debating issues while on the playground when they were reluctant to do so in the classroom. Many stimuli in the classroom may inhibit certain students from full participation. Such factors may include the fact that a teacher or other authority figure who ultimately passes judgment is present. On the playground, Deborah's students were not in the presence of the teacher. One challenge facing many teachers is to create an atmosphere where *all* students can demonstrate their competence in academic affairs.

Reading between the lines, or the effort to save face without directly saying no to someone, is at issue in Incident 69 ("Was Somebody Saying No?"). From Dr. Xi's point of view, Dr. Hastings may have been saying no, but may have been doing so in a polite way. Among some cultural groups, particularly in some Asian societies, it is considered quite rude to turn somebody down directly. That is, one never communicates a direct no to another, but implies such a response in an indirect manner. Rather than responding with a definite no, a person might say something like, "I will think about it for a while," or "I'll see what I can do." Individuals within the culture understand such a response to mean, in effect, no.

Related to this is Incident 78 ("The Sick Secretary"), in which Todd's approach to resolving conflict exacerbates an already difficult problem. Rather than openly criticizing Chungmin, his secretary, concerning what he believes to be a relatively minor problem, Todd must learn how to read her nonverbal cues and then how best to communicate that he wishes to resolve the dilemma. In the context of this specific situation, most of the interaction is carried out on the nonverbal level.

ROLES

"You can't tell the players without a scorecard" is a homily that is not always necessary to remember in one's own culture. People usually have sufficient information about others with whom they routinely interact during their everyday lives. On the other hand, this homily is a very helpful guide to follow when traveling abroad or when working in a cross-cultural situation. It suggests that the behavior others exhibit may, in fact, be incongruent with one's own expectations given the visual cues received by either party.

A role can be viewed as a set of behaviors one engages in that is specific to a certain position one holds, be it ascribed (e.g., mother, wife, female) or achieved (e.g., bank president, professor). We all hold certain behavioral expectations of those in specific roles (Biddle, 1979; Dunbar, 1994): nurturance from a mother, clear lectures from a professor, and so on. These roles in themselves are culture bound and determined by the community or the culture at large. Thus individuals are socialized into their roles, as well as into ways of interacting with others in their roles. Because socialization is such a potent process, certain values, behavioral patterns, and expectations are internalized and become a basic part of the player's personality. Roles become institutionalized when certain values, expectations, and behavioral patterns are exhibited by the community at large. People generally strive to conform to the expected and shared norms or values of their societies.

Roles are often defined by the appearance of individuals and by the "artifacts" with which they surround themselves. As we expect certain behaviors from those in certain roles, we make judgments about appropriate and inappropriate behavior. For instance, some visual cues of a police officer in American society include a dark blue uniform with a badge on the shirt, black shoes, a hat with a badge, and a gun worn in a holster. Certain behaviors are expected from a person exhibiting such cues, and we would say that she or he is acting appropriately in asking to see a driver's license, assisting those who need help, or speeding down the road in an automobile (with flashers on, of course). We would say this person is acting in an inappropriate manner if we were to see him or her waiting on tables in a restaurant, preparing for surgery in a hospital, running away from the scene of a crime, or stopping a car only to meet its physically attractive driver. Behaviors that diverge from what we expect can be quite unsettling. This point was made evident to one of us while counseling a young student a few years back. This particular child had an extremely difficult time accepting the fact that Anwar Sadat, the president of Egypt, had been assassinated by men who, on the outside, appeared to be Sadat's soldiers. For her, the most disturbing aspect of this incident appeared to be something to the tune of "what you see may not be what you get"—a difficult and traumatic realization for a young child to wrestle with, if not for many adults as well.

Individuals assume a number of different roles in their daily interactions with other individuals, groups, and organizations (Mullavey-O'Byrne, 1994b). The role adopted depends upon the task to be done. Productive, efficient, and healthy persons are able to shift roles as needed (e.g., from participant to leader, from employee to spouse) and understand the appropriate behaviors in each context. Such individuals should not have any great difficulty realizing that those who play by different rules (e.g., have different cultural frameworks) will themselves adopt different roles and have differing expectations.

Family

A variety of different roles, expectations, and situations may arise in the cross-cultural context. The family, for instance, is one institution that has many culturally determined boundaries placed on it (Kagitçibasi, 1990; Kim, Triandis, Kagitçibasi, Choi, & Yoon, 1994). To begin with, the word *family* can refer to either or both the nuclear family or the extended family, and the importance of these may differ. In many societies, for instance, a public announcement of engagement cannot be made until the intended spouse has been approved by the extended family into which he or she intends to marry. In some cases, it may even be the fiance's extended family itself that must be approved.

Deference to specific generations or individuals within families differs across cultures. In many Latin American as well as Arab societies, the aged are venerated, and most, if not all, major decisions are deferred to them. The opposite seems to be true of European American culture, in which youth is idolized and people are admired for remaining youthful. Rather than receiving deference in society or in the family, American elders are often segregated from the mainstream—placed in old-age homes or "golden age" apartment complexes. This arrangement keeps them at a distance from the immediate lives of those in the rest of society, while allowing younger generations the freedom of conscience that goes with knowing they are being cared for.

The roles of children differ from culture to culture as well. The old adage "Children should be seen and not heard" is adhered to strongly in many cultures, especially in those that revere the aged. A child growing up in such a culture may seldom have his or her opinion solicited. Rarely would he or she be encouraged to participate in adult conversation or decision making. In such societies, until children reach the age of adulthood (which varies from culture to culture also), they are expected simply to observe the elders around them.

At the opposite extreme, again, are some families found in the United States that defer to their young. Such families actively seek contributions, feedback, and participation by children in the hope that this will help them to develop the skills necessary to live independent lives in their society. Awareness of the differing perspectives that exist cross-culturally regarding children's roles is important, especially for those who travel with their children and wish to include them in many activities. Many cross-cultural anecdotes center on Americans who have shown up at social gatherings with their children when the hosts did not expect children.

Familism refers to the close identification and association with family. In some societies, familism is such a strong value that socializing often excludes outsiders such as neighbors, friends, and work associates. In many Mediterranean countries (as well as in others), such strong family orientation may cause outsiders to internalize feelings of rejection and isolation when they are not invited to join with friends and coworkers in their friendly family gatherings. Sojourners should be aware that any such exclusions are not the result of their own actions, but simply reflect association preferences specific to certain cultures.

One final concern regarding families that is worthy of mention concerns the mental health and adaptive capacities of the family members who travel with the principal sojourner (the individual whose work, schooling, or other needs prompted the family to move) (Schwartz & Kahne, 1993). In many instances, companies go to great expense to prepare employees for extended experiences in other countries through language and cultural instruction, yet provide little, if any, preparation for accompanying spouses and children. It is critical that spouses, especially nonworking spouses, be prepared to handle the forthcoming changes as well (research is now showing that a spouse's satisfaction is a key determinant in the success of an overseas sojourn for a family). Although spouses may be eager to work (even in a volunteer capacity), in some countries limited numbers and varieties of roles may be open to them, especially to wives. In other nations, it may be difficult for spouses to acquire work permits. Sojourners should be aware of the possibility that their spouses will have a difficult time finding suitable roles in a new culture, and that they may develop a sense of worthlessness as a result.

Sex Roles

Related to roles in the family are distinctions between the roles that males and females play in a culture (Eagly, 1987). Male and female intimate relations and interactions constitute an extremely sensitive issue from culture to culture. The cues that are typically transmitted with regard to intimacy in one culture can easily be misinterpreted in another. The rituals of male-female interaction are so complex and varied that we cannot possibly provide information relevant to all the cultures across which people may interact. We want only to emphasize here that sojourners and others interacting cross-culturally should be aware of this potential source of misunderstanding. They should seek out cultural informants (Brislin & Yoshida, 1994b), either experienced people from their own cultures or hosts who have observed the comings and goings of many sojourners, who can educate them about common mistakes. Thus prepared, they will be less likely to be misunderstood in their interactions with others.

Again, the area of role expectations becomes apparent with regard to traditional versus modern roles of men and women in societies (Moghaddam, Ditto, & Taylor, 1990). Although many nations appear to be modernizing, it is not uncommon for sojourners to find themselves in encounters with individuals or institutions that are deeply influenced by the historical traditions of their countries and cultures. In many nations of Africa, Asia, and Latin America, for instance, women are rarely found in positions of authority, high respect, or responsibility—for the most part, they hold only those positions traditionally afforded them.

Application to the Culture Assimilator
Incidents: The Family

It often occurs that individuals expect of others what they expect of themselves in certain roles and in the roles acted out in their cultures. As with many aspects of cross-cultural contact, expectations of appropriate behavior differ from culture to culture, and the role expectations that individuals have for themselves, their family members, and hosts may lead to conflicts. In Incident 22 ("A Night Out"), the acceptable behavior of children is the issue. Whereas it is common (and, in many families, expected) for American children to initiate discussion and actively explore their environments, unafraid of asking questions, nearly the opposite is expected of Belizean children. The Usher family, in this case, was not prepared for the activity of the American children, and the Thomases were not aware that the actions of their children would contradict the expectations of their hosts.

In Incident 27 ("Next-Door Neighbors"), Chris and Margaret felt as though they were disliked by their neighbors because their social invitations were always turned down. Likewise, Chris and Margaret were not included in any of their neighbors' social gatherings. The issue of familism is the crux of the problem here. In many cultures, interactions with people other than family members are kept to a minimum. Fellow workers, neighbors, and casual acquaintances are usually not included in social gatherings in the home, as that is a place typically reserved for the family.

The main issue in Incident 82 ("The Mother-in-Law's Visit") centers on the roles and expectations of extended family members. Mrs. Reyes from the Philippines, who was visiting her daughter and son-in-law in the United States, assumed that Tom would give equal attention, care, and concern to all people close to his wife—his mother-in-law included. Tom appeared put out by Mrs. Reyes's intent to stay 3 weeks longer *and* to invite her other children. Because of Tom's reaction, Mrs. Reyes felt rejected in her role as a mother-in-law.

The needs of family members who accompany sojourners are taken up in Incident 81 ("Problems at Home"). Although events at the workplace shaped up pretty well for Mr. Zale, things at home appeared to be falling apart for everyone. The root of the family problem was the lack of attention and preparation given to Mr. Zale's wife and children, who also had to adjust to new social surroundings, neighborhoods, recreational outlets, and language. A significant part of the preparation for overseas living should focus on the principal sojourner's family members, as they can be a critical factor in the satisfactory adjustment of the total group.

Application to the Culture Assimilator Incidents:
Males and Females

Males and females often misinterpret each other's intentions within their own cultures, let alone across cultural boundaries. A common occurrence of the misreading of interpersonal cues during a male-female inter-action is the root of the problem in Incident 23 ("The Personal Touch"). Jack, while in conversation with an attractive Filipino woman, made the mistake of reading her verbal and nonverbal cues of animated conversation, personal talk, and touching as signs of flirtation, as he would interpret them at home. These actions, however, are considered simply appropriate con-versational style within the host culture and should not have been inter-preted as revealing any further intent.

Misinterpretation of cues is also involved in Tamako's announcement that she has an American boyfriend in Incident 26 ("The Southern Gentle-man"). Whereas Jack had been brought up in a society that paid consider-able attention to social graces and polite gestures, Tamako was not accus-tomed to such niceties, especially from a member of the opposite sex. Tamako misread Jack's friendly gestures as signs of attraction.

The issue of sexual harassment in American universities is the key point brought out in Incident 93 ("The Feelings and Conversations of a So-journer"). This is not an uncommon occurrence, and such issues should be brought to the attention of sojourners studying in American universities. Just what is expected regarding the quantity and quality of individual attention, especially between members of the opposite sex, is a sensitive issue that can easily be misread by those involved in the interaction, as well as by outsiders looking in.

The root of the problem in Incident 63 ("Who's in Charge?") is tradi-tional versus modern roles of women. In this case, Janice was acting in an authoritative capacity for her company that, in the eyes of Mr. Yamamoto (the Japanese company's representative), a woman would not traditionally hold. Hesitation to accept a woman as the person in charge is a common occurrence in some cultures. Women who have roles of responsibility may often be referred to in cross-cultural interactions as secretaries. Addition-ally, Incident 8 ("Healing Wounds") brings out the issue of gender-based role behavior. Mr. Mohamed, an elderly Saudi Arabian immigrant to Australia, clearly defines what he finds to be acceptable behavior across gender lines. Even when hospitalized, he will not allow women who are not close family members to bathe and dress him. When his needs are not understood and he is assigned a female attendant, Mr. Mohamed reacts with rage—not an uncommon response when cultural expectations are not met.

Incident 30 ("A Foreign Guest") also deals with expectations concern-ing the roles of women. Although Mrs. Dalton felt extremely put out by John's assuming behavior and demands, John was simply acting as he would toward women in his home culture. John's upbringing impressed upon him that certain roles bring with them certain responsibilities. He did not, therefore, feel the need to exercise politeness in relation to what he saw as Mrs. Dalton's duties, which he assumed were well known to his hosts.

IMPORTANCE OF THE GROUP AND IMPORTANCE OF THE INDIVIDUAL

The concepts of individualism and collectivism are among the most comprehensively studied of all the concepts in the field of intercultural communication (Brislin & Yoshida, 1994a, 1994b; Kim et al., 1994; Triandis, Brislin, & Hui, 1988). It has been suggested that the distinction between individualism and collectivism is perhaps the single most important concept to understand in explaining problems in intercultural encounters (Bhawuk & Brislin, 1992; Hui, 1990). People socialized in individualistic societies seek out, and are rewarded for achieving, their own goals. That is, they tend to set their own goals, make their own plans, and then "do their own thing" in pursuit of their goals. People in collective societies give more attention to the goals and needs of the group and do not focus primarily on their own personal goals. That is, they emphasize their group allegiances, look out for the needs of the group, and are more likely to integrate group goals with their own goals. Hofstede's (1980, 1991) major study, referred to earlier in the essay on work, suggests that the United States is the most individualistic of all societies in the world. Other nations that rank high on this dimension are Australia, Canada, Great Britain, the Netherlands, and New Zealand. Nations that score high on collectivism are primarily those in Asia and South America. Thus the stage is set for myriad possible conflicts that have their origins in the differences between individualism and collectivism.

We can explore some of the origins and ramifications of each orientation. When two or more people come together for the purpose of achieving a mutual goal, a group has been formed. Although many different kinds of groups form and develop (e.g., work project groups, family groups, social groups), certain characteristics emerge that are common to them all. The very nature of groups introduces many complex interactions, conflicts, and pressures that do not exist when individuals work alone. Certain social norms and controls tend to develop among the members of a given group as safeguards against these potential problems. The behaviors of group members relative to one another thus become stabilized over time as participants become linked in their striving toward a common goal and reinforce each other's membership in that particular group. A group's goals can range from broad (e.g., enjoyable free time) to specific (e.g., completion of an agreed-upon task). As a result of these developments, affective ties between group members strengthen; group members begin looking out for one another and become concerned about each other's feelings and welfare (Homans, 1950). Any one individual within the group has a strong support network made up of other group members.

The collective nature or group-oriented behaviors of individuals can be found to a greater or lesser degree among persons within a given country and culture. Take, for example, the Japanese, who, more than most people, live in groups. The family, school, and company provide identity and status. Once a person has been accepted into a certain group in Japanese society, he or she is a member for life. Hence a strong reciprocal bond forms between the institution and its members. The fate of the group becomes important to the individual members; thus the successes and failures of the group become the successes and failures of the individual (Kashima & Callan, 1994).

Explanations for most present-day behaviors in Japan can be traced to earlier times. The solidarity of the group in Japan has its roots in the agricultural needs of the people long ago. Irrigation for rice farming required coordination and cooperation among the members of a village community if they expected to harvest a suitable crop. Villages developed tight-knit communities where the welfare of the group became more important than the welfare of the individual. Thus the Japanese developed a habit of doing things together. This habit persists today and works as well in factories, businesses, and schools.

The phenomenon of group cohesiveness and conformity to social norms that is evident in many Asian and Latin American cultures is not found as readily among most Euro-Americans. Western cultures tend to place greater emphasis on the dignity of the individual and self-worth, as well as on individual achievement and individual privilege. The idea that humans are free and morally responsible creatures is a relatively new one in human experience and is often attributed to the important role that science and the Industrial Revolution have played in people's lives. The phenomenon of individuality seems to be gaining ground; it is reinforced by such worldwide circumstances as increasing mobility, increasing urbanization, and increasing access to formal educational opportunities, as well as improved communications. As a result of the detachment and autonomy these developments encourage, traditions become difficult to maintain, as families and other once-cohesive groups split and individuals encounter different traditions (Moghaddam et al., 1990; Triandis, 1994).

Yet humans are social creatures. Regardless of the extent to which individuals seek autonomy, people cannot talk of individuality without reference to the group. In a traditional society, people hardly think of themselves as distinct from the group. They are so totally immersed in the culture and traditions of the group that they are not even aware of accepting them. Just as people are not usually aware of the air that they breathe (unless, of course, it is altered in some way), people in collectivist societies are rarely aware of the traditions of the group (unless they are being challenged or changed). People internalize the customs of their societies, and their communities become their world. Many individuals from traditional societies, for example, cannot answer the question, Where would you like to live if you could not live in your native country? It is just not conceivable to them that there is anywhere else to live.

Yet, as we have noted, the degree to which people identify with and defer to the group differs between nations and between cultures. The degree of tolerance toward conformity and nonconformity also differs, with more group-oriented cultures obviously demanding a higher degree of conformity than those that are more individualistic in nature. The extent to which people are expected to cooperate with others is closely related to individualism and collectivism also, as is the degree to which individuals feel they must reciprocate kind gestures from others (Cialdini, 1988; Graen & Wakabayashi, 1994).

How might differences in individualism and collectivism affect sojourners or other persons interacting across cultures? As we have suggested, individuals are often unaware of the patterns that guide their behavior. Thus, when they confront situations that are different from their past experiences, they have a tendency to interpret events, and respond to them, from their familiar perspectives. For example, imagine that a salesman from a Japanese firm has been transferred to the company's American headquarters for a 6-month period to learn the sales approach of the U.S. branch. He arrives well dressed, eager to work, and expecting to be welcomed into the work family. To his disappointment, after being greeted and introduced to others in the company, he is simply shown to his office and told the territory for which he is responsible. With no group support, no direction, and no knowledge of local procedures, he is expected to be aggressive and to chart out his own plans for success. Rather than jumping in and taking charge, however, he feels lost, ignored, and pressured to make decisions in areas about which he is not knowledgeable. Further, he does not feel such decisions should be solely his responsibility. Coming from a collective culture, he is looking for a supportive group. The reverse often occurs when the Euro-American goes to Japan to work. In that case, however, the more individualistic and aggressive salesman plunges in full steam ahead, oblivious to the fact that group expectations, group rewards, and group cohesiveness override the decisions and quick actions of any one person. Coming from an individualistic culture, the Euro-American is looking for opportunities to use his own skills, expertise, and knowledge. He is not as likely to look for a group into which he can integrate himself.

Application to the Culture Assimilator Incidents

How one individual defines a person, as a loyal group member or as someone able to make decisions utilizing his or her personal freedoms, is the root of the problem in Incident 64 ("Engineering a Decision"). M. Legrand, a Frenchman working for a Japanese firm in France, values his personal freedom and exercises his right to turn down an overseas job offer. Mr. Tanaka, the Japanese general manager, assumes it is M. Legrand's responsibility as a company employee to accept the position. A conflict thus arises over the values of orientation to the company and orientation to the self.

Incidents 110 and 107 stress the importance placed on group harmony and conformity to social norms. Many cultures are quite intolerant of individuals who deviate from the behavioral norms of the group. In Incident 110 ("Not Accepted by Her Peers"), Tomoko was rejected by her schoolmates because her behavior did not quite fit their expectations. Having recently returned to Japan after spending 4 years in the United States, Tomoko had acquired many traits and behaviors that were different from those of her peers. This phenomenon is quite common among Japanese who have spent time overseas. They return with a somewhat different perspective on life and a different behavioral repertoire to call upon. Thus they stand out as different in their own country. The returned mechanic in Incident 107 ("Back Home in Japan") also had new and different experiences during his job placement in Libya. Some of those behavioral changes carried over upon his return to Japan, and he did not conform to social norms while on the job. His department head's concern centered on the desire for harmony among group members.

Incident 11 ("The Trip to the Mountains") is also concerned with the issue of individual versus group orientation. Chen Li-men invited David (an American student) to go hiking with him in the mountains of Taiwan. David was obviously disappointed when Chen Li-men showed up on the day of the hike with 25 other hikers. For Chen Li-men, who came from a group-oriented society, it was normal to undertake leisure activities with a large group. David, who came from a more individualistic society, had assumed that he and Chen Li-men would be hiking alone. In many countries, once group ties are established, they represent lifelong commitments. Consequently, people do not enter into groups lightly. This concern causes the difficulty in Incident 80 ("The Delay"). Junko and Robert wanted to get married, but her Japanese parents were slow to give their blessing. They were delaying because they wanted to find out more about Robert's background, as they realized that the group ties formed by marriage would include the people in Robert's extended family.

In Incident 101 ("Office Hours"), Karl was quite disappointed when students came to see him during his office hours to talk about seemingly trivial concerns and basic material that had already been presented in class, rather than to expand upon these ideas and concepts. What was not evident to Karl was that his American students saw these office hour visits as a means for their professor to get to know them as individuals. Rather than allowing themselves to be lumped together with a large group of students, many successful American students seek out ways to stand out and become known entities in their classes. One way to accomplish this, especially for students who may be weak in class work, is to meet with the professor whenever possible and thus become known to him or her. The primary purpose of such meetings, then, at least from the student's viewpoint, is to become better known as an individual.

The issue of social orientation is brought out in Incident 6 ("The Invitation to Dinner"). Mr. Yung and his family from Korea, who were living in the United States, were having a difficult time adjusting to the fact that Americans in general do not just casually drop in on each other at home for social gatherings. Rather, social engagements are scheduled well in advance. Although Americans enjoy their leisure time and social activities, these do not occur as spontaneously as they might in Korea, which is a more socially oriented society.

Incident 20 and Incident 1 both bring forth the issue of conforming to socially expected norms of behavior, with special regard to the role of socialization practices in the rearing of children. In many countries, particularly in Latin America and Asia, children are socialized at an early age to conform to social norms. In Incident 20 ("The Rock Concert"), Judy's suggestion that she and her friends attend a rock concert, a normal activity for teenage girls in the United States, is not seen as appropriate, and her Mexican friends fear negative consequences if they go against what is expected of them. In Incident 1 ("A Packed Lunch"), the teacher requested that the American child bring a lunch to school that was similar to everyone else's (not a typical American lunch), so that the child would not stand out from the group.

The phenomenon of reciprocity is fundamental in Incidents 5 and 37. Incident 5 ("One Good Turn Deserves Another") relates how Mr. Wong and Mr. Chang, longtime friends, have exchanged obligations of assistance and loyalty to each other for quite some time. Neither hesitated to request a favor from the other. This system of long-standing reciprocity, far less common in Western cultures, binds families and friends for many, many years. In Incident 37 ("The Gift Exchange"), Keiko reciprocated the kind gestures of her friends. She had been socialized to believe that she must not be in debt to others, and that she must solidify relationships by reciprocating kindness. When her college friends dug up some old household goods for her new apartment, Keiko returned their kindness by presenting them with some of her precious personal belongings. Although the items given to her were not equal in monetary value, they nevertheless were of use to Keiko at the time. Because she had little money with which to purchase gifts, she was forced to give away her prized personal possessions.

RITUAL AND SUPERSTITION

Rituals pervade some aspects of all societies to varying degrees and may exist both as commonly agreed-upon societal forms and as more idiosyncratic individual forms (Denzin, 1994). Rituals may serve as social communication (e.g., shaking hands or bowing; Brislin & Yoshida, 1994b), to invoke power (e.g., calling upon the assistance of supernatural forces in a prescribed manner), or as a statement or reinforcement of belief, or to create order in an otherwise seemingly chaotic world (e.g., the Christian service of Holy Communion). The term *ritual* is thus used somewhat confusingly with regard to a wide range of phenomena: the established rules and procedures of religion, the culturally imposed manners and conventions of society, and even the compulsions of individuals. In its most common use, however, and in the sense generally used by anthropologists and sociologists, *ritual* implies some standardized behavior in which the relationship between the means and the end is not intrinsic. Rituals are therefore not based on facts but rather on symbolic concepts. Let's take greetings and "conversational openers" as examples. These are often ritualistic in that they are related to symbols (the importance of good relations among people) but have no necessary direct relation to the symbols. The typical American greeting of "How are you?" does not call for a detailed list of one's aches, pains, and recent disappointments. In other cultures, typical greetings include "Where are you going?" "When did you last eat?" and "Thank you for yesterday" (or the last time people were together) (Brislin & Yoshida, 1994b). Conversational openers are also sometimes ritualistic and do not call for specific responses. Sojourners are often surprised when they are questioned about matters that they consider personal (e.g., "Do you have a boyfriend or girlfriend?" asked of young and attractive individuals). There are a number of reasons for such questions, and they relate more to symbols than to demands for specific information. One reason is that in-group membership is being negotiated, given that such information is shared among members of close-knit groups (see the essay on in-groups and out-groups in Chapter 13). Another reason for such questions is simply to stimulate a conversation or to keep one flowing. For example, in some cultures either of us might be asked the personal question, "How much in royalties do you receive for this book?" This is not necessarily a request for specific information, but rather a means of developing positive interpersonal relations. The proper response is simply to keep the conversation going, whether or not one chooses to answer the question. We might say, "You know, royalties are handled a lot differently than most people think. One of the interesting decisions about this book dealt with the color of the cover." Note that this response does not reveal anything about royalties, but still shows an interest in keeping up our end of the conversation.

Rituals are often performed as part of relationships—there are rituals of kinship, of ties to others, of participation in and connection with the organic, psychological, and metaphorical realities of the society. They are related to key areas of human life—birth, death, cleanliness (Fernea & Fernea, 1994), illness, sexuality, and sense of community (Kim et al., 1994)—and are concerned with binding people's feelings and behavior into the social fabric. Put more simply, rituals can be viewed as bodily action or participation in relation to symbols. The action is social in that it generally involves groups of people sharing sets of expectations, though it may be performed in private (e.g., prayer). This sense of the term *ritual* should be distinguished from what ethologists and psychologists term ritualistic or superstitious behavior. In this latter use, the person generally places no subjective meaning on the act—it is a learned habit repeated periodically, often a behavior coincidentally reinforced in association with another rewarded action (e.g., a person always bets on gray horses because he once won a large sum of money on one).

Superstition likewise is a term loosely and inconsistently applied to a range of acts and beliefs, but it generally carries more pejorative connotations than *ritual*. Some anthropologists regard superstition as degraded or degenerate ritual, the context of certain ritualistic practices being lost with cultural changes and only the habitual action or vague fears persisting as superstitions. Jahoda (1969), looking at this subject from a cross-cultural perspective, discusses the difficulty of forming any definitions and concludes that there is no objective method of distinguishing superstitions from other beliefs or actions. He holds that the most we can achieve is a consensus that a particular act or belief is regarded as superstitious by a particular society or culture at a particular time. This stems from the impossibility of categorizing phenomena as rational or irrational because reasoning varies across cultures and with the evolution of knowledge within cultures.

The question of rationality is central to the way in which ritual and superstition are regarded by various cultures and in particular their devaluation by modern Western societies (Mullavey-O'Byrne, 1994b). Jahoda (1969) provides evidence of many beliefs in Western cultures that were formerly thought to be grounded in rational or scientific fact that now, because of changes in knowledge or cultural viewpoints, would be regarded as quaint or superstitious. He also shows that actions that may be defined as irrational in terms of a current consensus are still prevalent at all levels of Western society (see also Bocock, 1974). Cultures cannot be divided into the "enlightened" and the "superstitious," only the more or less superstitious.

Nonscientific cultures are not immersed in a world of irrational forces but rather have their own universes of symbols and relationships that are sensible and intelligible within the confines of their knowledge. Moreover, scientific cultures generally admit to only one reality—an objective rationality—and so cannot comprehend the whole context of the actions and beliefs of more intuitive or less secular cultures. Their viewpoint, though objective, lacks the robustness that comes from approaching an event from a range of perspectives. The correspondences and relationships in the rituals remain partially obscured, and the acts are thus seen as without apparent force or reason.

In addition, there is evidence that superstition is linked to fundamental rational modes of thinking and responding to the environment. Jahoda (1969) suggests that this is the inevitable by-product of the constant scanning for patterns in which we engage (see the essay on categorization in Chapter 13). These patterns of knowledge are established and evolve from a state of partial information about phenomena in all societies. The principal difference between scientific and other approaches is merely that science obliges one to verify and test for the assumed patterns by standard methods, though even the processes of verification and acceptance can be shown to be heavily influenced by cultural factors. Further, part of the scientific method includes admission of what remains unknown or unexplained. It seems unlikely that superstitions will be eradicated by the progress of science or secular education or that rituals will lose their salience. The need for symbolization, which is intellectual as well as emotional, is basic to individuals and societies. Acts and beliefs may change and may even seem to be obscured by the materialism of many secular societies, but the need for this extra dimension persists.

The implications of the above discussion for those living and working across cultures are that they should (a) maintain an awareness of the salience of rituals to other cultures and not deliberately transgress or ridicule such beliefs (Barna, 1994), (b) be cautious in assigning the label *irrational* to particular acts or beliefs on the basis of partial knowledge of the host culture, and (c) recognize the force that rituals or superstitions may hold for the host culture and be prepared to make allowances for this influence.

Application to the Culture Assimilator Incidents

The problems and uncertainties inherent in labeling behavior of another culture as rational or irrational are demonstrated in Incident 4 ("A Few Beers"). In this incident, John unwittingly violated a taboo that condemns personal contact with the left hand and so caused offense. Even if he had been aware of such a prohibition, he quite possibly would not have taken much notice of it, as he may have seen it as based in irrational superstition. But to Indonesians and to people in many other Asian and African cultures, this practice has a perfectly rational basis. In these societies, there have in the past been (and still are in some cases) very limited facilities for washing, and so traditionally one hand (the left) has been used for attending to bodily functions and other unclean tasks and the other has been used for eating, personal contact, and so forth. Thus the origins of this taboo are found in a rational, hygienic practice, but to an outsider operating from a limited knowledge of the culture it seems without logic and may be belittled.

In Incidents 3 ("Betting on the Bull") and 68 ("The Shinto Priest"), a lack of comprehension of the salience of rituals in other cultures is exhibited. In Incident 3, George failed to see any significance in bullfighting beyond that of competition, a sport, and so offended his colleagues. He comes from a society that is more secular and materialistic, where the symbolic significance of many acts and beliefs has been largely forgotten or trivialized. To the Spanish devotees, however, the ritual of bullfighting is central to their cultural identity and is seen as an intense drama that glorifies their concept of *pundonor* (honor and dignity) in the struggle of life and death. It is an act that reminds them of their cultural inheritance and provides an extra dimension to life beyond utilitarian, day-to-day activities. This belief (or lack of belief) in an extra dimension to life is also seen in Incident 68 in the conflict between the Japanese and American executives. The Americans were unable or unwilling to accept that a spiritually based ritual had any place or force in their company. Their viewpoint was objective, but it was also culture bound and narrow. Further, it failed to acknowledge the superstitious behavior of their own American workers who were ready to believe in a jinx on the company and the importance of psychological as well as material motivation to the employees. The Japanese had exhausted to their satisfaction all routine, practical measures that could be taken, and it thus seemed rational to them to seek reassurance through other (spiritual) means. The problem (discontent resulting from belief in a jinx) had arisen from a basically superstitious assumption, and it thus seemed logical to acknowledge this and seek a solution in the same sphere of beliefs. Whether the Americans had any faith in the Japanese proposal or not, they should have been willing to accept that the ritual was important and could be effective within the context of Japanese culture, which was an integral aspect of their company.

A related issue is presented in Incident 92 ("Making Friends"). In this case, John, a practicing Jehovah's Witness, was forbidden to participate in school holiday celebrations. Such issues are becoming increasingly common in many schools in the United States as well as in other multicultural nations, presenting schools and communities with opportunities to begin a dialogue concerning religious freedoms and school practices. In some localities, the solution of choice when cultures clash is to allow children to be excused from classrooms during holiday celebrations or, and in some cases, when potentially objectionable or controversial content is to be covered.

HIERARCHIES AMONG PEOPLE:
CLASS AND STATUS

Whenever more than a few people come together to work on a task, a hierarchy is established that leads to accepted norms concerning who is considered the leader and/or who can give and who should accept directions (Bochner, 1994; Hofstede, 1991). Anthropologists study hierarchies under such rubrics as "division of labor"; sociologists refer to such concepts as "class" and "status"; psychologists look at the phenomena of "leadership" and "deference to others." The criteria for placement in a hierarchy vary from culture to culture and from task to task within any one culture. They might include age, birthright, election by peers, expertise in a topic area, family name, formal education, sex, and even physical attractiveness. No matter what exact terms are used or what the exact criteria are, some people within cultures are at the tops of certain hierarchies and consequently possess more status than others. These people have certain rights and expectations, such as the expectation of deference from others, the right to speak first at a meeting, the expectation that others will accept directions, and the expectation that their opinions will affect decisions.

Four aspects of people's need to form hierarchies, and to find their places within them, are especially important in cross-cultural encounters. These include (a) discovering the criteria for hierarchical placement in the culture in which one is living; (b) reacting to how any one individual is treated with respect to placement in the hierarchy (in some cases, international sojourners will find that they have much lower status than in their home countries; in others, they will find that they have higher status); (c) given that there are many, often overlapping, hierarchies, finding one's way through the bureaucracy of another culture; and (d) reacting to how others are treated within the host country. Status is a phenomenon strongly affected by emotions and judgments of right and wrong. Sojourners are sometimes upset when they discover that certain people in the host country have few rights and seem to be the target of discrimination supported by both norms and laws.

Social Class

One of the criteria for placement in hierarchies is the social class into which a person is born. In Euro-American societies, typical determinants of social class include income, the respectability of one's occupation, level of education, and perceived desirability of the neighborhood in which one lives. In judging class status, difficulties arise for Euro-Americans when other criteria are added with which they have little familiarity, such as family name and a person's patrons or sponsors. Another difficulty is that the respect given to a certain indicator of social class may be different from country to country (Sinha, 1990). A good example is the relative status of elementary and high school teachers in Japan and the United States. In Japan, teaching is a respected occupation, and an honorable term, *sensei,* is used for members of that occupation. In the United States, on the other hand, teaching is not an especially respected profession. Many American teachers tell stories about being introduced to people at parties who, when they find out they are teachers, move on to initiate conversations with others who might be of higher status. An American teacher on a sojourn in Japan, then, would experience an increase in status. A Japanese teacher visiting the United States would experience a decrease in status.

Language interpreters may also find that their status changes as they move across cultural boundaries. American interpreters often report that their status increases when they work in Europe, for example. Bilingual persons skilled in both Spanish and English sometimes hide their Spanish skills while they are living in the United States because often Spanish speakers are considered to be of lower status (e.g., they are mistaken for Mexican laborers) than monolingual English speakers (Freimanis, 1994).

Loss of status can cause feelings of mild depression and annoyance, and orientation programs for sojourners should include discussion of this issue. Trainers in such programs should caution trainees against feeling personally discriminated against when they meet the status loss that accompanies many sojourns.

For many people, social class is a difficult concept to see in their everyday lives. Americans, for instance, grow up with the belief that they belong to a relatively classless society. When they experience life in other cultures and see behavior that is strongly influenced by class standing, they frequently become upset. For example, Americans are often uncomfortable in situations where servants are common, and are upset to see servants treated with (what Americans consider) a lack of the respect due any human being. Of course, Americans also exhibit behaviors that are based on class (Offermann & Gowing, 1990). For instance, if a banker's daughter brings home a young man she has been dating or wants to date who is from another racial group and whose parents are wage laborers, her parents may reject the young man. One reason may be racial—her parents may object to her seeing a young man from another racial group. We would probably call this racial prejudice. But another reason may be based on class—her parents may not like the idea of their daughter seeing the son of wage laborers. Americans do not even have a commonly used term for this situation—*class prejudice* is barely adequate because it sounds rather academic, given its infrequent use in everyday life. Even though there may be no common term for them, such situations are probably familiar to most American readers.

Even though all societies have class structures, it is always easier for people to see flaws in societies other than their own. People become familiar with the various occupations and status levels of their own societies and do not think about them very much unless they take courses in sociology or are confronted with differences while living in other societies. Take the example of countries in which the very rich members of the upper classes are accustomed to having servants. Sojourners should be aware of such class distinctions and should not be too quick to condemn or deliberately flout them so as to embarrass hosts. Abrupt removal of such distinctions would in many cases completely disrupt existing social balances, and the elimination of servants could create massive unemployment. Sojourners should remember that the eradication of class distinctions, if they hold this as a social ideal, is something that can proceed only very gradually.

Power

Given that some people have high status, they also have more power than those who are lower in the status hierarchy (Brislin, 1991). One form of power is the ability to control the behavior of others. Power holders are dominant over others and are able to control those others such that the power holders' goals are achieved. A powerful person differs from an influential person in that other people perceive that they have more choices about their behavior when the latter type of person makes a suggestion.

We mentioned previously that some sojourners experience an increase in status. Often, such people are from highly industrialized nations and are sojourning in those parts of the world variously called "less developed," "Third World," "technologically developing," and "the South." Sojourners from highly industrialized nations are often given more status in these countries because of where they are from, not because of any inherent qualities they may have (Kidder, 1977). However, some of these sojourners quickly come to believe that they are personally deserving of deference and respect.

Sojourners must realize that they will sometimes be given more status, and consequently more power, than they are accustomed to having in their own countries. They may be unprepared for the intoxicating effects of power—as the common expression has it, power can go to a person's head (Brislin, 1991). David Kipnis (1976), who has done extensive research on people's reactions to the acquisition of power, warns that four changes can take place: People who acquire power (a) grow to like power for its own sake; (b) begin to degrade their coworkers and to take credit for work that coworkers do; (c) become isolated from criticism, because no one likes to bring bad news to power holders; and (d) exaggerate their own self-importance.

Bureaucracies

Hierarchies among people are a fact. Unfortunately for people who are trying to understand them, hierarchies often overlap, so that it is often unclear which hierarchy a person should approach to accomplish a certain task (Goldstein, 1994; Sinha, 1994). For instance, an immigrant who is trying to discover the amount of money he or she owes to the government might need to approach a department concerned with immigration, another concerned with taxation, another concerned with labor, another concerned with foreign relations, or some combination of these. Further, individuals in any one hierarchy are very protective about the activities that give them status. Their right to approve or disapprove proposals in a certain area, or to put a stamp on a certain document, or to be the source of information on a certain topic, becomes part of their self-concept. The term *territoriality,* which comes from animal behavior studies, is sometimes used to describe the feelings people have about the activities they have the right to administer. Interestingly, the need to work through hierarchies, sometimes called working through the bureaucracy or cutting through red tape, probably differs from country to country only in degree, and not in kind. All countries have bureaucracies—the problem is to figure out how to satisfy one's needs in a specific bureaucracy. People within any country are familiar with their own bureaucracies and have learned ways to obtain the benefits those bureaucracies have to offer. Sojourners, of course, have to work their way through unfamiliar bureaucracies. It is the unfamiliarity, rather than the fact of bureaucracy itself, that is frustrating. It is interesting to note that people who write letters of recommendation for potential Fulbright grantees (who compete for one of the world's most prestigious sojourn opportunities) are asked to assess applicants' responses to bureaucracy.

According to the guidelines provided, the letters of recommendation should contain information on an applicant's "ability to cope with administrative, bureaucratic, and other frustrations."

Application to the Culture Assimilator Incidents

There will always be a tendency among sojourners to view other societies from the perspectives of their own cultures, with which they have extensive experience. Consequently, misunderstandings are frequent in situations involving concepts that sojourners view differently than people in the host society. Social class is a prime example. As mentioned previously, people do not think very much about social class; they tend to assume that the stratification of societies is pretty much the same everywhere (that is, the same as in their own societies). This view is often challenged by specific encounters in other cultures. In Incident 36 ("The Soccer Game"), Dave Mitchell was unaware that certain sports have class followings in Great Britain that are different from those in the United States. Given that soccer is often played by middle-class children in the United States and that U.S. soccer fans come from no particular classes, Dave never considered that there would be a problem in inviting his son's British friend to a game. But the British boy's mother had objections; she may have been worried about (a) the social acceptability and appearance attached to her son's attendance at what she understood to be a sport of the lower classes, or (b) the boy's safety, given that hooligans sometimes disrupt soccer games.

In Incidents 32 ("The Guest Meets the Maid") and 19 ("The Woman in Black"), the Americans are trying to be as egalitarian as possible. This is a value to which they have long been exposed. The American Declaration of Independence asserts that "all men are created equal." When the Americans in these incidents encountered sharp distinctions between upper-class hosts and their servants, they become very uncomfortable.

Given the facts of hierarchies and social stratification, behaviors associated with status levels are often different from culture to culture. In Incident 65 ("Can I Extend My Stay?"), Dr. Hong correctly viewed Dr. Brown as a high-status person. Hong incorrectly assumed, however, based on that fact, that Brown could perform the same sorts of influential behaviors in the United States that a person of similar status could perform in Korea. Hong was subsequently upset when Brown could not unilaterally extend Hong's sojourn. He misinterpreted Brown's explanation of "administrative difficulties" as a face-saving way of saying no. In reality, Brown was bound by a complex set of administrative guidelines. In Incident 94 ("Oh! So Proper!"), Martha surely knows that because she is the teacher, she is of higher status than her students. However, she fails to realize the importance of this basic fact among some of her Asian students. When Martha tries to ignore status boundaries by asking a student to call her by her first name, she causes discomfort rather than a favorable learning environment.

In Incident 69 ("Was Somebody Saying No?"), assumptions concerning who can make decisions are at the forefront. From Dr. Xi's point of view, someone with the very high status of Dr. Hastings should be able to make his or her own decisions about the use of time. A person of such high status should not have to receive permission from a set of administrators. This is one benefit of high status (from Dr. Xi's point of view)—a certain amount of removal from petty bureaucracies. When Dr. Hastings talked about having to consult administrators, however, Dr. Xi inferred a message in this and no longer considered Dr. Hastings to be the high-level individual he had previously believed he was.

When people sojourn, downward and upward shifts in their status relative to the host culture can cause problems. In Incidents 50 ("The Immigration Officer") and 96 ("Participation in a Seminar"), Felipe and Michael both experience status loss. Felipe is a senior official in his own country, but he is detained upon arrival in the host country like some laborer trying to immigrate illegally or someone trying to smuggle drugs. Michael is from a country in which the role of "graduate student" is a very high-status label. In the United States, however, he is not treated with much deference or special respect because (a) there are so many other graduate students at the university and (b) being a graduate student is not an especially high-status position to begin with. In Incident 12 ("His First Job"), in contrast, Mark Burke experiences a sudden increase in status and power. People defer to him, ask for his opinion, request that he lecture at universities, and invite him to parties that important people attend. The sudden increase in status is intoxicating, and Mark does not handle it well. For instance, he begins to devalue the task that brought him to the host country and instead spends time with the important people he has met. Many Western sojourners forget that it is not they, themselves, to whom hosts are deferring, but to their roles as educated members of highly industrialized nations.

As with so many other aspects of cross-cultural interaction, sojourners tend to interpret the status-related behavior of hosts as personally directed at them. This is the case in Incident 51 ("They Are Talking About Me"), in which Alan reacts strongly when he overhears his name being used during hosts' conversations. Another example is the set of events people experience when they have to work their way through a bureaucracy. In Incident 43 ("Lengthening Her Sojourn"), Susan needs to complete a set of papers so that she might extend her residence in the host country. She becomes irritated at all the forms and supporting documents she has to provide. It is easy to empathize with her plight, but what should be remembered is that a major factor underlying the burden of rules and regulations is their unfamiliarity. If a sojourner in Susan's home country wanted to lengthen his or her stay, the rules would be equally complex. The best advice for a sojourner who wishes to work through a bureaucracy is to find a host guide. This is especially critical because many basic ways of approaching and entering bureaucracies are not written down. Instead, they are part of oral tradition that "everyone" is supposed to know. "Everyone," of course, refers to citizens of a country who have been socialized there—it is easy to forget that sojourners have not had a lifetime of exposure to the bureaucracies of the host country.

VALUES:
THE INTEGRATING FORCE IN CULTURE

For it so falls out
That what we have we prize not to the worth
Whiles we enjoy it, but being lacked and lost,
Why then we rack the value.
     —William Shakespeare, *Much Ado About Nothing*

I value my garden more for being full of blackbirds than of cherries,
and very frankly give them fruit for their songs.
     —Joseph Addison

A single object can be looked upon with favor or disfavor, and can be valued more at one time than another, as Shakespeare and Addison both suggest. The innate worth of objects may be far less important than the thoughts that are attached to them. Values are the weights with which people evaluate or judge their world. People's values permeate the whole of their existence and are a major factor in determining what sorts of human beings they are and how they will behave (Bohm, 1980; Feather, 1994). People make judgments and draw conclusions about what is and what is not of value. These judgments give rise to certain presuppositions from which people act with little or no conscious awareness. These presuppositions, learned during childhood, play a pervasive role in everyday life and are meaningful in all arenas of people's adult experiences.

Rokeach (1979; see also Schwartz, 1992) notes that "values are core conceptions of the desirable within every individual and society. They serve as standards or criteria to guide not only action but also judgment, choice, attitude, evaluation, argument, exhortation, rationalization and one might add attribution of causality" (p. 2). (See the essay on attribution in Chapter 13.) Thus values are the constructs, groupings, and orientations by which people decide what is normative, preferred, or obligatory of members of their societies. The values of any given society dictate what is a desirable or undesirable state of affairs. At the same time, values "are the resultants of societal demands and psychological needs, they are learned and determined by culture, society, society's institutions, and personal experience" (Rokeach, 1979, p. 2).

Because values are the products of basic human and societal needs, the number of human values is small, and they focus on similar important concepts the world over (Schwartz, 1992). Values reflect a culture's view toward such central issues as politics, economics, religion, aesthetics, interpersonal relationships, morality, and the environment. Cultural differences and conflicts arise from the fact that individuals and societies order these values in differing hierarchies. These conflicts can be found in various spheres of life as values concurrently occur on personal, organizational, institutional, societal, and cultural levels. The magnitude and extent of the conflict depends on the level of the value—for instance, an individual disagreement in contrast to a disagreement over a land border between two nations. Another salient factor is how committed people are to a given value. Because we learn and develop our values as we grow from childhood to adulthood, they are affected by factors in the surrounding environment, society, and culture. Although individuals themselves form or order their own values, they are influenced in this by the values held by others in their cultures.

Conflicts often arise for people working and living across cultures when they try to function within their own common or familiar value systems while at the same time needing or wanting to identify with other systems.

If an individual is very committed to a particular value system and comes into contact with another that is quite different, a dilemma arises. The individual must recognize and address the reality of a culturally diverse world in which value systems are ordered differently. Attention can be placed on the structure or hierarchy of the particular values involved. Values can shift, adjust, change, or be reinforced as a result of experiences. These instances occur when people are faced with inconsistencies, incongruities, or hypocrisies (Devine & Zuwerink, 1994). For instance, people who live in societies where achievement through an individual's own efforts is valued will experience conflict when living in societies where achievement is attached to a person's family name or the patrons a person is able to cultivate (see the essay above on individualism and collectivism).

To evaluate various value systems effectively, individuals must first scrutinize and understand well their own value hierarchies or groupings. In this way, they should be able to discern the differences between their own system and those systems with which they come into contact. For Americans, the value placed on individual freedoms in U.S. society often leads to cross-cultural clashes. Many Americans believe that the concept of freedom includes the right to express oneself openly, and if such expression leads to slight property damage (e.g., painting slogans on walls, denting someone's automobile while on a protest march), then the penalty should be light. Although they agree that society should do what it can to combat crime, Americans as a whole are willing to err in crime fighting on the side of individual freedoms. Examples of this leaning toward individual rights include the many laws in place to protect the rights of people accused of crimes and the values placed on the concepts that "the punishment should fit the crime" and that there should be no "cruel and unusual punishment."

The leaders of (and many average citizens in) other countries also recognize the value of individual freedoms, but they place a higher value on a crime-free society. In 1993, most Americans read extensive coverage of a court case in Singapore involving an American teenager charged with vandalism. What seemed to many Americans a petty offense that called for a stiff fine was treated much more severely by Singapore authorities. The adolescent was jailed and also beaten with a bamboo cane. Many Americans decried the severity of the penalty, but many commentators in both Singapore and the United States pointed to the extremely low crime rate that has resulted from such severe measures. As another example, one of our friends remembers traveling in Malaysia a few years ago. Before planes landed there, the flight crews routinely announced the severe penalties (including death) in Malaysia for possession of drugs. Malaysian authorities may recognize the place (and even the value) of moderate adolescent rebelliousness, but this tolerance does not extend to experimentation with marijuana, as it sometimes does in the United States. People who have not experienced intercultural contact that has called for self-examination are rarely aware of their own presuppositions concerning their views of the world. In instances of values confrontation, people's natural tendency is to blame the things they can see and easily formulate in their minds, rather than to examine ideas in the preconscious (Epstein, 1994; Pedersen, 1993). Difficult situations seem to call for an appropriate set of values, but because situations are dynamic (even in a system with which one is familiar, but more so in a system with which one is not), there is no one set of appropriate values. Bohm (1980) suggests that "what is needed is an intelligent perception, from moment to moment, of what the right values are for the actual situation at the moment. That is to say, we have to be sufficiently free of attachment to past conclusions so that we are able to see each idea, each emotional response, each action, each relationship at its proper value without any persistent tendency toward bias and distortion" (p. 21). It is impossible to have such a free-flowing arrangement, however, because the result would be chaos. People need to have some foundation or focus on which to base their thinking and judgments. Individuals living and working in cultures other than their own need to move toward less rigid compartmentalization of the fixed presuppositions on which they base their value hierarchies. This flexibility should allow reason to flow freely in new ways so that it can adapt to fresh perceptions. In actual cross-cultural encounters, these perceptions deal with areas as personal and concrete as posture and spatial distance in the presence of another person, or can be as abstract as concepts of honesty and control of the environment. The perceptions include one's own personal likes and dislikes as well as some of society's customs and rituals.

Application to the Culture Assimilator Incidents

Values are an integral part of human life, and value-related behaviors occur on all levels of human activity. Incidents 28, 95, 2, and 41 all deal with values on a personal level, with issues ranging from the concrete ideas of spatial distance to conceptions of cleanliness and other personal norms dictated by societies' customs and rituals. In Incident 2 ("The Unsuccessful Dinner Party"), the ideas that Mei Ying held, contrasted to those of Alice, were not based on opinions concerning sterile conditions but rather on what each one had learned from the society in which she had grown up and with which she was familiar. Both Mei Ying and Alice were uncomfortable with each other's idea of cleanliness and hygiene.

Incidents 28 ("Rooming In—or Out?") and 95 ("Failing to Appear at the Appointed Time") deal with individuals' relationships with others as formed by their societies. In Incident 28, Pitchit's approach to the problem he and Jack have surprised Jack and caused him to think of Pitchit as unreasonable. Both of them saw that assertiveness might solve the problem, but their value rankings of that particular trait were very different. Jack saw assertiveness as a sign of strength and good adjustment, whereas Pitchit saw it as being very disruptive, disagreeable, and face threatening. In Incident 95, Mariko also saw a problematic situation as face threatening and one that should be avoided. She valued being polite and not hurting the other person's feelings over being frank. This kind of behavior is also valued by Euro-Americans, but is perhaps not as high in most people's value hierarchies as it is in Mariko's. People adjust or modify their less central or less important values to agree with their central or important values when there is a conflict between the two. The value Mariko placed on politeness was so high that no compromise was possible. In Incident 41 ("A Pacific Paradise?"), Barbara's adjustment difficulty seems to stem from her inability to satisfy a need she has—that of privacy. Whereas in the local environment privacy is not valued, Barbara feels a great need for periods of solitude.

Incidents 79, 17, 18, and 7 deal with philosophical concepts such as views of God, religion, the environment, and responsibility. Such a principle is at work in Incident 17 ("A Natural Disaster?"). Although Frank and the Guatemalans conceivably believe in the same God, they have different conceptions of just how this God works. These conceptions were formed by the value arrangements of the societies from which they came, and neither Frank nor the Guatemalans can understand the other's perspective. The problem is heightened by the fact that they feel they are dealing with the same deity. In Incident 79 ("Bringing Him Home to Dad"), Nazilah and Scott are confronted with a different perspective on what is proper and normal behavior for young men and women than they have been operating under. Here the conflict is between concepts formed in the past, as tradition dictates, and concepts formed in more modern times, as the present society encourages. The question for the couple is, When do we involve our parents in our relationship? Different cultures have very different guidelines to help answer this question. Adding to the confusion is the idea or value placed on the roles given to each person. In Incident 18 ("A Borrower or a Lender Be?"), Fua and Bill have different concepts of what roles a friend should play and how much personal responsibility people should have. The social system and support network to which Fua is accustomed does not coincide with the system that Bill knows. As frequently happens in cross-cultural encounters, the people involved are confused by two value systems that give different guidelines for behavior. In Incident 7 ("Foreign Bureaucracy"), Robert is offended by the host people's definition of normal payment procedures, because it coincides with his own definition of bribery, a practice that he feels is immoral. However, he sees nothing wrong with a payment system that includes tipping certain people. If he could view the problem with more openness and change his own concept of tipping to include situations other than the ones he normally encounters in his own society, he would not have such a conflict.

In all of the incidents mentioned above, sojourners are confronted by values or norms that are different from those they are accustomed to; if they stay locked into their usual ways of thinking, the conflicts remain. However, if they can somehow allow their thinking to be freed from fixed presuppositions based on their own value systems, then they can adjust to their new situations. At times, such adjustment will be comfortable, as in Incident 7, where the similarities between "payment" and "tipping" become clear. At other times, the adjustment will be less comfortable, but perhaps the sojourn can still continue without debilitating stress. For example, feminists from Euro-American countries may be upset to observe the limitations placed on the movements of, and opportunities for, women in some Arab countries. Total acceptance of these values on their part will be rare, but it is possible that they can develop an understanding of the different value system that is in place. The important thing to remember is that all societies have different value hierarchies, or arrangements for their values. Discovering what those hierarchies are is the key to learning about and adjusting to life in other cultures.

13

THE BASES OF CULTURAL DIFFERENCES

Confrontation with myriad differences is common to all extensive inter-cultural interactions, especially in highly diverse, multicultural nations such as the United States, Canada, Australia, and Great Britain. Similarly, as the world becomes more globally interconnected, the potential for increased intercultural interactions between and among many different groups significantly increases. Clearly, it is impossible to prepare individuals for every conceivable difference they may encounter, even in a long training program devoted to one specific culture. What can be done is to provide a framework for understanding the kinds of interactions and responses that might potentially occur, as we have attempted to do in the essays in Chapters 11 and 12 (Barna, 1994; Brislin & Yoshida, 1994a, 1994b). A third part of this broad framework consists of the *underlying reasons,* or *bases,* for various specific cultural differences. Our treatment of these underlying reasons is intended to promote understanding of why people behave as they do, given an awareness of how they organize knowledge, learn new material, and make judgments. The focus here is not on the knowledge itself, but on the underlying reasons that certain knowledge areas exist in the forms they do, as well as how the knowledge is used.

People's thinking cannot remain static in this fast-moving world. People must acquire new information to meet the new demands they face. The *manner* in which this is typically done, regardless of the exact knowledge to be learned, differs from culture to culture. Because people cannot react to every bit of information to which they are exposed, they organize information into categories (Fiske & Taylor, 1991). When a given category becomes important to a culture's survival, it is broken up or differentiated into smaller units. The practical result is that if people from other cultures do not differentiate a knowledge area in the same way, they may be seen as ignorant or at best backward. In people's interpersonal relationships, one of the major reasons for both categorization and differentiation is the basic human need to form in-groups and out-groups. In-groups consist of people who can be trusted, whereas out-group people should be kept at a distance. With their knowledge as a base, people make sense of their worlds. A basic feature of this sense making is causal attribution, that is, making judgments about the causes of the behavior people observe, both in themselves and in others (Triandis, 1994). People living and working across cultures have to decide whether others are truly helpful or simply polite, and whether they want new contributions from would-be advisers or simply to be left alone. What is considered appropriate knowledge differs, as do the attributions that follow from that knowledge.

CATEGORIZATION

At any one time, diverse and numerous stimuli demand to be assimilated and understood by the human mind. In order to manage this complex task, people organize and group elements together to form categories to which they are able to respond (Fiske & Taylor, 1991). Aspects of categories and the process of categorization are woven into every facet of life. Categories help to shape the values, beliefs, norms, roles, and attitudes of a society. Thus, as Triandis (1983) says, "the category is probably the most important element in the analysis of subjective culture" (p. 106).

People use categorization to deal effectively and efficiently with the complexity of their world. For instance, people divide food into such categories as breads, meats, sweets, and fruits; activities into work, play/sports, and leisure; animals into fowl, domestic, and wild; and even people into children, elderly, male/female, family, and friends. The various elements of the world that confront a child are organized into categories during the process of socialization. The final sets of categories that adults use, then, reflect the cultures of which they are members (Bruner, Goodnow, & Austin, 1956; Rogoff, 1990). Detweiler (1980) conceives of categorization as "the classification of sensory input from the world. . . . [It is] a theoretical concept which seems to be particularly important in an intercultural context. . . . The way information is believed to be organized or grouped in meaningful ways in human memory" (p. 277). Examining categorization more closely, one finds that "some categories are formed because they help people adjust to their world. Group labels such as ethnicity, sex, or religion are categories of this type. The boundaries which might separate groups

[, however,] are not rigid. Rather they can be manipulated at will to serve one's needs and to attain one's goals" (Brislin, 1981, p. 75). For instance, students may use the category *Caucasian* most of the time to describe themselves, but may suddenly switch to *Irish* or *Slovenian* if scholarships for people of these ancestries are made available.

Other cultural aspects of a society are also reflected in the organization and analysis of their categories, that is, the domains covered, their size, the criteria used for their formation, as well as the faculties used to determine or to discriminate among the levels of various criteria. The concept of the *prototype* is also crucial in the analysis of categories. For many categories there is one set of criteria or attributes that characterizes the clearest example of that category and serves as a convenient summary. For instance, for most people, the prototypic image of a bird is of one that flies and is rather small, perhaps 8 or 9 inches from beak to tail feathers, brown in color, and commonly found in the front yards of many homes in their neighborhoods—perhaps a sparrow or a robin. Most people do not think first of a chicken, an ostrich, or a penguin, although all of these are birds and share all the common characteristics of birds. Although category membership is based on the particular cluster of attributes that epitomize the "best exemplar" of that category, no one attribute or set of attributes can be seen as either indispensable or sufficient for membership in the category (Rosch & Mervis, 1975).

When people have gathered individual elements together and formed categories, they tend to use these categories in their thinking while downplaying the separate elements. Instead, they emphasize similarities, and seem to have little awareness of differences. Areas of conflict may arise in intercultural interactions when there are major differences in the ways people categorize the same sets of behaviors. When different systems are in operation and either party makes a judgment based on one or the other system, errors or inappropriate behavior may occur. These errors bring about erroneous expectations (Brislin, 1993). "Individuals who are socialized in the same culture categorize and interpret situations and behaviors similarly and therefore have similar expectancies. However, socialization in different cultures yields different categorization resulting in different meanings and expectations. Thus variations in the way things are categorized has an impact on both meaning and expectations" (Detweiler, 1980, p. 279). Consider the dog. All people, regardless of where in the world they are socialized, would describe the dog physically in similar ways; yet they have learned to place the dog in different categories depending on their particular socialization (Cushner & Trifonovitch, 1989). Many people reading this book grew up in communities where dogs were common; perhaps many kept dogs as pets themselves in their homes. Of all the animals represented in the world today, the dog is one that many would place in the category of *family member, household pet,* or *companion.* A devout Muslim, in contrast, might place the dog in the category of *dirty or disgusting animal,* similar to how many others would place a pig—as an animal to be avoided at all costs. Someone living in the South Pacific, on the other hand, might place the dog in the category of *food.* Misunderstandings occur because the same stimulus object can often be categorized in several different ways, depending upon who is doing the categorizing and for what purpose. One goal of cross-cultural training, then, is to make people cognizant of categorization differences (Detweiler, 1980; Lieberman, 1994).

However, awareness alone is insufficient. Kealey and Ruben's (1983) research has shown that people who are most aware of their perceptions, both in their personal and subjective aspects, tend to experience the most intense culture shock or maladjustment. In other words, the most knowledgeable people become the most disoriented (see also Adler, 1992). One reason for this interesting finding centers on the concept of expectation. If people have set ideas (or narrow categories), their adjustment is often slow—if they adjust at all. Lack of adjustment to new cultures can mean that individuals behave in them just as they would in their own cultures. Those with broader and more sensitive perspectives, however, tend to be more open to new ideas and new people. This particular trait causes them to be affected by their new experiences to a greater extent, which, in turn, causes the disorientation that is often called culture shock (Bochner, 1994; Furnham & Bochner, 1986). People living and working across cultures need to be aware that they will lose their familiar cues and will be confronted with unfamiliar stimuli and events. Internalization of this fact should lessen incorrect expectations and inappropriate behavior. Sojourners and others interacting cross-culturally should be encouraged to think of things in their new environments not as strangely different, but as excitingly new. This may help them to form new categories that will help them adjust.

Often, certain categories are so central to an individual's thinking about particular groups of people that he or she will be resistant to changing them, and will use them again and again. Because people behave according to the categories they have organized and not the individual factors, these categories often become stereotypes that do not allow for variation (Triandis, 1977, 1994). A strong adherence to stereotypes frequently leads to prejudice (see the essay on prejudice and ethnocentrism in Chapter 11), because stereotypes, which usually are not based on firsthand contact, are often negative or hostile. Generally, a stereotype is any sort of summary generalization that obscures the differences within any group of people (Brislin, 1981, 1993). One reason stereotypes exist is that they enable people to organize a lot of information in a short period of time. In difficult and unsure situations (such as those that often confront people living and working in cultures other than their own), people find it tempting to grasp for any information that will help them make appropriate interpretations. Once a stereotype label is attached to a person, all the information from that stereotype comes to the surface, where it can easily be put to use. For instance, in attempting to relate to a British businessperson he or she has just met, a sojourner may rely on such stereotypical characteristics as reserved, sportsmanlike, interested in cricket, likely to "keep a stiff upper lip" in times of stress, and has an opinion about the monarchy. Although it is tempting to fall back on stereotypes, especially in the face of obstacles to obtaining accurate information in an unfamiliar culture, sojourners must be careful not to overuse stereotypes, and must be especially careful about making decisions based on them. Again, individuals need to strive for greater awareness of the limits of what they know and how they think. As with other learned behaviors, a person can change, expand, develop, and adapt the ways he or she categorizes (and stereotypes) others, *if* he or she is aware of them. The misuse of stereotypes is disconcerting to all parties involved (Barna, 1994).

There is another aspect of categories that must be examined. As previously mentioned, categories help to define and determine the roles people have as they interact in their societies. As experience and contact with people in those defined roles increases, expectations as to certain behaviors associated with those roles also increase. Generalizations about these defined roles become reinforced, and expectations about the behavior of a person in a particular situation playing a particular role become part of a larger pattern (Brislin & Pedersen, 1976). When people have had limited encounters with others in certain roles, they may not know what to expect or what is expected of them. In cultures that have had no exposure to individuals in particular roles, hosts are more likely to miscategorize those individuals (Hamnett, 1983). Because categories link patterns between one culture and another, there is a danger that people will use unfamiliar categories in inappropriate places and sometimes impose their own cultures' categories on situations where hosts' categories are more suitable (Brislin, 1981). Making changes in people's categories, and thus in their thinking, is not always easy, but it is essential if certain political gains, for instance, are to be made. The recent signing of various Middle Eastern peace accords demands that people who previously categorized each other as *enemy* begin to reexamine their categories and to recategorize each other at least as *potentially peaceful neighbor.* Similar reexamination of categories must be part of any significant political upheaval, such as the reunification of Germany, the breakup of the Soviet Union, the changes in the former country of Yugoslavia, and the changing relations among the factions in Northern Ireland.

Sojourners and others interacting cross-culturally should be encouraged to become more aware of the categories they hold as well as to investigate potential new categories that other cultures may have to offer. In this way, they may be able to both expand and adjust their own categories, as well as learn a great deal about their host cultures. In cultures in which outsiders have rarely been encountered, a new set of categories may need to be developed. These new categories should include aspects that reflect mutual conceptions of hosts and sojourners. Special attention should be given to those aspects that are unique to the host society and to which sojourners must specifically adapt. The quality of flexibility is especially helpful, and wise people who interact extensively across cultures will learn to cultivate this characteristic in their lives (Gudykunst, 1994; Paige, 1993).

Application to the Culture Assimilator Incidents

As we have noted, a common occurrence in the process of categorization is stereotyping, or the summarizing of elements or traits about people that masks the differences among those elements (Brislin, 1981). This is the key principle in Incidents 14, 98, 10, and 67. In Incident 14 ("It's a Great Day for the Irish"), Henry from Hong Kong reacted to the Irish name O'Neil and interacted with Mr. O'Neil on the basis of his previous stereotype of Irish Americans and his knowledge of Irish history. Although it may be tempting to grasp at all the knowledge one has to provide common ground with hosts, sojourners should avoid using previously formed categories or stereotypes in such a manner.

In Incident 98 ("Special Educational Needs"), Qin Yu became frustrated at the American teachers' lack of distinction between her own Chinese culture and that of the Japanese. In teaching Sue to repeat a phrase characteristically associated with the Japanese, the teachers ignored the historical animosities between Japan and China. Qin Yu was inadvertently associated with her historic rivalry, an association she abhorred.

Betty Bradley in Incident 10 ("Foreign Policy Discussions") was placed in a similar situation. Her position as a foreign graduate student afforded her many new opportunities, but it also placed new constraints upon her because of the expectations her hosts had of people in that category. As one sent to study in another country, she was treated as a representative of her country, in effect, a sort of ambassador. The hosts' own conceptions of students and student interests included a repertoire of political, foreign policy, and economic ideas. Betty did not fit into their preconceptions of an intelligent student and thus experienced the discomfort of being excluded. Sojourners should be encouraged to find out, if at all possible, the expectations their hosts attach to the categories into which they are likely to be placed. With such knowledge, they may be able to avoid certain difficult situations.

There is also another principle operating in Incident 10 that can be seen more clearly in Incident 67 ("Skillful at Getting Grants"). This principle involves what might be called placement into a negative category by association. In the incident, Herb was trying to institute an excellent and useful project on an international basis. He had even managed to procure funds for the project. Ironically, that was precisely his problem. People are often suspicious of projects for which someone else is underwriting the cost. They are apt to wonder if the funding agency has some motive behind the project's stated purpose. This is particularly true in certain countries, and officials of those countries make attributions about researchers based on their projects' funding sources. People cannot easily separate themselves from their sources of support, whether those are agencies, corporations, or governments. Sojourners should be aware of this and should be careful with whom they interact, because connotations associated with categories may be transferred to them.

In contrast, hosts can also place, or rather misplace, individuals in inappropriate categories. Incidents 88 and 54 elaborate aspects of such troublesome occurrences. In Incident 88 ("From Providence to San Francisco"), the hosts in San Francisco, having no previous exposure to a similar individual, misplaced Joao, the Portuguese boy, in the category of Spanish-speaking people. This offended Joao, who resented being placed in a category other than the one in which he actually belonged in, and thus contributed to his deviant behavior. In Incident 54 ("The Shopper and the Vendor"), Brian from Hawaii was also miscategorized. As he had no other suitable category in which to place Brian, the vendor conveniently placed him into one with which the vendor was familiar. Sojourners may be placed in similar predicaments, facing unfamiliar categories and being unsure how to use them. They may apply one of their own more familiar categories when a host category would be far more accurate and useful. Sojourners, then, must think in terms of expanding their own categories or of building new ones according to the current (new) stimuli.

As people expand their categories, they may find that the previously acceptable limits of their categories have become unacceptable. Incident 49 ("Taken Into Custody on Drug Charges") deals with this issue. Hans-Martin and Paul's category of what constituted legal and acceptable behavior differed from that of host country officials. People should be careful not to impose their own cultures' categories where they may not be appropriate. Things that are included or acceptable in one's own country may not be in other countries. Sojourners should try to be flexible concerning their own category boundaries. They should expect that some host categories may be narrower than their own. They must be willing, therefore, to include some new items in their own categories while at the same time deleting some they had formerly included. Sojourners and others interacting interculturally will find that having more flexible boundaries will make it easier for them to adjust to other cultures.

DIFFERENTIATION

Mr. and Mrs. August Ringling of Baraboo, Wisconsin, had seven sons, who, in the late 1800s, built the Ringling Brothers Circus into the largest traveling entertainment spectacle the world has ever known. Given their success, other circus impresarios attempted to imitate aspects of the Ringling show so as to cash in on the public's desire for amusement. One of the things they imitated was the use of the word *Brothers* in the names of their circuses, as if use of the word would connote the bigness and greatness of the original Ringling show. Even circuses originated and managed by single individuals incorporated *Brothers* in their names. Knowledgeable circus people knew which circuses were actually managed by brothers (e.g., Ringling Brothers, Christiani Brothers); which were managed by a single, respected professional who used *Brothers* after his name (e.g., Charles Hunt, who managed Hunt Brothers Circus); and which were managed by individuals who made up names, and so created nonexistent people, because they sounded good (e.g., Cole Brothers Circus). Knowledge of these differences allowed circus people to tell insiders from outsiders. For instance, visitors would be regarded as ignorant if they showed up at the Cole Brothers Circus lot and asked to talk to one of the Cole brothers.

Psychologists use the term *differentiation* to refer to the distinctions people make within concepts such as *Brothers* in the circus. Differentiations are thus the separations people make within concepts (Fiske, 1993). Often, the degree of differentiation marks the level of knowledge a person has about a given topic. Automobile racers must recognize differences among many types of carburetors, whereas everyday drivers might be barely able to find the carburetors in their own cars. Gardeners know about many types of fertilizers; stamp collectors know the differences in value among various first-day covers from the 1920s; and elementary school teachers know several methods of teaching children to read. To communicate well with gardeners, stamp collectors, or teachers about their areas of expertise, one must use terminology that indicates one's knowledge of these various distinctions.

In cross-cultural experiences, people must learn how concepts are differentiated among those with whom they will be interacting. When people from different groups do not make the same distinctions within a concept, misunderstanding and ill feeling can result. Triandis (1975) gives an example based upon the experiences of American sojourners in Greece; the differentiation occurs within the concept *politeness*:

> Some Americans find Greeks extremely rude. They come to this conclusion from observations of Greeks in public settings—subways, busses, streets. They fail to realize that Greeks have two sets of social behaviors; one set is used with their ingroup, and another with their outgroup. In an ingroup, which a Greek defines as "family and friends and other people who are concerned with my welfare," Greeks are extremely polite. In outgroups they are rude. If the sample of behavior to which a foreigner has access is limited to outgroup social behavior, he will mistakenly assume that all Greek social behavior is rude. This will, of course, have consequences for his own social behavior. Once he assumes that the other person is rude, he is likely to behave in a rude way toward him, which will elicit rude behavior, thus confirming his preconceptions. A cycle of poor relations can then be generated. (p. 67)

Because the Americans in this example fail to recognize that the problem stems from their lack of understanding concerning the differentiation of a concept, there is nothing to break the cycle of assumption, behavior according to the assumption, and reinforcement of the assumption (Pedersen, 1993).

Cognitive complexity is a phenomenon related to differentiation. If people make many differentiations within a certain problem area or subject area, they are said to be cognitively complex rather than cognitively simple (Triandis, 1994; Wade & Bernstein, 1991). If people can deal only with the economic aspects of a technical assistance project, for instance, they are considered cognitively simple. On the other hand, if they can deal with the historical, economic, political, social, cultural, and management aspects of a project, they are considered cognitively complex. Davidson (1975) makes a case for a relationship between cognitive complexity and success on a sojourn:

> The relation between complexity and cross-cultural effectiveness is assumed to exist because a cognitively simple person has a single framework within which to evaluate the observed behavior of others in the target culture. Thus, when a behavior which he does not understand takes place, he is likely to evaluate it ethnocentrically. A complex person, on the other hand, has several frameworks for the perception of the same behavior. He might, for example, suspend judgment and obtain more information before evaluating the behavior. (p. 80)

In a study of Peace Corps workers assigned to Truk, an isolated collection of islands in Micronesia, Detweiler (1980) found empirical support for the proposed relationship. Cognitively complex Peace Corps volunteers were more likely to stay longer on Truk, and to complete their 2-year assignments, than were cognitively simple volunteers. The cognitively complex people in this case might have been able to use their multiple frameworks to find activities that were challenging to them. They might have become interested in learning some of the local language, learning about Trukese fishing methods, or participating in community activities above and beyond their specific Peace Corps assignments.

The concept of differentiation itself is culture general, but, as Brislin and Yoshida (1994b) point out, the content and criteria that are involved may vary, and it is important that individuals crossing cultures learn the distinctions. For instance, a smile may be interpreted as happiness in one culture and as cunning in another. Wearing informal clothing may be appropriate in certain business settings, but inappropriate in others. It is essential for individuals to learn to distinguish the appropriateness of certain behaviors in given contexts and circumstances.

Sojourners will often find themselves in social situations where they have to make differentiations in order to meet their goals in the host society. The following example is similar to one presented by Yoshida (1994). Assume that an American college student (Anne) is studying in Japan. She has joined a club devoted to playing classical music, and all the members agree to chip in money to buy 25 copies of sheet music for a chamber piece by Mozart. The leader of the club mentions that if the members buy 25 copies in bulk, there is a substantial savings compared with each member buying his or her own. However, Anne already has a good copy of the piece by Mozart. Should she chip in money to buy another copy for herself? Yoshida agues that she should consider doing so, and one reason involves understanding the differentiation between goals. On the one hand, there is the task-oriented goal of having a copy of the music so that people can learn the piece. On the other hand, there is another goal of joining in a cooperative effort (see the discussion of individualism and collectivism in Chapter 12) and not calling attention to oneself as a person with a demand that may interfere with group harmony. In her own culture, Anne might not differentiate so sharply between the two goals and might not give each the attention it deserves. In her own culture, she might say to herself, "I have a copy and don't need another, and others probably don't expect me to chip in money since they wouldn't buy another copy in similar circumstances." In Japan, however, she should recognize that the concept of group goals should be differentiated into at least two types: task and social. By contributing the money, she is showing her willingness to be a cooperative group member.

Application to the Culture Assimilator Incidents

In Incident 58 ("The Proposal Process"), Stan Brown did not make an appropriate differentiation within the concept of friend. Based on his socialization in his own country, Stan felt that friends could make a number of different contributions to one another. "Social companion" and "critic of ideas for the purpose of betterment" were two such contributions. If he made these contributions in his own country, New Zealand, such behavior would be seen as perfectly appropriate. In the Philippines, however, these two contributions are differentiated. A friend is certainly a social companion, but he or she is not expected to be a critic of one's ideas, at least in public. Stan, with every good intention, gave input about Jose's proposal at a public meeting. Jose interpreted the input as negative, and thus saw Stan as not acting like a friend.

Differentiation among concepts often runs counter to what people expect, and consequently there is frustration due to unconfirmed expectations. Ideally, it seems that immigrants who are established in a community would welcome new arrivals who come from the same home country, and even help the newcomers in their adjustment. However, such help and support are not always forthcoming. In Incident 100 ("The Local Gang"), the behavior of the people involved points to a strong distinction between local-born children of immigrants and newly arrived immigrants. Where outsiders might expect the local-born Filipino adolescents to welcome a recent arrival and member of their ethnic group, in actuality there was rejection. The new immigrants did not speak either a Filipino language or English in the same way as the locals. The new immigrants did not have the "right" friends, and they had different ways of dressing, different interests, and so forth. Apparently, obvious and visible aspects of behavior such as language use, friendship networks, and dress are more important to adolescents than shared ethnic heritage. This distinction between established immigrants and new immigrants, even though all originate from the same country, is frequently found in various parts of the world.

Of course, differentiation occurs within concepts other than those dealing with friendships and interpersonal relationships. In Incident 76 ("Quoth the Raven, 'Nevermore' "), Carl overgeneralized from observations of Japanese behavior at a company party. He thought that the informality at the party could also be found at a business meeting a few days later. His expectation was not confirmed, and Carl made a serious blunder at the meeting. In the language of this essay, Carl should have been advised to differentiate between behavior at the party and at work rather than to expect similar behavior at both places.

In Incident 67 ("Skillful at Getting Grants"), Herb made a differentiation within a concept and the hosts did not, and this differing perception caused problems. Within the concept of funding for projects, Herb made a distinction between the project itself and the source of the funding. In his own culture, Herb had developed project ideas and then sought out funding. If a source wanted to fund his work, that was fine with him as long as he could remain independent. In some other cultures, however, there is no distinction drawn between a project and its funding source. A project is seen as a reflection of the organization that sponsors it. Because Herb's project was being funded by a source that stimulated images of a military presence, the hosts were gravely concerned and treated Herb accordingly.

THE IN-GROUP/OUT-GROUP DISTINCTION

An aspect of human behavior found in every culture is the division of people into in-groups and out-groups (Banaji & Prentice, 1994; Brislin,

1993; Levine & Campbell, 1972). An in-group is made up of those people who are psychologically close to an individual and those with whom he or she feels comfortable and secure. Members of an in-group can be called upon in times of need. An in-group, then, consists of people who seek each other out, who have close and warm relationships, and who share their experiences with each other. Out-groups, on the other hand, consist of those people who are excluded as much as possible from one's everyday experiences. Out-groups contain people who are avoided, who are actively discouraged from seeking membership in one's in-group, and who are often distrusted. People who are considered inferior and not worthy of the benefits a society has to offer (e.g., jobs, schooling, citizenship) are also classified as out-group members.

One of the difficulties sojourners face is that members of their in-groups are almost always left behind, in their home countries. A person may travel with his or her immediate family, but other in-group members such as close friends and extended family members are almost never included in travel to the host country. Consequently, sojourners want to establish new in-group ties in their host countries so that they can feel comfortable and feel that they are members of a group upon which they can depend in times of trouble. Most often, however, it takes a good deal of time for hosts to become comfortable enough with sojourners to make overtures concerning the formation of in-group ties. The conflict between sojourners' desires to form in-group relationships and hosts' wariness of committing themselves to outsiders is often the basis of misunderstandings (Triandis, McCusker, & Hui, 1990). Sojourners should remember the following three facts:

1. Hosts have in-group ties with family and friends and do not have as great a need as sojourners for new interpersonal relationships.
2. Many hosts have had experiences with sojourners in the past and will make their decisions about offering in-group membership with new sojourners based on those experiences.
3. People in some cultures make sharp distinctions between their in-groups and people from other cultures.

The experience of needing to form new in-group ties is common to those who cross many kinds of culture lines or who enter already established groups. Within a given culture, teachers who are new to a particular building or system, or businesspeople who are new to a particular company, for instance, may find that it takes a considerable amount of time for them to establish the in-group relationships they need in that context to feel fully at home.

Sometimes, the relationships between in-groups and out-groups lead to feelings that do not follow from an individual's experiences in his or her own country. American sojourners in Greece, for instance, frequently report stories such as the following. An American citizen arrives in Greece and meets host counterparts on the job. Very quickly, the Greek coworkers ask personal questions of the American about salary, family, religion, and personal political preferences. Taken aback by what are considered intrusions into private areas, the American makes negative attributions about Greeks and does not seek out any further contact with them.

The key to such a situation centers on the issue of who is considered a member of the in-group. Most Americans' in-groups consist of family and friends. Excluded (with rare exceptions) are foreigners who have recently arrived in the United States. For Greeks, in contrast, the in-group includes family, old friends, and visitors to their country who seem to have goodwill toward Greece. Thus the Greeks in the above example are offering in-group membership with their personal questions and expect that the American will want to participate in such discussions, as they are typical of in-group communications. What the Greeks see as a compliment, then, the American takes as an insult (i.e., invasion of privacy). An understanding of the relationship between in-groups and out-groups, and of who is considered an in-group member, would reduce this problem.

Application to the Culture Assimilator Incidents

In Incident 87 ("Informal Gatherings of People"), Fumio wondered why he was not invited to Friday afternoon gatherings to celebrate the end of the workweek. The reason was that such gatherings were composed of in-group members, who felt they could relax with each other. A less well-known person, such as a sojourner, would detract from the informality of the gatherings. The explanation for hurt feelings is similar for Incident 27 ("Next-Door Neighbors"), in which Chris and Margaret wondered why they were not invited to their neighbors' home. In many countries, activities that take place inside the home are limited to family members. Family ties are very strong, and kinship relations provide the core of people's in-group identification. In such cultures, it is rare that people outside the family (fellow countrymen who are not kin as well as sojourners) will be included.

All countries undoubtedly have gatherings to which in-group members only are invited. In Japan, such gatherings can consist of activities held after the sojourner has been given adequate attention. Once, when one of the developers of this package of training materials was in Japan, he was taken to a bar by Japanese hosts one evening and was later put into a cab to be transported back to his hotel. After his exit from the evening, his Japanese hosts went to two more bars on their own. In this way, they were able to entertain their guest and then later relax among themselves. Others have told us that this appears to be a common pattern for entertaining guests in Japan.

Many cultures have certain expectations about the behaviors of in-group members, and if potential group members are unable to engage in these behaviors, they are rejected. In Incident 10 ("Foreign Policy Discussions"), Betty Bradley discovered that she was no longer invited to beer hall gatherings by her German acquaintances. The reason was that she was unable to participate in political discussions, a favorite activity of German students. If she wanted to spend time with these Germans, be accepted into the in-group, she would have to prepare herself by becoming current on various political topics, such as arms control, social changes in the new Germany, and conflict in the former Yugoslavia and the Middle East.

Cultures differ in the amount of attention given to sojourners. Visitors to the United States frequently comment that Americans are polite during initial interaction but then seem indifferent when they meet a visitor a second or third time. For instance, foreign students may be introduced at a faculty meeting and made to feel welcome, but those same students seem forgotten by faculty members a few days later. This leads to charges of American insincerity. In Incident 21 ("The Welcomed Visitor"), Dave was upset when he stopped being the target of special attention. In many cases, however, such inattention is a sign that hosts have accepted the sojourner into the in-group. Dave's hosts felt that he now "belonged" and did not feel the need to make special gestures toward him anymore, such as presenting him with the best food. As one experienced sojourner told us, "I knew that I was accepted when people stopped telling me how well I spoke the local language."

LEARNING STYLES

Researchers and practitioners in recent years have been giving an increased amount of attention to the ways people learn, particularly in cross-cultural settings (e.g., Cole & Means, 1981; Cole & Scribner, 1974; Cushner, 1990a; Cushner, McClelland, & Safford, 1992; Hofstede, 1986).

Although the institution we call *school* is in many ways similar from country to country, the socialization practices in the home and the family that influence an individual from the earliest age may differ markedly. This, in turn, may play an important role in the ways individuals are taught and in how they learn how to learn. Learning styles at home may be different from the learning styles teachers expect students to possess upon entering school. It has been suggested that the problems in school faced by many cultural minority members and immigrants lie here, at the interface between the culture of the home and the culture of the school (Ogbu, 1982).

Sojourners in countries other than their own, as well as individuals working in cross-cultural settings in their own countries, who have the responsibility of teaching (as educators, technical advisers, social workers, counselors, or managers) should take into account the manner in which individuals learn best and not assume that they have transferred new concepts and information to others merely because they have given verbal instruction (Taylor, 1994). Often, after engaging in a lengthy explanation of some concept, a teaching sojourner will ask if the students understand, and they will respond that they do. However, their subsequent actions will make it obvious that this is not true (Brislin & Yoshida, 1994b). Sojourners must remember that many times their students or trainees will say they understand what the sojourners have been trying to teach simply out of respect for the individuals doing the teaching.

Many potential differences in learning style are worthy of exploration. For instance, Western-style schooling usually requires students to learn in out-of-context situations. That is, individuals first master their language and acquire symbol utility and then abstract rules and concepts from books and spoken language for possible application at later times and places. In many non-Western, less technological societies, in contrast, particularly those without long histories of written languages, learning is accomplished in context, that is, by doing what is to be learned with the actual object at hand. Hunting and gathering societies, in which young males accompany the adults on hunting expeditions from a relatively early age, offer an example of in-context learning. The child learns through active involvement and participation with the adult teacher in the hunting process, with his contributions being of some value to the task at hand, not by passively observing procedures and techniques for future application. He is immediately rewarded when he masters the required skills and completes a kill, not by internalizing the procedure and reproducing it in symbol form (either orally or in writing) upon command.

Preferences for group versus individual learning constitute another potential area of differences in the ways people learn best. In many collective societies, individuality is not a goal; rather, group participation is expected and aimed for. Children of Hawaiian ancestry, for example, come under the guidance of their older siblings very early in life. Parents interact with their children as a group, not so much as individuals. As a result of this kind of upbringing, children learn to learn best from siblings and peers in group situations, not from one adult, as is typical in Euro-American cultures as well as in the school setting.

Learning styles may also differ from individual to individual within a given culture. For instance, some individuals prefer a concrete experiential mode of learning in which they succeed through actual manipulation and visualization of materials. Others prefer to learn in an abstract reflective manner, where they can be presented with ideas, think about them for a while, and arrive at some summary concepts on their own. Similarly, the ways in which people present information and argue or make their points may differ. Such variety typically exists throughout societies, but many cultures tend to stress one style of learning over others.

As a concept within such academic disciplines as psychology, communication, and education, "learning styles common within a culture" has more intuitive appeal than research-based support, and thus has generated considerable debate. Judith Kleinfield (1994), for instance, has searched long and hard for evidence of a learning style among Native Americans that is different from that of the majority of Americans, but cannot report any solid evidence for such a style. There are several reasons for the lack of research-based support for the existence of culturally determined learning styles. One is that just because people in some cultures learn well using a certain style, we cannot conclude that people in other cultures will learn poorly if that style is introduced in the classroom. Assume that people in a Native American culture learn well through cooperative group effort. Does this mean that middle-class European Americans will not learn new material through well-introduced, well-administered cooperative group efforts? The answer is no (Johnson & Johnson, 1987). Group learning can be effective in many places, as long as it is introduced carefully and students are given practice in its use to compensate for their prior unfamiliarity with a cooperative style. Kleinfield (1994) suggests that "the concept of learning styles is useful when it reminds teachers to create rich and interesting classrooms where children can learn in many different ways" (p. 156). She gives the example of a science lesson for children in a remote Eskimo village. The teacher tried to introduce the concepts of "calories" and "energy transformation" through a lecture but had little success, and the eyes of students indicated that they were bored. Later, he asked the children to attend a steam bath, an event of importance in their village's culture. The children observed what happened to water when it was in the form of gas, when it was solid, and when it was liquid. They became interested in the principles behind the changes and asked new questions, such as, "What happens to the steam when it goes out the steam bath when someone opens the door?" Kleinfield (1994) concludes the example by pointing out that the teacher had adapted the science lesson to the cultural setting and that "he would probably say that he had adapted his teaching to students' learning styles" (p. 156).

Application to the Culture Assimilator Incidents

The issue of in-context versus out-of-context learning is the crux of Incident 90 ("Careful Preparation of Lectures"). Robert spent 5 days teaching his Hawaiian clients the operation and maintenance of machinery from text and diagrams, but Hawaiians, like many other people, typically learn in context, by using the actual objects they are learning about and having the opportunity to practice new skills. In such learning, concepts and rules are rarely discussed, but are acquired after repeated experience and example. Robert's frustration and subsequent failure resulted from his use of inappropriate instructional techniques given the needs of his particular students.

The focus in Incident 91 ("Teaching Third Grade"), also evident in Incident 90, is the issue of group versus individual learning. As Marie discovered, Hawaiian children respond to group rewards and achievement recognition more favorably than they do to being singled out individually (as do learners in many other cultures that value the group's needs over the individual's). They also learn more and faster in group situations where assistance can be given by peers as needed.

Teacher-student interaction and its impact on teaching and learning are at issue in Incident 86 ("The New ESL Teacher"). George's rather informal approach and individual orientation were practices that were quite unfamiliar to his Japanese students, as they would be to many other Asian students. Many students who come from group-oriented cultures and from schools where teacher-student relationships are rather formal and structured have difficulty with the relative informality of American educational practice. Although new learning styles can be taught and learned, it may be wise, at least in the beginning, for teachers to establish an atmosphere conducive to the expectations and practices students naturally bring to class.

Incident 83 ("The Assessment of His Efforts") presents the issue of learning style differences from the student's perspective. What is deemed important and often necessary within one culture to show evidence of scholarly mastery or merely to explain a topic may not satisfy the requirements or expectations of another culture. Tal was from a culture in which his elders taught him that everything that can be associated with a concept or idea is relevant and should be included to relate an idea satisfactorily to another. In contrast, Tal's British professors expected him to communicate his thoughts in a precise manner, with arguments directed at central issues. The British professors found Tal's approach scattered and undisciplined. Clearly, a style based on learning in one culture can, unfortunately, interfere with education in another.

A story concerning cross-cultural cognitive development is often related about a research group's work among the Wolof in West Africa. Wolof adults were given a task to do, and they consistently responded to it according to Piaget's concrete operational stage of cognitive development (considered to be attained by children at roughly ages 11 to 15). When asked why they did not respond as would individuals in Piaget's formal operations stage (roughly ages 16 and older), their response was, "What, answer as a fool would?" The message here is that accepted and expected ways of responding may in fact be culturally determined and not universal expressions of cognitive development or chronological age.

Cultures differ in the ways in which the individuals who live in them teach and in the ways the people learn. Sojourners who hope to be effective in a teaching capacity must take these considerations into account.

ATTRIBUTION

The former mayor of New York City, Ed Koch, had a verbal trademark. Upon meeting a constituent, he would ask, "How'm I doin'?" thus requesting evaluative feedback on his performance as mayor. The fact that Mayor Koch expected people to answer his question points to his understanding of two fundamental thought processes among humans: (a) People observe the behavior of others and make judgments about those others, and (b) people also make judgments about themselves based in part on the reactions of others.

Research concerned with how people judge others and themselves, carried out largely by psychologists, has been done under the label of *attribution research* (e.g., Jones, 1979; Yan & Gaier, 1994; Zimbardo &

Leippe, 1991). Attributions are the conclusions or judgments people make about the things that happen in their worlds; in this context, we are concerned with attributions concerning people's behaviors: whether other people (or the observers themselves) are competent, well intentioned, effective, naive, power hungry, pressured by external forces, and so forth. Causal attributions are judgments concerning the *reasons* for people's behaviors. For instance, assume Peter helps John with a task. John is likely to ask himself questions (although maybe not consciously) about why Peter is helping him: "Did Peter help me out because of his altruism or did he help me out so that I would be indebted to him in the future?" John might also make attributions about himself: "Why did Peter help me? Did he think that I couldn't carry out the task by myself? Does this mean that I'm incompetent?"

Another example from the experiences of a foreign student adviser might help explain the concept of causal attribution. A male graduate student from Saudi Arabia who is studying in the United States has a term paper assigned to him by a professor. The student turns in a paper, but the professor marks it "F" and writes "plagiarized" on the front page. Plagiarism is a problem that demands disciplinary action at American universities, but given that the student is from overseas, the professor calls the foreign student adviser on campus rather than the college dean. The professor asks, "Is there something going on here that I don't know about? I don't want to see this student expelled from school." The action of the professor indicates attributional ambiguity concerning the cause of the student's behavior. He doesn't know whether (a) the attribution should be one he might use for an American student, such as "He got caught—he's a cheat," or (b) there is another, as yet unknown, attribution that would make interpretation of the problem less severe. This professor, incidentally, should be applauded for calling the foreign student adviser. Some professors, behaving quite reasonably according to widely accepted norms in academia, would go to the dean, and the student would face a major disciplinary hearing.

Some theories that have been developed by attribution researchers are worthy of consideration. When we analyze the behaviors of others, we have a strong tendency to use trait labels. In the example above, the trait label would be "he is a cheat." Furthermore, when we analyze the behavior of others we are much less likely to take into account any immediate factors in the situation or social context. This error—making trait judgments about others and failing to take into account situational factors—has been called the fundamental attribution error (Ross, 1977). It is probably more prevalent in cross-cultural encounters than in intracultural ones because such encounters often involve behavior that is new and different for the sojourner, the host, or both (Bond, 1994). With so much behavior that is new, people will make causal attributions so as to explain to themselves what is going on. But when so many attributions are being made, they cannot all possibly be correct. In addition to sheer numbers, many attributions will be wrong because people will not have sufficient information about the other cultures (or sufficient information about people from the other cultures) to make valid conclusions (Gudykunst, 1994).

Advice for improving attributions centers on the general principle that situational factors should be taken into account. Situational factors are outside the individual in the sense that they are not a permanent part of the individual's character structure or personality. Situational factors include the presence of other people who might be affected by the individual's behavior, time pressures on the individual, and the individual's lack of a support system. Situational factors also include experiences to which people have been exposed in their personal histories. People are able to make situational attributions about themselves because they have plenty of information about the pressures in their own environments and about their personal histories. But when they are making attributions about others, this information is frequently absent. Thus they tend to make trait attributions—if a person plagiarizes, he is a cheat.

The good foreign student adviser, however, knows that there are situational factors at work in this plagiarism incident. Many foreign students have grown up in cultures where knowledge is not necessarily always attributed to the developers of that knowledge. In contrast, Euro-American students are trained to credit the developers of knowledge when discussing their work (e.g., if one is discussing the theory of relativity, one must mention Einstein). Knowledge in many cultures is considered to be open, usable by anyone, without constant reference to the scholars who developed that knowledge. Thus when this foreign student writes a paper without citing his scholarly sources, he is employing a familiar strategy. But writing without citation is considered plagiarism by Euro-American professors. When the situational factors in this case are taken into account, and it is understood that the student is behaving according to his previous training, the attribution is quite different from "he is a cheat." Triandis (1977; Triandis, Kurowski, & Gelfand, 1994) has written of the need for sojourners and hosts to form "isomorphic" attributions, that is, shared attributions about people or incidents that take cultural differences into account. When sojourners and hosts make isomorphic attributions, their misunderstandings and conflict decrease because they understand each other's interpretations of behavior. To develop the ability to make isomorphic attributions, people must understand why and how attributions are made. One contributing factor in the making of a final attribution is the vividness of the incident in which the individual is directly involved. Vivid, personalized incidents overwhelm people's attention capacities and seem to carry more weight than they should in the formation of final attributions (Bond, 1994). Consider the following example. John is searching for housing in the country to which he has been assigned. He buys a guidebook put out by a group of concerned sojourners who want to help newcomers make their way in the host country. The developers of the guide sampled the opinions of 200 sojourners concerning good housing possibilities, and the book specifies several good neighborhoods. John then happens to name one of these neighborhoods to a person he has recently met and who has been helpful in John's adjustment. The friends says: "I know that area. My wife's cousin lived there and didn't like it. This person found that it had poor bus service and was too far from stores." What does John do?

There is a strong tendency, which all of us have, to place a great deal of weight on personal input. This input is given to John orally, probably with some colorful gestures, in contrast to the dull manner in which information is presented in the guidebook. But examine the situation more closely. The cousin is 1 person, and the guidebook was developed based on a survey of 200 people. So John now has input from 201 people, and the weight of the evidence is still strongly in favor of the neighborhood he was considering. However, the vivid, personalized input is likely to have more impact than simply 1 of 201 pieces of information. This tendency to react to vivid events is especially common among sojourners because they are exposed to many new and exciting events. But what is new and exciting is not necessarily important. Sojourners should keep this point in mind and ask themselves, Am I overreacting to a vivid incident directed at me, personally? Is there other information I might use before coming to a conclusion?

Application to the Culture Assimilator Incidents

In Incidents 57 ("Breakfast at the Cafe") and 53 ("Trip to the Public Market"), the sojourners are overreacting to vivid events in which host behavior is directed specifically at them. Gunnar feels that he has been overcharged, probably assuming that the waiter is trying to cheat him.

Rather than lashing out at the waiter, a wiser procedure would be to determine if there is other information besides Gunnar's assessment of the waiter's intentions. If this had been done, Gunnar would have discovered that there was restaurant policy, common in Spain, that would have explained the waiter's behavior. Jane Jefferson, in Incident 53, is understandably upset that someone in the host country shouted at her. She is especially upset because, as a sojourner anxious about her adjustment, she is seeking out pleasant events to reassure herself that her sojourn will be a positive experience. But this incident should not affect all aspects of her sojourn. It is best to put the single incident aside and not overinterpret it as predictive of all future experiences.

Difficult problems can sometimes be lessened in intensity, although probably not eliminated, by an understanding of how people make attributions. In Incident 84 ("A Secretary's Work Is Never Easy"), Mrs. Simpson is addressed in an unpleasant, demanding manner by a sojourner. The strong tendency is for her to take the incident personally. But there are aspects of the incident that might permit other attributions, which would consequently lessen the stress that Mrs. Simpson feels. One aspect is that the sojourner is addressing the role Mrs. Simpson is playing, not Mrs. Simpson herself. The other aspect is that the sojourner is accustomed to addressing servants and is addressing Mrs. Simpson in this familiar manner. If Mrs. Simpson thinks about these possibilities and changes her conclusions about the event (called *reattribution*), she will not feel so strongly that she is being personally attacked.

The fact that the sojourner is accustomed to dealing with servants, or more generally is using a style of interaction that has developed over many years, is one type of situational factor that should be taken into account in making an attribution. Another type of situational factor may be the immediate pressures facing an individual. In Incident 71 ("Learning the Ropes"), Helen Connor is surprised to hear a Japanese coworker criticize his bosses while drinking in a bar, because she had always thought that the Japanese were careful about public decorum. Rather than attribute to her coworker the trait of aggressiveness, however, Helen should take situational variables into account. Two such variables are the pressures that the Japanese coworker has recently experienced and the disappointment he has recently felt. Such considerations might lead Helen to conclude, "His reactions are not so different from what mine would have been."

The question of honesty and ethical behavior in business practices is at issue in Incident 72 ("Are There Ethical Issues Involved?"). In the incident, Jack and Herb become quite frustrated by what they believe to be unethical behavior on the part of their Chinese associates; that of inquiring into details that might be regarded as highly technical trade secrets. The Chinese want to learn advanced technology, and they do not see any ethical difficulties in asking pointed questions meant to discover advanced knowledge among businesspeople who are proposing joint ventures. What the Chinese might consider good business practice—to learn from others with advanced technology—Jack and Herb see as overstepping boundaries, especially before any real joint agreement has been reached. On the other hand, the Chinese might perceive their behavior as good business, just as people from the United States (and many other parts of the world) feel that it is good practice to do business in China because of low labor costs. The ability to understand the motivations behind the behaviors of others, or the ability to make isomorphic attributions, is an essential element of productive joint ventures across cultures.

REFERENCES

Adler, N. J. (1992). *International dimensions of organizational behavior* (2nd ed.). Boston: PWS-Kent.

Adler, N. J., & Matthews, K. (1994). Health psychology: Why do some people get sick and some stay well? *Annual Review of Psychology, 45,* 229-259.

Albert, R. (1983). The intercultural sensitizer or culture assimilator: A cognitive approach. In D. Landis & R. W. Brislin (Eds.), *Handbook of intercultural training* (Vol. 2). Elmsford, NY: Pergamon.

Allport, G. (1954). *The nature of prejudice.* Reading, MA: Addison-Wesley.

Anderson, L. (1994). A new look at an old construct: Cross-cultural adaptation. *International Journal of Intercultural Relations, 18,* 293-328.

Aoki, J. (1991). *Effects of the culture assimilator on cross-cultural understandings and attitudes of college students.* Unpublished doctoral dissertation, Southern Illinois University at Carbondale.

Ball, D., & McCulloch, W. (1993). *International business: Introduction and essentials* (5th ed.). Homewood, IL: Irwin.

Banaji, M., & Prentice, D. (1994). The self in social contexts. *Annual Review of Psychology, 45,* 297-332.

Barna, L. (1994). Stumbling blocks in intercultural communication. In L. Samovar & R. Porter (Eds.), *Intercultural communication: A reader* (7th ed., pp. 337-346). Belmont, CA: Wadsworth.

Berscheid, E. (1994). Interpersonal relationships. *Annual Review of Psychology, 45,* 79-92.

Bhatkal, R. (1990). *Intercultural sensitivity training for preservice teachers using a culture-general assimilator with a peer interactive approach and media analysis.* Unpublished doctoral dissertation, University of Nebraska, Lincoln.

Bhawuk, D. P. S. (1990). Cross-cultural orientation programs. In R. W. Brislin (Ed.), *Applied cross-cultural psychology* (pp. 325-346). Newbury Park, CA: Sage.

Bhawuk, D. P. S., & Brislin, R. W. (1992). The measurement of intercultural sensitivity using the individualism and collectivism concepts. *International Journal of Intercultural Relations, 16,* 413-436.

Biddle, B. (1979). *Role theory: Expectations, identities, and behaviors.* New York: Academic Press.

Bochner, S. (1994). Cross-cultural differences in the self-concept: A test of Hofstede's individualism-collectivism distinction. *Journal of Cross-Cultural Psychology, 25,* 273-283.

Bocock, R. (1974). *Ritual in industrial society*. London: Allen & Unwin.

Bohm, D. (1980). On insight and its significance for science, education, and values. In D. Sloan (Ed.), *Education and values*. New York: Teacher College Press.

Bond, M. H. (1994). Continuing encounters with Hong Kong. In W. J. Lonner & R. S. Malpass (Eds.), *Psychology and culture* (pp. 41-46). Boston: Allyn & Bacon.

Bowlby, J. (1988). *A secure base*. New York: Basic Books.

Bransford, J. (1979). *Human cognition: Learning, understanding, and remembering*. Belmont, CA: Wadsworth.

Brislin, R. W. (1981). *Cross-cultural encounters: Face-to-face interaction*. Elmsford, NY: Pergamon.

Brislin, R. W. (1991). *The art of getting things done: A practical guide to the use of power*. New York: Praeger.

Brislin, R. W. (1993). *Understanding culture's influence on behavior*. Fort Worth, TX: Harcourt Brace Jovanovich.

Brislin, R. W., Cushner, K., Cherrie, C., & Yong, M. (1986). *Intercultural interactions: A practical guide*. Beverly Hills, CA: Sage.

Brislin, R. W., Landis, D., & Brandt, M. (1983). Conceptualizations of intercultural behavior and training. In D. Landis & R. W. Brislin (Eds.), *Handbook of intercultural training* (Vol. 1). Elmsford, NY: Pergamon.

Brislin, R. W., & Pedersen, P. (1976). *Cross-cultural orientation programs*. New York: Gardner.

Brislin, R. W., & Yoshida, T. (Eds.). (1994a). *Improving intercultural interactions: Modules for cross-cultural training programs*. Thousand Oaks, CA: Sage.

Brislin, R. W., & Yoshida, T. (1994b). *Intercultural communication training: An introduction*. Thousand Oaks, CA: Sage.

Broaddus, D. (1986). *Use of the culture general assimilator in intercultural training*. Unpublished doctoral dissertation, Indiana State University, Terre Haute.

Bruner, J., Goodnow, J., & Austin, G. (1956). *A study of thinking*. New York: John Wiley.

Burgoon, J., Buller, D., & Woodall, W. G. (1989). *Nonverbal communication: The unspoken dialogue*. New York: Harper & Row.

Byrne, D., & Kelley, K. (1981). *An introduction to personality* (3rd ed.). Englewood Cliffs, NJ: Prentice Hall.

Cialdini, R. (1988). *Influence: Science and practice* (2nd ed.). Glenview, IL: Scott Foresman.

Cole, M., & Means, B. (1981). *Comparative studies of how people think*. Cambridge, MA: Harvard University Press.

Cole, M., & Scribner, S. (1974). *Culture and thought*. New York: John Wiley.

Cummins, J. (1981). Four misconceptions about language proficiency in bilingual education. *NABE Journal, 5,* 31-45.

Cushner, K. (1989). Assessing the impact of a culture-general assimilator. *International Journal of Intercultural Relations, 13,* 125-146.

Cushner, K. (1990a). *They are talking about me! and other stories about exchange students*. New York: AFS Intercultural Programs.

Cushner, K. (1990b). Cross-cultural psychology and the formal classroom. In R. W. Brislin (Ed.), *Applied cross-cultural psychology* (pp. 98-120). Newbury Park, CA: Sage.

Cushner, K. (1994). Preparing teachers for an intercultural context. In R. W. Brislin & T. Yoshida (Eds.), *Improving intercultural interactions: Modules for cross-cultural training programs* (pp. 109-128). Thousand Oaks, CA: Sage.

Cushner, K., & Landis, D. (in press). The intercultural sensitizer. In D. Landis & R. Bhagat (Eds.), *Handbook of intercultural training* (2nd ed.). Thousand Oaks, CA: Sage.

Cushner, K., McClelland, A., & Safford, P. (1992). *Human diversity in education: An integrative approach.* New York: McGraw-Hill.

Cushner, K., & Trifonovitch, G. (1989). Understanding misunderstanding: Barriers to dealing with diversity. *Social Education, 53,* 318-322.

Davidson, A. (1975). Cognitive differentiation and culture training. In R. W. Brislin, S. Bochner, & W. J. Lonner (Eds.), *Cross-cultural perspectives on learning.* Beverly Hills, CA: Sage.

Davis, B. (1972). *The ripe harvest: Educating migrant children.* Coral Gables, FL: University of Miami Press.

Deal, T. E., & Kennedy, A. A. (1982). *Corporate cultures: The rites and rituals of corporate life.* Reading, MA: Addison-Wesley.

Denzin, N. (1994). Ritual behavior. In R. Corsini (Ed.), *Encyclopedia of psychology* (2nd ed., Vol. 3, pp. 324-325). New York: John Wiley.

Detweiler, R. (1980). Intercultural interaction and the categorization process: A conceptual analysis and behavioral outcome. *International Journal of Intercultural Relations, 4,* 275-293.

Devine, P., & Zuwerink, J. (1994). Prejudice and guilt: The internal struggle to overcome prejudice. In W. J. Lonner & R. S. Malpass (Eds.), *Psychology and culture* (pp. 203-207). Boston: Allyn & Bacon.

Dolphin, C. (1988). Variables in the use of personal space in intercultural transactions. *Howard Journal of Communication, 1,* 23-38.

Dowling, P., Schuler, R., & Welch, D. (1994). *International dimensions of human resource management* (2nd ed.). Belmont, CA: Wadsworth.

Draguns, J. (1990). Applications of cross-cultural psychology in the field of mental health. In R. W. Brislin (Ed.), *Applied cross-cultural psychology* (pp. 302-324). Newbury Park, CA: Sage.

Dunbar, E. (1994). The German executive in the U.S. work and social environment: Exploring role demands. *International Journal of Intercultural Relations, 18,* 277-291.

Eagly, A. (1987). *Sex differences in social behavior: A social role interpretation.* Hillsdale, NJ: Lawrence Erlbaum.

Epstein, S. (1994). Integration of the cognitive and psychodynamic unconscious. *American Psychologist, 49,* 709-724.

Erez, M. (1994). Toward a model of cross-cultural industrial and organizational psychology. In H. C. Triandis, M. Dunnette, & L. Hough (Eds.), *Handbook of industrial and organizational psychology* (2nd ed., Vol. 4, pp. 559-607). Palo Alto, CA: Consulting Psychologists Press.

Feather, N. (1994). Values and culture. In W. J. Lonner & R. S. Malpass (Eds.), *Psychology and culture* (pp. 183-189). Boston: Allyn & Bacon.

Fernea, E., & Fernea, R. (1994). Cleanliness and culture. In W. J. Lonner & R. S. Malpass (Eds.), *Psychology and culture* (pp. 65-69). Boston: Allyn & Bacon.

Fiedler, F., Mitchell, T., & Triandis, H. C. (1971). The culture assimilator: An approach to cross-cultural training. *Journal of Applied Psychology, 55,* 95-102.

Fiske, A. (1991). *Structures of social life.* New York: Free Press.

Fiske, S. (1993). Social cognition and social perception. *Annual Review of Psychology, 44,* 155-194.

Fiske, S., & Taylor, S. (1991). *Social cognition* (2nd ed.). New York: McGraw-Hill.

Freimanis, C. (1994). Training bilinguals to interpret in the community. In R. W. Brislin & T. Yoshida (Eds.), *Improving intercultural interactions: Modules for cross-cultural training programs* (pp. 313-341). Thousand Oaks, CA: Sage.

Furnham, A., & Bochner, S. (1986). *Culture shock: Psychological reactions to unfamiliar environments.* London: Methuen.

Glaser, R. (1984). Education and thinking: The role of knowledge. *American Psychologist, 39,* 93-104.

Goldstein, J. (1994). *International relations.* New York: HarperCollins.

Gosnell, P. (1983). *University incidents: A workbook in cross cultural communication.* Rio Piedras: University of Puerto Rico.

Graen, G., & Wakabayashi, M. (1994). Cross-cultural leadership making: Bridging American and Japanese diversity for team advantage. In H. C. Triandis, M. Dunnette, & L. Hough (Eds.), *Handbook of industrial and organizational psychology* (2nd ed., Vol. 4, pp. 415-446). Palo Alto, CA: Consulting Psychologists Press.

Gudykunst, W. (1994). *Bridging differences: Effective intergroup communication.* Thousand Oaks, CA: Sage.

Gudykunst, W., & Hammer, M. (1983). Basic training design: Approaches to intercultural training. In D. Landis & R. W. Brislin (Eds.), *Handbook of intercultural training* (Vol. 1). Elmsford, NY: Pergamon.

Gudykunst, W., Wiseman, R., & Hammer, M. (1977). Determinants of a sojourner's satisfaction. In B. Ruben (Ed.), *Communication yearbook 1.* New Brunswick, NJ: Transaction.

Hall, E. (1959). *The silent language.* Garden City, NY: Doubleday.

Hall, E. (1966). *The hidden dimension.* Garden City, NY: Doubleday.

Hall, E. (1983). *Dance of life.* Garden City, NY: Doubleday.

Hamnett, M. (1983). Oceania: Cross-cultural adaptation. In D. Landis & R. W. Brislin (Eds.), *Handbook of intercultural training* (Vol. 3). New York: Pergamon.

Handy, C. B. (1976). Culture and structures. In *Understanding organizations.* Middlesex, England: Hazell, Watson & Viney.

Hansel, B. (1988). Developing an international perspective in youth through exchange programs. *Education and Urban Society, 20,* 177-196.

Hawes, R., & Kealey, D. (1981). An empirical study of Canadian technical assistance: Adaptation and effectiveness on overseas assignment. *International Journal of Intercultural Relations, 5,* 239-258.

Helson, H. (1964). *Adaptation level theory.* New York: Harper & Row.

Hilgard, E., Atkinson, R. C., & Atkinson, R. L. (1975). *Introduction to psychology* (6th ed.). New York: Harcourt Brace Jovanovich.

Hofstede, G. (1980). *Culture's consequences: International differences in work-related values.* Beverly Hills, CA: Sage.

Hofstede, G. (1986). Cultural differences in teaching and learning. *International Journal of Intercultural Relations, 10,* 301-320.

Hofstede, G. (1991). *Cultures and organizations: Software of the mind.* London: McGraw-Hill.

Hofstede, G., & Bond, M. (1988). The Confucius connection: From cultural roots to economic growth. *Organizational Dynamics, 16*(4), 4-21.

Homans, G. (1950). *The human group.* New York: Harper & Row.

Hui, C. H. (1990). Work attitudes, leadership styles, and managerial behaviors in different cultures. In R. W. Brislin (Ed.), *Applied cross-cultural psychology* (pp. 121-141). Newbury Park, CA: Sage.

Ilola, L. (1991, April 3). *The use of structured social interaction with the culture-general assimilator to increase cognitive problem solving about intercultural interactions in an ethnically diverse population.* Paper presented at the annual meeting of the American Educational Research Association, Chicago.

Jahoda, G. (1969). *The psychology of superstition.* Harmondsworth: Penguin.

Janis, I., & Mann, L. (1977). *Decision making.* New York: Free Press.

Johnson, D., & Johnson, R. (1987). *Learning together and alone: Cooperative, competitive, and individualistic learning* (2nd ed.). Englewood Cliffs, NJ: Prentice Hall.

Jones, E. (1979). The rocky road from acts to dispositions. *American Psychologist, 34,* 107-117.

Jones, W. (1989). Racial attitudes. In C. Wilson & W. Ferris (Eds.), *Encyclopedia of southern culture* (pp. 1118-1120). Chapel Hill: University of North Carolina Press.

Kagitçibasi, C. (1978). Cross-national encounters: Turkish students in the United States. *International Journal of Intercultural Relations, 2,* 141-160.

Kagitçibasi, C. (1990). Family and socialization in cross-cultural perspective: A model of change. In J. Berman (Ed.), *Nebraska Symposium on Motivation, 1989* (pp. 135-200). Lincoln: University of Nebraska Press.

Kashima, Y., & Callan, V. (1994). The Japanese work group. In H. C. Triandis, M. Dunnette, & L. Hough (Eds.), *Handbook of industrial and organizational psychology* (2nd ed., Vol. 4, pp. 609-646). Palo Alto, CA: Consulting Psychologists Press.

Katz, D. (1960). The functional approach to the study of attitudes. *Public Opinion Quarterly, 24,* 164-204.

Kealey, D., & Ruben, B. (1983). Cross-cultural personnel selection, criteria, issues, and methods. In D. Landis & R. W. Brislin (Eds.), *Handbook of intercultural training* (Vol. 1). New York: Pergamon.

Keating, C. (1994). World without words: Messages from face and body. In W. J. Lonner & R. S. Malpass (Eds.), *Psychology and culture* (pp. 175-182). Boston: Allyn & Bacon.

Kelman, H., & Ezekiel, R. (1970). *Cross-cultural encounters.* San Francisco: Jossey-Bass.

Kerrick, J., Clark, V., & Rice, D. (1967). Lectures versus participation in the health training of Peace Corps volunteers. *Journal of Educational Psychology, 58,* 259-265.

Kidder, L. (1977). The inadvertent creation of a neocolonial culture: A study of Western sojourners in India. *International Journal of Intercultural Relations, 1,* 48-60.

Kim, U., Triandis, H. C., Kagitçibasi, C., Choi, S.-C., & Yoon, G. (Eds.). (1994). *Individualism and collectivism: Theory, method, and applications.* Thousand Oaks, CA: Sage.

Kim, Y. Y. (1994). Intercultural personhood: An integration of Eastern and Western perspectives. In L. Samovar & R. Porter (Eds.), *Intercultural communication: A reader* (7th ed., pp. 415-424). Belmont, CA: Wadsworth.

Kipnis, D. (1976). *The power holders.* Chicago: University of Chicago Press.

Kleinfield, J. (1994). Learning styles and culture. In W. J. Lonner & R. S. Malpass (Eds.), *Psychology and culture* (pp. 151-156). Boston: Allyn & Bacon.

Kochman, T. (1981). *Black and white styles in conflict and communication.* Chicago: University of Chicago Press.

Lambert, R., & Bressler, M. (1956). *Indian students on an American campus.* Minneapolis: University of Minnesota Press.

Lambert, W. (1972). *Language, psychology and culture.* Stanford, CA: Stanford University Press.

Landis, D., & Brislin, R. W. (Eds.). (1983). *Handbook of intercultural training* (3 vols.). Elmsford, NY: Pergamon.

Levine, R., & Campbell, D. (1972). *Ethnocentrism.* New York: John Wiley.

Lieberman, D. (1994). Ethnocognitivism, problem solving, and hemisphericity. In L. Samovar & R. Porter (Eds.), *Intercultural communication: A reader* (7th ed., pp. 178-193). Belmont, CA: Wadsworth.

Malpass, R. S., & Salancik, G. (1977). Linear and branching formats in culture assimilator training. *International Journal of Intercultural Relations, 1,* 76-87.

Manson, S. (1994). Culture and depression: Discovering variations in the experience of illness. In W. J. Lonner & R. S. Malpass (Eds.), *Psychology and culture* (pp. 285-290). Boston: Allyn & Bacon.

March, J., & Olsen, J. (1980). *Ambiguity and choice in organizations.* Bergen-Oslo Tronson: Universitetsforlaget.

Marin, G., & Marin, B. V. (1991). *Research with Hispanic populations.* Newbury Park, CA: Sage.

Maslach, C. (1978). The client role in staff burnout. *Journal of Social Issues, 34,* 111-124.

Meichenbaum, D. (1977). *Cognitive-behavior modification: An integrative approach.* New York: Plenum.

Moghaddam, F., Ditto, B., & Taylor, D. (1990). Attitudes and attributions related to psychological symptomatology in Indian immigrant women. *Journal of Cross-Cultural Psychology, 21,* 335-350.

Moore, M., & Levitan, L. (1993). *For hearing people only* (2nd ed.). Rochester, NY: Deaf Life.

Mullavey-O'Byrne, C. (1994a). Intercultural communication for health care professionals. In R. W. Brislin & T. Yoshida (Eds.), *Improving intercultural interactions: Modules for cross-cultural training programs* (pp. 171-196). Thousand Oaks, CA: Sage.

Mullavey-O'Byrne, C. (1994b). Intercultural Interactions in welfare work. In R. W. Brislin & T. Yoshida (Eds.), *Improving intercultural interactions: Modules for cross-cultural training programs* (pp. 197-220). Thousand Oaks, CA: Sage.

Offermann, L., & Gowing, M. (1990). Organizations of the future: Changes and challenges. *American Psychologist, 45,* 95-108.

Ogbu, J. (1982). Cultural discontinuities and schooling. *Anthropology and Education Quarterly, 13,* 290-307.

Pacino, W. R. (1989). Gender stereotypes and gender roles in cross-cultural education: The culture assimilator. *International Journal of Intercultural Relations, 13,* 57-72.

Paige, R. M. (Ed.). (1993). *Education for the intercultural experience.* Yarmouth, ME: Intercultural Press.

Pedersen, P. (1988). *A handbook for developing multicultural awareness.* Alexandria, VA: American Association for Counseling and Development.

Pedersen, P. (1993). Mediating multicultural conflict by separating behaviors from expectations in a cultural grid. *International Journal of Intercultural Relations, 17,* 343-353.

Peplau, L., & Perlman, D. (Eds.). (1982). *Loneliness: A sourcebook of current theory, research and therapy.* New York: John Wiley.

Pruegger, V., & Rogers, T. (1994). Cross-cultural sensitivity training: Methods and assessment. *International Journal of Intercultural Relations, 18,* 369-387.

Ramirez, H. (1992). *The effects of cross-cultural training on the attributions and attitudes of preservice teachers (LEP instructors).* Unpublished doctoral dissertation, University of Illinois, Urbana-Champaign.

Rimmon, S. (1977). *The concept of ambiguity: The example of James.* Chicago: University of Chicago Press.

Rogers, J., & Ward, C. (1993). Expectation-experience discrepancies and psychological adjustment during cross-cultural reentry. *International Journal of Intercultural Relations, 17,* 185-196.

Rogler, L. (1994). International migrations: A framework for directing research. *American Psychologist, 49,* 701-708.

Rogoff, B. (1990). *Apprenticeship in thinking: Cognitive development in social context.* New York: Oxford University Press.

Rokeach, M. (1979). *Understanding human values.* New York: Free Press.

Rosch, E., & Mervis, C. B. (1975). Family resemblances: Studies in the internal structures of categories. *Cognitive Psychology, 7,* 573-605.

Ross, L. (1977). The intuitive psychologist and his shortcomings: Distortion in the attribution process. In L. Berkowitz (Ed.), *Advances in experimental social psychology* (Vol. 10). New York: Academic Press.

Ruben, B., & Kealey, D. (1979). Behavioral assessment of communication competency and the prediction of cross-cultural adaptation. *International Journal of Intercultural Relations, 3,* 15-47.

Schachter, S., & Singer, J. (1962). Cognitive, social, and physiological determinants of emotional state. *Psychological Review, 69,* 379-399.

Schaufeli, W., & Janczur, B. (1994). Burnout among nurses: A Polish-Dutch comparison. *Journal of Cross-Cultural Psychology, 25,* 95-113.

Schwartz, C. G., & Kahne, M. (1993). Support for student and staff wives in social transition in a university setting. *International Journal of Intercultural Relations, 17,* 451-463.

Schwartz, S. (1992). Universals in the content and structure of values: Theoretical advances and empirical tests in twenty countries. In M. Zanna (Ed.), *Advances in experimental social psychology* (Vol. 25, pp. 1-65). San Diego, CA: Academic Press.

Shirts, R. G. (1976). *Rafa Rafa: A cross-cultural simulation.* Del Mar, CA: Simile II.

Singelis, T. (1994). Nonverbal communication in intercultural interactions. In R. W. Brislin & T. Yoshida (Eds.), *Improving intercultural interactions: Modules for cross-cultural training programs* (pp. 268-294). Thousand Oaks, CA: Sage.

Singer, M. S. (1993). Starting a career: An intercultural choice among overseas Asian students. *International Journal of Intercultural Relations, 17,* 73-88.

Sinha, D. (1990). Interventions for development out of poverty. In R. W. Brislin (Ed.), *Applied cross-cultural psychology* (pp. 77-97). Newbury Park, CA: Sage.

Sinha, J. (1994). Culture embeddedness and the developmental role of industrial organizations in India. In H. C. Triandis, M. Dunnette, & L. Hough (Eds.), *Handbook of industrial and organizational psychology* (2nd ed., Vol. 4, pp. 727-764). Palo Alto, CA: Consulting Psychologists Press.

Siple, L. (1994). Cultural patterns of deaf people. *International Journal of Intercultural Relations, 18,* 345-367.

Stephan, C., & Stephan, W. (1992). Reducing intercultural anxiety through intercultural contact. *International Journal of Intercultural Relations, 16,* 89-106.

Tannen, D. (1990). *You just don't understand: Women and men in conversation.* New York: Ballantine.

Taylor, E. (1994). A learning model for becoming interculturally competent. *International Journal of Intercultural Relations, 18,* 389-408.

Taylor, J. (1953). A personality scale of manifest anxiety. *Journal of Abnormal and Social Psychology, 48,* 285-290.

Textor, R. (Ed.). (1966). *Cultural frontiers of the Peace Corps.* Cambridge: MIT Press.

Thiagarajan, S., & Steinwachs, B. (1990). *Barnga: A simulation game on cultural clashes.* Yarmouth, ME: Intercultural Press.

Triandis, H. C. (1975). Culture training, cognitive complexity, and interpersonal attitudes. In R. W. Brislin, S. Bochner, & W. J. Lonner (Eds.), *Cross-cultural perspectives on learning* (pp. 39-78). Beverly Hills, CA: Sage.

Triandis, H. C. (1977). *Interpersonal behavior.* Monterey, CA: Brooks/Cole.

Triandis, H. C. (1983). Essentials of studying cultures. In D. Landis & R. W. Brislin (Eds.), *Handbook of intercultural training* (Vol. 1). New York: Pergamon.

Triandis, H. C. (1994). *Culture and social behavior.* New York: McGraw-Hill.

Triandis, H. C., Brislin, R. W., & Hui, C. H. (1988). Cross-cultural training across the individualism-collectivism divide. *International Journal of Intercultural Relations, 12,* 269-289.

Triandis, H. C., Kurowski, L., & Gelfand, M. (1994). Workplace diversity. In H. C. Triandis, M. Dunnette, & L. Hough (Eds.), *Handbook of industrial and organizational psychology* (2nd ed., Vol. 4, pp. 769-827). Palo Alto, CA: Consulting Psychologists Press.

Triandis, H. C., Kurowski, L., Tecktiel, A., & Chan, D. (1993). Extracting the emics of diversity. *International Journal of Intercultural Relations, 17,* 217-234.

Triandis, H. C., McCusker, C., & Hui, C. H. (1990). Multimethod probes in individualism and collectivism. *Journal of Personality and Social Psychology, 59,* 1006-1020.

Tygiel, J. (1983). *Baseball's great experiment: Jackie Robinson and his legacy.* New York: Oxford University.

Tzeng, O., & Jackson, J. (1994). Effects of contact, conflict, and social identity on interethnic group hostilities. *International Journal of Intercultural Relations, 18,* 259-276.

Wade, P., & Bernstein, B. (1991). Culture sensitivity training and counselor's race: Effects on black female clients. *Journal of Counseling Psychology, 38,* 9-15.

Wang, Z. M. (1994). Culture, economic reform, and the role of industrial and organizational psychology in China. In H. C. Triandis, M. Dunnette, & L. Hough (Eds.), *Handbook of industrial and organizational psychology* (2nd ed., Vol. 4, pp. 689-725). Palo Alto, CA: Consulting Psychologists Press.

Webster's Third New International Dictionary Unabridged. (1966). Springfield, MA: Merriam Webster.

Weldon, D. E., Carlston, D. E., Rissman, A. K., Slobodin, L., & Triandis, H. C. (1975). A laboratory test of effects of culture assimilator training. *Journal of Personality and Social Psychology, 32,* 300-310.

Whorf, B. (1956). *Language, thought and reality* (J. Carroll, Ed.). New York: John Wiley.

Witte, K. (1993). A theory of cognition and negative affect: Extending Gudykunst and Hammer's theory of uncertainty and anxiety reduction. *International Journal of Intercultural Relations, 17,* 197-215.

Worchel, S., & Mitchell, T. (1970). *An evaluation of the effectiveness of the Thai and Greek culture assimilators.* Seattle: University of Washington, Organizational Research Group.

Wrightsman, L., & Deaux, K. (1981). *Social psychology in the 80's* (3rd ed.). Monterey, CA: Brooks/Cole.

Yan, W., & Gaier, E. (1994). Causal attributions for college success and failure: An Asian-American comparison. *Journal of Cross-Cultural Psychology, 25,* 146-158.

Yarbro, C. L. M. (1988). *An assessment of the ability of the culture-general assimilator to create sensitivity to multiculturalism in an educational setting.* Unpublished doctoral dissertation, University of Houston, College of Education.

Yoshida, T. (1994). Interpersonal versus non-interpersonal realities: An effective tool individualists can use to better understand collectivists. In R. W. Brislin & T. Yoshida (Eds.), *Improving intercultural interactions: Modules for cross-cultural training programs* (pp. 243-267). Thousand Oaks, CA: Sage.

Zedeck, S., & Cascio, W. (1984). Psychological issues in personnel decisions. *Annual Review of Psychology, 35,* 461-518.

Zimbardo, P. (1970). The human choice: Individuation, reason, and order versus deindividuation, impulse, and chaos. In W. Arnold & D. Levine (Eds.), *Nebraska Symposium on
Motivation.* Lincoln: University of Nebraska Press.

Zimbardo, P., & Leippe, P. (1991). *The psychology of attitude change and social influence.*
New York: McGraw-Hill.

AUTHOR INDEX

357

SUBJECT INDEX

ABOUT THE AUTHORS

Kenneth Cushner is Associate Professor of Education and Director of the Center for International and Intercultural Education at Kent State University. He received his doctoral degree from the University of Hawaii at Manoa while on scholarship with the East-West Center. He is a frequent contributor to the professional literature in intercultural education, conducts professional development activities for many professional educational associations worldwide, and has developed and led international education programs for young people and educators on five continents. He is coauthor of *Human Diversity in Education: An Integrative Approach* (1992). He enjoys playing guitar and percussion instruments, and is also interested in photography.

Richard W. Brislin is Senior Fellow and Project Director at the East-West Center in Honolulu, Hawaii. He received his Ph.D. in psychology from Pennsylvania State University. In addition to teaching and conducting research, he directs yearly programs for college professors who want to develop intercultural course work and for cross-cultural trainers who want to expand their skills. His recent books include *The Art of Getting Things Done: A Practical Guide to the Use of Power* (1991), *Understanding Culture's Influence on Behavior* (1993), and *Intercultural Communication Training: An Introduction* (1994). He enjoys playing banjo, pennywhistle, and Irish folk harp.